READY FOR THE RIDE

An Autobiography

of

John Thomas McLeod

Ready for the Ride
Copyright 2020 by John Thomas Mcleod
Cover design by Sarah Leafblad
Published by Lulu.com

ISBN: 978-1-716-350139 (paperback)

TABLE OF CONTENTS

PREFACE

AT THE END OF WWI when my mom was ten years old, she took the streetcar downtown, shook the hand of General Pershing, and was excited to see the handsome uniformed American servicemen that her older sisters sometimes brought home for dinner. Since her mom was born just four years after the civil war, even that didn't seem like ancient history to me as a little kid in the 1940s. So much has happened since the start of the civil war, however, it seemed incomprehensible to my youngest granddaughter that my grandparents were born so long ago. That's when I realized I was the connecting generation between the civil war and the iPhone 11. I was born halfway between each.

Since stories tie us to our past and provide a foundation for our future, I finally decided to just go ahead and retrace my steps. The process of gathering information, recalling events and writing them down made me think about where I've been, what I've done during these 80 years, and what's important. By writing my story, "Ready for the Ride," I've come out from behind myself, at least part way, as my family, siblings and others may learn.

Plans and dreams are precarious and can come crashing down after just one poor decision or one imprudent act. In this digital age, where nothing disappears, there are many more potential traps and pitfalls, different from those I encountered. No one can keep living casually, unethically or immorally and achieve God's ideal vision for their life. Overall success or failure is due to a handful of decisions. Making a decision leads one way. Not making a decision, which is also a decision, leads another way. Be bold, think ahead and make wise ones so that you will finish well the race you are running. Time flies

PART I: 1940-1945

IT'S A BIG WORLD

1. IOWA CITY, IOWA

IT WAS A ROUGH START. It wasn't supposed to be that way. Certainly not at the University of Iowa Hospital in Iowa City. But the truth is, that's the way it was. After all, it was only 26 years after doctors started doing more good than harm, since many people think 1914 was the turn-around year.

The little boy didn't breathe right away as the doctors dipped him first in cold water, then warm, then cold, then warm, until finally he gasped his first croupy breath. He probably aspirated some amniotic fluid containing meconium. Hopefully, you'll get through life without ever hearing about that again. It causes wheezing, coughing, shortness of breath and susceptibility to lung infections.

Next, on the little boy's first day, the doctors circumcised him and gave him a smallpox vaccination on his right rear cheek. That didn't work out so well. There was a lot of crying every time his diapers were changed and often in between. A week later when he arrived home, his Grandma Middleton took one look and screamed, "Take that boy back!"

Considering that his mom, Esther Jane, was so heavily drugged for her first deliveries and after one of them even asked the doctor three days later, "Have I had the baby yet?" it's a wonder that her second little boy even pulled through. This all started on May 16, 1940. Welcome, John Thomas McLeod, into the world.

The University of Iowa Hospital soon stopped doing circumcisions and smallpox vaccinations until after the first week. Modern medicine finally caught up with the Jews who knew over 2000 years earlier that it should be done on the eighth day. Medical advances took another small step forward. I'm glad I could make a difference.

From 1938-1942, my dad, Arthur Manning McLeod, was doing research at the University of Iowa for the Dean of the College of Engineering, Professor F.M. Dawson. Dad was inventing all kinds of things including fish ladders, grease interceptors, siphon breakers to prevent contamination of drinking water, and an anti-slam check valve. Unfortunately, the University of Iowa kept all the patents, or we might have been rich. Before that, Dad earned his civil engineering degree in 1928 from the University of Wisconsin (UW) in Madison, an architectural engineering degree in 1932 from the University of Illinois in Champaign, and a hydraulic engineering master's degree in 1938 from the UW.

Professor Dawson also had kids and one of them invited my brother Paul, who was 4 ½ years older than me, over one day for lunch. Mom was curious about how the upper crust lived and wanted to know how the lunch tasted. Paul replied, "Yes, it was really good. They had more pans on the table than we do."

I had a big appetite and by three months had doubled my weight to 16 pounds. I'd drink four 7-oz bottles of diluted Carnation milk, plus orange juice, pablum, cod liver oil and 2 teaspoons of calcium.

One evening before Mom and Dad went to the movies, Mom nursed me, gave me a bottle, and left thinking I'd be full and happy. When they returned a few hours later, Mom asked Grandma how I did. She said, "I gave him a bottle and he went right to sleep." At eight months, just when things were going well, I got pneumonia but eventually fought it off with sulfa and sedatives. No penicillin yet. That would come later.

In April 1941, we moved from Olive Court to a more spacious house and yard in nearby Coralville. That's because on May 15, 1941, just a day before my first birthday, my sister Mary Jane was born. She entered this world without suffering from any medical mishaps and never seemed to catch as many "bugs" as I did. Years later, for a year or two in grade school, she was also taller and could run faster, much to her delight. She has also relished the fact that for one day a year, she was just as old as me. I'm over it now.

Mom was a bit obsessed with how much food I consumed and kept detailed records. In my baby book she mentioned I drank a quart of fresh unpasteurized milk from the neighbor's cow every day and ate plenty of vegetables from the garden. Fresh was the key word. Mom always wanted to start boiling the water before picking the beans."

At one year, I tried to sneak up on Robins and imitate birds. In fact, my first word was "bird." According to Mom, I was a friendly, jolly kid who liked to throw toys. She also wrote that I was unusually strong, but since she was barely 5' tall and not even 100 pounds, how could she tell?

At 17 months I had the chickenpox for three weeks, but at my next check-up, the doctor said, "He is a fine boy and I haven't seen a better behaved one." Mom loved hearing that.

A couple months later, they cut off all my blond curls and called it my first haircut. Paul, who was almost six, lamented, "Now he doesn't look pretty." I'm glad I got over that stage a long time

Esther Jane & Mary, Paul, John, & Art
December 1941

ago. Years later, Paul used one of my baby pictures and won a cutest baby contest. Being a good, honest doctor with a clean conscience, he admitted the fraud and gave up his prize.

On December 7, 1941, Japan attacked Pearl Harbor. Mom was very worried about the future of her three kids growing up in a world being devastated by war. Both Mom and Dad were born in 1908 and they still had memories of WWI, the war that was supposed to end all wars. She feared that the stories they'd heard about mustard gas and other atrocities might be repeated.

When I was 23 months old, Mom wrote, "John turns the clothes basket upside down and gets in the apple tree by himself. He often escapes from the fenced yard to play with the neighbor's dog and loves to climb up and over our trapeze swing set and seems very sure of himself." Just when things were going well, I got the measles. Mom made sure the shades were drawn to protect my eyes, and that I drank a lot of water and stayed in bed so I wouldn't have any complications. Mom always took good care of us at home and she never worried about getting sick herself.

John McLeod, 23 Months

2. MOVING TO MADISON

IN SEPTEMBER 1942, we left our rented house in Coralville when Dad got a new job at the U.S. Forest Products Laboratory (FPL), located at the north end of Highland Avenue in Madison, Wisconsin. During the war, Dad did research on wooden airplane propellers, gliders, and PT boats to learn where wood could replace metal. Other researchers were testing hundreds of different types of wood and construction techniques – anything to assist the war effort. Aunt Oral, Mom's oldest sister, born in 1899, also worked at the FPL as a Secretary-Office Manager in the Research and Publication Department.

In early 1943, after staying two months at Grandpa and Grandma Middleton's house at 1831 Green Street, Rockford, Illinois, we moved into a cozy, three-bedroom brick home at 2221 Chadbourne Avenue, Madison, Wisconsin. It was right in front of West High School and cost $6500. Their monthly mortgage was $40, and many people thought they would have a hard time paying such an amount. You would never guess that the original owner purchased it through a Sears Roebuck catalog. In those days, Sears would pay the buyer $1 for any board that had a knot. A lumberyard today would go broke doing that.

3. IT'S TOUGH TO BE TWO

BEING 2 COULD BE FRUSTRATING. I couldn't reach the bathroom light switch no matter how much I stretched on my tip toes. Wouldn't a 2-year-old Chimpanzee just get a chair?

Such Restraint!

Mom wrote "John and Mary get along well and are so loving sometimes. He also likes Sunday School and enjoys picture books, which until now, he only wanted to throw." She also wrote that I could talk "Quite plainly at times but would often cut my sentences short." To save time perhaps. Breaking early habits doesn't come easy as I still tend to finish other people's sentences.

Several times in the next few years I'd get the croup and would sleep on the davenport pillows placed in the bathtub. So, I could breathe easier, Mom and Dad made the room so humid that the wallpaper started peeling off the walls. Up in the corner, above the tub, one of those big, round electric heaters, that glowed coppery-red, helped heat the room, and our old toaster was used as a hotplate to boil water. I surely didn't make life easy for Mom and Dad, but they always did their best to take care of me. Years later, Mary said, "I knew our parents loved us when I saw how hard they worked to take care of you." She never seemed to get sick.

4. TAKING A WALK

DURING THESE YEARS, I ENJOYED visiting Uncle Frank and Aunt Oral. They lived in an old house at the end of Highland Avenue, north of old University Avenue. Their acre lot was eight blocks from our house and came with cats, dogs, ponies, and sometimes chickens. At three, I begged to ride a young colt named Rosey O'Dea. Uncle Frank was an antique dealer, or "picker," and had a lot of old stuff sitting around. We drove and walked over there so often that I soon learned the way. One day when I was about three, I decided to go by myself. I walked around the side of West High School and then down Highland Avenue to the busy corner at University Avenue by the Rennebohm Rexall drug store. A minute later, Uncle Frank, who was working out in his front yard, was more than just a little surprised to see me walking up his driveway alone. Since he had just heard some tires screeching down at the corner, he asked, "How'd you get across the street?" I said, "The cars just stopped." Aunt Oral then called Mom, who said I was just playing around in the yard. Ah, those were the days – when you could do dumb stuff and not get in trouble or go to jail.

In 1943, Mom went to Minneapolis for three weeks to have her goiter removed and to recover at her sister Gladys's house. When she returned, I felt sorry for her as I tenderly touched the scar on her neck. Shortly after, I got the mumps on both sides. Anytime a doctor diagnosed one of those childhood illnesses, the Health Department showed up and put a big quarantine sign on the front door warning people to stay away. Dad had to move out and go to Frank and Oral's house for the week. For him this wasn't too inconvenient because he only had to walk across the railroad tracks to work at the FPL.

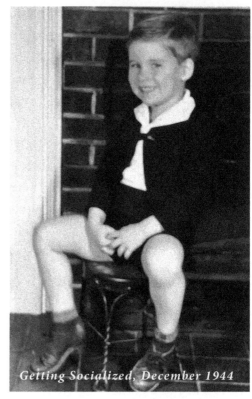

Getting Socialized, December 1944

Mary and I shared one upstairs bedroom while Paul slept in the other. Both had closets with a window that opened to the roof, so of course we crawled out to enjoy the view. We were always careful so Mom wouldn't worry. One day Paul also crawled out on the roof with Haakon Bakken, a kid three years older who lived across the street. When Haakon and Paul peered down the narrow chimney flue, Paul realized that it wasn't possible for big fat Santa Claus to get in the house that way — and it became the saddest day in his life. That was a whole year after Paul asked Mom, "Why am I the only kid in second grade who believes in Santa Claus?" Both bedrooms were remodeled by Dad who cut out the walls under the front and back roof so Mary and I could keep our beds tucked in the newly created space, giving us more room to play.

At three years, Mom wrote, "John is a little bossy with Mary" but later in the year we were "singing and playing together, stacking blocks, having tea parties and enjoying our many books." Most remarkably she wrote, "John is very lovable and easier to manage than previously." Best of all, just a year later, "He seems to be over his cough." The one thing positive about being congested was that Dad would rub my chest with Mentholatum when I went to bed. It felt so good I never wanted him to quit. Today it's not so easy to find this old remedy in most drug stores – but it is still my favorite medicine.

Sitting next to Grandma Middleton on the piano bench, while she played and sang "Redwing" and "In the Garden," was a time I remember fondly. She often helped by doing the dishes and when she did, I'd sometimes poke the flab on the back of her arms back and forth and laugh. She was a good sport and even laughed along with me. On our Sunday visits to Rockford, she cooked good chicken dinners when we showed up. Grandma loved us kids and I enjoyed snuggling up next to her. She was born on April 19, 1869, just four years after the civil war and died on January 26, 1948, when I was seven. Grandpa was five years younger but lived to be 93. He was a tough little guy who enjoyed his big vegetable garden on his vacant lot next door. If you sat next to him at dinner, he'd grab you above the knee and give you a horse bite or steal something off your plate.

On September 2, 1945, WWII ended. For us, it was a big day. Several of us kids marched back and forth making our own parade in front of West High School as we banged spoons on Mom's saucepans chanting, "We won the war! We won the war!" That meant Mom and Dad could get rid of the ration books, stop saving tin cans, stop making laundry soap out of lye, and life could return to its normal state of frugality. Everyone backed WWII, the last war that we fought to win.

For a few more years the milkman continued to deliver several quarts to our back door. About 3" of cream rose to the top of the bottles which we had to shake unless Mom wanted it for whipped cream. When the milkman walked behind our house, we sometimes sneaked some ice chips out of his truck to suck on during the hot summer days. This all ended about the time they started to homogenize milk.

After the war, in 1946, Dad's job at the Forest Products Lab ended but he was soon offered a job for $10,000 a year in Gary, Indiana. That was a big amount, but when they went to Gary to check it out and look around the town, they decided that "It was no place to bring up a family." He soon decided to start his own architectural practice and worked on his own until 1951. After a year or so, he was making about $4,000 and was driving all over the state, supervising the construction of the schools and other buildings he designed. It was enough to get by and to keep paying off their monthly mortgage.

Since Mary and I had birthdays just a day apart, we sometimes celebrated them together at Uncle Frank and Aunt Oral's house. They didn't have any kids, so we were surrogates which they enjoyed part time. We played a lot of games, had gunny sack races, and ate a lot of cake and ice cream. Oral had an old cleaning lady, Mrs. Kane, who I thought was 100 years old. Despite this, I challenged her to a race, and yes, I was a wee bit embarrassed when that skinny little lady took off in a flash and beat me. Luckily, no one was paying much attention.

Uncle Frank wasn't so involved with our birthday celebrations. He was older than Oral and had a pot belly. We got along great and talked and did things together. One morning, about 6:00 a.m., I walked over to his house and could see him sitting in his antique armchair, one that had springs at the bottom of the front legs. Instead of knocking on the front door, I sneaked down the outside stairs, crept up the basement stairs and knocked loudly on the kitchen door to scare him. It worked. He quickly threw open the door and stood way back to avoid an immediate confrontation. It was just me. Only then did I realize I was lucky I didn't get hurt or even shot.

5. LIMBURGER CHEESE

SINCE UNCLE FRANK KNEW that I thought I was tough, he asked, "Go pick up that board by the garage and bring it to me." Well, this board was only about 5' long, 8" wide and an inch thick. Easy, I thought, but this was no ordinary board. It was a solid steel plank and too heavy for me to carry. I lifted one end before I realized he had gotten the best of me. He had a good laugh. He also had a little banty rooster that chased me around the yard. Another hearty laugh, which he remembered many times over the years. He also tried to get me to taste his favorite Limburger cheese. That was absolutely the worst smell ever. "Just like dirty feet," he said.

Ready for the Ride

Frank spent a lot of time driving around southern Wisconsin looking for antiques, and according to an appraiser I met years later, was a "famous picker." He pulled his trailer everywhere just in case he found some valuable furniture at a bargain price. One day when I traveled with him, we went to Cobb and all-around Southwestern Wisconsin. He knocked on some old lady's door, and as we sat and talked at her kitchen table, he started bargaining for a few old teacups. After some time, he turned to me and asked, "What would you pay, John, for this cup?" I answered, "Ten cents." They laughed and he got the cups.

Frank and Oral had a lot of beautiful antiques and glassware. When they had company over for dinner, she would often set the table a day earlier to make sure everything was just perfect. When my visit encroached on their mealtime, they sometimes asked if I would join them. A few times, when I called Mom to get her permission, I asked, "What are you making for lunch?" The first time it was funny, but I quickly learned that comparing menus was a poor way to accept or decline an invitation. But that isn't when Frank sometimes joked, "Come again when you can't stay so long." He occasionally said that to be funny. They usually used a set of clear, red dishes and sometimes pewter cups, until they found out that lead could kill you. Most of all, I admired their

"Old Colonial" sterling silver and especially admired the fluted spoons. Oral promised me I would someday be the beneficiary, but they never signed their will. When Frank died a year after Oral in July 1970, his sister, Lottie, ended up with everything. Even though Lottie never knew it, the joke was on her. Because of the great depression, Frank never trusted the banks, so he kept $50,000 cash stashed in the basement freezer in a container marked "strawberries." In her haste to throw out all the old food, Lottie never noticed. Uncle Frank had confided this to Paul's wife, Elaine, who was the only other person who knew about his stash.

Uncle Frank always carried a lot of money in his wallet because he had to be ready to buy an antique whenever the opportunity arose. One day he even showed me a $1000 bill. I think that's how he impressed Oral when they first met.

In his quest for antiques, Frank stopped by a farm where he had been trying for 25 years to buy a big cast iron pot. The lady was stubborn, however, and wouldn't sell. Finally, Frank asked, "What do you use that pot for?" She said, "To water my chickens." Frank said, "You shouldn't do that. One day a chicken will get up there on the rim and fall in and drown." She replied, "One did yesterday. You can have it." He knew just what to say.

Years later, Frank and Oral drove over to Babcock Hall on the UW campus to get a couple of those big, delicious ice cream cones. It was busy so he double-parked in front while Oral waited in the car. Just then, a university policeman drove up, got out of his car, and started writing out a parking ticket. Oral, of course, got upset and started arguing with the cop. Just then Frank walked out with a cone in each hand. He quickly sized up the situation and ordered, "Oral, get back in the car." He then took the cop aside and explained, "Ever since she started going through that 'time of life,' I can't do anything with her." The cop replied, "My wife is the same way," and he ripped up the ticket.

PART II: 1945-1952
LEARNING THE THREE R'S

6. RANDALL ELEMENTARY SCHOOL

A FEW DAYS BEFORE KINDERGARTEN, I asked Mom, "How come Mary can say the alphabet and I can't?" She quickly taught me, and I was up to speed. Grandma McLeod said it backwards, but I never bothered to learn that. One way was enough. Mom believed that she wasn't supposed to teach us school stuff. That was the teacher's job.

In September 1945, I started school at Randall, Madison's oldest elementary school in use, built in 1908, the same year Mom and Dad were born. I would walk or run the three blocks in about five minutes. I liked my teacher, Miss Drews. Kindergarten was fun, but the silly part was putting our heads down on our desks for ten minutes to rest after we drank a carton of milk and ate a cookie. Who needed to rest? We only had school for a half day. I went in the morning and I always woke up early.

When winter arrived, Mom made me a wool coat with a pointed hood. On my way to school, big Johnny Schmitz, who lived across the street, sometimes yelled, "Here comes Johnny, the little girl-boy." I thought it was kind of funny, but it made Mom angry.

Before Christmas, I got a sore throat, rash, and a fever. Sure enough, I had another one of those childhood diseases, scarlet fever. Another quarantine sign was placed on our front door. Dad (Paul too, so he could continue going to school), moved out of the house. Mary played outside my door, so we could see each other and talk. She never seemed to get sick but everyone else never got closer than the front door. I took sulfa every four hours and after three weeks, Doctor McDonough took another throat culture. It was still positive, so he gave me penicillin. Yes, I was growing up in the modern medical age. I took penicillin for two days. Only two days? But it didn't work. That meant more sulfa for the next three days. Anyway, the Health Department took down the quarantine sign after four weeks. Finally, I was allowed to play just a little because Mom was worried too much exercise might damage my heart. After more than six weeks, I returned to kindergarten and finished the school year.

My carefree life continued all through my years at Randall where we never had any homework but did pay close attention in class. That's the way it was and that's the way we liked it. Nobody wanted homework.

7. SIX JOHNS

MY FIRST-GRADE TEACHER, Miss Ziegler, taught us how to read "Dick and Jane" books, write, add, subtract, and tell time back when clocks had hands. The day after we learned to tell time, I was asked to teach Bill Lautz, as he had missed a day of school. I felt so important. Years later, after I learned that Mom and Dad thought Miss Ziegler was a bit sarcastic, I recalled an incident that happened on May 16, 1946. She asked Peter Mueller, "Why are you all dressed up?" Peter excitedly answered, "Because I'm going to John McLeod's birthday party." He had to say my last name because there were six

"Johns" in our class. Then she turned to me and asked, "Why did you invite him?" I didn't answer but thought it was a strange remark. Her other remarks went over our heads.

One day I climbed the birch tree at West High, by the corner of Ash and Van Hise Avenue, when the branch broke, and I fell about 10' to the grass below. Although greatly relieved that I had just missed some big landscaping boulders, I ran home crying. To test if my arm was broken, Dad asked me to pick up an old Raggedy Andy doll. When I couldn't, we drove to the hospital where I got an X-Ray and a plaster cast for two weeks to protect my greenstick fracture. While I still had the cast on my arm, Paul came home after a week in the hospital recovering from a hernia operation.

Even though I had written Paul a couple of "sympathetic get-well" letters, I thought this was my chance to beat him in wrestling. After all, my arm was a club, and surely, he must be in a weakened condition. It soon became obvious, however, that the doctor had neglected to tell him to avoid heavy lifting as he threw me across the living room onto the sofa with a loud crack. We instantly stopped, pulled out the sofa and saw that the broken frame had punctured the material. We pushed it back against the wall and Dad never said a word.

By the time my cast came off, I could throw a baseball just about as well with my right hand as with my left. However, I was left-handed, like Dad, and proud of it, so I reverted. Strangely enough, I continued to throw underhand with my right. Later, that became a complication when I was the pitcher on our 9th grade homeroom softball team. I couldn't wear a glove because if someone hit the ball to me, I had to take it off before throwing to first base.

8. PICNIC POINT

IN FIRST GRADE, Steve Emlen, who became my best friend, moved from out East to a big, 2-story house at 2621 Van Hise Avenue, just on the other side of West High. His phone was easy to remember because it was 32621. His dad was a professor who taught classes about birds and animal behavior. Steve also loved birds, and I think he even knew more about them than I did. When he said that Kirtland's Warblers only nested in Michigan, that was something I didn't know even though I pretended I did. Sixty years later, a few of those little warblers decided to move west and are now nesting in Adams county in central Wisconsin.

We spent many hours together going on bird hikes. Most often, our destination was Picnic Point which was a mile-long peninsula that stuck out in Lake Mendota. We rode our bikes down Allen Street, crossed under the Milwaukee Railroad bridge and began our bird watching. Everywhere past that point was an open, swampy landfill. Now, of course, it is filled with the big UW hospital and dozens of other university buildings. There's no more green space except for a few practice and baseball fields. We then turned left at the lake and went through the entrance to Picnic Point. Along the path, we sometimes observed hundreds of tadpoles swimming in little puddles of water, and Leopard Frogs were everywhere. Alongside the marsh we saw red-wings, wrens, warblers, gulls and just about everything possible. On some days in

May, we counted over 100 different species. On the grassy hillside near the entrance, there were well-defined clumps of red pines where we sometimes found Great Horned Owls dozing with one eye open watching our every move. Under the pines we searched through the needles for owl pellets, those little dry balls of regurgitated, gray fur and bones. When we broke them open, we usually found the skeletons of field mice. On some days we even found mice with their brood of a half-dozen, tiny, pink, squeaking babies. Every trip was a new adventure.

9. A NICE EVEN NUMBER

ON JUNE 17, 1947, my youngest sister, Margaret Joanna, was born. She came home on a warm, sunny afternoon and there were several of us kids who came in the house to look at the new arrival. That made four of us now, two boys and two girls — a "nice even number" Mom said.

Just a year earlier, when Mary was visiting Cave of the Mounds, she had made a wish at the wishing well for a little sister. Now she had one. Many years later when someone asked Mom how she had spaced out her kids so well, she said, "When I thought it was time to have another child, Dad was only too happy to oblige."

Before Mom was married, she dreamed of having 12 kids and had names for all of them. Reality set in later when she realized it wasn't so easy giving birth. Or maybe it was about money or just too much work. Anyway, by this time she was 38 and they had settled on four. It was certainly a better time to have kids. The war was won two years earlier, Dad was getting established in a new career, they had their own house, and the country was optimistic. Harry Truman had been President for over two years and famously had a sign on his desk that said, "The Buck Stops Here."

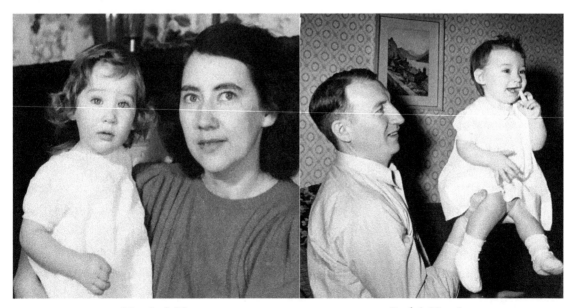

Margie & Mom   *Dad & Margie*

Second grade went okay. My teacher, Mrs. Campion, was an older lady who must have been a good disciplinarian. Once she put little Michael Patterson over her knee and gave him a good spanking, but I can't remember anything he did that was so disrespectful. Most of us were always well-behaved, as I remember it, perhaps because the teachers were able to do something about it.

During second grade, Mary, Margie, and I came down with whooping cough. With three sick kids, it was a tough time for Mom, and for Dad who cared for me at night. I was always the sickest and coughed so hard I lost my lunches. I missed six weeks of school and everyone in my class sent me get-well letters which were fun to read. I had some terrifying nightmares and still remember one. I was sleeping in Mom and Dad's bed and the door was half open, which made it easy for a monster to stand in the doorway. For the longest time, he flashed colored lights all over the room and I was terrified. Towards the end of the ordeal, after the monster retreated down the hall, a little yellow chick ran around in circles. Then it was over.

For Christmas in 1947, I received a basketball, a microscope, and a kitten. The kitten was unusual, as my mother never wanted any animals in the house. A few times we had dogs, but they were "outside" dogs and none of them ever lasted more than a few weeks before they ran off or got hit by a bus. I used my 44-power microscope and spent many hours looking at tiny objects on the small glass slides. I quickly discovered that light had to be able to pass through whatever I was looking at, which was disappointing. In our stockings, which we hung up on the mantle above our fireplace every Christmas Eve, we would get an assortment of small objects, such as little magnetic "Tricky Dogs" (one of my favorites), pencils, candy, little toys and also oranges. For Mom and Dad, who had to fill the largest knee-high socks we could find, this took some time, so they almost always included a large orange. When they were little kids during WWI, eating an orange was a special treat, but for me, they were just "fillers." WWII had ended two years earlier, the economy was booming, and we ate oranges and grapefruit quite often. Mom wrote that I had even gone shopping with Paul and spent some of my hard-earned money on presents for others. Maybe that was the moment when life started being not completely about me. I'm still working on that.

10. WISCONSIN'S CENTENNIAL SUMMER

MAY 29TH, 1948 WAS 100 YEARS AFTER President Polk signed a congressional act admitting Wisconsin into the union. Because of that, on Saturday with thousands of others, I watched the big centennial parade around the capital square celebrating statehood. I felt lucky to be alive on such an historic day.

All summer, and during a lot of subsequent summers as well, we'd hop on our bikes and head to Willows Beach on Lake Mendota where we often spent the whole day, free from worries and having fun. What more could a kid want? In the 1940's, the lakes and beaches were clean until August, when the weeds increased. There wasn't much algae until lawn fertilizers and phosphorus detergents became a big issue with the growing population. Despite this, I did get a lot of middle-ear fungus infections. After several visits to my ENT, old Dr. Brindley said to Mom, "If I had ears like his, I'd never go swimming again." I didn't follow that advice, but I did start using ear plugs. We got plenty of exercise each summer and more than enough sun. Too much in fact. My skin was so light that I never could get a good tan. For that, I blame Dad and his red hair. That's why I thought Mom called him "Brick."

That summer and the next, Mom enrolled me and my sister Mary in the University Laboratory School held at Washington Grade School. I later wondered if it were to improve my reading or just to get me out of the house.

Mary came home the first day and told Mom that she had met a girl with beautiful curly hair and wondered if she could invite her to lunch after school. Sure enough, it all worked out and little Patty Hamilton came to lunch. Mom was a little surprised to see that Patty was Negro, as we said at the time, and pleased that Mary didn't even seem to notice. Patty had an older brother Harry, two years ahead of me, and a younger sister Muriel who was a couple years younger than Patty. Their father, Harry Sr., had a Ph.D. in Chemistry and did research at the Forest Products Lab when Dad was there. When the war effort ended, Dad later told me that Harry Sr. was the first one laid off. Velma, his wife, was the first full-time African American teacher hired in Madison and taught at the Madison Vocational and Adult School for many years. Later a middle school was named after her. Our families became good friends, and we enjoyed a number of holiday meals together. It was about that time that Mom and Dad joined the National Association for the Advancement of Colored People (NAACP). The Hamiltons were charter members and just about the only black family I ever saw in Madison. Young Harry received an $8000 graduate school scholarship to study astronomy at the UW. That was a lot of money.

I grew up almost without ever meeting any other minorities or knowing anything about prejudices or the slang terms associated with each nationality or race. Mom was most conscious of that and she kept us all in line. Once when I used the phrase, "He Jewed me down" she quickly explained why I was never to say that again. Until then I had no idea that it was derogatory.

Dad & His Sisters, 1917

Just before school started, I took a Greyhound bus to Fort Atkinson, about an hour from home, to spend a week visiting my Aunt Marge and Uncle Earl Bienfang and my two cousins, Joanne, and Judy. By this time, my Grandma Bertha McLeod also lived with the Bienfangs in their old brick house along the Rock River at 714 Riverside Drive. Grandma's husband, who was born just one year after the civil war on July 6, 1866, had died years earlier at 45 on May 12, 1912, just after Dad turned four. Ever since, Grandma supported her four kids, Clara, Marge, Dad and Hazel, and herself by sewing. Earning a living by sewing always seemed just about impossible to me, but when she showed me how to thread a fine needle, I was amazed. She first licked her fingers, straightened the thread, and then simply threaded the needle without even looking. At eight years old, it took me several attempts.

During and after the summer of 1948, I earned a little money selling greeting cards and mowing lawns with our old push mower. A few times I mowed the lawn of Aldo Leopold's widow, who lived on Van Hise Avenue at the front corner of West High school. I also pulled weeds from the flower beds and rock gardens at the home of Forest and Leonore Middleton in Shorewood Hills, a small village a mile or two west of our house and north of University Avenue. For what weeding I did, I was paid $0.25 an hour, but the best part was being rewarded with a cold bottle of "Dad's Old-Fashioned Root Beer" that they kept in the old cistern. After Dad graduated from the University of Illinois in 1932, he remodeled their old stone house. It was a big project, but Dad was able to fix and repair just about anything. He also drafted the plans to remodel the big, white Winterble house that still stands close to the west end of the new UW Hospital. Since he was willing and able to do any type of work, they always had enough money even during the depression, which was one of the best times of their lives. Movies only cost a nickel.

Forest Middleton was my first cousin twice removed. I never knew what that meant until 70 years later when my sister Margie explained he was Grandpa Middleton's cousin. In high school, whenever we took achievement tests with questions about relationships more complicated than aunts, uncles and first cousins, I just went on to the next question. We didn't have many relatives and I never did learn anything about family connections beyond that.

When Forest and Leonore were first married, they went to Japan for a couple years where he worked for some big company. While they were there, much of Japan was destroyed by the terrible earthquake and fires of 1923. Forest, who was working in Tokyo, couldn't return home to Yokohama by train since the tracks were destroyed and nothing was working. He had to walk for 22 miles among the fires and chaos. When he finally arrived at their third story apartment, he found it had been flattened. After a day of searching for his wife, he gave up and decided just to get on the ship and go home as they had planned. Then the unimaginable happened. Several days later they came face to face at sea.

11. THIRD GRADE

MY TEACHER, MISS NESS, was young and pretty and we thought she was the best. We spent a lot of time memorizing multiplication tables. I also started reading the Thornton W. Burgess books, including Lightfoot the Deer, Jenny Wren, Reddy Fox, and many others. Those books taught me quite a bit about how the various animals and birds behaved, which was interesting to me. Years later, I bought a complete set of all his books, most of which I had never seen, at the antique mall in Columbus, Wisconsin. Shortly thereafter I gave them to Molly Mae, my oldest grandchild, when she was in third or fourth grade. Although she read them all, they didn't turn her into a bird watcher.

Molly was born December 11, 1999, 100 years after Aunt Oral, so, if she takes good care of herself, she'll have a good chance to live in three different centuries.

In January, Mary and I started piano lessons at Mom's suggestion. Every Wednesday noon we hurried home from school so we could eat lunch and still have time for our lessons taught by an older lady, Verna Vath. After just over a month, we performed in our first recital on Monday evening, February 9, 1948, held at the Esther Vilas Memorial Hall in the old YWCA at 120 State Street. Mary was second in the program and played "My Little Toy Drum." I was next and played Hayden's "Surprise Symphony." Paul, who was far more proficient, came much later in the program and played the "Chicago Express." At our next recital June 16th, Mary and I played a duet, "The Clock Man," in addition to our separate pieces of "Ruffy and Tuffy" and "Swans on the Lake." Our last recital together took place on June 21, 1949, when Mary played "The Spinning Song" and I played "The Caissons Go Rolling Along." Shortly after finishing John Thompson's First Grade Piano Book, I told Mom, "You're just wasting your money on music lessons."

About 6:00 a.m. one morning, I started pounding out my lesson on our old upright piano, located just down the hall from Mom and Dad's bedroom. Dad must have been up late the night before because all 6'4" and 235 pounds of him came storming down the hall in his pajamas and ordered, "Stop playing that darned piano right now." That was that. Shortly after everyone agreed that I could stop lessons. Yes, I had the opportunity to learn how to play, but I didn't care that much about it and doubted if I would ever be proficient like Paul. Mom asked, "Are you sure you won't mind not being able to play when you're older?" I didn't care. They thought I had enough other interests to keep me busy. Other than my interest in birds, I don't know what all those other interests were. My favorite classes were art and recess. In fact, I even took art lessons from an artist who had a studio on the Capital Square. I was doing well in school, at least well enough to keep my parents from commenting. Years later, when Mom was over 100 years old, she mentioned that Mrs. Vath had said, "If you ever decide that paying for so many lessons is too expensive, make sure John continues." I almost died laughing. Mom must have had a memory lapse, no doubt about it. Or was it simply a sad example of a partially wasted youth? Back then, kids were supposed to have fun. That was my goal.

That summer Mom enrolled me in summer school held at Edgewood Catholic High School. It was ridiculously easy. When we had spelling tests, the nun would first write the word on the blackboard so we could get a good look at it. Then she would erase it and we'd write it down. I thought that was stupid. How could anybody ever miss a word? I wondered what I was doing there but I didn't complain too much because afterwards, I could walk down to the wooded shore of Lake Wingra and explore. I'd catch baby toads, bring them home and put them in our sandbox under the plum tree. After a few days in such a dry place, I noticed the toads started to shrivel up. To see if they were alive, I put a small pocket mirror in front of their noses to see if there was any moisture on the mirror. There never was. Then I'd set them under the rhubarb leaves in the garden and, lo and behold, would later find them looking less shriveled. That was one of my first science lessons.

After school, I looked forward to eating Mom's fresh homemade bread. On an empty stomach, there was nothing better than a couple of thick, warm slices covered in butter. On cold winter mornings before breakfast, when we had run out of homemade bread, Dad sometimes gave me $0.35 and sent me to the corner bakery to buy a loaf of hot fresh bread and pecan rolls, which kept me warm on the way home.

To save money, Mom sometimes bought a plastic bag of white oleomargarine which contained a little orange cherry of food coloring. It was often my job to pop the cherry and squish the bag for several minutes until it all turned a more acceptable yellow color. When we visited Grandpa and Grandma in Rockford, Mom sometimes bought a case of colored margarine, which was illegal to sell in Wisconsin, the dairy state. One time at the grocery store, Grandpa, who was quite deaf, embarrassed Mom when he loudly told the cashier that his daughter came all the way from Wisconsin to buy margarine. Butter tasted better, no doubt about it, and better than all those tasteless buttery spreads that were concocted years later. Mary said, "Life is too short to eat margarine." She was right.

I occasionally listened to some radio programs such as "The Lone Ranger" and "Sgt. Preston and his Dog Yukon King." My brother also listened to "The Shadow," and the announcer who said, "Who knows what evil lurks in the hearts of men. The Shadow knows," but that voice and sound effects were too scary for my imagination. Sunday nights were the best when all of us listened to "Fibber McGee and Molly" and "Phil Harris and Alice Faye." One night after school, Pete Mermin asked me over and all we did was listen to the radio. I had thought we were going to play outside and have fun, but we just listened. His dad had once upon a time won the state spelling bee in Connecticut and Pete, later, earned all kinds of advanced degrees.

12. WHAT DO YOU PREFER?

WHEN MOM GREW UP in Rockford, there were a few blacks who rented in the neighborhood. Nobody ever wanted to sell them a house even though they were good neighbors. As a little girl, in about 1917, Mom enjoyed talking to Mrs. Lewis. One day she asked her, "Do you prefer to be called colored or Negro?" Mrs. Lewis stood up straight and replied, "I prefer to be called Mrs. Lewis." Years later, Mom said she learned a good lesson that day. Grandpa Middleton treated everyone with respect and was color blind. Dad, who was born in Mobile, Alabama, might have had a quite different experience if he hadn't returned to Wisconsin when he was just six weeks old. His dad was a policeman in Mobile and I ended up with his Billy club. It is a short little club but when you tap yourself on your head, it hurts.

The most repeated story about Mom was when she ate 23 ice cream cones at the Dairyman's Rock River Cruise in 1918 when she was nine. Unlike her little brother, John, who ate too much of everything else and got sick, Mom concentrated on ice cream. However, when the man dishing out the ice cream said, "Little girl, haven't you had just about enough?" she was too embarrassed to ask for more.

13. LOOKING "HUSKY"

I DIDN'T MISS A DAY of school in the fourth grade. Mom said I looked "husky." To her, that meant solid and healthy. To me, it meant "Just a little chubby." I did have a little baby fat, so I knew I was right. That's why I hated the word.

My teacher, Miss Kienzle, motivated us with a big chart where we could stick gold stars after our name if we got a perfect score on a quiz. I remember that little Johnny Walsh got the most stars for one six-week period. He was a good athlete, could run faster than any of us, and was the organizer and pitcher on our little-league baseball team. His dad was a lawyer and the head boxing coach at the UW. From little Johnny Walsh, who was a lot smaller than me, I learned that I was not a boxer. I was more of a flincher. His dad had obviously taught him the basics.

During each spring and summer, Steve Emlen and I continued to spend a lot of time going on bird hikes. During weekends especially, we would leave at first light and be gone for hours. A few times we rode out past Nakoma, down Seminole Highway and parked our bikes by the railroad tracks. We then walked west along the narrow tracks that cut through Dunn's Marsh. Sometimes we went wading out into the swampy black muck and would see a variety of birds, such as Least Bitterns, Sora Rails, ducks, and grebes and we'd get dive-bombed by Black Terns. When the trains roared past, powered by those huge, black steam engines, we would crouch down at the water's edge about 4' from the tracks. We did our best to calculate just when and where the engines would blast out the scalding steam. Luckily, we never had to roll over into the water. The engineers must have been beside themselves as they roared past two little kids. No worries. We knew what we were doing.

Our little league baseball team was sponsored by a plumbing company, Hyland Hall, and each summer, after fourth, fifth and sixth grades, they would buy us new nylon jerseys. Our team would play at one of the ball diamonds down at Vilas Park, where they also had a sandy beach on Lake Wingra and a free zoo. We would hop on our bikes, ride about eight blocks to the park, play our game and ride home. I don't remember anyone's mom or dad ever attending a game. In those days, kids were expected and trusted to do things on their own. If mine had come to watch, I don't think I would have played. Playing out in right field, where I was probably looking at a bird, I wouldn't have wanted my dad watching as a fly ball sailed over my head. Paul claims he witnessed such a scene.

One day when Dick Caswell and several of us rode down the street from my house on the way to a game, a Robin flew over and hit him in the face with a bird bomb. Then a second later, another did the same thing, a double whammy. We could hardly believe it. We all thought it was about the funniest thing we had ever seen, as Dick struggled to wipe off his face on his long-sleeved jersey.

Dick Caswell invited several of us to his birthday party to see a "Frankenstein" movie. It was terrible. We were all so scared that several times we had to leave the theater. When I've seen clips of those old movies in recent years, they look ridiculous, almost funny. But this was before we were conditioned by TV which our family didn't get for ten more years. At least we could go to the movies back then for just $0.25. Just a few "Looney Tune" cartoons were worth the money.

Our family, especially during my grade school years, went on a lot of family picnics to places such as Parfrey's Glen and Baxter's Hollow near Baraboo, and Stewart's Park in Mt. Horeb. In the fall we collected black walnuts and hickory nuts by the gunny sack and camped all over northern Wisconsin and Upper Michigan. We also enjoyed visits with our aunts, uncles, and cousins from Detroit (Uncle John and Aunt Elizabeth Middleton and their three daughters, Nancy, Mary and June), in Rockford (more of my mom's family, including my Grandpa Clarence and Grandma Josie Middleton, Uncle Bill Middleton and his daughter Janet, Uncle Ralph and Aunt Dorothy Middleton and their three kids, Richard, Tommy and Judy), and in Fort Atkinson (Grandma McLeod, Uncle Earl and Aunt Marge Bienfang and their two daughters, Joanne and Judy). We'd all just come and go without warning. It was usually a big surprise. Living so close to Uncle Frank and Aunt Oral made it easy for them to come over often. We all enjoyed that a lot. During the week, we often took rides in our 1939 Ford to enjoy the sunsets overlooking Blackhawk golf course in Shorewood Hills. I loved going but Paul didn't. He complained they all looked alike. Years later we discovered he was color blind like Grandpa, who passed the recessive, sex-linked gene to Mom and then Paul. Being color blind never seemed to bother Paul, but I'm glad I wasn't one of the 50% of boys who got it from Mom. It sure would have hampered my bird watching.

The Hyland Hall Baseball Team at George Hall's House
Bob Wright, John Lorimer, John McLeod, Tippy Cantwell, Andy Anderson, Tom Nedderman,
Johnny Walsh (lying down), Jim Dallman & Dick Caswell

14. ONE PENNY PER BRICK

THE FIRST TIME DAD remodeled our house, he tore out the thick brick pillars that held up the front porch roof and replaced them with smaller wood posts. He also moved the steps to the front of the house and away from the driveway so water wouldn't pour off the roof and freeze on the steep steps. When my classmate, the loquacious little Victor Cassidy, walked by, he asked, "Don't you think the architect of this house knew best how it should look?" Maybe so, but he didn't have to live in it. It was no surprise to us when Victor became a magazine editor in Chicago. After all, his dad, Fred, was an English professor at the UW, who started collecting and organizing the thousands of colloquialisms from all over the country that were compiled and later published in the "Dictionary of Regional American English," a huge project that has gone on for years.

Dad's next home project was adding a one-car garage with a small office for Dad and a larger bedroom above. To prepare for the construction, Dad asked me to clean the mortar off all the bricks that came from the old garage that was knocked down. I sat for two weeks pounding off the mortar with an old brick hammer and earned one penny per brick. I was okay with the pay. After just five bricks, I could buy a candy bar. Best of all, I got my own bedroom with a view of the backyard and no longer shared a room with Mary and Margie. By the time I was in ninth grade, I moved into Dad's little front room office, which he had to remodel, and my old bedroom became the piano room.

After completing the addition in 1949, Mom and Dad had a chance to buy, from a friend and salesman, a new chest freezer and refrigerator for the bargain price of $34 each. To them, it was a big gamble because there was no warranty, but after much discussion, they bought them. Fifteen years later in 1964 they repainted the refrigerator when they moved to their new house, and then it lasted for about 20 more years after that. Most younger people would have purchased a new, bigger model but Mom and Dad had gone through the Great Depression. Once you've gone through that, you're *ruined* forever. That means you'll be frugal for the rest of your life. The freezer lasted 64 years until 2013 when we sold the house after Mom died.

15. SUNDAY SCHOOL

DURING THESE YEARS, our family always attended the big downtown First Methodist Church on Wisconsin Avenue, just a block off the Capital Square, where my parents were married on Memorial Day in 1933. Even as kids, we dressed up in our Sunday best. In fourth grade, I got a new black sport coat with pink flecks and some new stylish narrow ties. Sunday mornings were usually interesting, but I did suffer through a few rather boring Sunday School teachers, like Dr. Straughn, who smoked cigars even in his office. For years I tried to get him to stop because I thought a doctor should know better, but he kept smoking until the end. Smoking to me was such an unacceptable habit, I literally could not leave the matter alone. To this day, whenever I see someone smoking, I feel compelled to make a comment encouraging them to quit.

My next Sunday School teacher, Mr. Wolf, occasionally brought some Wisconsin football players to class. One of them, Harland Carl, #41, was a speedy halfback who was 5'9" and 165 pounds. No wonder he was injured a lot, but back then the tackles only weighed about 225. I never knew why he brought them, but we were glad to meet them. Sometimes we'd skip Sunday School and walk a block up to the Walgreen's drugstore on the Capital Square, buy some candy bars and maybe a pack of Juicy Fruit gum. We'd be back in time for church to listen to Dr. Abbey's sermons, which were way above my head.

16. THE 1940s

DURING THE DECADE OF THE 1940s, a lot happened. Franklin Roosevelt was President, WWII started and ended, Harry Truman became President and then beat Thomas Dewey in a squeaker, the first atomic bomb was dropped, the Marshall Plan helped rebuild Europe, the Berlin airlift saved West Berlin from the communists and the list goes on. One of the things that I remember was the trivial controversy over the singing ability of Truman's daughter, Margaret. To confirm my memory, I looked up an example. On December 6, 1950, the Washington Post music critic wrote a review of a concert by the president's daughter: "Miss Truman is a unique American phenomenon with a pleasant voice of little size and fair quality ...she cannot sing very well ... is flat a good deal of the time — more last night than most at any time we have heard her in past years ... has not improved in the years we have heard her ... and still cannot sing with anything approaching, professional finish."

President Truman's response: "I've just read your lousy review of Margaret's concert. I've come to the conclusion that you're an 'eight ulcer man on a four ulcer pay.' It seems to me that you are a frustrated old man who wishes he could have been successful. When you write such poppycock as was in the back section of the paper you work for, it shows conclusively that you're off the beam and at least four of your ulcers are at work. Someday I hope to meet you. When that happens, you'll need a new nose, a lot of beefsteak for black eyes, and perhaps a supporter below! Pegler, a guttersnipe, is a gentleman alongside you. I hope you'll accept that statement as a worse insult than a reflection on your ancestry." Over the years it seems as if nothing has changed in politics.

Grandma McLeod was born on April 2, 1876, and died on May 24, 1950, at the hospital in Watertown. Her death was very strange according to the story Dad told me. When Grandma was a little girl, a gypsy lady read her fortune and foretold the day she would die. After two days in the hospital, she died on the appointed day. I attended her funeral, the first one for me. When I saw her in the open casket, I couldn't get her cold image out of my mind. After that I never wanted to go to another funeral and fortunately didn't have to for many years. I still dislike lingering in front of an open casket and don't want to remember people looking that way.

17. TEN YEARS OLD

I BEGAN FIFTH GRADE WHEN I WAS TEN. That is when we started having different teachers for each class. The new, enthusiastic music teacher, Mrs. Kline, had been my music teacher during summer school a few years earlier at Washington School. She replaced the retired Mrs. Moultrie, who we called Mrs. Moldy, and started a boys' choir. Because of my "beautiful" soprano voice, I was chosen to sing the second verse of "We Three Kings" in the Christmas program. I did okay but that was my last solo.

I also got a pet hamster which I kept in a small wire cage on my dresser. I played with him quite a bit, but when I moved the cage to replace the newspapers underneath, I realized that he had been drinking too much water in between changes. Forever after my dresser top was stained. I felt guilty but nobody ever said anything about it. I didn't either.

My science teacher, Mr. Paul Olson, limped because he had a wooden leg. Once when we were talking about the weather, he offered to sell us for just $1.00, a $10,000 life insurance policy in case we were ever hit by lightning. Since none of us had ever heard of this happening, we all declined. And what could a dead person do with all that money anyway? He told another story about a man on a camping trip who ran out of toilet paper. When he got to the store, he was so embarrassed that he asked the clerk for wiping paper. I know we must have learned a lot of science that year but that's what I remember. I found out many years later that a Wisconsin wildlife conservation area was named after him for his statewide conservation efforts. I'd see him again later in eighth grade.

18. BETTY GRABLE

ONE DAY AT RECESS, someone forgot the soccer ball. I ran back to our homeroom and found it full of sixth graders. Steve Ely said, "Here comes Betty Grable." When I got home, I asked Dad, "Who's Betty Grable?" After learning she was a movie star famous for her beautiful legs, that became the last day I ever wore shorts to school. Years later Mom said she had tried to get me to wear long pants, but I resisted saying, "No, I can run faster in shorts."

After school one day, Steve Emlen and I were walking home when a half dozen of those same sixth graders started chasing us so they could spank Steve on his birthday. His birthday was in August, but the chase was still on. We ran all over the neighborhood, doubled back towards Randall, and didn't get caught until we were at the corner of Chadbourne and Roby Road, overlooking the Randall school playground. Right away big, chubby Wally Rhodes grabbed me, but I quickly got him in a headlock and threw him to the ground. It was a stalemate. If any of those sixth graders, all standing in a circle around me, did a thing to me or Steve, they knew I could punch Wally in the nose with my free left fist. That's the way we remained for twenty minutes. Finally, a lady from a nearby house must have called the school because old Mrs. Henry, the Superintendent, walked up to the corner and broke it up. Wally was humiliated. After that, he avoided me all through high school. He later owned the "Rhodes Travel Agency." Those sixth graders learned a lesson, and that was the last fight I ever had.

19. STOP AND FRISK IN 1950

ONE WARM AFTERNOON, two of my classmates, twins David and Dennis Pearson, who lived on the other side of West High, and I were up in front of the high school when a police car drove past. Dennis yelled, "What are policemen made of?" I had heard that before, so we all yelled, "dirty yellow coppers." As you can imagine, the policeman stopped his squad car, and since I lived just a few feet away, I was taken home first. Dad came to the door and listened to what happened and then responded, "I don't understand it. He has never done anything like this before." Even to me, that comment sounded so trite that I could hardly believe he said it. Back in the house, Dad said, "You need to get some new friends." That was easy. I didn't see them much anyway. I knew it was wrong and heeded his advice.

I couldn't understand why it was legal to buy firecrackers in Wisconsin if you couldn't blow them up. I never bought any myself but my buddy, Steve Emlen, somehow got his hands on a cherry bomb. At the corner, right in front of West High School, he lit one just as a policeman turned onto Ash Street. We both tore down the street past my house and ran up Burmeister's driveway two houses down. I kept on running, doubled back, jumped over the fence into my backyard where I hid in the raspberry bushes. I was safe but Steve decided to lie down on the ground and hide under the lilac bushes next to the garage. With his lights on bright, the policeman pulled into the driveway, got out of his squad car, and started looking around with his flashlight. Poor Steve was panicked as the beam of light missed him by inches. Then it was over.

Every boy has a compulsion to shoot at stuff and that's why I made a slingshot. From a willow tree, I found the perfect crotch, cut it to size and peeled off the bark. Next, I cut two strips of rubber from an old bicycle inner tube and from a small piece of leather made the part that held the ammunition. It was one fine, well-balanced, powerful slingshot, better than the ones in the store with rubber tubes. One day when I was messing around, I took aim at an English Sparrow. Bam, it was a direct hit. But instead of instant death, the poor sparrow fluttered around in agony. I knew right away that I had to put him out of his misery, so I walked over, stepped on him and crunched him into the pavement. I felt sick. That was the last time I shot at a living creature. It was much more fun when I almost hit the target. Then I could yell, "Did you see how close I came?" That's when I learned that "Nothing good happens when little kids are just messing around."

My friend Steve had a pet Hill Myna bird which could very clearly say at least twenty different phrases, like "Wise up bud," "Good morning" and "It's going to be a rather stormy morning I'd say." It also had a loud wolf whistle. When it eventually died, I asked him if he was going to stuff it. Steve replied indignantly, "No, would you stuff your brother?" I didn't understand that pets seemed to become members of the family. At our house pets never were.

20. OFF TO FLORIDA

IN MARCH 1951, when I was in fifth grade, all six of us piled in the car for a trip to Florida during Easter vacation. As Dad started the car, Mom said, "Aren't you going to lock the front door?" After rummaging around the house looking for the key, Dad locked the door, then walked out through the unlocked basement and garage doors and we began our whirlwind ten-day vacation. I thought, "What was the point of that?" We never had locked it before.

We briefly stopped in Nashville, Tennessee, where we walked through the capital. It was a grubby building with old geezers sitting around spitting tobacco into the dozens of big, brass spittoons regularly spaced up and down the hallways. Compared to Wisconsin's beautiful and spotless capital, it was a shock. When I re-visited the capital and the downtown area years later, the capital and the whole downtown area had been transformed.

As we drove through the deep south, I noticed that there were a lot of "Whites Only" and "Coloreds Only" signs by drinking fountains and all over the place. Why would they do that? I walked past a park bench that an old Negro man had just finished painting and he posted a handmade sign reading, "Weet Pant." That seemed funny to me. We've come a long way since those days. Thirteen years later the 1964 Civil Rights Act was passed.

I was constantly on the lookout for birds. I kept my only bird book under the front car seat. It was our huge John James Audubon book, "Birds of America," with pictures of all his paintings. I had it memorized and pulled it out to confirm my observations whenever I saw a new bird. A year later when I turned eleven, Paul gave me a real bird-identification book. It was Roger Tory Peterson's "A Field Guide to the Birds of Eastern North America." That guide was a huge improvement and I didn't need a forklift to carry it. A few years later, Peterson gave an Audubon screen tour lecture at West High School, and I got him to sign my well-used book.

Next, we stopped in southern Tennessee to visit Sally, whose deceased husband had worked at the Forest Products Lab with Dad. She was a down-to-earth, very friendly and generous person who helped take care of Grandma Middleton for six weeks after she broke her leg. After her husband died, she moved into a run-down southern "mansion" in rural Lewisburg with old Jack Grey who always had a little bit of white scum on the corners of his lips. I was intrigued by the way he rolled his own cigarettes and licked the paper to stick it together. On Easter morning, the only Sunday of the year that Sally didn't go to church, we enjoyed her fresh baking-powder biscuits, bacon, and eggs which she had collected a few minutes earlier. We then had an Easter egg hunt and visited the Milky Way Farm where a prize bull had just sold for $65,000, a record. We saw a $15,000 bull, which still seemed expensive to me.

After passing hundreds of signs for hundreds of miles advertising Lookout Mountain in Chattanooga, Tennessee, we decided to stop and see all seven states: NC, VA, SC, GA, AL, MS, and KY. The view was great, but I wasn't so sure that anyone could see the seventh state 120 miles away. It was just a little too hazy for that.

Once in Florida, we visited all the tourist attractions including the old fort at St. Augustine where the movie, "Distant Drums," starring Gary Cooper had just been filmed. A little farther south, at Marine Studios, we played catch with the dolphins after the show with a small innertube. Then we went swimming and drove our car on the wide, flat Daytona Beach where they had car races.

My favorite place was Silver Springs at Ocala, now located just off I-75 in north-central Florida. We took a glass-bottomed boat into the jungle and peered down 80' to the bottom of the crystal-clear spring. I saw some new birds, including anhingas, or snake birds as they were called. When they swam, only their long necks were above the water and they did look like snakes. At Bok Tower near Orlando, while everyone else listened to the chimes, I went bird watching. While I sat silently under the azaleas, a big black snake, about 5' long, slithered right in front of me. It never saw me.

Florida's first theme park, Cypress Gardens, started in 1936. Three years later they planted a banyan tree and many additional beautiful plants, flowers and exotic trees. It was a beautiful place and there were even pretty southern belles, dressed up in fancy gowns with hoop skirts to add a touch of southern charm. We also watched the Tommy Bartlett Water Ski Show. Years later I was surprised to learn that the travelling show, which originated in Chicago in 1952, settled in Wisconsin Dells after its second stop. Cypress Gardens is now called Legoland. They still have the botanical gardens and Tommy's water ski show, but most people bring their kids to see the various structures made from Legos. Even the southern belles are made from Legos. When my daughter and son-in-law visited us in Florida years later, their two boys wanted to see Legoland. I made sure they didn't miss the best part and was surprised to see how far the banyan tree had spread out.

One of the highlights of the trip for Mom was stopping at all the "Free Orange Juice" stands along the highways. There were dozens of them, and we were always hot and thirsty without air-conditioning. They served fresh, cold juice in little paper cups and we always asked for as many refills as we dared. There were millions of orange trees, mile after mile, and dozens of tractor trailers full of oranges parked alongside the Minute Maid frozen orange juice factory. We had an interesting tour, but I was most surprised that the oranges shipped around the country were dyed to make them look more attractive. Where there weren't orange trees, the pastureland was populated with Brahman cattle, an American breed developed from cattle from India. We thought they must be better adapted to the hot, Florida climate. Where the land hadn't been cleared, there were tall pines and thousands of palmettos. In 1950, Florida had just 2.8 million people. Compare that to 22 million in 2020.

21. KEY LIME PIE AND RED UNDIES

I WAS AMAZED AT the endless, beautiful beaches along the Atlantic coast and found the Everglades to be a wild paradise. From Miami, we drove 120 miles to Key West, over one long bridge after another. One was seven miles long, and from one island to the next we never saw any billboards. Little sister Margie sang, "London Bridge is Falling Down" all the way. Once when we looked down from a bridge, we saw four huge Manta Rays swim under us. At Key West we stayed in a newer motel with air-conditioning. It cost $10 and was the most expensive place we stayed. For dinner I ordered green turtle steak. It was a very fine-grained steak which fortunately, for the giant sea turtles, is no longer on restaurant menus. Paul had wanted to go deep sea fishing but at the last minute, three-year-old Margie scraped her sunburned back while trying to climb an old woody bush. I thought, "How could that happen?" I didn't care that we weren't going, but Paul, who loved fishing, was disappointed. That was the same day we bought a key lime pie. After we drove for miles trying to find a shady picnic spot, Margie slipped as we got out of the car and sat in the pie. Luckily, it was covered with wax paper so we could still eat it. It was delicious despite the imprint.

By this time, we were all sunburned as we headed to Jacksonville, where we saw a dozen flamingos shivering in a pool at 18 degrees. As we continued north into the Appalachian Mountains, we stopped to have a short snowball fight and yelled, "Ouch, my sunburn." By nighttime, it was even colder in Highland, North Carolina. Since we rarely looked for a place to stay until late in the day, we were lucky to find a room because the town was pretty much closed down for the winter season. We were warned to be quiet because some newlyweds occupied a nearby room, and they had been told that no other travelers would be staying the night. We behaved, but in the morning, Margie couldn't find her red undies, and although we searched high and low, they never were found. We figured a mouse, or something larger, must have dragged them off in the night. It's been a family mystery for years.

The Smoky Mountains were beautiful. The hills were lush with greenery and little creeks were everywhere, tumbling down the moss-covered boulders. I could have stayed there for weeks, but we had to get back on the road. To get home, we drove on two-lane roads through dozens of small towns before we arrived in Wisconsin. Just a few years later, thanks to President Eisenhower, construction began on the interstate highway system, which was developed for defense reasons, in order to move military equipment faster from one side of the country to the other. Years later, Mom said she wished she would have taken us out of school more often for trips.

22. BACK TO RANDALL

ON THE FIRST DAY OF SCHOOL after our Florida trip, my homeroom teacher, Miss Simonson, asked, "Would you like to tell the class what you did on your vacation?" She sure caught me off guard because I couldn't seem to think of the many great things we had seen and done. I was disappointed with myself that I pretty much blanked out. Two days later, the penny postcard arrived that I sent to the class a week earlier. That just made it worse.

School was going fine in fifth and sixth and my grades were okay. A grade of "S" meant satisfactory and I got a lot of those along with an occasional "S+" which was like and "A." I don't remember getting S minuses, but I didn't get 44 S plusses like Mary did on one of her six-week report cards. I thought perhaps her teachers were easy graders. Best of all, we didn't have any homework except for a couple hours in sixth grade. In that year, we took a standardized reading test and I scored at grade level 7.6. Not too shabby. A couple of the smart girls scored a 10.6 and one at grade level 11. They both became professors. Lois, who scored 10.6, was my girlfriend for a while in sixth grade. She even invited me to the "Twirp Twirl" dance in high school but moved to Washington, D.C. for our senior year. Barbara, who had the other top score, won the Randall school spelling bee. I had spelled my way into the quarter-finals but then missed a few days of school and the next round because of our vacation to Florida. But I watched the finals. One of the last words was "mere." Barbara very quickly responded, "Do you mean a female horse or a mere trifle?" I was lost. I knew that a mare was a female horse, but a mere trifle. What was that? And it was only a four-letter word. At that moment I was glad I had been in Florida for over ten days and could still bask in the knowledge that I had almost qualified to be in the contest. After all, I had memorized hundreds of words that were listed in a newspaper supplement for all of us to study. That burst of interest in spelling did help me in the years to come, but I never developed a love for reading, just for reading's sake, where I might have come across other "mere trifles." Fiction was a waste of time so I tended to read only books that were "true," where I could learn facts. In retrospect, that was a mistake. I didn't seem to realize that by reading more I might have learned to read faster and with more comprehension. I was always busy doing other things and still am.

23. REACHING MY GOAL

FOR THE LAST SEVERAL MONTHS, I had wanted to buy a pair of binoculars for birding. To earn money, I knocked on doors and shoveled a lot of snow. One morning I worked for about four hours and made $5. I was pooped. I kept busy all winter, and by spring I had earned the $41.80 needed to buy my new 7x50 Novar binoculars. They didn't have a center focus, but I used them so much that I could quickly turn each eyepiece, so they'd be properly focused for every distance. Dad took my wood burner and neatly wrote, as only an architect could, my name, address and date inside the leather case. I carefully guarded them with my life and still have them today. That was April 10, 1951, just before I was 11 years old.

Working hard for those binoculars taught me an important lesson. Because it was my hard work and my money, I took excellent care of them. When we rode our bikes, I always carefully secured them in my bike's carrying case behind my seat. My friend, however, used his parent's binoculars and one day wasn't so careful. One day his fell out of his bike's carrying case and smashed onto the street as we sped under the Milwaukee Road bridge. I thought, "How could he not have fastened the straps?"

Mrs. Mary Walker, President of the Madison Audubon Society, lived just a couple blocks from my house and took both Steve and me under her wing and sometimes went with us on our hikes to Picnic Point. She would tell us ways to identify each bird and encouraged us to read about them when we got home. She also took us to some of the Madison Audubon Society meetings.

Cub Scouts was somewhat interesting to me for a couple years, but since our family had done a lot of camping every summer, the outdoor part didn't add much. For one merit badge, I had to do some kitchen activities, such as making breakfast and taking out the trash. I woke up early in the morning and started making oatmeal, which we ate quite often, but by the time everyone else was up and ready to eat, it was getting thicker and drier and I was worried it was no longer fit for human consumption. When Mom entered the kitchen, she simply added some more water and stirred. It tasted great. Taking out the trash, however, was more of a problem. From then on, I was expected to take it out for the rest of my life. That just didn't seem right.

24. A SPECIAL PLACE

RANDALL SCHOOL WAS A SPECIAL PLACE. It's located on the near west side at the corner of Spooner and Regent Streets, just west of the UW Stadium and Field House. Many of the university professors lived in and around this area and since there was no busing in those days, a lot of the kid's parents were professors. I never thought about this until later in high school, but I was going to school with a lot of smart kids who were expected to do well. That was fortunate because I have often wondered how I would have turned out under different circumstances. Randall was a special place. I mean, how many grade schools have a fight song?

There's a school at ten North Spooner Street,
Randall, its Randall,
You'll find this school is hard to beat,
Randall, Randall School

Shouting loud and clear,
We raise a cheer for Randall,
We work with a vim, we never give in.
We're out to win for Randall.

And how many grade schools also have a Loyalty Song?

We stand up to cheer for the school we love best,
We face toward our flag red and white,
The red is for courage to face any task,
The white for the truth and the right.

Tis here we prepare, to do and to dare,
At Rand-all School, our Rand-all School,
We aim to play fair and learn how to share,
At Rand-all School, our Rand-all School!

Words and music were by Helena Moultrie and her 6th grade class in 1946. And who was in 6th grade in 1946? My brother Paul. No wonder he knew all the words.

25. POLITICS

THE SUMMER AND FALL OF 1952 was a presidential election year pitting General Dwight D. Eisenhower against the supposedly more intellectual Adlai Stevenson. The general, of course, was well-known and popular because he had been the Allied Commander during WWII. I would have voted for him. My friend Steve, however, came from a Democratic-leaning family so he hoped his family's choice would win. I was pleased when Eisenhower won in a landslide, but our differing opinions didn't make any difference to us in our quest to collect as many campaign buttons as we could. At every opportunity we took the bus downtown and stopped at the Republican and Democratic campaign headquarters asking for buttons. We collected a variety of "I Like Ike" and "We Need Adlai Badly" buttons, which I have kept ever since in a wooden box that I later made in seventh-grade manual arts class. Someday, I thought, those buttons are going to be worth a lot of money. The box is already antique.

That year Gaylord Nelson was running for re-election to the Wisconsin State Senate when Steve and I encountered him at the Democratic headquarters. He introduced himself to us, firmly shook our hands, looked us straight in the eyes and asked, "Are you boys going to wear these buttons and give some to other people?" We promised we would but were glad to get out of there as I felt his eyes pierce my guilty soul. We certainly had no intention of giving them away. In 1958, he became the Wisconsin Governor and four years later became a three term U.S. Senator. He's best remembered as the founder of "Earth Day."

Years later, during his re-election campaign in 1968, Green Bay Packer ex-coach and General Manager, Vince Lombardi, praised the democratic Senator Nelson as the #1 conservationist at a banquet in Oshkosh, WI. That was turned into a TV ad that infuriated the Wisconsin Republican Party and Vince's wife, Marie, who was a staunch Republican.

26. THE KOREAN CONFLICT

I CLOSELY FOLLOWED THE KOREAN CONFLICT, from June 1950, to July 1953, with great interest in "The Capital Times," Madison's afternoon newspaper. Every day I looked at the map and watched the progress as our troops gained or lost ground. When they made it all the way north to the Yalu River, I wanted them to attack China and take them over as well while we still could. Nobody listened and look at the mess we're in today. About 2,500,000 people, including 55,000 Americans, died in the stalemate. That was a lot of people, considering we never even declared war.

I read every war story every day because three recent West High School graduates, all close neighbors, were over there fighting. Gil Colucci lived right across the street and I wrote to him regularly. In February and March 1952, he wrote back that he had been severely injured and was recovering in a hospital in Japan from bullet wounds and blood clots. A few months later, when he returned home, he brought me an empty hand grenade and told me a few war stories. He took me to watch several of his city-league softball games. He was a first baseman and a powerful home run hitter even though he had a brace on his leg.

One day, Dad saw an ad in the Capital Times for a Craftsman lathe and a sander. When we went to pick them up, Dad was surprised to see that the seller was his old manual arts teacher at Tomah High School. For the next couple years, I spent many hours in our basement making bowls and other creations such as tiled cheese plates and bowls for cracking pecans. I made piles of shavings and I'm sure I breathed in way too much sawdust.

PART III: 1952-1958
MADISON WEST

27. AT MADISON WEST

IN THE FALL OF 1952, everyone in our class at Randall started seventh grade at West Junior High School. No longer did I have to walk three blocks to school but could leave home, run past the vacant lot on the corner, cross Ash Street and be in class in just about one minute. I was never tardy to class my whole life and would never be able to brag that "I had to walk six miles to school uphill both ways."

Seventh grade went well except for Social Studies taught by old Mrs. Karow. I didn't care for her so I wasn't conscientious about my homework. For my second six-weeks grade, I got a D. Dad said I had to buckle down and do better. Following brother Paul with his straight A's, who Mom sometimes chastised for studying too much, and followed by Mary, with all her S plusses, put on the pressure. My next six-weeks grade was a B and that D was my last unacceptable grade.

English class was spent mostly learning to write. If our assignment was to write a 200-word theme, I would count the words to make sure I complied. Sometimes I'd ask Paul to correct my work, and he would cross off unnecessary words, which then made me worry I wouldn't have enough. We also spent a lot of time diagramming sentences, learning about nouns, verbs, adjectives, adverbs, prepositions, and conjunctions – the list seemed endless. By the end of the year, I was used to the big school and all was going well.

Everyone looked forward to the auditorium programs attended by all 2000 junior and senior high kids. We heard a variety of speakers and programs, including a movie of the first atom-bomb explosion, and a demonstration of a microwave oven. When the speaker cracked open an egg on a napkin, placed it in the oven and in just a few seconds pulled out a cooked egg, we were amazed. However, a long time passed before microwaves were available in the stores. Raytheon, which owned Amana, sold its first countertop "Radarange" in 1967 for $495.

Seventh grade was also a very social time. I attended a lot of parties where we slow-danced with our girlfriends. My new love was Marjorie. There was a lot of kissing going on at those parties which were usually held in darkened basement recreation rooms, a safe distance from the parents upstairs. By eighth grade, these parties came to an end, at least for me, and I settled into a somewhat more serious existence. By then, another boy, Carter Anderson, was trying to get Marjorie's attention. He learned that her new favorite popular song was "Lady of Spain," and asked me to go downtown with him to buy the record. Maybe you remember seeing those little "45 rpm" records with the big hole in the middle that cost $0.85. Then we took another bus to her home, off Mineral Point Road, just a few blocks past Forest Hill Cemetery. I still wonder why I agreed to go with him since Marjorie and I had since drifted apart. However, I do remember getting home that evening. Instead of running home across the street right after school at 3:30, I didn't show up until five hours later. Fortunately, there were no serious repercussions. According to the 1950 census, Madison had just 96,056 people and nobody worried much about safety. We were all free-range kids.

My best friend, Steve Emlen, missed all those seventh-grade activities because his family spent the year in Southern Rhodesia, now Zimbabwe, where his dad was conducting research. That year I was by myself on my many excursions to Picnic Point and the surrounding area.

Guess Who Still Believes in Santa Claus?
Margie, Mary, John & Paul, 1953

28. EASTER VACATION

DURING EASTER VACATION IN 1953, we drove to New Orleans, via Nashville and Lewisburg, with Uncle Frank and Aunt Oral. In Mobile, Alabama, we visited Bellingrath Gardens with its elegant 10,500-square-foot mansion on 65 beautifully landscaped acres. In Biloxi, Mississippi, we loved the beaches, took an excursion to a fort, and Dad and Paul finally went deep sea fishing. In New Orleans, we ate dinner one night at the famous Antoine's Restaurant, the first in New Orleans which opened in about 1840. It was very formal, and we probably looked a little out of place. It was the first time I had ever seen waiters in tuxedos. They brought our food with several plates stacked up their arms. I had a big salad for $0.85 and chicken for $2.25. For all of us the bill was $35, a huge bargain today but a big chunk out of our trip's budget. We also went down to the Port of New Orleans and watched big stalks of bananas being unloaded from ships. They were then dipped in some liquid to kill off the bugs and snakes. Any bananas too ripe for shipping (any that were even slightly yellow) were tossed aside and we could take all we wanted. A lot of army tanks destined for Korea were being loaded onto ships.

After leaving New Orleans, Uncle Frank led the way as we drove over some very long bridges, thanks to Governor Huey Long. Just as he went around a sharp curve to the right and approached a narrow bridge, he met a big semi-truck. I could see Frank's shoulders tense up with both hands tightly on the steering wheel as we quickly slowed down to avoid the crash. But he squeezed between the guard rail and the truck, missing each by just inches and we continued almost as if nothing happened.

In Natchez, Mississippi, we toured several ante-bellum homes surrounded by huge live oak trees loaded with Spanish moss. When we asked the guide where we could stay at night, she suggested the home we were visiting. It was a grandiose place with 18' ceilings, but she didn't mention that at night trains roared by just outside the window. As we continued home, we stopped in Hot Springs, Arkansas, drove through the Ozarks and on to Camdenton and Lake of the Ozarks in Missouri. In Iowa City we visited the place where Dad used to work and the house where we lived in Coralville — which no longer was out in the country.

Except for one night in Natchez, we always stayed at motels. Uncle Frank, being the antique dealer and bargain hunter that he was, became the self-appointed negotiator when it came to how much our rooms were going to cost. He would enter alone and inquire if a couple of rooms were available. Then he'd say, "I don't mind paying the $7 but my poor brother-in-law has all those kids and can't afford that much." We'd split the difference. He got a kick out of doing it and we thought he was clever.

29. MY AUTHORLESS BOOK

I WAS MORE CONSCIENTIOUS in eighth grade, stayed on the honor roll, and except for one time, always did my homework. The one time I didn't happened in English class, taught by Mrs. Karsten. When she assigned us to do a book report, I could easily have read one of the classic comics which summarized some well-known books, as I had done once in the past. This time, however, I chose to do nothing. When the time came to give my report, I continued to say that I wasn't ready, until the last day, when Mrs. Karsten said, "Doing something is better than a zero." That made perfect sense. I knew I would need a lot of 100s to overcome a zero. So, I stood up and proceeded to describe my book, "Robin Hood." I hadn't ever read a book about Robin Hood, but a year or two earlier, had seen the movie. As I began to describe my authorless book, I quickly realized I didn't remember quite as much as I had hoped. Soon I had the whole class laughing and we all had a great time that morning. I later saw in her grade book that I received a "3" out of "10." I still got an "A" that six weeks.

American History was taught by grumpy Mrs. Little, and I argued with her about my test answers. Years later I learned that her husband had been severely injured by mustard gas in WWI. That taught me a lesson. You never know what's going on in people's lives unless you really know them. It's never a mistake to step back and learn why people act and do the things they do. That newfound knowledge, however, seldom kept me from making some "over-the-top" remarks from time to time.

I enjoyed being in the Boy's Junior High Glee Club and continued to sing in the school chorus all through high school. Our teacher, Mrs. Huxtable, was a little dynamo and she got the best out of us. She had wanted to be a professional pianist, but I heard her hands were too small. Our chorus class was large, about 80 kids, and she maintained excellent discipline. A few years earlier before I entered West High, however, she stomped her high heeled shoe through the foot-high wood platform that was made so she could see everyone. When we had a substitute, however, things sometimes got out of hand. On rare occasions, our unacceptable behavior started when someone passed around a note saying, "At 3 o'clock, slam your books down on your desk." Our indiscipline only lasted a few seconds.

Manual arts was my favorite class in seventh and eighth grades. It even gave me some useful, lifelong skills. Our projects included a shelf, which my parents later used in the downstairs bathroom of their new house, a metal wall lamp that I still have in my basement workshop, a small ironing board that my mom used for years and that wooden jewelry box that still holds my collection of campaign buttons. Once when I was painting, our teacher, Mr. Fallon, said that I painted like a Scotsman. I had no idea what that meant but soon learned. Yes, the Scots were cheap, and I needed more paint on my brush. My dad said that the Scots weren't cheap, they were just poor and didn't have much. For many years after, I still had no idea about the various nationalities and the prejudices associated with each.

In seventh and eighth grades, a bunch of us boys went to Club Arrowhead at the Young Men's Christian Association (YMCA) on Saturday nights to play basketball. We also had dances and went swimming. Back then, boys always swam naked at the YMCA. Supposedly it was more sanitary,

Dinner at Uncle Frank & Aunt Oral's House

which seemed strange to me. Club Arrowhead was led by several UW Physical Education students who were practice teaching and learning how to manage a bunch of kids. One night, when our student leader was taking us home, his old car sputtered to a stop as we ascended the hill by Hoyt Park. Just then a policeman drove up behind and gave us a push. Somehow our bumpers hooked together, and the police car's bumper was jerked off. We tried not to laugh too hard until after we were on our way again.

At the First Methodist Church, Mary and I started confirmation classes taught by the Assistant Pastor. True to form, Mary was very conscientious and wrote out Biblical answers to all the questions in our workbook. I guess she did deserve all those S plusses. A few times, I plagiarized her work to make the class a bit easier. Shortly after, we became members of the First United Methodist Church. All through high school and university, I continued going to church and attended the Methodist Youth Fellowship (MYF). We planned a lot of social activities including bowling, ice skating, swimming, and weekends at Pine Lake Camp. In high school and beyond, it was also a desirable source for dates. At one of our worship sessions, some of which I led, I noticed that I had dated all six girls in the first two rows.

30. FOUR BROWN PELICANS

IN EARLY SPRING, Doc Emlen took Steve and me up to the flat grasslands near Plainfield, Wisconsin to watch the Greater Prairie Chickens "boom." Fran Hamerstrom and her husband, Frederick, had been studying them for several years, and we were going to help again as we had done before and for several years afterwards. Fran came from a wealthy Boston family, but her love for the outdoors was considered "unladylike" by her patrician father. She was Aldo Leopold's only female graduate student, earning a master's degree, and her husband was one of just three students who earned a Ph.D., also under Leopold, the "Father of Game Management." Over the years, while conducting their research to save the prairie chicken from extinction, they hosted over 7,000 helpers, usually university ornithology students, whom they called "Boomers," because that is the sound male prairie chickens make during their mating season.

The Hammerstroms lived in a huge, run-down farmhouse that needed a lot of paint and work that it never got. At night we slept in our sleeping bags on old camp mattresses in grubby conditions and were awakened at 3:30 in the morning to eat a breakfast of runny fried eggs and toast. Steve and I were then dropped off in the dark on the side of the road and were pointed in the direction of the blind we were to occupy. We climbed over a fence, crawled under the canvas blind, sat on a little bench and waited for the birds to arrive. We lifted the flaps and peeked out the windows to see the chickens as they flew into their booming grounds. It was our job, for the next three hours, to make a map of each male's territory, identify every bird by reading the numbers on their leg bands, and take notes of any other chickens or Sharp-tailed Grouse that might come to visit. During this time, we had to remain quiet and barely whisper as we watched a half-dozen birds stomp their feet, blow up their orange air sacs and strut around while making their booming sounds. Head to head with other chickens, they never crossed the line of their territory. It was quite amusing to see them strut back and forth. By about 7:00 a.m., the last of the chickens flew off and our day's work ended. We then climbed out from underneath the blind, secured the ropes and waited on the road to be picked up.

Once while we waited, back when we were in sixth grade, four Brown Pelicans flew over our heads. We couldn't believe it. Of course, none of the big shot ornithologists would believe two little kids. Not until a day later, when our observations were verified, did we receive an apology. After all, I had been to Florida where I had seen a lot of pelicans. We knew what we'd seen and probably could identify more birds than almost all the much older "Boomers."

31. THE SUMMER CONSERVATION PROGRAM

FOR FOUR WEEKS FOLLOWING EIGHTH GRADE, I attended a four-part summer Conservation Program organized by Paul Olson, that involved the Board of Education and the State Department of Conservation. Mr. Olson, you'll remember, was my fifth-grade science teacher but next became the Principal of the new Midvale Elementary School. A total of 26 kids from East and West High Schools participated.

For the first week, we worked in the woods with county foresters and learned what trees to cut, what cull trees to leave for birds and animals, and how to plant trees for pulp and wood. One of the kids found a little hognose snake, the kind that rears up like a cobra but is totally harmless. He was excited to show everyone, but as soon as one kid saw it, he came screaming out of the woods in a panic. I had never seen anyone so scared. My dad told me about how he found a nest of baby grass snakes and held about fifty of them in his hand at one time. Since then, I have been surprised at how many people hate snakes.

Game management was the topic for the second week. We piled up the tree tops we had cut down earlier for rabbit habitat and we learned about controlled burning. For the third week, we worked on Black Earth Creek, which later became a well-known trout stream. We collected rocks and stacked them so that the current would be diverted away from the bank and would run deeper and faster. We kept cool and wet for several days that week.

For the final week, we learned about contour plowing and other proper farming practices which reduced soil erosion. We even took a field trip to the Upper Mississippi Experimental Station in La Crosse, Wisconsin, and saw the hillsides where those farmers had learned their lessons. They were even leaving hedgerows for wildlife, which is what most interested me. Over 60 years later, I still don't see enough of those obviously smart soil-saving farming techniques being practiced. I get dismayed every time I see gullies and rows of corn going up and down a hill instead of around it. I thought that Louisiana, located at the mouth of the Mississippi, would someday become the largest state in the union due to erosion. We all earned one semester credit in science towards our high school graduation, but I wasn't too excited about that.

That was also the summer when we planted 500 White Spruce and 500 White Pine seedlings on Mom and Dad's new 4.3-acre land purchase. It was the highest hill for miles around, had a view of the capital five miles away and was located out in the country on Schroeder Road, then just a two-lane dirt road on the Southwest edge of Madison. Dad was able to come up with the $6000, which he paid in installments, thanks to an inheritance from his mom a few years earlier. Mr. Jay Rose, a member of our church, admired Dad and Mom, thought they would be friendly neighbors, and was glad to sell them the building site. The land was called Rosewood.

Mom wasn't sure she wanted to live out in the country so far from the old West High School neighborhood. She didn't drive and would be isolated. Besides, Rosewood seemed so dry. It was almost surrounded by farmland and populated by Bur Oaks with no underbrush because it had been grazed by cows. Paul and I even made a small nine-hole golf course. Just a few years after we planted all those pine trees, with help from Grandpa Middleton, the hill soon looked a lot greener. The squirrels also helped as they distributed a bushel of black walnuts that we had gathered on a picnic. By then we had almost forgotten what a miserable, thirsty job it was digging all those holes in the dry, rocky soil. For the next decade, it remained a picnic spot for some and a parking spot for others.

32. INTRODUCTION TO GOLF

IN SIXTH GRADE GYM CLASS we learned how to hold a golf club, but I never played at a golf course as many of my friends did regularly. My classmate, Jim Dallman, agreed to show me the ropes. We hopped on our bikes, rode past West High School to Glenway golf course and paid the $0.35 fee. Jim started first. He hit the ball hard but sliced it towards the houses across the street, where it smashed through a small window. It wasn't an auspicious start as the lady came running out of the house screaming and waving her arms. Jim quickly agreed that his dad would fix the window. We continued our game and I got a 64 on nine holes.

The second time I golfed was at the new Odana Hills course and got the same score. It was a more difficult course, but I was now in the tenth grade and two years older. Since I hadn't improved, that was the last time I ever played except for a few sponsored golf outings. The truth is, I didn't consider golf to be a sport. If you didn't get out of breath and work up a sweat, it was just a frustrating activity.

33. MAKING THE CUT

THROUGHOUT OUR GRADE SCHOOL YEARS, we had many rough-and-tumble tackle football games up in front of West High School, so when I got the chance, I tried out for the team. To my surprise, I was one of just five eighth graders who made the cut. Strangely enough, getting banged around was no longer so entertaining. So, a year later, in ninth grade, I didn't even go out. The coach, Don Page, who led the West High basketball team to a state championship in 1945, tried to talk me into it, but

I simply didn't want to. In such a large school I could see that there were a lot of other bigger, faster kids and I didn't see any future in it. The other four turned out to be all-city, some all-conference and one, Jim Bakken, a Parade All-American quarterback. He later played for Wisconsin and for many years was a kicker for the St. Louis Cardinals. He was out of my league. In gym class one day, we paired off to do "fake out" drills to see if we could get around our partner. When opposite Jim Bakken, I was the one who got faked out. Once, when I thought I had him, he jumped over me. He also became an all-state basketball guard as a sophomore, an anchor on the relay team, and a pitcher on the baseball team.

34. TWENTY-FIVE LAPS

ANOTHER TIME IN GYM CLASS, our teacher and high school basketball coach, Big Boomer Bob Harris, who was as big as Dad with a cleft lip and a big booming voice, had us all lined up in a row when he could see my lips moving. Yes, I had whispered something to Johnny Walsh in front of me. Boomer Bob boomed, "All right, the Great McLeod, always mouthing off, twenty-five laps." As I was running around the gym I thought, "What just happened?" At dinner I told Dad and he just laughed. The night before, at the parent-teacher conferences, Dad had "argued" with Boomer Bob stating that at our age, we should be having more fun playing sports with less emphasis on winning. Boomer Bob would have none of it. I'm not sure I did either. Living in the People's Republic of Madison, as it was later called, was slowly turning Dad into a Democrat. Later in life he even denied voting for Richard Nixon.

In science class one day we were asked to write a short one-page report on any topic we wanted. For some reason, my imagination failed me until I read an article about the new Lincoln sedan in an auto mechanics magazine. It was the first car with headlights that turned from side to side to follow the direction of the front wheels, a great idea. I rewrote the article in my own words and summarized it by writing, "Truly, Lincoln is the best car on the road." When I handed in my report, it sounded sappy to me then and more so today. That was the first and last time I ever heard about turning headlights. They probably got stuck when it snowed.

35. RUN, RAN, RUN

MY NINTH GRADE ENGLISH TEACHER, Mrs. Lowry, filled the entire blackboard with grammar rules every day. The whole year, so it seemed, we studied grammar. We diagrammed sentences, memorized the 36 prepositions that were followed by the objective case, learned to conjugate all the irregular verbs (today I run, yesterday I ran, and I have run in the past) and this went on and on. And yes, Mrs. Lowry, I know I shouldn't begin a sentence with "and" or "but," or end a sentence with a preposition or split an infinitive, but from time to time I'm going to do it anyway. Who made up those rules? They don't always make sense. Her class was interesting but proved to be a curse. Ever since, I have been just a wee bit critical of people's grammar, such as football and basketball announcers, many of whom never even learned how to conjugate the word "run." To this day, I tend to correct people while they are talking. My daughter-in-law, Sara, who is not one of the culprits, even gave me a T-shirt that says, "Just so you know, I'm silently correcting your grammar as you speak." Could I possibly have irritated someone? When my kids were little, I would correctly repeat what they said, and as a result, my son tested out of Freshman English at the UW in Madison just because the correct answer sounded better. That isn't normally the best way to pass a test, but in this case, it is. Nobody wants to think about grammar while they're talking.

I also took Latin for a couple years, taught by Teresa Kleinheinz. In this class we learned even more grammar, which fit in nicely with my English class. Every day we learned about ten new words. I

The Winning Hand: John, Grandpa, Uncle Frank & Paul

memorized them in the evening, got up at 6:30 to make sure I still knew them, and then got 100 on the quiz. What an easy way to get an "A." In tenth grade we translated a part of Julius Caesar's "The Gallic Wars" where I learned that "Gaul is divided into three parts." I also learned that when Brutus stabbed his friend Julius Caesar, poor Julius said, "Et tu, Brute?" which means "Even you Brutus?" Mrs. Kleinheinz reminded us that Caesar, even under such difficult circumstances, used the vocative case correctly. I later learned in English class that "Et tu, Brute" was written by Shakespeare.

36. A FAR WEST VACATION

TOWARDS THE END OF THE SUMMER, Mrs. Mary Hunt, and her daughter Peggy, were planning a long trip out West to pick up her son Dwight, who was attending a boy's camp in Idaho. Mary was asked to accompany Peggy, her close friend, and I was asked to be Dwight's companion. Dad and Mom didn't think I'd want to go but I jumped at the chance for a new adventure.

We left on August 14, 1955, and headed west past La Crosse to Rochester, Minnesota, where we admired the new 11 story marble buildings at Mayo Clinic, and onto Haplan Woods State Park, Pipestone National Monument, and the flatlands of western Minnesota. In South Dakota, the land of "infinite variety," I learned the word "arroyo," those narrow valleys surrounded by bare hillsides that are subject to flash flooding. We stopped at Pierre, the capital, and then crossed the Missouri River into sage brush country. We camped next to the dry Bad River, before entering the Badlands. We soon saw our first jack rabbit, a two-foot rattlesnake, which we almost stepped on, and ten golden eagles, all before arriving at the famous Wall Drug Store. On the third day we passed by Rapid City and drove through the Black Hills National Forest before arriving at Mt. Rushmore. The faces of Washington, Jefferson, Roosevelt and Lincoln were 60' high from their hairline to their chins. Then onto Custer State Park where we took a tour and learned that there were more Indians at the Battle of the Little Bighorn than Custer had bullets. We fed some grass to a group of fifteen burros, and then watched them stick their noses into everyone's car window.

Past Deadwood, we drove on to Sundance and could see Devil's Tower in the distance, appearing like a huge tree stump with vertical columns, 865' high, with about an acre and a half on top. We camped nearby, heard a lecture on the Black Hills and saw the prairie dog colony. Many of them were very tame and ate out of our hands, which allowed me to take close-ups using Dad's old 8mm Keystone movie camera. This was the first time I had ever taken movies and was able to use some of Dad's outdated rolls of film. I was pleased with the results. That was the beginning of an expensive hobby.

When we left Devil's Tower, I ran 2.6 miles for some exercise and the others picked me up after about twenty minutes. I needed the exercise but was sore the next day. Many times, before entering a small town, we would see signs that said, "Town Ahead." I guess they wanted us to slow down.

The next day in Billings, Montana, we bought gas for $0.34 per gallon. In Big Timber, the main drag was called McLeod Street. We then drove through a town called McLeod. It had two bars, a store, one filling station and a motel. We camped along the Boulder River, a beautiful spot with a view of Mt. Douglas. West of Bozeman, we saw some antelopes and continued to Helena and Missoula, where we stayed in the Shady Grove Cabins.

In Idaho, we drove over Lookout Pass to Mullan and then around Lake Coeur D'Alene, Idaho, where we picked up Peggy Hunt's younger brother, Dwight, at Arrow Camp. In Spokane, Washington, we went to see some relatives of Mrs. Hunt, the K.J. Kafflens. They weren't home so we set up camp at Riverside State Park. In the evening we went to a fair where I spent $0.93

riding the Octopus roller coaster. The first time I was terrified but by the fourth, not so much. Another ride, called the Hammer, was far worse. Somehow Dwight and I lived through it but would never do it again.

Back at the Kafflens, we waited until 9:00 p.m. before they showed up. They insisted we stay, as we had hoped, so back we went to the park, packed up our tent in the dark and spent a much more comfortable night in their luxurious home. The next day they showed us Spokane in their new Buick.

Mrs. Kafflen, Peggy, Mary, Dwight, John & Mrs. Hunt

We continued our trip west along the beautiful Columbia River and entered the Ginkgo State Petrified Forest. The museum contained many beautifully polished pieces of petrified wood. As we got closer to Seattle on Highway 10, the scenery changed from flat irrigated fields to high, jagged mountains in the distance. Once we arrived in Seattle, we started looking for some more relatives of Mrs. Hunt, Hal, and Sue Miles. That evening we peered through Hal's 165X telescope and were excited to see the rings of Saturn. They showed us around the long, narrow city of Seattle and the Boeing Air Force Base where we watched some huge B-52's take off. I was surprised to see so many civil defense signs and escape routes posted throughout the city. We continued past La Grande Dam, the largest arch dam in the world. We didn't pay the entrance fee into Mt. Rainier National Park because it was cloudy. Instead we visited Lewis and Clark State Park and continued south to Portland, Oregon, where we stayed with more relatives, Bill, and Janet Mayer. The next evening, they grilled huge pieces of delicious, fresh salmon. At home, Mom often made salmon loaf from canned salmon (the first meal she cooked after getting married), a wretched excuse for seafood.

From Portland, we headed west to Ecola State Park and Cannon Beach and viewed the Pacific Ocean for the first time in our lives. The scenery was fantastic, and I had a great time throwing bits of bread to the gulls that hovered over our heads on the edge of the cliff. The beach was beautiful, with huge rocky outcroppings sticking up in the surf. We also enjoyed swimming for several hours and saw where Lewis and Clark reached their destination and made salt from the sea water. Our journey continued past Mt. Hood, Mt. St. Helens, and Mt. Adams. Mrs. Hunt showed us where she had formerly lived, on top of a high hill called Council Crest, but most houses were gone and replaced by huge medical buildings with a great view of Portland. Twenty years later, in 1975, Mrs. Mary Hunt became a Peace Corps Volunteer teaching chemistry in Nairobi, Kenya.

Ever since we picked up Dwight, who would soon be an eighth grader, we discovered over and over that he loved trains. And yes, in the west there were a lot of long freight trains. Every time we saw a train, he got super excited and repeated, "How lucky can I get, how lucky can I get..." until the train passed. It just about drove me crazy. I had to remind myself over and over why I had been invited on the trip.

On the sixteenth day, we headed east along the Columbia River with its many sandbars. We passed Beacon Rock and stopped at several beautiful waterfalls including Multnomah Falls, 620' high. Next, we stopped at the Bonneville Dam which supplied power to much of the Northwest. We found the fish ladders interesting and even saw a sea lamprey fastened to a salmon. We followed Highway 30, the Columbia Highway, past Boardman where we left the river and went on to Boise, Idaho. A little farther we started seeing humorous signs:

"Sagebrush is free, stuff some in your trunk"
"Warning, Methodists, look out for Mormon crickets"
"Please do not feed the desert rats"
"Watch out for flying saucers and skunks"
"This is not sagebrush. This is Idaho clover"
"Danger, Skunk crossing"
"Don't just sit there, nag your husband"

By the Snake River we camped at Thousand Springs, where an underground river leaked through the rocks creating dozens of waterfalls. On our way to Shoshone Falls, we crossed over the Memorial Bridge, which is 476' above the Snake River and is one of the highest cantilever bridges in the world. We passed miles of potato fields and tall corn, just as in Iowa, before entering Utah.

In Salt Lake City, a city of about 200,000 people at that time, we again stayed with some more of Mrs. Hunt's relatives, Mr. and Mrs. R. N. Hunt. They had a big house and in the evening the maid served a huge, quite rare roast. One of the daughters said, "Father, would you please pass the blood." That is the kind of comment I might have made but certainly not in such a formal setting. Mr. Hunt had played basketball for Wisconsin and hoped someday to have five boys for a team. So far, however, he had four girls. Back then, girls didn't play basketball except in gym class. And they could only dribble the ball two times, I think, so they wouldn't get too tired. Title IX wasn't passed until 17 years later.

On September 1, 1955, we all went swimming in the Great Salt Lake. It had about 23% salt, compared to about 4% in the ocean, so this was a different experience. First, in many places all over my body, wherever I had a tiny scratch that I didn't even know I had, it stung. And it was impossible not to float. When standing in deep water, my head, neck and part of my shoulders stayed out of the water. We were warned not to swallow any, but of course I accidentally did and proceeded to cough and choke for several minutes. Fortunately, there were showers so we could rinse off the caked-on salt.

The next day we headed towards Denver, 566 miles away, and camped in the Routt National Forest, where the weather was clear and crisp. In the morning, our half-filled bucket of water was frozen solid, but we soon warmed up, cooked breakfast, and headed for Rocky Mountain National Park. After driving up Trail Ridge Road, and running around at Lookout Point, which was over two miles high, we quickly discovered how fast we got out of breath. At the highest point, the elevation was 12,183' above sea level. We saw Longs Peak, Tyndall Glacier and then entered Roosevelt National Forest where we camped a couple days. Once again, we performed our duties of putting up the tents, cooking, doing the dishes and packing up in the morning.

We visited the University of Colorado in Boulder, then on to Denver where we drove past the U.S. Mint, the capitol building, the Mormon Temple, the new Civic Center, and of course, the Union Train Station with its huge train yards. Dwight was in heaven. As we drove east, we went past Sterling and Julesburg and then along the Platte River in Nebraska and finally to a motel. It felt refreshing to get cleaned up, but the trains went by every ten minutes all night and every ten minutes Dwight got up to look.

On U.S. 30, we hardly saw any cars for 450 miles. The weather was perfect, and I could think of only one day when it rained, which was in the Black Hills, after we had already done what we wanted. At Cedar Rapids, we turned onto Highway 151, drove through Dubuque, the oldest town in Iowa, past Belmont, Wisconsin's first capital, and arrived in Madison after 24 days. It was a great adventure. A few days later I started tenth grade.

37. MADISON WEST HIGH SCHOOL

WHEN SCHOOL STARTED IN SEPTEMBER 1955, I weighed 135 pounds and was 5' 9." I had grown seven inches in the last two years. According to Mom, I was also "thinner than last year," which meant I wasn't so "husky." Brother Paul had gone out for wrestling as a senior and we had always wrestled quite a bit just for fun. I looked forward to tenth grade when I could also go out.

The wrestling room was small, crowded with sweaty kids, and almost without ventilation except for a small window to let in the winter air. The mats went from wall to wall and were covered with a heavy rubber sheet that we had to tuck in all around the edges. By the end of practice, the air was foul, and everyone was soaking wet. After practice we all took showers, yet we'd stuff our wet, sweaty clothes into our gym bags where they would ferment in our lockers until the next day. Every several weeks, Coach Hable had to suggest that it was once again time to take our gear home and get it washed as the ammonia smell was overpowering.

We started our practices with calisthenics and then learned some wrestling moves. Burt Hable had been a safety on the 1953 Wisconsin Rose Bowl team but unfortunately had never seen a wrestling match before he became coach. As a result, our progress wasn't as fast as it could have been. Burt's Ph.D. in History didn't help either, but we worked hard and respected him. After a few weeks I got noticed after two of us were in a mad scramble. Shortly thereafter I was picked to wrestle in an exhibition match against another 135-pounder on the visiting Lake Mills team. The kid I wrestled was probably inexperienced too but I'm quite sure he was better than me. He got me in a half-nelson and was starting to pin me when he committed the unforgivable sin of getting too far forward. I bridged out of it and pinned him with the same hold. What a way to start my illustrious career. We both learned a lesson that afternoon. My second and last exhibition match of the year was at Stoughton, just south of Madison. I got beat 2-0 in an uneventful match and was so tired after those six minutes, I could hardly walk to the shower. The old concrete shower stalls were narrow, and so much water poured out of all the spigots at once, I thought I was going to drown. I could barely breathe. Yes, I had to get in much better shape. Next year would be better.

At home we always had plenty to eat, and during wrestling season, at my request, we ate a lot of meat. I never thought about how much Dad got until one night when he grabbed the last piece of chicken and pronounced, "I do the work, I eat the meat." We all had a good laugh but I wondered about all the other times when he had eaten the gizzards, hearts, and chicken livers.

38. SNEAKING IN

BACK IN THE FALL OF 1952, I had cut out every single article about the Wisconsin football team from the afternoon Capital Times newspaper. I'm not sure why except that I was a huge Badger fan and had sneaked into just about every football game since I was in second grade. I also had a big, 3' long envelope that held all the clippings. Because I never met anyone else on that Rose Bowl team, I gave them to Coach Hable after keeping them for three years. I don't know if he ever looked at them.

By the time I was in tenth grade, hundreds of kids regularly sneaked into the UW football games and sat on the grassy knoll near the Northwest corner of the Field House. There were so many of us that the police finally threatened to take us downtown to the station where our parents would have to pick us up. That's when I took the threat seriously and stopped my sneaking. The consequences were not an acceptable risk even though it was quite easy to do. I simply picked out a couple that looked like they could be my parents and then maneuvered my way just in front of them. As I got to the turnstile, I'd look back at "my parents" as if to say, "They have my ticket," and boom, as soon as the ticket taker dropped his arm, I bolted free into the mass of people. It was easy.

Thanks to my connection with little Johnny Walsh and his dad, the UW boxing coach, I got a job selling peanuts and popcorn and could see the games while making about $7-8 bucks for a few hours of work. Little Johnny Walsh, however, did much better. Since he lived in the 2000 block of Regent Street, two blocks closer to the stadium than I did, he made a small fortune parking twenty some cars all over his yard at $5 and then $10 per car. That's why he could always buy the latest comic book at $0.10 a copy. He had a big trunk full of them. I hope he kept them because they would be worth a fortune now, way more than my campaign buttons.

For several years, Mom and Dad went out of their way to invite UW foreign students to Thanksgiving dinner. It was the Christian thing to do and we might even learn a little about another country. Maybe so, but I wasn't too excited about it. I just wanted to eat with our family and Uncle Frank and Aunt Oral. But they did what they thought was right and invited an African student who turned out to be from South Africa. That afternoon we all learned something new. Instead of getting a black student as Mom and Dad had assumed, he was a blond kid of Dutch heritage who strongly supported apartheid. It was an interesting conversation between Mom and Dad, members of the local NAACP, and our young guest. This was six years before Nelson Mandela was sentenced to prison where he languished for 27 years. A year after his release, he received the Nobel Peace Prize, and in 1994 became President.

In tenth grade, American History was taught by Raymond Quand, my homeroom teacher who got us under control the first minute we entered his room. He strategically placed his big, metal wastebasket between the door and his desk so that when he walked back into the room he could "accidentally" give it a swift kick. After the big bang, he yelled "Who moved the waste basket?" The message was clear. Don't mess with Mr. Quandt. Many years later, he became faithful friends with my dad and they often met for coffee at Rennebohm's Drug Store. I got all A's that first semester of tenth grade but then slacked off and got all B's the second. My parents never said a word but that's what kept me from graduating with honors a couple years later.

39. BACK TO FLORIDA

ABOUT A WEEK BEFORE EASTER VACATION, I got braces on my teeth. First an oral surgeon pulled four teeth, the fourth ones back on each side, to make room so my front teeth could be pulled back. A couple days later after my shiny platinum braces were cemented on tight, a wire popped off. My orthodontist put the wire back but then tightened it up and I spent the next week in misery with a sore mouth. That's how tenth grade Easter vacation began as we headed to Florida for the second time just before I turned 16.

After a few hundred miles, we ran out of gas about a quarter mile from some small town. When we finally slowed down to about 10 mph, Paul and I jumped out of the backseat and started to push as hard as we could. Let me tell you, running that fast from a dead start was quite a jolt. When we made it to the filling station Dad said, "We can't stop here. They won't accept my DX gas station credit card." Needless to say, we got gas, Dad paid cash and I was frazzled the rest of the day.

In Nashville, we visited Centennial Park and admired the beautiful replica of the Parthenon. Dad, who had studied Greek architecture, of course, knew all about it. He explained that the sides curved out a tiny bit so that they would look straight.

Again, we stopped in Lewisburg, Tennessee to visit Sally, whose husband had worked with Dad at the Forest Products Lab. One evening, to keep us busy, Sally arranged for Paul and me to go to a recreation center with three other kids, including "Little ol' Brenda," where we listened to a lot of loud "Rock Around the Clock" kind of music. We hated the music, so Paul and I walked back with Brenda to her house where we met two other boys and girls and a boy from Florida. Paul and I then watched TV while precocious Brenda and her sixteen-year-old friends necked and drank whisky. That night we learned that those small-town southern girls were way ahead of us.

After two days of driving, we stopped for the night in Ingles, Florida, a tiny spot on Highway 19. A couple hours farther south we stopped at the Sponge Docks in Tarpon Springs, a town settled by Greeks in 1887, and took a boat ride. A diver, dressed in an old diving suit, showed us how they formerly dove for sponges. An hour later, we crossed over the big bridges at Tampa to Bradenton where the Milwaukee Braves had their spring training camp. We soon stopped at a roadside stand advertising "All the orange juice you can drink for $0.10," where I drank four cups before we started to look for a place to stay. It was quite a search. We finally settled on a ranch house across the street from the beautiful beach at Siesta Key that cost $50 for three nights. For $11 more, we decided to stay an extra night to make our vacation even more relaxing. Until then, we had always travelled as far as we could, in order to see as much as possible during our allotted time. For us, relaxing on vacation was a new concept. Thanks to Paul's insistence, this trip was different.

At Siesta Key we enjoyed swimming and looking for shells. I still have that box of "antique" shells on a shelf in my garage but haven't looked at them since. They were fun to collect but then what? At my suggestion, we took a short trip over to Myaka State Park where I saw a lot of birds. On Friday we departed for home in time for school. Years later I asked Dad how much he spent on our ten-day Easter vacations for the six of us. He replied, "I took $400 and spent about $250."

40. A REAL JOB

I WORKED AT A DAIRY QUEEN located just west of the Shorewood Hills Village entrance on University Avenue from March 22nd until October 17th, 1956. That first day on the job, I washed walls and dishes from 4:00 right after school until 8:30 p.m. when I rode my 3-speed Schwinn home in the rain. I was recommended for the job by Ronnie Burmeister who had worked there the year before and lived two houses down from us on Chadbourne Avenue. It was my first real job that required a social security number, which eventually arrived on June 20th. On most summer days, I opened the business, made the cones, sundaes, milk shakes and soft drinks, while making change from the cash drawer. In fact, I didn't buy my first handheld calculator until 18 years later in 1974. Back then the DQ menu was limited — no hot dogs or hamburgers. On weekends, or whenever it was busy, my boss, Perry Shields, would be in charge. One of the important things I had to learn, which was quite simple, was making the curl on the top. Only Dairy Queen did that. When mixing shakes, I always held the cup so that they would be extra thick. To show the customer just how thick they were, I'd sometimes tip the cup upside down. A minute or so later, after the shake had a moment to warm up, there was sometimes a disaster in the parking lot when the customer showed off doing the same thing.

I hated making banana splits because they took too much time while the line outside the window grew longer and longer. I usually bought bananas first thing in the morning next door at the new PDQ store and filling station. PDQ was short for "pretty darn quick" and was started by one of Dad's Optimist Club member friends, Sam Jacobson. Soon PDQs were all over

Madison. One morning when I went to buy a few bananas, the door accidentally locked behind me and I couldn't get back in. Now what? As I walked around the store to see where I could break in, I noticed that the little front serving window was unlocked. Being a skinny, 145-pounder I jumped up and squeezed through. I don't know how many people must have seen me as they drove down University Avenue. I never heard a word about it.

I was convinced that DQ was better than any of the other soft-serve outlets like Tasty Freeze. I got paid $0.75 per hour which was just okay but since I didn't quit before the season ended, I received a bonus of $0.05 for every hour that I had worked. That helped.

During the summer, I took drivers' education in front of West High School with a new 1956 DeSoto with a push button automatic shift and passed my driver's test in downtown Madison the first time. That was a relief. The policeman's only suggestion was that I come to a stop more gradually. Until I got my license, I thought I knew how to get everywhere. Once behind the wheel, however, I discovered I wasn't always so sure.

Grandpa Middleton, who was 84, shocked Mom when he called and said, "I'm getting married next week. Come on down for the wedding on July 14th." I'm sure he was hoping to get a wife who could bake fresh homemade bread and do some of the cooking. But the tables were soon turned when his new wife, Ida, was confined to a wheelchair. Suddenly he had to do even more heavy lifting.

Over a month later on September 23, 1956, Dad attended a Methodist Layman's Conference at the Green Lake Baptist Assembly where he played a round of golf with his fellow laymen. Before long, Dad's score card soon reflected the fact that he played golf less than once a year. To remedy this situation, his partner suggested that he should hit a hole-in-one. On the very next 130-yard hole, he did, and was presented with a small trophy with a round hole in the "1."

On October 13th, the afternoon newspaper, The Capital Times, was delivered to the DQ front window with the headlines, "UW Freshman Student Murdered." The victim was Tommy Middleton, as well as his younger sister, Judy, my cousins from Rockford. Uncle Ralph's wife, my Aunt Dorothy, had shot her two youngest children. Richard, the oldest, was fortunately away at school at Harvard. As I read, it seemed as if it had happened to strangers. I couldn't believe it. We later learned that Aunt Dorothy had been suffering from some well-concealed mental problems which I had never noticed. They were well-concealed perhaps because nobody ever talked about such embarrassing issues. After the murder trial, Dorothy succeeded in committing suicide in a mental hospital. Of course, that didn't resolve all the issues and hard feelings between Uncle Ralph and Mom, who never could figure out why Ralph was upset with her. She didn't know what more she could have done.

For the next five or six years during the school year, I continued to work for Perry Shields, my former boss at the DQ, who became the custodian at the First Congregational Church at the corner of University Avenue and Breese Terrace. He lived inside the church in a small apartment. On Saturday mornings, I'd dust and sweep the sanctuary and Sunday School rooms.

That way I got a little extra cash on a regular basis and I'm sure Mr. Shields greatly appreciated me doing a lot of his work. I also washed the exterior second story windows. I had a safety harness around my waist with straps that fastened to hooks stuck in between the bricks on each side of the window. A few of the hooks were a bit loose in the old mortar but they always held, and I survived.

41. MY JUNIOR YEAR

IN ELEVENTH GRADE, I took Advanced Algebra, English, and Biology. In Algebra, I got excellent grades but never understood why I was doing what I did or how I would ever use it. I was basically memorizing equations to pass tests, which meant I'd soon forget all I had learned. As a result, that was the last math class I took in high school. Maybe Mr. McCloskey wasn't as perceptive as I thought or maybe I should have asked for explanations.

At the time, I was glad I didn't have old Mrs. Lugg for math, partly because she looked cross-eyed and taught the kids to use a slide rule. For sure I would have forgotten how to use one of those. There was no future in that technology. Being a professional architectural engineer, my dad was extremely adept at using one and carried it with him all the time. He could quickly get the answer to the second or third decimal point and solve problems published in his engineering magazines, but had a hard time explaining simpler problems to me. Maybe it was a lack of hard work on my part. Or maybe I needed a few more IQ points. I certainly wasn't my dad.

A year later during our high school graduation show, which was a spoof on our class and in part to make fun of the teachers, one student wrote a skit about Mrs. Lugg. Two girls, one dressed as Mrs. Lugg and another as a student, walked quickly across the stage from opposite sides and bumped into each other. With books flying, Mrs. Lugg said, "Why don't you look where you're going?" The student replied, "Why don't you go where you're looking." I hope she never heard about that.

I had an interesting English teacher, Miss Holstein, in both eleventh and twelfth grades. We read a lot of interesting literature including the adventures of Ulysses, Greek mythology, Oedipus Rex, Homer, Jonathan Edwards' "Sinners in the Hands of an Angry God" and for two weeks, excerpts from the Bible. Reading such highbrow literature made me feel, well, just a wee bit more educated. Miss Holstein once told us how new acquaintances would make mental notes to remember her name. Sometimes they would call her Miss Jersey or Miss Guernsey. She was a big woman.

We also read poetry written by English and early American poets. Once or twice in school we had assignments to write poetry which I dreaded. Dad, however, could recite hundreds of poems. On Valentine's day he composed this poem for Mrs. Dora Hanson, who lived next door with her husband Oscar, a retired tobacco farmer from Edgerton:

"At the smart age of ninety-three
She's good at quoting poetry.

She's sharp as anyone can be
In gay or serious repartee.

Though she has earned a train of attendants
She strongly maintains her independence.

If you on her a favor press
She returns it to you with interest.

As a hostess she is always gracious
And plies you with food on all occasions.

From just a snack when you walk in the room
To a three-course dinner on Sunday noon.
Also, if I am any judge
She makes the best of chocolate fudge.

She's a very special person you see
And has won our hearts completely.
That is why we bring this rhyme
To ask her to be our Valentine."

Once I said random words to see if Dad could recite a poem containing that word. I was amazed when he did. A few years earlier while we were driving home, Dad started to recite a long poem, "The Captain's Well," that he had memorized for an eighth-grade school program in 1922. He got through most of it. I asked, "How can you still remember it?" He replied, "I'm interested in it." Dad was interested in just about everything.

Biology was my favorite class, and Mr. C. J. Antoine was my favorite teacher. He knew I was an avid birder so when the time came to learn the names of some birds, he deferred to me. It was a little awkward, but I guess I didn't mind. One time on a test, he asked how to eliminate White Pine Blister Rust. For fun, I wrote down two ways. The first was to eliminate all the gooseberries, the host, or you could also cut down all the White Pine trees. He commented that he would provide the axe and a flashlight. I didn't get any extra credit.

We also had to take Health for a semester, where we learned about the two terrible sexual diseases that would afflict us if we ever strayed off the straight and narrow. The pressure on us seemed extreme and everyone I knew led a straight and narrow life. We all knew that if we ever got one, the government would ask us about all our girlfriends and then interview them. We also saw a lot of movies about the importance of driving carefully. The memorable line in one of them, as the family was speeding on a mountain road with a load of kids, was, "Don't worry, I know this road like the back of my hand," as their van went flying over the cliff. We also learned a little about life and term insurance and memorized, "A family that prays together stays together," and other sayings. This actually happened in Madison in the 1950's. Health was taught by old Willis Jones, the track coach. His dad had been Dad's track coach back in 1927 when Dad was Wisconsin's best freshman miler. Dad also ran cross country and got down to 168 pounds. At 6'4," his BMI must have been low. Back in Tomah High School, he always lapped his nearest competitor on their quarter-mile cinder track. In 1926, his time running the mile in high school was a little under 4 minutes, 30 seconds.

42. MAKING THE TEAM

OF COURSE, I WENT OUT FOR WRESTLING. Without last year's seniors, my life became a little easier. As a sophomore, I sometimes practiced with Chuck Dykeman who was all bones and elbows. It just plain hurt to wrestle him. As a junior, my main opposition was now a senior, Bob Bing. He was also a 145-pounder and wanted desperately to beat me out. When he could, he'd even go downtown to the YMCA and lift weights in his attempt to get stronger, but he already was. He could lift 135 pounds above his head. I could never have done that. He never beat me but was a first-string high school miler, and later at Wisconsin became a cheerleader. Then he got to lift cheerleaders. It all worked out.

Coach Hable was still trying to teach us various wrestling moves, but this year our team had a secret weapon — a new sophomore, Steve Martin, whose dad, George, was the Wisconsin wrestling coach. Steve sometimes took us down to the Wisconsin wrestling room where Coach Martin would show us some clever tricks. A day or so later, we'd try them out during our Friday afternoon matches. My favorite was the "Single Wing Lock" which we called the "Chest Cruncher." Once when we were wrestling East High School, our most hated opposition, I pinned my opponent in 45 seconds. The next time I wrestled him, he was defensive, but I got him again with the "Chest Cruncher." I had a lot of fun with that hold. Nobody ever saw it coming.

Our team had never won a dual match against East High School, but we were sure we could this year. The night before the match, little Johnny Walsh, our 128-pounder, was working when he noticed a "Salt Tablet" dispenser. The sign said, "If you feel hot and tired, take a tablet." He thought that if one were effective, eleven would be much better. When he got home and told his mother, she immediately called the doctor who said, "Stick a hose down his throat." Well, after drinking water all night, he weighed in overweight and had to forfeit the match. He wrestled anyway but now it was just an exhibition match. Although Johnny won by a pin, East High got the five points and won the match. How could that happen? He is the one who got all those gold stars in fourth grade.

Paul, Margie, Mary, & John

Every other year, the music teacher, Miss Huxtable, directed a musical play. This year she chose "Naughty Mariett," and there were a couple kids able to sing the lead parts, Jeff Dean, a junior, and Emily Curless, a senior. I just had a small part, a dancing scene with several others. Dancing was not one of my abilities, but I don't remember any groans from the polite audience. My sister Mary, however, did have a major dancing part.

43. ALL SUMMER AT PINE LAKE

IN THE SUMMER OF 1957, I was one of two lifeguards at Pine Lake Methodist Church Camp near Westfield, Wisconsin. Since I had to have a physical exam, Mom called Dr. McDonough, who got me through all those childhood diseases. He took one look at me, dutifully filled out the form and asked her, "Don't you think he's a little old to still be seeing his baby doctor?" Mom and I were a bit embarrassed.

I also had to take a lifesaving class at the old downtown YMCA, but time ran out and I never did get certified. In fact, I wasn't even a particularly able swimmer. When we swam back and forth across the lake one weekend, I used my favorite stroke, the dog paddle, but when on duty, I either stood on the pier or watched from a boat to save anyone in trouble. I did save a couple little girls when they were being tested to see if they could swim out to the raft. Halfway there, one hollered, "Save me." A second later, another third grader yelled, "Save me, too." They were so little that I could easily drag them to the nearby rowboat. Nobody ever inquired about my credentials and that was fine with me.

The other lifeguard, Dave, and I did all kinds of other tasks: washing the pots and pans, taking out the garbage, and other odd jobs to keep the place clean and orderly. One morning when burying the garbage, we backed the old Ford pickup truck too far into the sandy hillside, got stuck and spent the rest of the morning furiously shoveling sand.

I had advantageous connections to get the job. The Director of the camp, Mr. Bill Marsh, was the Principal of Central High School, went to our Methodist church, and was a close friend of my dad. Dad had also designed the large main dining hall and several new cabins at the camp. As a kid, I also worked for Bill and his wife, Louise, pulling weeds at their home over near Vilas Park.

I was well acquainted with Pine Lake Camp. Every summer, beginning in grade school, I spent a week there, swimming, sleeping eight of us in a big army tent, playing games, meeting new kids, and dating plenty of girlfriends. Back then it cost just $14 a week, which was a great deal for my mom and dad because they got a vacation too. It was eight years of camp crammed into just three months. And I got paid the grand sum of $287.50 for the summer.

44. BEING A BEST FRIEND

AS A JOKE, I WROTE A MUSHY LOVE LETTER to a pretend girlfriend and mailed it "by mistake" to Steve Emlen, my best buddy — but was disappointed not to get a reply. At the end of the summer, I asked him why he never mentioned the mix-up. His mom chimed in and said, "When he saw the letter wasn't for him, he didn't read it and wouldn't show it to anyone. My joke was a flop, and for a moment I was disappointed — but quickly realized that Steve was my best friend.

In May, a year before I headed to Pine Lake, Steve Emlen, and I each got new pets. Two fledgling Great Horned Owls had been abandoned and rather than letting nature take its course, Steve's dad, the zoology professor, somehow ended up with them. Steve's owl, "Melvin," resided in a small pantry in their newly acquired stucco house at the corner of Van Hise and Bascom, just a couple blocks from mine. I made a big cage for my owl, "Herman," in our backyard. Dad and I went to the city dump and found some 4'x8' sheets of heavy paneling which we used to make the sides of his cage. The inside measured about 3'x4', where Herman slept during the day plus a screened front porch so he could observe the world at night. As soon as I finished the cage on June 1st, I picked up Herman from Steve's house.

To feed a large owl, you must either be an expert small game trapper or have a easy source to get such food. Thanks to Steve's dad, we had a source. Doc Emlen took us to the UW lab where they did experiments on white rats. When they died, they were tossed into a chest freezer where we helped ourselves. Steve had a big machete, which I used to chop the frozen rats in cross sections while Steve used a paring knife to cut each slice into quarters. We then bagged them up and put them in our freezers, to the delight of our mothers. We hand-fed our pets once each day.

This all happened in the days when we were free, before the days of the DNR, the Department of Natural Resources, which now even prohibits kids from collecting bird feathers. What would the DNR do if they found out that the widow across the street, old Mrs. Colucci, had given me a stuffed Great Blue Heron, a Red-Throated and a Common Loon, a Wood Duck and Gadwall? Once we dressed up the heron to imitate a stork for a baby shower. Years later I gave the heron to a friend who was a science teacher at a Christian camp in the Poconos in Pennsylvania. The DNR later made him dispose of it. My stuffed birds are now over 100 years old, but I doubt if I could claim the "grandfather clause."

During the summer of 1957, Herman also accompanied me to Pine Lake Camp. There he ate a more upper-class diet of left-over raw steaks, hamburger and an occasional squirrel or mouse that the campers dragged in. One brought me a mouse that had its hind leg caught in a trap so it could hardly walk. I put it on the end of Herman's perch and watched it crawl slowly toward his feet. I wondered, "Would Herman know what to do after being hand-fed all his life?" As the gimpy mouse started to climb over his foot, it happened in a flash. Herman's other foot lifted, and all four talons completely pierced through the mouse's little body, two on each side, while its big hooked beak decapitated the poor critter at the same time. If I had blinked, I would have missed it all. Instant death. Herman still knew what to do.

One stormy night at the Emlen house, Steve's mom, Ginny, was home alone when she heard clicking noises coming down the hall, closer and closer, towards the living room where she was trying to read. She was almost frozen with fear when she decided she had to stand up and see who was coming. Peering around the corner, at first, she didn't see a thing but suddenly noticed Melvin walking toward her. The pantry door had blown open and Melvin had a glimpse of freedom. At the end of the summer, I brought Herman home from camp and after a year let him go free in the UW Arboretum, not far from where the lilacs bloom every spring. He flew off toward some big Red Pines and disappeared.

45. A CANOE ADVENTURE

COACH GEORGE MARTIN took a small group of us West High School wrestlers to northern Wisconsin on a canoe trip down the Flambeau River at the end of the summer. George and his son, Steve, had their own canoe while Steve Emlen and I used his somewhat deteriorated wooden "Old Town" canoe that had been coated with fiberglass to keep it from leaking. I had never canoed in whitewater but Steve, who had given canoe lessons, assured me we would be fine. I sat in the bow and Steve in the stern so he could steer and shout orders. As we headed down the raging river, which was several feet higher than normal thanks to some heavy rains, I quickly caught on and we were doing well. After a few hours, we had negotiated many difficult rapids, where others in our group had failed, and were growing in confidence. As we congratulated ourselves, after passing through the roughest spot, we encountered several high waves as the bow lifted and slapped down hard on the water. The force ripped the canoe in half from the right gunnel to the left, which was all that connected the two halves. As we slowly sank, we laughed our heads off, but for the next two miles, until we finally could get to shore, we hung on for dear life as we bounced over one rock after another. I don't know where the canoe ended up; I just hope no one spent too long looking for bodies.

The next day we rented an aluminum canoe and headed to another famous whitewater river, the Brule. It was also flooded and flowing fast as we entered the water. Steve and I once again were doing quite well when we came to some wild looking rapids up ahead. We pulled to the side, looked at the rapids, and picked out our route. All was going fine as we paddled furiously downstream. Suddenly, however, we bumped dead center into a big boulder and came to an abrupt stop. As I turned my head to look back at Steve, the raging water quickly turned the canoe sideways, filled it up with water and bent it backward into a "V" around the rock. We both stepped out into the waist deep water and tried to free the canoe. When George and Steve arrived minutes later and saw our predicament, they stopped to help. After struggling for 20 minutes, we succeeded in lifting it off the rock which fortunately was close to shore. We bent it back into shape, lugged it up the hill and waited to get picked up. The last scene revolved around George discussing the accident. Surely the outfitter had insurance. I think we set a record: two canoes in two days.

Steve & John —defeated by the Brule

46. THE SPACE RACE

THE SOVIET UNION LAUNCHED THE FIRST artificial earth satellite, Sputnik 1, on October 4, 1957. It emitted pulses that were followed by amateur ham radio operators around the world until the batteries died three weeks later. It soon fell to the earth on January 4, 1958. It was a big deal, however, as it seemed evident the U.S. had fallen behind the Russians in the space race that accentuated the cold war. There was suddenly an increased emphasis on teaching science and technology and the "missile gap" became a big issue in the 1960 presidential election.

47. ONE MORE YEAR

IN THE FALL OF 1957, I WAS 6'1" and weighed 180 pounds as I started my senior year at Madison West High school. I took all the standard classes including Physics, Chemistry, and English. It was a successful year. The football team dominated and went undefeated for the first time in school history. The basketball team didn't make it to the state finals after finishing second the previous year. Our old nemesis, East High, won instead for the first time ever. In the semi-final game, East beat West by scoring the last 11 points and held on by stalling for a 2-point victory. The last time West won State was 1945 and they wouldn't again until 1992.

Our wrestling team did well, as five of us made it to the state meet. That was quite a success and much better than in past years. For me, it was satisfying to win almost all my matches my senior year. At the state meet, I was also pleased to place in the top eight out of sixteen in my weight class held at the UW Field House. Steve Martin did the best by placing second. That year Dave Neal at 165 pounds and I at 155 were elected co-captains by our teammates, which helped me feel my time on the mat was an especially satisfying experience. Wrestling gave me a lot of confidence. And it got me in top shape. I had a 6-pack and that word "husky" was no longer applicable. A girl in chemistry class even said I had skinny legs. I took that as a compliment because it confirmed I was no longer husky. Because I had lost 25 pounds by eating less than 1200 calories a day to get down to and maintain my wrestling weight, the student editors of the yearbook wrote, "Master Dietician" under my picture.

Our senior class had 340 kids. Forty-one got honors and I was number 57. When I was talking to a UW admissions officer later that fall, he seemed to think, after learning I was a West High graduate, that I wouldn't have any problems at the UW. West had a great reputation. Most of the kids were pushed by well-educated parents. That is why I had to study several hours every night to keep up. Everyone I knew was going somewhere to university. On our wrestling team, five kids had fathers who were head coaches at the UW, four others were professors, and my dad was the only one who didn't have a Ph.D., but he did have the equivalent education. After high school, it never occurred to me that I wouldn't go to the UW. That's just what you did. When one classmate said she was going to Colorado, I wondered why anybody would do that when the UW was so close. My best friend, Steve Emlen, headed for Swarthmore, wherever that was. He knew. As I mentioned, his family had come from out East. Steve later earned his Ph.D. from Michigan and became a well-known behavioral ecology professor at Cornell. All my close friends ended up getting Ph.Ds. I have often mentioned the smart kids at West High, because it made me feel like I was one of them. What path would I take?

48. EXPLORING EUROPE

FIRST, I WAS GOING TO EUROPE with a group of 24 kids, from ninth to twelfth grades, to help promote positive international relations. Mr. and Mrs. Engelke and Mrs. Robert Hamill were our leaders. Mr. Engelke was the Principal of Nakoma Grade School, and his wife, Marion, was quite a well-known, local artist. Years later she gave me one of her mountain paintings for a wedding present. Mrs. Hamill was married to Rev. Hamill, pastor at the Wesley Foundation Methodist Church, across from the Chemistry Building on University Avenue. One of their two sons, Tim, would be a helper on the trip since he spoke German after spending a year in Germany living with Evert Helms. Evert, in turn, was presently living with the Hamills and attending West High. In addition to Evert, there were two other foreign students at West, both American Field Service (AFS) students, a girl from Sweden and a boy from Italy. Five decades later, they both attended our 50th West High School reunion. By then, kids from 80 different countries attended West — the same as the UW. The scholastic level didn't drop but the football team suffered with the influx of all the new soccer enthusiasts.

The name of our group was the Teens Overseas Project, and we were "Toppers." Several kids were from a Methodist church in Naperville, Illinois but most of us were from Madison. Starting September 29, 1957, most of the group started to attend monthly meetings to prepare for the trip. I was later included and wondered why nobody thought I would want to go. When I heard about it, I jumped at the chance. We learned that the trip was going to cost $690 and we were supposed to take $25 spending money. The cost included $340 for the round trip voyages by ship, the plane ride to West Berlin, boat rides across the English Channel, and train and bus transportation all over the continent, plus food and lodging mostly in Youth Hostels that cost $1 each night. My sister Mary and I had each saved enough money for the trip.

Brother Paul also flew to Germany that same summer with his classmate, Jim Dohr. They were half done with Medical school and this would be their last free summer. Paul had ordered a 1958 VW Beetle for $965 and the two of them drove all over Europe. Paul shipped it home for about $400 and it became our second car. I was the one who used it the most after I mastered the manual shift. It didn't take long but when I took drivers' education, you'll remember, I had learned on a push-button shift DeSoto.

Several days after graduation, Dad and Mom drove us to Montreal, via Niagara Falls, where we later boarded the 10,000-ton converted cargo ship, the "Arosa Star." On the way, I lost my wallet and spending money for the summer. It must have slipped out of the pocket of those slippery, nylon wash-and-wear pants when I got out of the car somewhere in Indiana. It's probably fortunate that it happened then. I never had a wallet before and needed to be more careful. Fortunately, Dad replenished my money supply.

In Montreal, the night before we boarded the ship, we went to a fancy French restaurant so Mary, and her friend, Peggy Hunt, could practice their French. Peggy and her mom, you'll remember, had taken us out west three summers earlier. For dinner, Peggy ordered something new, calf brains. That was too much for me.

On June 17, 1958, we boarded the ship, the Arosa Star. It was not luxurious but was outfitted to haul a lot of people — mainly students. Two of us were crammed into a tiny room with bunk beds and the big bathrooms were down the hall. The food was great, however, and I ate plenty of it. There were a lot of movies and other activities including a big masquerade party. With help from Mary and several other girls who provided various articles of clothing, I dressed up complete with oranges, and a sign that read, "I dreamed I went to Europe in my Maidenform Bra." There were prizes for the most beautiful, the most original and the funniest. I placed third and won the boobie prize in the funniest category. The Captain handed out a big candy bar to the winners and kissed the girls. Since I was dressed as one, I gave him a kiss, flexed my muscles and the crowd roared with laughter. The "I dreamed I went to…" ad was a common radio and TV ad at the time.

A bit later that evening, Mary and I danced the Tango, surrounded by dozens of cheering kids. Mary was quite an accomplished ballet dancer and taught dozens of little kids in our basement for several years. She later performed with the Madison Civic Dance Guild and the Wisconsin Ballet Company and even spent one summer dancing in New York. On several occasions she also tried to teach me a few dances with limited success. This was my most famous moment, but Mary and I are the only ones who remember it.

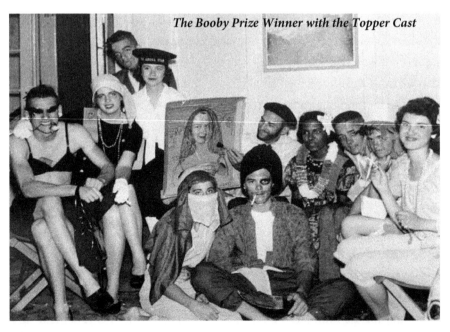

The Booby Prize Winner with the Topper Cast

The voyage was calm until the eighth day when the winds topped 60 knots and the waves crashed over the deck. During the storm, I walked down to the rear deck and watched the raging ocean as we dropped about 20' and then seconds later, I could see for miles. I never got seasick, but it seemed that most of the 850 students did. It was awful. The bathroom floors were covered with vomit and the passengers barfed over the railings which blew in the wind for hundreds of yards behind the ship. When we arrived in Plymouth the next day, the weather was beautiful.

We boarded a small boat which took us to customs and then survived a harrowing cab ride down the wrong side of the road. Each time we met another car on our way to the train station, we were close to a head on collision. Also, I wasn't used to first looking right before stepping off the curb, which twice almost got me killed. Our first night was spent in a youth hostel on a lumpy straw mattress. We were now ready to start our European trip, just thirteen years after the end of World War II.

In Exeter, we visited the cathedral, completed in 1339, and the Guild Hall, remodeled in 1330, where we met the Mayor. They were elegant buildings where we saw some swords, gold chains, hats, and pictures from around 1066. We were served fancy sandwiches and cakes and I ate as many as I dared. We then met at the Mint Methodist Church where the English kids were noisily running around, and some were even smoking. I thought they would have been more reserved.

The next morning, we washed our faces in ice water and took the train 180 miles to London, seeing a lot of sheep and scarecrows along the way. Once in London, we visited Westminster Abbey, had a tour through Parliament, walked around Trafalgar Square and at Piccadilly Circus saw the cuckoo pop out of the big clock at 7:00 p.m. On Sunday morning, in Westminster Abbey, we sat in the half where the service was not taking place. Then we wandered around Hyde Park where people got on their soapboxes and said anything they wanted. They could even disparage the Queen without fear of arrest. As we departed, one Irishman said, "Cheerio American. I like you. I see you have some intelligence." Yes, there were a lot of crackpots. Next, we watched the changing of the guard at Buckingham Palace, where several locals did their unsuccessful best to make the guards laugh. Then we walked to St. Paul's Cathedral, which wasn't as big or beautiful as Westminster Abbey. A day later, we visited the Tower of London and London Bridge. From London we took a train to Colchester and on to Harwich where we boarded a ship to the Hook of Holland.

49. ON THE CONTINENT

AFTER A SHORT TRAIN RIDE TO ROTTERDAM, we arrived at a large, well-organized youth hostel and took a shower that was so cold I thought my hair would freeze. Welcome to the continent. On July 3rd, we left Rotterdam for the Hague. Six of us then went on a tour of the Peace Palace where the League of Nations was created. I even sat in the U.S. chair. Nearby we walked into a restaurant, not fancy on the outside, but inside the waiters all wore tuxedos. Since we were the only customers, we received their full attention. Patty Caves was chewing on a cigar shaped piece of bread when she laughed, and a chunk got stuck in her windpipe. She choked for the next ten minutes. It was quite a scene. When we saw the tuxedos, we should have known enough to leave. Patty was the one who brought her own private ketchup bottle. I couldn't believe it. We once had ketchup at home, but the half empty bottle sat on the shelf for a year before Mom finally threw it away.

After an hour of shopping, I asked a man for directions. He first gave us an interesting tour of the town before finally putting us on a bus to our destination — but when we arrived, he was already there talking with Mr. Engelke. He then led our whole group to the youth hostel which was about five miles away. Without his help, we might never have found it. We learned that he had been in the underground during the war and was no doubt incredibly grateful to Americans. This newer hostel was built in 1953 and even had hot water.

The next day we took several trains and trams to Alkmaar, where on Fridays they had a huge cheese market, with hundreds of people buying and selling. Coming from Wisconsin, it was a little slice of heaven and I couldn't resist buying a chunk. Then more trains to Amsterdam, where we met a Mr. Diks who was our guide for the next few days. He showed us the Rembrandt house where the famous painter had lived for over thirty years. It was turned into a museum and filled with his paintings. After visiting Anne Frank's house, a bit depressing, we toured the canals, and six of us walked behind the train station through the red-light district. We should have avoided that. For the next few days in Holland, I saw a lot of old houses, windmills, the Zuider Zee and a few bombed-out churches and buildings.

50. GERMANY

ON JULY 7TH, THE TRAIN TOOK US from Amersfoort across Holland to Hannover, Germany where we stopped at the America Haus. Late that evening, we boarded a 60 passenger Pan American Airlines flight to West Berlin. We landed just after midnight, took a bus to a Methodist camp about an hour away from the city center. We finally got to bed at 2:15 a.m. It was a poor place with old buildings and cold water.

For the next few days, we met with German students and went in and out of East Berlin. West Berlin was a thriving, busy city, jammed with bicycles, cars, and people. As soon as we entered East Berlin on the subway, everyone suddenly stopped talking and the mood turned grim. East Berlin looked as if World War II had just ended a month earlier. There were huge piles of rubble and big empty buildings that were still uninhabitable and looked ready to crumble. The streets were almost empty of vehicles and people. We saw the bomb shelters, Russian war memorials and the bunker where Hitler committed suicide. The difference between life under capitalism and life under communism was unbelievable! On the border between East and West Berlin, we visited the Brandenburg Gate which was completed in 1791. It was severely damaged in 1945 but was repaired by the governments of both East and West Berlin. Three years after our visit, it was closed off when the Russians built the Berlin Wall in 1961. After five days in Berlin, we flew back to Hannover and took the train to the medieval city of Goslar.

In Göttingen, each of us was farmed out to a German family for the next three days. This was all arranged by Dr. Helms, the father of Evert, who as I mentioned had been a student at West High the past year. I stayed with Jochen Piep who spoke adequate English, because all students were required to take six years of it in high school. His parents were away, and he was at home with some friends, one of whom was a baker and an accomplished cook. We spent a lot of time talking, asking, and answering questions. One simple question that I asked was, "Why do German kids only listen to American popular music?" Jochen said, "Because the lyrics are so stupid in German." I could have said the same thing — dumb lyrics and foul words never sound offensive in a foreign language. I also mentioned that it seemed the Germans were a lot bigger and stronger than the average Englishman. Jochen said, "Yes, but the English have a lot of willpower."

At Jochen's house, on July 14th, I had a real bath. The water was so dirty I had to refill the tub to rinse. For three days we talked, went to a play, toured the city, went swimming, visited the city hall, rode on his brother's motorcycle, climbed to the top of a tall tower on a hill overlooking the town, bought a gold watch for $24.16, attended a meeting at the International Club where we discussed "Atomic Power for Germany" moderated by Dr. Helms, went to a dance, visited a high school, played their basketball team, attended a Biology and a Latin class taught by an ex-Nazi in Hitler's secret service, and listened to Mr. Engelke give a speech in German at the school assembly. Jochen said he could have understood him better in English. Jochen was a great host and even tried to iron my wash-and-wear pants. He quickly discovered, however, that his hot iron was more than a match for the seat of my nylon pants that melted on his iron. He felt embarrassed but I could get along without them. From then on, I sometimes used the lederhosen (short leather pants) that he had given me a day earlier. After all the shaking of hands (some of the girls cried), we said goodbye to our hosts and climbed aboard a yellow school bus which carried us around the continent for the next month. Our bus towed a trailer full of our suitcases and Topper bags.

We drove all day and passed through Kassel, Fulda, Bamberg and arrived in Nuremberg at our youth hostel that looked like a castle. We continued driving the next day through Ansbach, Dinkelsbuhl, Nördlingen, Donauwörth, Augsburg, Schongau and Füssen before seeing a couple of castles in Neuschwanstein and Hohenschwangau. After three rainy days the sun came out just in time to see the Dream Castle that is on all the tourist posters. The Alps and the scenery were beautiful.

51. AUSTRIA, LICHTENSTEIN, SWITZERLAND, AND ITALY

WE SAID GOODBYE TO GERMANY, crossed into Austria and arrived at a newer hostel where we went swimming on July 19th. The water was perfect and a great way to take a bath. That evening we saw Smetana's opera "The Bartered Bride" on Lake Constance with the Vienna Symphony Orchestra, the Vienna State Opera Ballet, and the Bregenz Festival Choir. It was the best show I had ever seen and the setting over the water was perfect. Our $2 seats weren't the best, but I could see all their facial expressions with my binoculars.

On Sunday morning we attended a small Methodist church begun by the Swiss as a resettlement center for Hungarian refugees. Our group sang "Fairest Lord Jesus" and "Swing Low Sweet Chariot" during the church service as we did on several other occasions. The rest of the day we travelled through the mountains past the Pestalozzi Children's Village and Vaduz, Lichtenstein, before we quietly sneaked into our hostel three hours late in the town of Maloja, Switzerland. The next morning, we hiked part way up the mountain, and just before boarding our bus to Italy, we bumped into Dr. Helms, from Göttingen, who was also on vacation. We drove past Lake Como, where there were palm trees, and onto Chiavenna and Lecco, before arriving in Milan, Italy. There we saw Leonardo da Vinci's "The Last Supper" as well as "Jesus and the Two Robbers on the Cross," on the opposite wall. The next day we visited The Duomo, the third largest Catholic cathedral in the world. It's the one with the tall spires and on all the postcards. You couldn't enter with bare elbows or knees, but my Bermuda shorts and the rest of me was mostly covered by my raincoat. A few people stared but I was used to that.

Then off we went to Genoa and Varezza. Our hostel was on the Mediterranean and the swimming was refreshing with big waves. When it started to rain, we shook the pebbles out of our suits and ran back to our hostel. After dinner, Patty Caves, whose dad owned the Caves Buick dealership in Madison, and I walked down the hill and sat on some rocks just short of the waves and spray. It was beautiful as the moon came up.

On July 23rd, we drove through Torino, Pinerolo, Perosa, Argentina and Prali on our way to Agape, where we stayed at the Second International (Protestant church) Camp located halfway up a mountain close to the French border. The camp was founded in 1947 to study the teachings of a Reformed Waldensian Pastor, Tullio Vinay, who started the movement in the twelfth century to follow Christ in poverty and simplicity. They later joined up with the Calvinists and were greatly persecuted by the Catholics.

The main topic discussed was "The Equivocal Position of the World of Today with Regards to War," an esoteric sounding subject of dubious interest to most everyone in our group. All the lectures were translated to and from English, French, German and Italian. The Italian translator seemed to speak with his flailing hands and arms, and sometimes looked like a contortionist, especially when an Italian Senator was speaking. We listened with earphones or in groups with our own simultaneous translator standing off to the side of the speaker. We didn't attend all the lectures, but sometimes went hiking to enjoy the mountain scenery.

Breakfast always consisted of bread and cocoa. The other meals were bread, noodles and potatoes or rice. Protein was still too expensive to serve to a bunch of poor campers so soon after the war. The day when our group oversaw setting tables and washing dishes, I had never seen a kitchen so greasy in all my life. There was no soap and we rinsed the dishes, pots and pans with cold water. The handles of the pans were so slippery, we could hardly hold them. Fortunately, only a few in our group got sick. To make matters worse, two of the younger boys decided to drink three bottles of wine which they bought in the village below. They not only needed help getting back up the mountain and finding their rooms, but once in the upper bunk, my ninth-grade roommate repeated what he had done during the storm on the "Arosa Star" the day before we arrived in Plymouth. And I got stuck cleaning it up with my bare hands and a washcloth.

After a couple days, brother Paul and his friend Jim Dohr, showed up with our new 1958 Beetle. We washed it in the stream below the camp, but by the time we drove back up the mountain, it was dusty again. We sneaked them into our dorm room where they slept one night on the floor before they set up their tent. They stayed four days before they left for Berlin.

In the afternoon, four of us went down to the village and had a steak dinner for $0.60. Back at the camp, we met and listened to Martin Niemoller, the German theologian who was in prison for eight years under Hitler. He became best known for his poetic speech:

"First, they came for the communists, and I did not speak out -
  Because I was not a communist.
Then they came for the trade unionists, and I did not speak out -
  Because I was not a trade unionist.
Then they came for the Jews, and I did not speak out -
  Because I was not a Jew.
Then they came for me — and there was no one left to speak for me."

After ten nights we left Agape on August 2nd. The Italians were sad to see us go and waved at our bus until we were out of sight.

52. FRANCE TO SWITZERLAND AND BACK

WE CROSSED INTO FRANCE just after lunch, and yes, their Alps looked the same as the Italian Alps. By dinner time, we arrived in Grenoble and stayed at the Students' Hotel. It had spring beds, desks, restaurants, and warm water. We ate ham, smoked fish, two kinds of potatoes and noodles. The next morning, we attended a Catholic church, the first time for me, but got nothing out of it because it was all in French and Latin. We then drove the rest of the day to Geneva, Switzerland. Although we arrived early at the hostel, we didn't get back from dinner until 10:00 p.m., and by then all the beds were filled up. They kicked out a bunch of kids, but we had to double up, two to a single bed. It was hot and miserable, and we had to turn over in unison. It was funny, however, when some French kid fell out of bed and screamed.

Geneva was an attractive city and we all enjoyed walking along the lake. We toured the United Nations building, viewed Mt. Blanc and did some shopping. After borrowing $20 from Mary, I bought my sister Margaret a music box shaped like a Swiss house for the grand sum of $5.89. Over 60 years later, Margie said, "I certainly do remember that!" Later we celebrated Mrs. Hamill's 62nd birthday, who you'll remember was one of our three group leaders. She got a kiss from everyone and was so happy that she had tears in her eyes. Then we headed back to the same hot, stuffy hostel where kids were even sleeping on the floor between the beds.

In Dole we saw the cathedral that was taken over by the Protestants during the Reformation. At the time of Calvin, all the idols or statues were removed, making the transformation complete. Next, we visited the headquarters of the World Council of Churches, which occupied several small houses, presumably to save money. In the evening, Rob Engelke, a ninth grader, got out his guitar and did a great imitation of Satchmo. He was good, and later, while still at West High, bought a Corvette with his earnings from giving guitar lessons.

We then drove 285 miles to Dijon, Bourges, and Aubigny-sur-Nere where we stayed the night. The next 100-mile day was easier as we passed Gien and saw the cathedrals in Orleans and Chartres, with their magnificent stained-glass windows, before arriving in Bierville. They were big but not as elaborate as those in Milan. At a cost of $0.25, we toured Versailles and the Palace, begun in the early 1600's by Louis XIII. It was huge, ornate, and filled with hundreds of statues. The Hall of Mirrors was beautiful, with many intricate tapestries and clocks, but the outside fountains weren't turned on. That happened only at night on the first and third Sundays. The gardens were also in the process of being restored to their former glory. From there we could see the Eiffel Tower and were soon in Paris where we stayed the next four days.

Notre-Dame Cathedral, Paris

That evening we hopped on an old Mercedes bus to visit the Basilica of the Sacre-Coeur and had a wonderful night view of Paris before walking past the Moulin Rouge. On Sunday morning, we entered Notre Dame Cathedral. It was immense, and the two huge rose-shaped stained-glass windows were the most colorful and impressive of any that we had seen. The organ music was beautiful, and as my eyes were directed upward, it gave me a strange, tingly feeling that God was in this place. I'm glad I could see it before it almost burned to the ground in April 2019.

French food had a great reputation, but our lunch that day was cow's cheek, which looked like blubber and octopus. The "meat" seemed to be mostly cartilage and had some hairs on it. Mary handed her French-English dictionary to a woman at our table and she pointed to the word "nostril." I didn't touch it. Mr. Engelke later admitted that he was glad he didn't have any of that in his stomach. Strangely, the food we had in England was the best. I guess that's because England was less damaged in the war and their breakfasts were much like ours.

Our two hours in the Louvre, where we had time to see only a fraction of the artwork, was still memorable. We saw the Mona Lisa, Venus de Milo, and Winged Victory, along with hundreds of statues, even mummies and little figurines. I was pooped and had a sore throat, so I walked back to our Student's Hotel where I showered and napped to finish the day.

We wandered around Paris in small groups and finally ended up in a perfume shop. I bought five small bottles: Ooh la la, Miss Dior, Balenciaga, Replique, and Ma Griffe cologne. I imagined that they could be some future gifts for my mother. Yes, that's the story. There went another $15.77 but I did get a 25% discount plus a small bottle of cognac which could be for Grandpa. I was now down to my last $10. We then walked to the Arc de Triomphe and saw Napoleon's Tomb inside the "Hotel" des Invalides. We took three elevators to reach the top of the Eiffel Tower, 984' high, and enjoyed the view of Paris including Montmartre and the Opera.

53. THE WORLD'S FAIR

AFTER PARIS, WE BOARDED A TRAIN for the 175-mile trip to Brussels, Belgium, and the 1958 World's Fair. Our first night we saw the "Atomium," which was 335' high and the main feature, celebrating the atomic age. We all thought the fair was fantastic. The U.S. pavilion was a big round building where we watched a style show and color TV for the first time in our lives. At the end of the day we walked six blocks in the rain to our miserable hostel. Then we hiked up three flights of stairs to a crowded stuffy room holding 100 kids. The washroom was down a fire escape, in the rain,

Atomium
Photo by fotografierende on Unsplash

to the floor below. At 11:00 p.m. a kid almost got kicked out for making a loud trumpet noise.

After the hostel made us sandwiches (a piece of brown bread inside of two white slices), which undoubtedly saved them money, we spent the day visiting the pavilions from Italy, Switzerland, France, Finland, Argentina, the Congo and Russia, where they had a replica of Sputnik, launched the previous October. That afternoon we took a bus to Diest where some 2000 kids were attending a Youth Hostel Rally in an open-air theater. We slept on the floor in a big school gymnasium. I still had an inflamed sore throat, so the next day I stayed there alone and slept while everyone else was at the fair.

When the sun first peeked through the windows of the gym, Mr. Engelke was lying on his back next to me making quite a rumble. So, I reached over and gently pinched his nostrils together. He missed his first breath as his lungs slightly expanded, then he missed the second as his lungs expanded further. By his third attempt to inhale, he gasped in desperation and woke up. We all laughed our heads off waking more than just a few tired fair goers. He always said that if his snoring bothered us, we should wake him. I'm not sure he meant it, but he was a good sport.

Along with those 2000 kids, we all boarded a chartered train and once again headed to the fair. A couple of us forgot our meal tickets which admitted us into the fair, but that didn't matter to the gatekeeper who let us in anyway. After another long day at the exposition, which was a precursor to EPCOT in Florida, we again boarded the 10 p.m. train back to Diest.

More trains the next day, four hours to Antwerp and six hours to Rotterdam, where a few of us went to a Dean Martin-Jerry Lewis movie, "You're Never Too Young." It was funny but our reserved seats in the second row were way too close. A third train took us once again to the Hook of Holland where we went through customs and boarded a ship to cross the channel back to England. The ship was a great improvement over the rickety old trains, and I got a short but energizing night's sleep on the overnight ride. Before we disembarked at Harwich, we had a delicious ham and egg breakfast which made us almost giddy with delight. On the continent, every breakfast consisted of bread with marmalade plus something hot to drink.

54. BACK TO BRITAIN

AFTER WE LEFT THE FAIR in the old coal-burning train, I made the mistake of sticking my head out the window and got a cinder in my eye which drove me crazy. Every time I blinked it scratched my eye, so I tried holding my hand tight against my eye with limited success. When we reached Colchester, another Topper guided me to a clinic, where a doctor lifted my eyelid and quickly removed it with a Q-tip, giving me instant relief.

At our next stop in Haverhill, we went to a Congregational Church and met our host families where we stayed for two nights. My friendly hosts, the Corkindales, had a 17-year-old boy, David, and a 14-year-old girl named Pip. I slept in a cushy double bed, which was heavenly after youth those hostel beds, until they woke me up for ham and eggs. In England, ham and eggs became a habit.

From Haverhill, our group went by bus to Grimes Graves, where we saw the flint mines from about 2300 B.C. The flint was dug out using deer antlers and was used to make axes and other tools. We climbed down a ladder into a tunnel holding candles to light our way. Mining flint was a job only a Roman slave would do.

That evening in Haverhill, we watched a TV program about segregation in America. It was alarming to see the hate, and as an American, embarrassing to watch. Living in Madison, I rarely saw a black person, and Mom and Dad were even members of the local NAACP. It was still six years before the 1964 Civil Rights Act.

As the racial situation started to improve in the U.S., England was being increasingly populated by Pakistanis, Indians and Africans coming from the many Commonwealth countries. Since the European Common Market was formed, member countries have been virtually invaded by millions of refugees from the Middle East and Africa. When this happens too fast, new immigrants don't get assimilated but remain in large enclaves where they don't even have to learn the local language. This creates little countries within the country and starts to change the culture. Since a country with too many cultures doesn't have any culture at all, you can be sure this will lead to serious problems in the future. In the U.S., we have always prided ourselves that our immigrants turn into Americans and adopt our customs. With certain groups, however, that is no longer happening.

The next morning, I said goodbye to the Corkindales. Their family was extremely friendly and courteous and made me feel at home. As the train chugged past their house, I stuck my head out the window and waved to David and Pip. No cinder in my eye this time. For the next eight years, Pip sent me letters, Christmas cards and presents including a sweater, a scarf, books and even a silver cigarette holder which, of course, I never used. I kept responding to her letters and by1965 she even started signing her letters, "Love, Pip." I would see her again in late August 1966, when she arrived in Madison hoping to find a spouse.

By lunch time we arrived in Cambridge, toured the University, I bought a few cigars for Grandpa, which was the most incongruous thing I ever did, and ate a hamburger at Wimpey's. The afternoon train took us to Ely and the next day's train to Coventry, Kenilworth and on to Leamington Spa. Then we visited Warwick Castle, Shottery and then Stratford-on-Avon where we went to Anne Hathaway's cottage and William Shakespeare's birthplace. It cost us two shillings, or $0.28 to enter. I enjoyed the garden as well as some delicious plums I plucked off a tree. Later, Mrs. Engelke admitted that she picked a few mulberries as well. That evening we saw "Twelfth Night" in the Shakespeare Memorial Theater. We had excellent seats in the center of the second row of the balcony. It was a great theater and the scenery was amazing.

The next morning, I was the first one through the food line, and since I finished before the last was served, I went through the line again. I had lost eight pounds despite spending an extra $25 on food since we left. The girls, however, gained just about the same amount. We then boarded a train to St. Briavels, Hereford, Gloucester, and Chepstow and a long bus ride to Monmouth in Wales where our hostel was in a castle. The weather was awful.

On Sunday morning, we attended the Church of England, which was way too ritualistic for me. The weather was still awful and cold when we later hiked a couple miles into the Forest of Dean, where the Romans dug for iron. The next day we took a train to Bristol, another to Bath, and a third to Salisbury. From there we visited Stonehenge, a prehistoric monument in Wiltshire, which was again being restored. Three of the sarsens (bluestones), about 13' tall, were re-erected and set in concrete bases to keep them from tipping over. A fourth train took us to the port of Southampton. Until I arrived in England, I had never been on a train. My curiosity was satisfied.

Our European adventure was nearly over. Just one more night in a hostel, where we ate another English sausage and egg breakfast, completed our chores (this time we cleaned the washroom), drove to Pier 30 in seven taxis, got our passports stamped, and boarded a tender which carried us out to the "Arosa Kulm," the sister ship to the "Arosa Star."

55. ALMOST HOME

WE DEPARTED FOR HOME on August 26, 1958. After our ship had been at sea for four days, the "RMS Queen Mary" passed us, and a day before we arrived in New York, it passed us again returning to England. I wasn't upset by the slow speed of our little ship. I needed sleep and food, and realized I was more run down than I had thought. Sleeping for 18 hours the first day was a clue. By the end of the ten-day voyage, I was back to normal.

As we floated past the Statue of Liberty, New York harbor was overcast, and the ocean was smooth as glass. We docked on September 5th, one day overdue. If you want to visit the RMS Queen Mary, which was launched in 1934, just go to Long Beach, California where it is now a hotel.

Before three of us left New York City in Mrs. Engelke's car, we quickly drove by Times Square, the Empire State Building, the Metropolitan Museum of Art, Central Park, down Broadway, through the Holland Tunnel and ran nine red lights on the way to our Howard Johnson's resting spot in New Jersey. After swimming in the pool and soaking in the tub, I finally got clean. A day later we were back home in Madison.

A few days after returning home, I got a phone call from a man who said he had found my lost wallet. He was at the Mayflower Motel on the beltline, not far from Park Street. He said he would return it if I would meet him at the motel. What would I do? It sure sounded fishy to Dad and me. So, we called the cops who went with us. I got my empty wallet, and sure enough, he had a record in Indiana and was arrested. I never did learn his intentions.

Times were changing. Most stores in Madison were now open on Sundays. I didn't think it was a great idea. It was just one more day for people to work.

56. DAD'S BUSINESS

DAD AND BILL KAESER were architectural students together at the University of Illinois and became partners in 1951. Their partnership was different than most because Bill's family was the beneficiary of the Pet Milk fortune. As a result, he didn't need or care if he received any money from the business. On the other hand, his social connections probably resulted in a lot of business. He became a well-known architect in Madison while Dad kept in the background, made the presentations to drum up new business, did the structural work on the buildings and houses they designed and supervised the construction.

In the late 1950's, their business improved greatly when their firm, "Kaeser and McLeod," won the contract to design the Cuna Mutual Insurance World Headquarters on Mineral Point Road on Madison's West side. That's when Dad's income increased to about $18,000 a year and we had money for ice cream twice a week. The office also paid Mom to type the dozens of pages of detailed specifications for all their projects, which was at that time a miserable job with four carbons. It was lucky she had attended Brown's Business College in Rockford right out of high school where she learned to type — not just for Dad but also for our school term papers.

Their designs were influenced by Frank Lloyd Wright, and they even worked on Wright's 1955 design of Madison's Lake Monona Terrace Convention Center, which Wright first conceived in 1938. Dad was frustrated with the design because he said, "There is just no way structurally to support it." The Madison City Council effectively nixed the big project in 1957 when they voted to lower the building's height by 20 feet. In 1959, the 20-foot law was repealed, and Wright died the same year. The council also complained it would be too expensive at an estimated cost of $4 per sq. ft. even though a new civic center in Phoenix cost $25. Perhaps the real reason why Madison's old guard didn't want to have anything to do with him was because Wright had a reputation as a womanizer, expected to get everything for free because he was a genius, and was even more imperious than they were. My frustrated Dad said to me, "What this city needs is about a hundred first class funerals." Finally, the Monona Terrace did get built in 1997, four years after Dad died. By then, new building materials made it all possible, and the younger generation of Madisonians no longer remembered Wright in a negative way. It took Madison from 1938 to 1997 to get it done. Congratulations, finally.

If you walk from the capital building down to the new Monona Terrace Civic Center, you can see, if you take time to look, two tiles in memory of Dad that were generously donated by Paul to help fund the project.

PART IV: 1958-1963
THE UNIVERSITY YEARS

57. ON WISCONSIN

I STARTED SCHOOL at the University of Wisconsin in September 1958. I had been in the last class of Wisconsin high school graduates that didn't have to take an entrance exam, like the ACT or SAT, to enter the UW. So why would I? I didn't worry because I had gone to West High School. After all, it was a special place with all those Randall School students.

Paul helped me register for my classes, including Biology, Physics, Chemistry and English. To sign up, we just had to walk to the buildings where the classes were held and pick the class and hour we wanted. We also made sure that my classes wouldn't all have their final exams scheduled on the same day. That's all I had to do to enroll at the UW.

All freshmen boys were required to pass a test to avoid taking physical education. It included sit-ups, push-ups and rope climbing. The big heavy football players were inept at climbing up the rope. On that test, it was the little, skinny kids who excelled.

ROTC was compulsory for all the boys. We first learned about M1 rifles from WWII and had target practice. Although I had never gone hunting, I was steady enough to earn my expert marksman medal. When a 3-star General came from Chicago to pin on our medals, there were only eight of us honored that day in the UW Field House. When the General came to me, he asked, "Have you ever fired a rifle before?" I crisply replied, "No sir, just a BB gun." The General broke out into a big grin and proceeded to the next cadet.

Because of all the Vietnam anti-war protests around the country, ROTC became voluntary as soon as I completed my two years. The Captain who taught our class and promoted me to Sergeant my sophomore year, hoped I would continue ROTC and become a commissioned officer. That meant I would be obligated to Uncle Sam for three years. I chose not to and continued to avoid the draft with college deferments.

58. OUT FOR WRESTLING

WRESTLING PRACTICE STARTED in October, and I began getting some excellent coaching. Coach George Martin was fantastic. While wrestling for Iowa State, George had been a national champion at 165 pounds in 1933. He was ineligible for the 1936 Berlin Olympics because he had just been hired a year earlier as the new Wisconsin coach, and was no longer considered an amateur. He did, however, pin the U.S. silver medalist several times in practice matches.

Although wrestling was popular in Iowa, Oklahoma and Pennsylvania, there weren't any Wisconsin high schools that offered the sport back in 1935. Coach Martin quickly realized that his new job would be difficult without a lot of competitive high school wrestling programs. By the time I was in high school, 80 schools offered wrestling. The number is now close to 350 and he is very well-known in wrestling circles as the father of Wisconsin wrestling. He's now in the Wisconsin, Iowa, and National Wrestling Halls of Fame.

In 1958, the NCAA didn't allow freshmen to compete at the varsity level. That was fine with me because I had a lot to learn. Every night after school, from about 3:30 to supper time, we practiced, got in better shape, and learned a lot of new moves. Matches were now nine minutes. In high school, that seemed like a week.

In the meantime, West High also got a new coach, Don Hafeman. He had been a three-time high school state champ, did the same in the Big Ten, and later became the Superintendent of the Madison School District. Thanks to Don, West High soon had a much better team. One of the best wrestlers was Breck Johnson who was undefeated all year at 165 pounds. If I had been back in high school knowing what I did then, he would have clobbered me. Just as I had done a year earlier, Breck came down to the UW wrestling room for some extra practice before the state meet. After wrestling with him for a while, I was amazed at how much stronger and better I had become. As they say, you don't get better without tough competition and I had been getting plenty of that. At the end-of-season wrestling banquet, several of us freshmen received our Badger numeral sweaters.

59. TO GUARANTEE A SOCIAL LIFE

TO IMPROVE MY SOCIAL LIFE, Paul suggested that I buy two season coupon books so I could attend all five university plays at the Union Theater. That meant I had to find a date. I looked no further than my Biology class where I met Janet, a nursing student. Using our blue 1958 VW Beetle, I even took her home one weekend and met her parents in River Falls, where her dad was a chemistry professor at River Falls State College. That evening we all drove into Minneapolis to see "Oklahoma." We dated for a year and typically went to movies at the Orpheum or Capital theaters on State Street, followed by pizza at Paisans on lower State Street. Such a date cost $5 — $3 for pizza and $1 each for the movie. I think she dumped me for Marty Garrity, who had scored 44 points for Shawano in the high school basketball tournament a year or so earlier. That was fine with me because unlike Janet, I didn't want to play baseball. After that, I dated a lot of different girls for the next year. In addition to the plays, there were a lot of other events to attend at the student union, such as Ella Fitzgerald with the Oscar Peterson Trio and the Travel Adventure series of films and talks.

Paul had always kept track of all the money he spent each year, so I did the same. Tuition was less than $200 per year, books about $70, and everything else (clothes, dates, and all other miscellaneous expenses) amounted to just over $600. I lived and ate at home and rode my bike to class. I had some old military saddle bags draped over the rear tire which held all my books and papers needed for the day. My trusty three-speed Schwinn was the same bike that I bought used from Paul for $52 when I was ten. Paul felt guilty that he had charged his little brother so much for his bike, but I was happy. I drove it thousands of miles for over thirteen years and it never gave me any problems. My parents were happy too, because I could usually get where I wanted without needing a ride. They never had to pay any of my college expenses except room and board. For them, it was as if we were still in high school, as all of us earned enough each summer for the next year.

During Wisconsin's "cool" months, I always wore Levis, a long-sleeved, white shirt and a sweater all through high school and university. To save Christmas money, Mom knitted me a red wool sweater but after I wore it a few times it got baggy. She willingly redid the bottom half but then it didn't look as smooth as the top because the yarn was wrinkled from her first attempt. To solve the problem, she ripped it all out and started over for the third time. I was surprised at her stamina and I wore it for several years.

Easter vacation in 1959 was the third time we drove to Florida. Paul and Mary, however, stayed home. Paul was in medical school and wanted to study for exams, while studious Mary wanted to spend as much time as possible with her boyfriend, Sean Austin. I wasn't about to turn down a vacation because I could always study later. Besides that, we were going on a two-day private, guided Audubon tour of the Everglades. The guide pointed out many birds I had never seen before and I had a great time. I even made an 8mm. movie with my Bolex camera that I had purchased a year earlier. When we returned home, we discovered that Paul and his friends had eaten all the T-bone steaks in the freezer. I thought it was funny, but Mom and Dad never bought a half cow again after that.

Both Paul and Mary were more studious and somewhat better at delayed gratification than I was. Mom and Dad possibly thought that I was trying my absolute best in school. If they did, they were sometimes mistaken. I studied hard, but sometimes just enough to do okay, and in retrospect it all worked out fine. The truth is most everything I learned never helped me earn a nickel. I would never be a doctor, Mom joked years later, because I had chewed the lead paint off the back of my highchair.

60. WORKING FOR THE FEDS

DURING THE SUMMER OF 1959, I got an interesting job as a Tour Leader at the USDA Forest Products Laboratory, thanks mostly to Aunt Oral, who worked there for 38 years. To get the job you want, you need connections. Although she retired shortly after, she continued getting calls about different projects and publications from the distant past since she knew where everything was kept. On the government salary scale, I was a lowly GS-3, and my annual income would have been $3495.

For my first week on the job, I followed my predecessor, a 28-year-old law student, as he led the daily tours. I learned where to go and what to say as we wound our way through each department where an incredible variety of research was being conducted, such as making paper, treating wood to withstand the weather, testing the strength of telephone poles with a million-pound press, sandwich construction, and packaging materials. They were researching just about anything you could imagine regarding wood. After a week, I was on my own, felt confident to lead the tours alone, and met a lot of interesting people from all around the world.

When I wasn't leading tours, I worked in the Research, Publications, and Information Department where all the research papers were assembled that were written by the dozens of Ph.D. researchers. We stacked the pages in reverse order around a big round table that slowly rotated. As each page passed by in front of us, we'd pick them up, one at a time, assemble and then staple the booklets. It was easy if we kept our fingers moist with glycerin. When work was slow, I was told to "accidentally" skip a page, or two. Then we had to sit and wait for the table to make another revolution before that page came around a second time.

Another custom was taking coffee breaks. I didn't drink coffee and certainly didn't want to eat donuts or junk food. And who needed a break? I sure didn't. This was frustrating to me. When I had a job, I wanted to get it done. So while everyone disappeared for a half hour, I decided to improve my typing skills on the new electric typewriters. After a few days of this, however, I was told to go on coffee breaks with everyone else because "It didn't look professional for me to be in the office just practicing." I was surprised that my initiative was squelched. I had no choice but to get used to coffee breaks. That was my first exposure to "government work."

61. NOW A SOPHOMORE

MY SOPHOMORE YEAR AT THE UW was about the same as the first except I had to study more. One elective class, Art History, was taught by Professor James Watrous. His daughter, Lynn, was my sister Mary's friend from high school. It was interesting to learn about those old, famous European artists such as Michelangelo, Rubens, Bruegel and many more. I did need a little more culture.

Many years later, my wife and I, along with her sister and husband, visited the Milwaukee Art Museum, so the Preservator, James De Young, my wife's cousin, could give us a tour. When he heard that I had taken a class taught by Professor Watrous, he was envious. At the time, I didn't appreciate the excellent and well-known professors that I had. But thanks to James De Young, we did appreciate our private, and remarkably interesting behind-the-scenes tour of the museum just days before he retired.

I really enjoyed Psychology taught by Prof. Harry Harlow, who was famous for his maternal separation and isolation experiments on rhesus monkeys. He was interesting and funny but for six weeks he departed to be a visiting professor at Ohio State. We in turn got one of their professors who said, "If you will," after practically every sentence. After a few weeks, it was so annoying that I decided to count the times he said it. In just one lecture, I counted 47 "If-you-wills." I think that was a precursor to "You know."

62. WRESTLING IN THE BIG 10

AS A FRESHMAN, I COULD EAT WHATEVER I WANTED, including three or four big sandwiches made with Mom's homemade bread, an apple, a cookie and usually two thirds of a quart of milk. There was a milk vending machine in Birge Hall where I had my various Biology classes. For $0.10, I could get a third of a quart, but I soon learned that if I twisted the dial at just the right moment, two containers would fall out into the tray below. Once I even got three. Freshman didn't have to think about anything except trying to get better.

As a sophomore, however, I could wrestle for real and had to watch my weight. Luckily, my appetite decreased, and one sandwich sufficed. When I occasionally ordered a piece of pie or cake for lunch at the student union, I discovered that I was sluggish and slow during practice. I could hardly believe it made such a big difference. Most people, I thought, would never realize just how drastically the food they eat affects their well-being and performance — unless they were in top condition.

Just as in high school, my prospects improved because some of the best wrestlers from the year before had graduated. I wasn't sure how I ranked among everyone who would be in my 167-pound weight class. Then I twisted my knee. Nothing too severe but Coach Martin didn't know if I would be ready. A couple weeks before the first scheduled match, he casually mentioned to me that he was a little worried that one wrestler "might not be able to compete, and now you have a sore knee." I thought, "That means he thinks I'm on the first team." His little off-hand comment did wonders for my confidence. It is amazing how confidence affects performance. I was always quite a bit taller than the kids I wrestled. I mean, look around. How many wrestlers are tall? Once back in high school while we weighed in, a kid on the other team was overheard saying to his teammate, "Who is that big kid?" When little Johnny Walsh told me that, I knew I would win. Another time, when we wrestled Purdue in a Big Ten match, my balding opponent's name was Sampson. Guess what? I lost when I shouldn't have. If only I hadn't skipped so many Sunday school classes, I would have known that Sampson lost all his strength when Delilah cut his hair.

Wrestling that year went well. To get a letter I only had to win more than I lost. That I did and got a varsity "W" on my new Wisconsin Badger red cardigan sweater. I never wore my letter sweater more than a few times, as it always seemed a bit pretentious, but it did give me the confidence that I could walk down the street and not be overly concerned about my physical well-being.

Three College Wrestlers
Steve Martin, John McLeod & Steve Emlen

There is one match that I remember far better than any of the others. It was against Cornell College from Mount Vernon, Iowa which had beaten Wisconsin 18 to 14 the previous year. It all started when Coach Martin said, "John, for our next match, you are going to be wrestling heavyweight." I said, "What? Are you kidding? I only weigh 174 dripping wet." Coach replied, "Don't worry, he's not that big." I thought, just what does that mean? Ten pounds bigger would be a lot. To make matters worse, I had been sick on Monday and missed a hard day of practice. I wondered if I could even go for nine minutes. When we weighed in, I got my first glimpse of him. He was much shorter, muscular, and weighed 195. Not good, but I had a plan. I would try to stay away from him the whole first round and hope he couldn't take me down.

After grabbing his thick arms, which felt like legs, I knew that was my best hope. Around and around we went for the first three minutes. At the beginning of the second round, I lost the coin flip and he chose up. I knew I had to escape fast before he ground me into the mat — and I did in a flash. Now I was winning one to nothing. After another minute of going around and around, I could see he was getting mad. He charged into me hard and I fell straight backwards. I turned over at the last possible second and pinned him so fast with a lateral drop he didn't even know what happened. It was a move I had practiced many times just in case someone would try to push me around. He stormed off the mat and didn't even shake hands. When my old high school wrestling buddy and co-captain, Dave Neal, read that I had pinned him in 4:22, he was amazed. Dave had been mauled by the same guy.

It was during this time that I started dating Nancy, my sister Mary's friend from their Integrated Liberal Studies program. She was majoring in Spanish and the humanities which was a far cry from anything that I cared about. We got along fine, however, and kept dating for the next few years except during her junior year abroad in Spain in 1961-1962. At the same time, Mary spent her year living abroad in Göttingen, Germany, where we had both spent a few days during the summer of 1958.

Aunt Oral thought Mom and Dad should never have let Mary spend the year in Europe all alone. It was simply too dangerous. Mom responded by posting an article on our hallway bulletin board, written by columnist Art Buchwald, titled "Innocent Wisconsin in Sinful Paris." It was a satirical letter from a mother to her daughter in Paris who mentioned all the murders, robberies and other terrible things that were happening in innocent Wisconsin. I don't know if Aunt Oral ever read the article but it no doubt made Mom feel better.

In the spring of 1960, Paul graduated from medical school and was now a doctor. He then headed to Duluth, Minnesota, where he did his internship and met a blonde nurse, Elaine Sundstrom, who became his wife. I finished my sophomore year, Mary her freshman year and Margie seventh grade.

During the summer of 1960 before my third year, I worked construction. I carried lumber, took the plywood forms off new concrete walls, and did anything the boss and the carpenters wanted me to do. I was a grunt. It was hot, hard work and it was the perfect job to toughen me up for the next wrestling season. I'm sure my dad was instrumental in getting me the job, as he was familiar with a lot of contractors. Before my first day on the job, Dad gave me some wise advice. He said, "Act alive." In other words, jump quickly when told what to do and keep busy. The second day I noticed a lot of football players weren't there.

63. MINOR SURGERY

AS A JUNIOR, I again went out for wrestling. All was going well except that I was still constantly getting sore throats. My tonsils would swell up on each side so I could hardly swallow, and I was constantly sucking on "Sucrets" to take away the soreness. I never felt sick, but I never seemed to get better. Dr. Brindley, my old ENT specialist, said I needed a tonsillectomy. So, after I had two Big 10 matches on Friday and Saturday, I went to Madison General Hospital on a Monday, the first day of Christmas vacation, where I stayed overnight before being operated on the next morning. That evening, I shared a room with two older men who just had abdominal surgeries, so it hurt when they laughed. With me in the room they laughed a little more. They couldn't believe it when I started doing push-ups in bed. After a while, a young pretty nurse walked in and asked me "Would you like a back rub?" I was totally unprepared for that question and couldn't imagine why she might think I needed one, so I said "No." A moment later I thought, "Was that dumb, or what?"

Bright and early the next morning, Dr. Brindley cut out my tonsils while I sat in a chair and was vaguely aware of what he was doing. After he finished, I awoke instantly as they wheeled me off to recover. That afternoon, when my sister Mary came to visit me with her Italian friend, Paola, I looked up and mumbled, "Just go away." I was in no condition or mood to talk. I spent at least one more night in the hospital. If you think spending that much time in the hospital sounds ridiculous for a tonsillectomy, just remember that my brother spent a whole week in the hospital for simple, minor hernia surgery back when he was twelve and I was recovering from my left arm fracture. Minor surgery, I discovered, is surgery done on someone else. By the time I had my tonsillectomy, doctors were no longer removing them in such big numbers, but I was super happy with the results and haven't had a sore throat since.

From what I heard, Grandpa Middleton was much tougher. When he needed his tonsils removed, he walked downtown to the doctor's office in Rockford and demanded, "Take these darn things out." Then he walked home. That's what Mom told me.

It took me all ten days of vacation to recover and after that I started to lose interest in wrestling. After a few more matches at the end of the season, I had a talk with Coach Martin and resigned from the team. It was then interesting to see how my sleep patterns changed. When I practiced every night after school, I went home, ate dinner, took a nap for an hour, and then studied until 10 p.m. When the season was over, I skipped the nap and stayed up the first night until 2:00 a.m. Then the next night, it was 1:00 a.m., then midnight until after a couple weeks, I was back on my old schedule. With more free time, my grades didn't get any better. I just became less efficient.

64. AN EXPENSIVE HOBBY

I SPLURGED $515 on a new 16mm Bolex, Swiss-made movie camera in the spring of 1961. When I paid the bill, I wasn't happy because just a week earlier, Wisconsin had passed a new 3% sales tax which meant I had to pay another $15. I bought a book about making movies which helped. Learning to edit was the biggest benefit of all. A roll of film, which lasted just three minutes, cost $6 to $8, and another $7 to have it developed, so I was careful not to waste any film.

I had already learned a lot about taking movies just from watching Dad's old 8-mm movies that he first took out west when I was just a few months old. In the summer of 1940, I stayed home with

Grandma Middleton while Dad, Mom and Paul made the trip. Dad found the mountains to be so impressive, he wanted to get them all in the picture at once, so he moved his new "moving" camera from side to side, up and down, around, and back again. The same thing happened with our baby and family pictures. Since watching them made me dizzy, I always used a tripod and did my best to properly expose the film. The following summer, I filmed the scenery, animals, birds, and flowers and then edited my first 16-mm movie. I'd show and narrate it, as well as several of my subsequent films, to different groups such as Dad's Westside Optimist Club and church groups.

65. GOTHIC, COLORADO

DURING THE SUMMER OF 1961, Steve Emlen returned home from Swarthmore. Thanks to his dad's connections, we both headed for The Rocky Mountain Biological Laboratory (RMBL), located in Gothic, just north of Crested Butte, Colorado. Once again, I was able to drive our VW Beetle and we agreed that I'd pay for the gas and Steve for any repairs. When we stopped for an oil change, I was reminded just how odd VWs looked when up on the hoist, because the rear tires hung down and tilted inward in an unnatural looking position. Taking advantage of this, I decided to get Steve from the waiting room and give him a shock. When he saw the car, I said, "Look at the way the tires

hang down. The axle is broken, and we are going to need a new one." The stunned look on his face was priceless. Neither one of us had any money for such a big repair. After a hearty laugh, we were soon on our way.

From Gunnison in Southwest Colorado, we headed 30 miles north to Crested Butte and then another nine miles up the twisting gravel road to Gothic. Crested Butte had once been a thriving town of about 5000 people with two hotels, dance halls, and several saloons. It all started in 1880 when it was reported that rich silver deposits were found in the area. A dozen years later, however, the town was mostly deserted when little silver was found.

RMBL got its start in 1930 when John C. Johnson, a Biology professor in Gunnison, bought the property for $200. When we arrived 31 years later, we found a few buildings, a dining room, several cabins, and some old weathered shacks from the 1850s. It was a beautiful valley,

Urban Cowboy

9400 high with flowers blooming everywhere, surrounded by mountains. Steve and I stayed in the oldest shack, the one where President Ulysses S. Grant was rumored to have stayed. We had to climb up an outside ladder to get into our room. There we found two old steel-framed beds with an old dorm mattress on each. That's all there was and all we needed.

The Director of RMBL was Dr. Bob Endres from Swarthmore College. Another well-known biologist there was Dr. Paul Erlich from Stanford, known as the butterfly man. A few years later in 1968, he and his wife, Anne, wrote "The Population Bomb" which startled people into thinking that the rapidly increasing world population would soon lead to mass starvation. It already was in India. But the "Green Revolution," which began in about 1970, reduced the threat, as new high-yielding hybrid corn and wheat varieties were introduced along with more effective herbicides.

I ended up working with Dr. Keith Justice, Director of the Sonoran Desert Museum in Arizona. He had an Atomic Energy Commission grant to study the movements of mice. For several days, I made 100 little wood boxes with a small opening so mice could go in and out. Next, I used a benzyne burner to cover kymograph paper sheets with a coat of greasy smoke which I then put in the boxes. These boxes were placed in a grid out in a field where the mice would enter looking for food. To identify how far each mouse traveled at night in search of food, I first had to trap the mice and cut off certain toes with my fingernail clippers so we could keep track of each mouse by their footprints. There was more to it than that, but I never did read any papers he might have written or learn why the AEC would be interested in the movements of mice.

One afternoon, while Dr. Justice and several of us were in his cabin talking, he pulled out a bottle of whiskey, walked outside and filled up the hummingbird feeder hanging in the middle of his big window. Immediately, one of the dozens of little Rufous Hummingbirds flew up, took a swig, and flew up into the closest tree where it continued to sputter and shake his head for the next ten minutes. It wasn't very scientific or kind, but we did laugh our heads off.

We also were able to do a great deal of hiking and traveling around that part of the state in my VW. When I spent a few cents more for premium gas, I discovered my VW could climb up some steep rocky mountain roads that it couldn't navigate with regular. It was a great summer of exploration. Mom, Dad and Margie also drove out to Gothic late in the summer and I found a great camping spot for them along Copper Creek in the mountains. 1961 was also the year when developers started quietly buying up land for the big ski resort now at Crested Butte.

At RMBL, Dr. Justice trapped a skunk under his porch and then performed an operation to remove its "scent" gland. I ended up taking "Skunky" home in a little wire cage. At night, while I camped along the side of the road, he managed to escape and got into my lunch and a loaf of bread. He made a huge mess and even chewed up some of the stuffing under the car seat. I managed to mostly clean it up, got him back in his cage and proceeded home. "Skunky" really wasn't all that tame. Paul, being a doctor, however, gave me two valium pills which I cut into pieces and fed to "Skunky." They worked. This fun lasted for about a week before I got the excellent idea of giving my new pet to Steve Martin. He gracefully accepted my gift and took it home, but then "Skunky" escaped the very next day. I assumed his mother was responsible but 60 years later, Steve admitted he was. My feelings weren't hurt. Keeping a skunk for more than a day was enough. It was the most original gift I ever gave.

Devil's Tower, Wyoming

66. BACK TO MADISON

MY SENIOR YEAR AT WISCONSIN again started smoothly and my classes were interesting. Just before Halloween, Steve Martin stopped by our house with a dead feral cat that he had shot with his bow and arrow in the stone quarry by Hoyt Park. He was quite pleased because feral cats kill unbelievable numbers of small mammals and birds each year, now estimated to be 12 billion mammals and 4 billion birds. I asked, "What are you going to do with the cat?" Suddenly, we had an idea. Dad made a noose, I stuffed an apple in its mouth, we went down to the lab where I was taking Comparative Anatomy, and we hung it from the pipes in the storeroom. The next morning, I overheard one envious graduate assistant say, "I wish I had thought of this when I was an undergrad." The professor, however, was hopping mad when he met his assistants in the elevator on their way to the incinerator. And that was the end of that.

67. ENCOUNTER WITH A BLONDE

IN JANUARY 1962, our Methodist Youth Fellowship (MYF) group had a swimming party at the YMCA. As Steve Martin and I were waiting in the lobby, a new blonde walked in and headed down the long flight of stairs to the girls' changing room. Partly to be funny, I followed her halfway down the stairway before I turned around. She never noticed but I noticed her!

During the party, I made Steve ask her various questions. I guess I was too bashful or immature to ask her myself, but I did muster up the courage to ask her to come to our get-together at Richard Klatt's house later for hot chocolate and donuts. She said, "I can't because I have to be back in my dorm by 10:00 p.m." Back then there were strict rules for girls. Since I had Dad's 1959 Chrysler Windsor, the one with the push button shift and the big tail fins, I promised I'd get her back on time. Then she said, "Yes." During the party, we played some cards. Although she had never played cards as a kid (they were called "devil" cards at her house), she became quite an accomplished shuffler after three months playing with the psych patients at the Mendota State Mental Hospital. By comparison, I couldn't shuffle at all. My dad always said, "Being a good card player is a sign of a wasted childhood." When we went to leave, I realized I had a new problem. Several other girls, some of whom I had dated, were also going with me. Who would I take home last? I chose the new blonde girl, Donna.

Then I realized I didn't even know her last name. About the only thing I knew was that she was a nursing student at the Methodist Hospital School of Nursing. Mom then mentioned that old Mr. Jay Rose, an old family friend who had sold us Rosewood, was in the hospital at Methodist. Maybe he could find out her name? I soon learned there were two nursing students named Donna and one was sick in the hospital. So, I visited the hospital. After finally finding the right room, I peeked in the door, but it wasn't the right Donna. I was getting closer. After a few more calls, I succeeded in learning her last name.

Donna De Young was impressed that I had tried so hard to find her. I was off to a successful start, except she thought I was too young. Was it my behavior at the pool or my youthful look? When she found out I had graduated from high school a year before her and had even been to Europe, she was more impressed.

Our MYF had a winter weekend scheduled at Pine Lake Camp and I wondered if Donna would be able to get away. She was in a full-time, three-year degree program to become a Registered Nurse, and was either going to class or working full time in the hospital, but she was free and gladly said yes. We spent the weekend walking in the snow, talking, and sitting in front of the big stone fireplace. She had two older sisters, Sharon and June, a younger brother, Mark, and lived in a small town an hour away called Friesland. She wanted to be a nurse like her two sisters because she didn't want to spend every summer for the rest of her life working in the canning factory or on a farm. One girl, Twila, from Patch Grove even sketched a picture of us.

On Valentine's Day in 1962, I gave her an elegant little box of candy. Something I said about getting candy for my mom made her think it had originally been for her. To this day she still wonders who the original intended beneficiary was. I never said and won't now.

We continued to date quite often. Once on a double date, we saw a sneak preview of "North by Northwest," starring Cary Grant at the Orpheum Theater. Before we got our tickets, Steve Martin and I bought popcorn at the Caramel Crisp Shop on the corner. They had better popcorn and it was cheaper. Donna was surprised, maybe even impressed, that "going cheap" didn't concern or embarrass us.

68. HEADING WEST

DURING THE SUMMER OF 1962, thanks again to Doc Emlen, I got another great job at the University of Colorado's Biological Research Station at Moran, Wyoming. Moran was in the Grand Teton National Park located just south of Yellowstone in Northwest Wyoming. I thought it was about the most beautiful place in the world, but because Yellowstone was the first, biggest and best-known Park, the Tetons were often overlooked by the hordes of tourists. I worked for Dr. Margaret Altmann, who was born in Germany in 1900 and left for America in 1933 as Hitler was gaining power. She became a professor at the University of Colorado and from 1948 until 1984 studied elk and moose behavior. I was her assistant.

On the way out west, I again drove our trusty 1958 VW Beetle with the fold-back sunroof. Steve Martin followed me on his BMW motorcycle to the Tetons and then continued to the RMBL in Colorado where I had been the previous summer. We left on a dark, stormy morning and the downpour persisted for at least 500 of the 650 miles we drove the first day. When we passed trucks or buses, poor Steve would almost disappear in the whirlwind of rain. A windshield would have helped. We slept that night on top of a pile of dirty bed sheets and towels in the laundry room of a motel in Pierre, South Dakota. It was free and we were grateful after traveling so far.

We stopped at several places including the Badlands, Mt. Rushmore in the Black Hills, and Custer State Park. As we drove along, mile after mile, Steve would get a bit frustrated because my 36-horsepower Beetle just wasn't able to go faster than 35 mph up the long slopes. At Wind Cave National Park, he had enough and went flying by me about 80 or 90 mph. In just a few seconds, he was so far ahead that I could hardly see him. Several minutes later, however, as I rounded a corner, there was Steve, out in the field straight ahead. Was he hiding from me? Well, no, he couldn't make the corner because of loose pea gravel and had even slammed through a barbed wire fence. Luckily only the headlight on his BMW bike was damaged, not enough to keep us off the road.

69. DETOUR IN MONTANA

WE NEXT STAYED A COUPLE NIGHTS with Paul and his wife Elaine at Malmstrom Air Force Base in Great Falls. Elaine was just about ready to give birth to their first child, David, who was born June 22, 1962, and Paul, a Captain, was working as an obstetrician. He had previously accepted a residency in Salinas, California, but when the "old lady" in the draft board saw the notice in the paper, he got an irate call saying he would be drafted because he didn't inform her that his address had changed. It still hadn't, of course, so he immediately decided to enlist in the Air Force. There he fortuitously received top-notch training in obstetrics and connections to Columbia Presbyterian in New York, the most coveted training hospital in the country, where he later completed his three-year residency. So, "thank you" old lady on the draft board for changing Paul's career path from psychiatry to Ob-Gyn. God works in mysterious ways.

Captain Paul & Cowboy John

Steve Martin and I then headed north to Glacier National Park in Montana. We arrived on June 6th and the wall of snow on the sides of the road was over 20' straight up. The next morning, we hiked seven miles up the Sperry Glacier Trail to Sperry Chalet, which was mostly covered with snow and wouldn't be open to the public for six more weeks. We were alone on the trail all day, and whenever we stepped next to a partially exposed boulder, which was warmed by the sun, we'd fall through the soft snow up to our waists. For a while, it was funny, but we eventually tired of pulling one leg out of the snow. We made plenty of noise to keep any bears away, drank out of the cold mountain streams, and admired the bright yellow Avalanche Lilies that covered the hillsides. It was a beautiful sunny day, and when we arrived at the chalet, we walked right up on the partially snow-covered roof and ate our sandwiches. Late in the day, as we descended the last mile of the steep trail, our wobbly legs hardly held us up.

That evening we turned off the main road onto a narrow, grassy road and discovered a small ranger's cabin still closed for the winter. It had an open front porch and was a perfect place to roll out our sleeping bags. Steve, however, first wanted to take a short walk along the stream. When he came back minutes later, I had already fallen sound asleep in my sleeping bag. So, what did he do? He growled and shook me. I was terrified and screamed in panic as I thrashed around in my zipped-up bag. My response was so realistic that Steve thought I was joking. Several years went by before I admitted to Steve that I had thought I was going to be dinner for a hungry Grizzly.

We then had a great time at the Walton Goat Lick where we got up close to the sure-footed Mountain Goats that we filmed as they effortlessly ran along the steep rocky slopes that gave way with each step. Driving south back to civilization, the engine sputtered as we started to run out of gas over 40 miles from the nearest town. My VW didn't have a gas gauge, but it did have a little lever that I flipped to the right, giving me one more gallon. That meant I could drive about 30 more miles. I had to be careful. I turned off the key and coasted when going downhill, and when I dropped below 35mph, turned it on again. After driving over 40 anxious miles, we made it. We continued to Devil's Tower, which I had seen seven years earlier, and finally arrived at Moran, Wyoming, in the Tetons. Steve then continued his journey to the RMBL at Gothic, Colorado.

70. MORAN, WYOMING

THAT FIRST EVENING, Margaret Altmann and I drove up to the top of Signal Mountain where she pointed out a herd of about 40 elk far below. I looked, kept looking, and looked a bit more before I finally saw them. I could always see a bird before anyone else, but this was different. It amazed me. How could I be so blind? Now I realized I had to learn to see elk and moose. After a few days I could and was soon much better at finding them than Professor Altmann. Later, and just for fun, when I drove up to Yellowstone, I'd stop my car along the road and intently look across a prairie through my binoculars — at nothing. In just a few minutes, there would be a line of cars behind me, also trying to look — at nothing as I drove off.

Most of our time was spent observing moose, as the elk had moved up into the high hills. I'd sit on a knoll overlooking the small ponds and marshy areas, wait for moose to appear, and fill out 3x5 note cards with my observations. I enjoyed hiking to places such as Jenny Lake, Hidden Falls, Swan Lake, and out-of-the-way spots where I would silently sit and wait for the wildlife to come to me. I was always heavily covered with mosquito spray because they surrounded me by the thousands. They continually bounced off my clothes, hoping to find a spot without spray. By the end of the summer, I was immune to mosquitoes.

Professor Altmann had a little dog, Butsy, who was often close at her side, and two horses, Lucky and Timber, which I groomed and fed. Together we used them a few times on day trips as well as on our four-day backpack trip into the Teton Wilderness. The first night, we planned to stay in a ranger cabin, when two other men rode up and staked their horses right next to ours. Margaret was not happy. Then their two hungry dogs gobbled up two huge plates of blue rat poison sitting on the cabin floor. All night long they regretted having done that, but they survived. They did, however, scare the horses at night which pulled over the hitching rail. I slept in the cabin with the two strangers while Margaret stayed in her tent, worried the dogs would vomit all over it. The next day we continued north into Yellowstone and were at least 15 miles from the nearest road. The scenery was beautiful and the next two nights were far better when we stayed in a forest service cabin with two rooms. We saw several hundred elk and a few moose and mule deer. The fourth day, we rode about 22 miles back to the biological station. Once we headed home, we never had to worry about getting lost. The horses knew the way. They also walked a lot faster as soon as they realized we were headed back.

Before the pack trip, Margaret taught me how to balance our two big packs on a horse by using a small statue of a horse, two mini-packs and a shoelace. I never needed to do that again, but throughout the summer I did have fun riding her horses out in the back pasture chasing coyotes.

One night we listened to George Schaller, one of Doc Emlen's former graduate students, give a seminar on mountain gorillas that he had studied in Africa. George confided to me that Margaret had told him "John is one of the best assistants I ever had," which I was pleased to hear. George later sent me a card mentioning his upcoming research in India and he said that if I continued to work with Margaret, he would see me again. I never did but I was interested in his work.

Whenever I got the chance, I took 16mm movies of the moose, elk, flowers and mountain scenery. Early one morning on my day off, I drove to Yellowstone National Park and passed through the entrance about 4:00 a.m. before the Park Rangers were on duty. As the sun came up, I intentionally ended up in the middle of a nursery herd of about 50 female elk and their calves. That's when I realized just how enormous they were as they calmly walked around me just inches away. As I crouched down filming and looked up at them, I wondered if I knew what I was doing.

On July 30, 1962, Margaret and I drove to Yellowstone to meet John and Frank Craighead, identical twins, who were doing research on Grizzly Bears. I was excited to meet them, having read their articles in National Geographic. I had even written to them a year earlier to see if they needed a research assistant, but they felt obligated to hire students from Montana State University. After they told us about their research, we enjoyed talking with their kids who entertained us with their tame pet Golden Eagle, Great Gray Owl, Sparrow Hawk (Kestrel) and Prairie Falcon.

We later returned in the evening and drove to a nearby dump where we saw about 35 Grizzlies. As soon as we arrived, they scattered but soon returned. They can outrun a horse and the big boars weigh up to 1200 pounds. They are so vicious they don't even turn their backs on each other. I had never seen a Grizzly but didn't take any movies. Margaret said not to.

In early August, brother Paul and Elaine came to visit. I arranged to have them stay one night in Margaret's cabin in the Teton Wilderness. I was able to show them around briefly until they left the next morning. Baby David was just over six weeks old.

Towards the end of summer, Margaret and I drove to Montana to see a herd of bison at the National Bison Range in Moiese, located in the Flathead Indian Reservation in Northwest Montana. Moiese was established in 1908 to help save the remaining bison. It was estimated that there had been sixty to eighty million bison, but by 1899, their number had dwindled to about 600 animals. It was an interesting trip to get up close and see some of the huge, 2200-pound bulls. Today the biggest herd is in Yellowstone, where they now number about 5000.

For a couple weeks before my duties were over, Steve Martin, who ended up working for Margaret the following summer, arrived from Gothic so we could drive home together. Against Margaret's wishes, we hiked up to the 11,200' Lower Saddle between the Grand and Middle Tetons, and then on my last evening, after doing the "fill out the index card routine" of plotting elk on the sagebrush flats Southeast of Signal Mountain, we drove to some wild areas where tourists seldom went. We soon came upon a herd of about 40 elk, and after watching them for a few minutes, I did the unthinkable. I chased them. We must have been bouncing along on the two-rut road at least 45 mph until we couldn't laugh anymore. What was I rebelling at?

By the end of the summer, I had earned $480, less my food, and had enough film to make a forty-minute movie. I copied and sold some of my best movies to Rev. Howard Orians (father of Dr. Gordon Orians at the University of Washington) who needed some moose pictures for his next Audubon Screen Tour film — similar to the one where I met Roger Tory Peterson in the West High School auditorium back in 1953. Peterson, you'll remember, made the first excellent bird identification guide. Margaret Altmann also asked me to make her a movie of my best moose and elk shots. I selected about 20 minutes of film that I edited and then had duplicated and sent it to her with a bill for $75 to cover my expenses. She didn't approve of my modest charge and sent it back. I was surprised that she expected me, a student, to incur all the expenses. After a summer of constraints, I suddenly realized why I had rebelled earlier.

From the middle of May until the first week of September, I didn't cut my hair and didn't shave the last six weeks. That's when I learned I should never grow a beard for any reason. It was too scraggly. For a few days back home in Madison, I did have a beautiful head of dark brown curls that made me look like a mountain man. Donna didn't know what to think when she first saw me. A few days later, I had the excess cut off at Joe's Barber Shop at the corner of Regent and Allen Street, just a block east of West High School.

71. ONE EXTRA YEAR

AS A LITTLE KID IN THE 1950S, looking around and thinking about what I'd do someday, words policeman, fireman, teacher, doctor, or lawyer came to mind. Although there were countless kinds of jobs, I never heard much about them. Years later I thought maybe someone should write a book listing the 100,000 plus different kinds of jobs that there are in the world and give a copy to every student or at least to every guidance counselor. In high school, we had three counselors, but I never talked to them. If the UW had them, I never knew it.

After almost four years at Wisconsin, I came to the realization that unless I went another year to earn my teaching credentials, I wouldn't be able to get a teaching job. Talk about a lack of foresight. What was I thinking? Weren't there any advisors to ask me what I was planning to do? I didn't even ask myself. Fortunately, school was so inexpensive that another year wasn't going to break my bank. Besides that, school was fun, a lot was going on, and I didn't have any obligations or worries.

I next signed up with the School of Education and took all the education classes I needed to become a high school Biology teacher. One class, visual arts, which introduced us to the various ways of making presentations, even included "flannel graphs." That's where the teacher placed little cut-out figures of felt onto a felt covered easel to tell a story. I had once seen that method used in an elementary Sunday school class and found it to be boring back then. That was the most useless class I took, and I found out why education classes had a reputation for being dull. It would have been more useful to learn how to use mimeograph machines which we had before the advent of duplicators and printers.

I was soon assigned to Schenk Middle School, located on Madison's far East Side, where I did my practice teaching. I taught five ninth-grade Biology classes for six weeks in order to meet the requirements. The students were divided by ability into three groups. One class was above average, one was below average and three were in the middle. I thought it was a terrible system. The smart kids were fun to teach and caught on quickly. The slow class was fun too because they would come up with such crazy, outlandish questions I sometimes thought we would all die laughing. The middle three classes, however, were deadly. Getting them to respond was harder than pulling teeth. There weren't any kids to lead or follow. I had never seen kids like that before.

Back in class after our six weeks of practice teaching, our professor, Dr. Pella, talked in glowing terms about what a "cracker jack" job one of the other student teachers had done. That was great but I wondered why I received a "C" because not once in the six-weeks period did anyone ever observe me teaching — not even the teacher I replaced. I was surprised at the lack of supervision but didn't care that much. I had worked hard and thought I did a rather adequate job of teaching. Teaching, however, wasn't exactly as rewarding as I thought it would be. I also wondered about my ability to be a stern disciplinarian if the need arose. In the middle of it all, I got in a car accident.

72. A CRUSHED BEETLE

ONE FRIDAY EVENING, I drove up Langdon Street on the UW campus right behind a big old sedan that signaled and turned right but then abruptly did a U-turn. Smash. I plowed into the driver's side, crushing the Beetles front end, banged my forehead on the chrome arm of the plastic sun shield and dented the dashboard with my knee. When I got out of the car with blood dripping down my face, the other driver's first words were, "Oh no, I just got my license back yesterday."

Even though the other driver again lost his license, this accident never should have happened. In a way, it was my fault. I was planning to turn right at that same corner to visit Nancy, whom I had been dating for a couple years, but suddenly decided to visit Donna whose apartment was straight up the street. Instead, I visited the Emergency Room and got four stitches in the middle of my forehead. My knee puffed up and I had to have it drained twice but all turned out fine. I healed and insurance paid $540 to fix the Beetle, which continued to be a reliable "peoples" car.

73. A CRAZY IDEA

WITH JUST OVER ONE SEMESTER SHY OF GRADUATING from the University of Wisconsin, Steve Martin, my wrestling buddy from high school, and I got the crazy idea of going to South America. It seemed more exciting than teaching. The fact that neither of us knew Spanish, didn't have any money or a way to get started on this venture, didn't enter our thoughts. We certainly weren't thinking about the draft and Vietnam. It was simply an exciting idea. To prepare for this unlikely possibility, I slightly altered my academic schedule for my next and final semester. I signed up for a geography class that turned out to be more about agriculture in South America. It was taught by an old professor who seemed to have the boring gene. Or maybe he just wasn't feeling well. All I can remember is that we learned way too much about "slash and burn" agriculture. To summarize, these Brazilian farmers expended tremendous effort cutting down the old-growth timber in the Amazon jungle, burned the trees and then for the next few years planted their crops in the rich untouched soil until the heavy tropical rains washed away all the nutrients and thin layer of soil, forcing them to start all over again. I found myself falling behind with the reading assignments and was trying to decide if I should drop the course before the approaching deadline. Suddenly fate intervened. The professor died and we had the choice of continuing with a graduate assistant or simply dropping the class. My decision was easy. I would finish the semester with just 12 credits and graduate in June.

Three of those credits were from a Wildlife Ecology course taught by Professor Joe Hickey. He was doing a research project on how tree trimming, done by the City of Madison to control Dutch Elm Disease, was affecting the Robin population which preferred to nest in elms. Since he knew who I was and that I had an interest in birds, he asked me to get up at 4:00 a.m. to count the singing males every few days for three weeks. I hopped on my bicycle, pedaled past West High School and Forest Hill Cemetery to a neighborhood just off Mineral Point Road and counted the Robins. When I gave Professor Hickey my data, he was surprised at how few I counted, so of course he checked and confirmed my results. Tree trimming proved to be an effective way to reduce the number of nesting Robins but an ineffective way to control the beetles. Soon millions of the majestic elms disappeared from the streets of Madison and many other cities.

Another class was, "Origins of Greek and Latin Medical Terms." Brother Paul had also taken the class and I used his book with all his notes. It was taught by Professor Howe, who lived on Chadbourne Avenue, just a few houses west of Randall school. He had a daughter who used to park cars on their front lawn during the football games and you could hear her yelling, "Paahk heeah, Paahk heeah," in her unmistakable English accent. In class, he sometimes joked about his "numskull" daughter who, I knew, went to Vassar after finishing tenth grade at West High. Prof. Howe went through the whole book, one prefix, root, and suffix at a time, describing the meaning and origin of each. By the end of the semester, I could look at any medical or scientific word and figure out its meaning. I got a 99 on the final exam. All I had to do was memorize the book.

Another class I took was "Fish Ecology," taught by Professor Arthur Hasler. His son, Fritz, had been in my Cub Scout troop in fifth and sixth grades, and our meetings were sometimes held at their house in the University Heights. Fritz also was my classmate in high school and later worked for NASA. My dad, along with his long-time partner, William Kaeser, designed the Hasler Laboratory of Limnology, as it was later called, along the shores of Lake Mendota just West of the Student Union at the end of Park Street.

Unfortunately, Dr. Hasler was replaced for six weeks by some visiting English professor. He obviously had no idea of our background as he wrote one extremely complicated fish population equation on the blackboard after another. None of us had any idea what he was talking about and fortunately none of us was ever asked to respond. We just sat there and listened politely. When Dr. Hasler returned, we never were tested to see if we had learned the material. I did write a paper on the life-cycle of the sockeye salmon and found it interesting that after they left their home streams in Alaska and elsewhere, they toured the Pacific in a big circle for five years before returning to the same stream to spawn and die.

74. TO FLORIDA AND BACK

DURING EASTER VACATION in April 1963, Steve Martin and I took off for Florida in my VW Beetle, armed with some AAA maps, and a vague idea of where we'd go. The car had a problem that occasionally prevented us from going over 40 mph. That saved us once from getting a ticket from one of the small-town sheriffs in Georgia but was otherwise just an irritation.

Since Steve was just getting interested in birds, he was amazed at how I could identify them by the way they behaved or flew, as we drove from one birding hotspot to another. Since the Everglades had been half destroyed by the previous year's hurricane, we hurried off to Key West, which for me was a huge disappointment after seeing it earlier in fifth grade. Since it had turned into a crowded, grubby, immoral community with billboards everywhere, we turned around and headed back up the Atlantic coast past Miami. The wide-open beach between Miami and Fort Lauderdale was beautiful without a hotel in sight, so that's where we spent the night in our sleeping bags. At Fort Lauderdale, the beach was packed with thousands of college kids who arrived every Easter to enjoy the surf, sand, and sun. Unlike most other vacationers, however, we applied so many layers of cream and oily suntan lotion that we could hardly wash them off. After getting sunburned on all my previous trips to Florida, I was happy to remain pale, but

Steve was a bit disappointed to return without a tan. In central Florida, we bought a half bushel of oranges, but they didn't last the day. Our ten-day whirlwind trip of 4400 miles was over the day before school started.

75. PASSING THE TEST

A FEW DAYS LATER, the unforeseen happened. A team of Peace Corps (PC) recruiters, including some big names, a Shriver and a Rockefeller, arrived from Washington, D.C. to initiate the Wisconsin Project, a major recruiting effort on the UW campus. The big liberal campus in Madison was the perfect place to start since many students had heard John F. Kennedy speak at the UW. I saw him at the packed UW Field House on October 23, 1960, during the presidential campaign. Many students were enthusiastic Kennedy supporters, especially since his "New Frontier" speech, when he accepted the Democratic nomination. His speech was not a set of promises. It was a set of challenges. He wanted to foster a new sense of national purpose, civic participation, and sacrifice.

The recruiters were accompanied by a radio and TV blitz about the Peace Corps, signed into law on March 1, 1961, wanting to find young people who were "Willing to take the toughest job you'll ever love." They said it would not be easy, but it would be rich and satisfying. During the first two years of John F. Kennedy's presidency, the PC had become a big deal. Young Americans were going to change the world. "Take the test," they said, "and we'll let you know in just ten days if you are accepted." That seemed fast. I heard some applicants had been waiting for over a year without an answer which made it difficult to plan ahead or accept a job. I thought if I couldn't pass the test after just completing five years at the UW, I would never be able to, so I took the test. There was nothing to lose

When I entered the UW in the fall of 1958, every freshman took a psychological test which asked many similar questions in different ways. Then a few weeks before these recruiters arrived, every senior again took the same test. It seemed as if they wanted to see how consistent we were with our attitudes and beliefs. As it turned out, the Peace Corps administered the same test. By then I knew what was coming and tried to be consistent.

Sure enough, as the recruiters promised, I received a letter just over a week later from the Peace Corps Director, Robert Sargent Shriver, Jr. It began, "Dear Mr. McLeod, I am happy to inform you that you have been chosen as a promising applicant to enter training for the Peace Corps Project described in the enclosed brochure ...."

Yes, I was accepted to begin Peace Corps training in the fall to eventually go to Guatemala – if I could get through training. First, I pulled out an atlas and confirmed that yes, Guatemala was where I thought it was. I found out several years later that an FBI agent had even gone to Gothic, Colorado later in the summer to confirm that I had been there and who knows what else. I think the agent wanted a short vacation.

In the meantime, I received at least 50 postcards from various high schools around the state asking me to come for an interview to be a high school Biology teacher. Until that moment, my whole life had revolved around the biological sciences, and the UW teacher placement bureau proved to be quite efficient. On the other hand, going to a foreign country, learning a new language, and travelling sure sounded more exciting than teaching. I'd be exposed to a whole new world.

76. QUICK DECISIONS AND CONSEQUENCES

MY DECISION SEEMED EASY. Without any altruistic motives, I quickly accepted. Would my whole life's direction be sidetracked for two years?

I thought most people, and I was one of them, make lifelong preparations for the way they want their lives to turn out. All my interests, all my hobbies and summer jobs, and all my studies were geared to teaching Biology. Then suddenly, in one moment, I became not one of those people. By simply jumping at what I thought would be an interesting and exciting adventure, everything was about to change.

A day later I picked up Donna and one of her friends from the UW hospital where she worked on the psychiatric ward as a Registered Nurse. On their way home her friend asked, "John, what are you planning to do after graduation?" Well, I had just found out. So, I blurted out, without thinking how it might affect Donna, whom I had dated for two years, that I was going into the Peace Corps and would be gone for a couple of years. Donna was stunned. She had other hopes and dreams.

That weekend Donna went home to Friesland, a small Dutch town of 352 people, to commiserate with her parents. They decided that she should call me at home to find out just what my intentions were. When she made the call, my mother answered and said, "John is in Neenah visiting his girlfriend." When I heard that, I said, "Mom, couldn't you have just said I was away for a few days." Anyway, when Donna confronted me a day later, I rather lamely stated that after talking with my brother, I decided that until I was positive and ready, I should wait before making any big decisions. We continued to date, going to the movies, and occasionally sailing on Lake Mendota, but I was simply not ready for anything more serious. The timing was not right.

In the past, I had dated a fair number of girls, usually just once or twice until I discovered that there were obstacles, such as religion, in the way of developing a lasting relationship. To be blunt, I chose not to spend my limited financial resources on a dead end. With Nancy, however, there were no obvious obstacles, so we continued dating. We never talked about the future. I think we both knew we didn't have much in common. She was more of a scholar, majored in Spanish, the humanities, and was content to just sit and read for hours. I preferred more activity and enjoyed being outside doing anything else.

On the other hand, my dad was quite proud that I had been accepted into the Peace Corps which he repeated a number of times to his friends — in spite of the fact that I knew, and had told him several times, I had only been accepted to start Peace Corps training. The rumors were that it would not be so easy. He obviously had plenty of confidence in me. I preferred to give myself an escape plan if I didn't make it through training or if I ultimately decided not to go.

77. OPTIONS AND OPPORTUNITIES

I HAVE SOMETIMES WONDERED, "Would I have taken the Peace Corps test if I had not previously had the crazy idea of going to South America with Steve Martin — even though we both knew it was doubtful our plans would ever materialize?" If I had decided to hold back instead of stepping forward to take the test, how would my life have turned out?

We make poor choices because of our presumptions, pressures, and expectations of others. Not making a decision is the same as making a decision. It just changes or postpones the result. Be bold. It gives you more options and leads you into all kinds of situations and opportunities. You can always fall back and regroup.

I was now a UW graduate with a Bachelor of Science in Secondary Education (BS-SED). Of course, I received a few cards from some relatives and friends but one from my Grandpa Middleton, who was

Grandpa Clarence Middleton and Mom

89 years old, is the only one I kept. He wrote, "Page No. 1 June Thursday the 20 — in the Morning after Breakfast — had a nice rain and it is 60 Degrees and the sun is shining. Sending 5 1 Dollars Bills for Graduation and good luck to you. Hope this gets through on time! Picked the peas yesterday and you can have a mess if you can get them by Saturday the 22. Goodbye C. D. Middleton 1831 Green Street Rockford Ill."

78. SOUTH DAKOTA

IN MID-SUMMER 1963, before Peace Corps training was to start, I headed to South Dakota for six weeks to band ducks. There I joined two Federal Game Agents from the U.S. Fish and Wildlife Service and two other Biology students hoping to get some field experience.

The task was simple. We drove along the miles of country roads until we spotted a considerable number of ducks on one of the hundreds of small ponds that dotted the landscape. We then waded into the pond, usually just up to our chests, and drove the flightless, molting ducks into a trap that we set up between two long wing nets. Most of the ducks, often more than a hundred at a time, were compliant and swam into the trap as planned, but others were sneaky and became almost invisible as they hid in the reeds and muck. After hauling the trap onto dry land, we identified, measured, weighed, and sexed the various kinds of ducks, teals, grebes, and coots before clamping a band on their legs. By the time we finished the paperwork, the constant hot, dry wind thoroughly dried our Levis just in time for the next pond.

Only once in deeper water did I get so tangled up in seaweed that I struggled five minutes to go just ten feet to shore. The agent joked, "Ya, we saw you but first we had to get those ducks." No worry, I was a lifeguard and could have struggled a lot longer. But it did surprise me how fast a person can get in trouble.

On one occasion, I encountered a huge Holstein bull grazing near some rusty abandoned farm equipment. Thinking that I could have a little fun and believing I could run to safety behind the old machinery, I began to tease it. When the bull started snorting, swinging its head from side to side and pawing the ground, one of the agents looked up and yelled, "Stop that and get out of there." Being a city kid, I didn't realize that Holsteins don't charge blindly, like in a Spanish bullfight, but look where their prey is going. Then I remembered the story about the bull that chased Grandma McLeod up a tree back on their farm near Tomah, Wisconsin. I never could visualize Grandma climbing a tree, but I guess she was young once too.

Later that evening, the agent gave me $5 to buy a six pack, but in my haste, I forgot my wallet. Without an ID, I returned empty handed, much to their amusement. At 23, I still had never drunk a beer, even after five years at the UW where you could order one in the student union.

We lived in motels and had an interesting summer listening to the tales of poachers and other lawbreakers recounted by the game agents. When the six weeks were up, we had banded 4,105 ducks.

UW Grad, 1963

In the previous months, Dad had designed a Frank Lloyd Wright-style home with big windows, two massive limestone fireplaces, clear redwood siding and a cedar shake roof, which he and Mom planned to build on the hill at Rosewood, their 4.3 acre lot off Schroeder Road, purchased a decade earlier. Schroeder Road was no longer a dirt road but was now a two-lane, paved street and the whole surrounding area was getting built up. All us kids except Margie, who still had two more years at West High, had left home and it was the right time for them to go ahead. Dad and Mom were now 56 and 55 and had plenty of energy to proceed with their dream.

When I returned from South Dakota, the foundation was about to be poured and my contribution was wrapping the Bur Oak trees with boards to keep them from getting damaged by machinery. I also re-stacked a big pile of cedar boards for the ceiling so they could air dry without warping. During and after construction of the house, Dad did a tremendous amount of back-breaking landscape work by making stone retaining walls all around the house. A year earlier I had knocked down a couple of old limestone buildings on a nearby farm giving him plenty of material.

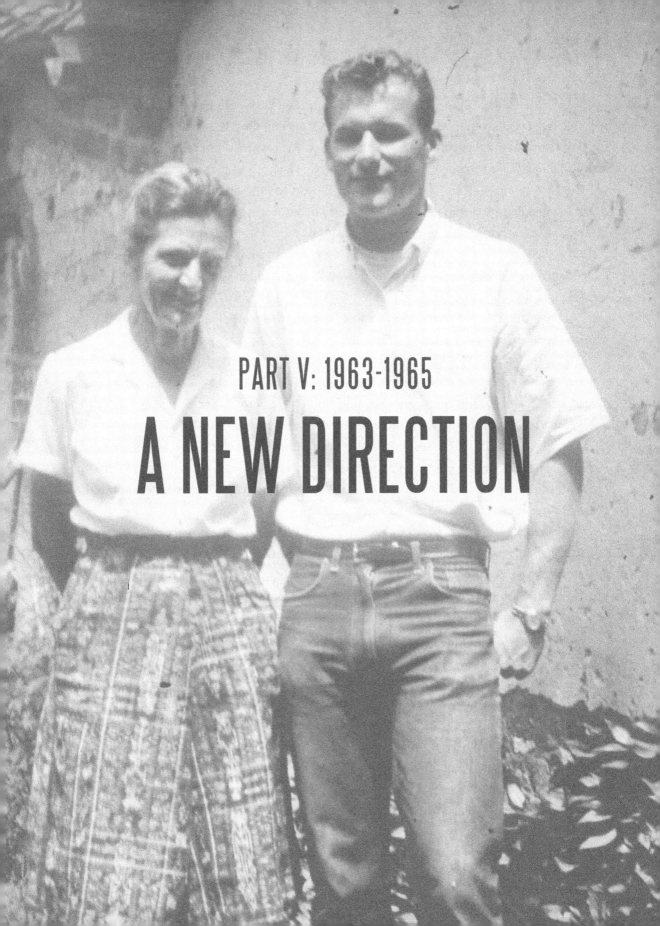

PART V: 1963-1965
A NEW DIRECTION

79. PEACE CORPS TRAINING

BEFORE I LEFT FOR PEACE CORPS TRAINING, I noticed that I was getting fingernail-size, scaly white spots all over my chest and shoulders that didn't get tanned in the sun. I went to a dermatologist at the UW Hospital who thought I had a fungus infection. He gave me some salve but a month or two later I still looked like a leopard. I'd find out the correct diagnosis later.

Our first month of Peace Corps training was scheduled to begin in September in Puerto Rico. At the last minute, however, it was abruptly canceled because of mosquitoes. An outbreak of Dengue Fever, also called break bone fever, had infected the trainers at the Peace Corps training camp, including the Director, Andy Hernandez. Andy later recounted how he had to ask a nurse to lift his folded arms off to his sides because he couldn't stand the pain and the weight on his chest. Canceling was the right decision but I was disappointed not to see Puerto Rico. In the meantime, I began to receive information from Peace Corps headquarters on what to take and when to arrive at New Mexico State University in Las Cruces, New Mexico.

On September 19, 1963, with a ticket in hand, I first flew from Madison to Chicago. While waiting for my next flight at O'Hare airport, it became rather obvious that new Peace Corps trainees all had a certain look. Eight of us had no trouble finding each other as we waited at the American Airlines departure gate. In just a few more hours, after stops in Fort Worth and El Paso, we took a Greyhound bus and taxis to the small campus of New Mexico State University. We ended up at the Regent University Dorms before meeting most of the others, who were playing touch football on a beautiful, sunny day. I was a little surprised to see that one of the quarterbacks was a blonde girl, Sue Peers. She was surprisingly athletic.

On September 24, an article was published in "The Round Up," the student newspaper at New Mexico State University. It said, "The last of the fourth group of Peace Corps volunteers to be trained at NMSU arrived Thursday. The group, called Guatemala III, consists of 45 women and 30 men, who will study for 12 weeks —10 on campus and two in the field — before being assigned to Guatemala for 20 months.

This is not only a training program, but a selection program designed to eliminate those who for some reason might lack qualities necessary for a PCV. Their first three days were spent taking psychological tests and physical examinations. Monday, they began classes. The average college student might balk at the schedule of the PC trainee. All will take 4-5 hours of Spanish per day. Some have had no experience with the language. They will also study the history, politics, culture and geography of Guatemala, American history and institutions, and world affairs. These subjects will add to their understanding of the natives of Guatemala. They will also take courses in health and physical education.

Girls will study such subjects as home economics, childcare, nutrition, clothing, and sanitation. Boys' courses will include carpentry, animal care, construction materials and gardening. The PC trainees will be in class an average of 10 hours per day, six days per week.

The program is under contract with CARE and will open with a school lunch program in Guatemala. They might then enter into community improvement projects, literacy programs, or the teaching of English. The program is very flexible and allows the volunteers to carry out those projects for which they feel there is a great need or interest.

Program coordinator is Jacob Tejada. Dr. Paul Duffield, head of agriculture services, is administrator and Dr. Samuel R. Skaggs, dairy professor, is in charge of the technical training."

The curriculum stated that we would have Spanish classes for 240 hours, area studies for 90 hours, U.S. history and government for 25 hours, world affairs for 25 hours, technical skills for 100 hours, physical education and health for 70 hours, Peace Corps orientation for 15 hours, and communism-in-action for 5 hours.

The last was a big deal because Fidel Castro had overthrown the Cuban dictator Batista in 1959. Then the U.S. failed to overthrow Castro in April 1961, during the Bay of Pigs invasion, and came close to nuclear war with Russia during the Cuban Missile crisis in October 1962. As a result, we were told that we could not have beards to imitate Castro. We were also not to have contact with U.S. Embassy or USAID officials, to avoid any political accusations that we were secret CIA agents.

All 69 of us were divided into eight Spanish groups. Group one consisted of trainees who had studied Spanish in college and group eight with those who had no language training. I started out in group seven because I had had two years of Latin and one year of German at the UW but was soon moved to group six a couple weeks later because the instructor must have thought I was doing better than some others. I wasn't so sure.

After breakfast, which started at 6:45 a.m., classes continued all day until at least 8:00 p.m. That's when I returned to my room to study Spanish and learn what I should have already learned during our four hours of classes. I learned by seeing and reading, not so much by hearing as we did in class. Trying to learn Spanish the same way that I learned English as a kid was frustrating to me. My roommate, Bill Pearson, was in the same boat.

The physical education part of our training included swimming. To keep from drowning, just in case we were thrown overboard, we had to float for 20 minutes with our hands and feet behind our backs. That was a relaxing way to stay alive without expending any energy, but it did take a few minutes to get relaxed enough to get into an easy breathing rhythm.

In the nearby Organ mountains, we rappelled down a rock wall and crossed over a canyon about 100' wide on a rope some 80' above the ground that our mountain climber leaders set up for us. Crossing the canyon wasn't scary but since the safety harness was made for a short person, several of us got our bunched-up shirts caught between the carabiner and rope which ripped holes in them and stopped us less than halfway across. Hand over hand, we pulled ourselves the rest of the way. We also had to run 600 meters and were tested to see how many pull-ups and sit-ups we could do in two minutes. I remember doing 64 sit-ups, the same as another trainee, Jim Corzine. Since we hadn't done any sit-ups for a couple years, we were both so sore that for the next week it took us several minutes to stand up straight after each class.

Most every Wednesday we got vaccinated for diseases such as yellow fever, cholera, tetanus, and smallpox, that would hopefully protect us from the awful array of tropical diseases to which we might be exposed. They also seemed intent on removing most of our wisdom teeth even though everyone had already gone to their home-town dentists. One Wednesday I received a typhoid shot, and just as my arm was starting to get inflamed and sore the next morning, the dentist pulled two of my wisdom teeth. It was a brutal and bloody procedure. When the dentist was finished, I slowly stood up. With my back just a few inches from the wall, he asked, "Are you feeling okay?" As I said, "Yes," I tipped back and bumped against the wall which kept me from falling. Only then did I realize that I wasn't quite as fine as I thought. Someone drove me back to the dorm where I slept for 24 hours straight. My stitches were removed the following Monday. Quite a few of us looked as if we had the mumps.

On October 13th, 41 of us took a one-day vacation by chartered bus to see the White Sands National Monument and Carlsbad Caverns. We took a three mile, almost four-hour tour of the cave, which was amazing. When they turned off the lights for twenty seconds, we discovered what it was like to be in total darkness. At 5:20 p.m., a swarm of some 250,000 bats came swirling up and out of the cave.

80. ALDAMA, CHIHUAHUA, MEXICO

OUR ENTIRE GROUP headed to the province of Chihuahua, Mexico, for two weeks in early November. We were divided into eight groups of eight, and each went to different rural towns. My group went to a town of 6000 people called Aldama, which was about 15 miles Northwest of Chihuahua. We stayed in the small, grubby, miserable "Hotel Aldama" with a muddy, puddle-filled courtyard. It cost $1.30 each night including two meals. Two law students from the University of Chihuahua, named Ángel and Gilberto, accompanied us. They were paid by the Peace Corps but didn't know where their stipend was coming from or that we were future PCVs. This was just part of their sociology class.

My small 8x11 whitewashed room had a cement floor, the ceiling was covered with logs, the only window was splashed with whitewash and the curtain was an old burlap bag peppered with holes. A 60-watt bulb hung by a cord from the ceiling and the door didn't close completely but the old screen door had a lock. I wrote some letters on a little wooden table and there was a small mirror on the wall flanked by two pictures of girls. I was too tall for the lumpy double bed which I shared with Bob Keberlein. Bob was from Menasha, Wisconsin and had studied Spanish for three years at the UW before signing up for the Peace Corps.

The first morning, Gilberto stopped in to see how we were doing, and he told the cook to boil the raw milk. After that we had hot milk on our soggy corn flakes. We also had bread, bacon, and an egg. He said they were going to order water from Chihuahua, that would come in a sanitary can, so we wouldn't have to drink so much Coca Cola. Coke was the only drink that was safe.

Gilberto drove our group (Bob Keberlein, Jay Jackson, Norma Wilder, Ramona Whaley, Judy Wilks, Ron and Jane Brousseau) several miles to an old Catholic church, built some 400 years earlier, that was now in total disrepair and occupied mostly by pigeons. On our way back, we walked for three hours along the river and met a class of 11-year-old kids on a field trip. Some were sitting in the muddy water fully clothed while one boy sat in his undies. A few had horses tied to a nearby tree. It was quite a scene, unlike any field trip I had ever seen. We chatted with them a while before continuing.

Later in the day, we talked with the Director at a primary school and visited a class where everyone seemed eager to learn. When school was over, we played basketball with some kids, who couldn't decide if they wanted to go home or stay and talk with all eight of us. Four in our group, including Bob and Norma, did most of the talking. For me, speaking was still a real struggle. Even though I was learning a lot of words, they didn't always make sense when they were strung together in a sentence.

Back at our "hotel," we ate some enchiladas with hot sauce. One drop for every three bites was plenty for me. Until then, the hottest food I had ever eaten was sharp cheddar cheese. At 10:30 p.m. Bob and I went to bed. It was a miserable night. The blankets were too small, Bob coughed all night, and in the morning, I woke up with Montezuma's revenge. I was the fourth one to suffer. The other four had to wait one more day. The hot boiled milk on corn flakes didn't help a bit.

On November 7, 1963, the Mayor of Aldama sent over a driver with a pick-up truck and took us to a well-kept hacienda several miles out of town. There was a big house, a pond, and adobe shacks for the workers. Since the owner wasn't there, we returned after an hour and spent the day listening to the radio and practicing Spanish with Ángel, our sociology student assistant. At 10:30 p.m., a three-piece marimba band showed up at the hotel to play for free beer. They sure livened up the evening.

First thing in the morning, we went to see the priest, who was always the most important person in town, but he was nowhere to be found. Instead we visited a five-bed hospital and talked to the doctor who claimed he had only lost two of the 1500 babies he had delivered in the previous six years. That evening we went to a benefit show at the Catholic school to be entertained by some well-known Mexican singer who didn't show up. Instead we saw a "Tarzan" movie with Spanish subtitles. You can imagine how much we all enjoyed it. When I got back to the room, I snapped my towel to kill flies until about 1:00 a.m. when my arm got too sore to continue.

After breakfast we drove 30 miles to Guadalupe, a small isolated village of 300, in an enclosed pick-up provided by the Mayor, who informed us we had to pay for the gas. It was a dusty road, but the desert scenery was beautiful as burros passed by with bundles of firewood. We also stopped to look at what was supposedly an abandoned uranium mine. In Guadalupe, everyone lived in adobe houses, and most of the fifty school kids were poorly clad or naked with bloated stomachs from poor diets. Somehow the people grew black beans and corn in the desert soil, but it was obvious the kids weren't getting enough of them. We then headed north to see a tributary of the Rio Grande where we all saw some coyotes and our first roadrunner.

On our return, we narrowly missed a head-on collision with another truck as it careened off the road. We stopped for a second, watched the other driver jump out to pick up his hat and then kept going. After seven hours of driving, we arrived at our hotel, where someone took us to a men's service club. Shortly after we entered, a band with about 15 kids playing trumpets, tubas and trombones blasted us out of our seats. The club's President introduced each of us, one at a time, as everyone clapped. He then offered us cokes, beer, or any drink we wanted. Judy Wilks took him at his word and requested tequila and brandy — and was kidded the rest of the evening. After the meeting, we broke up into small groups and they asked us questions until midnight. I didn't say much but was pleased that I could understand quite a bit when just two people were talking.

As Jay Jackson and I walked around town, we watched five cotton gins separate out the seeds as workers bundled up the cotton. We saw people making adobe blocks, like in Las Cruces, where we made an adobe oven and used it to cook a meal.

Early the next morning we observed the CARE school lunch program being prepared. The powdered milk was measured in two big wash tubs by a man using his bare arm to stir it. He then poured the milk into some big milk cans and placed them in a truck and drove off to pick up the beans prepared by some lady. A bakery made bread rolls, using CARE flour, and the food was then delivered to six schools with 415 kids. The same men's service club paid all the expenses.

Our two weeks in Aldama weren't all play and sightseeing. One afternoon we cleaned up the playground at a Catholic school, carried away rocks and dirt and made some seats around the edge. Early the following morning, the Peace Corps Project Coordinator, Dr. Jacob Tejada, showed up to see how we were doing. He seemed satisfied even though we were all still sleeping when he arrived with our mail. We had a meeting that night to help us prepare our final report.

The next day we went to a fiesta in San Diego, a 90-minute ride over more dusty roads. We rode in one truck while the Mayor, the Secretary, the Treasurer, and several policemen went in another. Along the way, we stopped at some hot springs, where it felt wonderful to get clean. In the evening, the Treasurer, who drank way too much tequila, tried to give me his curved folding knife as a remembrance of Aldama. He called it "saca tripas," or "pull out your guts." I told him it was a great knife, admired the bone handle, asked questions about it, and tried to give it back. We went back and forth several times until it seemed he would be hurt if I rejected it. Somehow, I ended up with it, which didn't seem right considering his inebriated condition. We were treated royally and after thirteen days away, returned to Las Cruces for several more weeks of training.

81. BACK AT NEW MEXICO STATE UNIVERSITY

ALONG THE WAY, THREE PC RECRUITS QUIT, while eight others were selected out for various reasons that were never divulged to us. Some we expected, like big Ed from Massachusetts who thought Chicago was a state, but a few others came as a surprise. One kid in the dorm room next to me, after getting the humiliating news, supposedly consumed eight double whiskeys and was so drunk that we could only see the whites of his eyes as he groaned with every breath for over an hour. Personally, I never worried about getting selected out.

As we walked back from our physical education class just before noon on Friday, November 22, 1963, we got the terrible news that President John F. Kennedy had been shot. Everyone alive that day will never forget where they were when they got the news. President Kennedy's most quoted line was, "Ask not what your country can do for you — ask what you can do for your country." With such beliefs, he'd be a conservative republican if he were alive today.

For the next few weeks, we continued our busy schedule as our instructors attempted to teach us a little about everything. We even learned how to slaughter pigs and chickens, just in case the need would arise. They started with a five month old hog, shot it between the eyes, picked it up by its hind legs with a chain, slit its throat, drained the blood, and dipped it in a tank of 145-degree water for six minutes to loosen the hair before scraping it off. Then they gutted it so it would cool faster. The next day they showed us how to cut it up into bacon and pork chops. Each of us also had to slit the neck of a chicken and hold it upside down to drain out the blood. That sure was a better way than cutting off its head and letting it flop wildly down the driveway as Uncle Frank had done when I was a little kid.

Because I had always thought about being a teacher, I inquired several times about getting into a teaching program. I talked to our Coordinator as well as the CARE-PC Director in Guatemala, Keni Kent, who indicated they would see what they could do. It never happened and in retrospect, I was glad. Such a job, with regular hours, would have been too restrictive. At the same time, I kept thinking that getting a job with an organization similar to CARE sure sounded more interesting than teaching. I was conflicted.

Training ended on December 16th and we all flew home for Christmas. The American Airlines flight to Chicago had a half-dozen seats filled up with huge Piñatas that several volunteers purchased on our week-end trips to Juarez. Once home, I packed my metal trunk we were all told to buy, had my shoes resoled, and the day after Christmas flew to Miami, where 58 of us rejoiced at the Hotel Lindsay Hopkins. We were going to Guatemala.

82. GUATEMALA HERE WE COME

AT 10:00 A.M. ON DECEMBER 27, 1963, 58 of us, including eight married couples, boarded a four-engine charter flight from Miami to Guatemala City. It was a beautiful day as we flew over Cuba and Guantanamo Bay. We had the run of the plane and enjoyed our celebratory four-hour flight. Our adventure to the "Land of Eternal Spring" was about to begin.

On the tarmac we were met by dozens of people, including a rowdy bunch of PCVs from Groups I and II who waved at us to get back on the plane while we still had the chance. The Embassy, USAID and Guatemalan government personnel were more reserved. Out on the runway, our pictures were clicked a hundred times before we breezed through customs and were bussed to the Palace Hotel in downtown Guatemala City. There we again met our CARE-Peace Corps bosses, Keni Kent and his able assistant, Tony Duran. After a few announcements, we were free to explore our new surroundings. During our first few days, we all must have looked like tourists because the taxi drivers constantly yelled, "Hey Mister, do you want a ride?" After a week or two when our demeanor changed, they stopped asking.

CARE was contracted by the PC to manage our group because in these early days, the PC didn't have enough of their own trained personnel. We were fortunate to have Keni and Tony Duran as leaders. They did a great job, and everybody admired them.

For the first week, we attended classes all day long at the cold, dingy Social Work School, listening to lectures in English and Spanish to acquaint us with some Guatemalan agencies and people. That was followed by a New Year's Eve party at the Guatemalan American Institute — where I first drank some punch laced with the awful local rum. At midnight, everyone kissed everyone in sight. We had made it to Guatemala.

We're Going to Change the World — or Ourselves

83. SINK OR SWIM

ON JANUARY 3, 1964, we each received an envelope with 35 Quetzales (Q35), equivalent to U.S. $35.00, given a destination and told to return three days later. My group of four included Ann Silverman, Doug Taber and Priscilla Takano who was from Guam. Priscilla knew a USAID employee, D.L. Crisostomo, who took us first to Lake Amatitlán, where we had a picnic, and then on to Escuintla, a hot, tropical city halfway down the mountains towards Puerto San José, our first destination. That last leg by bus was a new experience. A little kid in front of me stuck his head out the window and sprayed me with vomit. The people on the bus all had huge smiles on their faces, and I learned for the first time that this was one of their favorite kinds of humor. A bit later, a stoic Indian got soaked by a pig that was tied on top of the bus. He just sat there motionless and took it.

We found rooms at the Hotel Pacifica, a flimsy wooden structure without any amenities, but it was on the beach. We couldn't go swimming because our swimming suits were packed in our trunks, which had not yet arrived. At night, however, it was very dark, and our undies served us well. The weather was perfect but garbage and banana peels, which frequently wrapped around my ankles, gave me the creeps as I wasn't yet well acquainted with the ocean in Guatemala.

The next morning, we boarded a bus to Guatemala City, which first drove all over town for the next hour picking up people. Back to where we started, we resumed our trip up the steep hillsides. As we approached mile high Guatemala City, another bus passed us, which meant the race was on.

Uphill through Sololá

As we roared down a long slope and curved to the right, I could feel the tires on the right side lifting off the blacktop. I was sure we were going to roll down the steep bank to our deaths but somehow the driver kept it on the road. From Guatemala City, we boarded another old school bus and headed west to Panajachel on the shores of Lake Atitlán. At the end of a long day on the road, the red sky highlighted the four volcanoes surrounding Lake Atitlán. It was gorgeous. We stayed at the Maya-Azteca Hotel, cheap in every way.

At noon the next day, we bussed 2000' back up the hill in time to see the Indian market in Sololá where there were all kinds of vegetables, fruits and handicrafts for sale. As we walked past the stalls, the Indian women only came up to my elbows, and at 6'1" I felt gigantic. From there, we went on to Chichicastenango where we just missed the famous, weekly Indian market. We were supposed to talk with some PCVs from Group II but they weren't around. We didn't care, as it seemed to be a pointless task. On our third day, we had another long bus ride back to the Palace Hotel. I loved the Palace. It was an old "luxury" hotel with comfy beds and tasty food served by Indian women dressed in their traditional garb.

84. OUR DESTINATION

JANUARY 7TH WAS THE BIG DAY when Keni Kent announced where we would be stationed, and with whom. We had all made our requests. Would they be honored? I had decided that my best choice would be Marge Bradbury, a 64-year-old lady who had lived in Bolivia and Mexico where her husband had been a mining engineer. She could speak Spanish, which meant that I would be able to survive the first few months. I thought we could get along well, and she might even keep me out of trouble. Lo and behold, my request was granted, although several other PCVs were surprised at my choice. We would be living in San Pedro Ayampuc, a village just 12 miles Northeast of the big city. That was good. We could get to Guatemala City in about an hour. At the time, I don't think any of us appreciated how much work, time, and hundreds of dusty miles it took for Keni and Tony to locate sites and homes for all of us.

Marge Bradbury and John

The next day I woke up with Montezuma's Revenge and didn't dare venture too far from my hotel room. Meanwhile, Marge spent her time buying mattresses and other items we would need. On January 9th, we hired a taxi for Q7.50, and headed to San Pedro Ayampuc with our single camp-style mattresses tied on top and our new purchases packed inside. The cabby was so terrified going down the steep switchbacks as we approached San Pedro Ayampuc, I doubt he ever returned. The rutted, dusty main street to the plaza wasn't much better, but we made it. This would be our home for the next twenty months.

As we entered the circular plaza, we passed a medical dispensary and a big white Catholic church on the right and came to a stop in front of the school straight ahead. The village office, post office and jail were off to the left before the bakery. There was a huge Ceiba (Kapok), the national tree of Guatemala, in the center and the lowest branches were at least 40' above us. Although the Mayor, Ricardo Álvarez, supposedly knew we were coming, no one was there to meet us as we exited the taxi. A teacher, Francisco Garcia, finally came out of the school, quizzed us about America for a few minutes, and then said we could stay in the school where Marge and I each had a classroom to ourselves. Our "Welcome," as we found out later, was quite unlike the brass band reception that a few others received but we were here, and everyone soon knew it. Yes, they thought we were coming tomorrow. Everything would have been ready by tomorrow.

Marge in our backyard

We soon learned that it would take another week for our house renovations to be completed. Since we had more items to purchase, I left for Guatemala City after two nights and purchased a table, chairs, and two beds. Since I didn't know that I could have had them delivered to the bus, I had them sent to the Peace Corps office. Fortunately, a week later, Keni Kent and Tony Duran arrived with our stuff packed in their Jeep as it was cluttering up their office. We all knew I got away with free delivery and we all had a hearty laugh. At least they knew we were both adequately settled in our house. Luckily, we lived just an hour away.

Our house, surrounded by an 8' wall, was on the near right side of the big, grassy, open plaza, opposite the mayor's office and post office. I was happy with the central location where I could see what was happening. Marge and I each had our own 15'x15' bedroom with front doors and shuttered windows that opened onto the street. Our small kitchen had room for a table, two chairs, a five-gallon "Salvavidas" (lifesaving) water bottle for drinking water and a countertop where we placed our two-burner kerosene stove, some pots, pans, and utensils. We even had a few storage rooms, where I hung up a pole for clothes, and a covered back patio where we each had a little kerosene lamp, so we could read at night hunched over our books. The outdoor privy had been cleaned up. To keep the bees and flies away, I hung a Shell Vapona insecticide strip below the seat. We had our own 15' well which a couple Indians eventually cleaned out and limed. I bought a bucket, pulley and a rope and we were all set. Next, I bought a big wash tub, four bamboo poles and some shower curtains to make a private shower stall. In the morning, I'd fill up the tub, wait until the sun warmed up the water, and then we took turns having a stand-up sponge bath. After a few months, we were quite comfortable. During the first few weeks, however, we were dealing with a dusty, filthy mess. We had a huge amount of cleaning to do and junk and garbage to bury. Until I cleaned up the kitchen, we ate peanut butter sandwiches in Marge's room. It was extremely dry and dusty, but the rent was cheap. Our landlord, Miguel Ángel Morales, charged us $8 a month which we split. Our monthly Peace Corps salary was $115, and as I found out later, my basic food and living expenses amounted to about $35. I could save a lot of money.

Our first task was to try to organize a CARE school lunch program. Marge and I met with the teachers and the mothers' club. She did all the talking as I had a hard time understanding anything.

From then on, I spent a lot of time each day and night studying Spanish. Before lunch, it was usually my job to walk across the plaza to the little bakery where I bought fresh bread and some delicious little miniature loaves like banana bread. On the way over, I'd practice saying some version of, "I want to buy some bread," and hoped I wouldn't get too many questions that I couldn't understand or answer.

The first few weeks, I went on frequent shopping trips to Guatemala City to buy all kinds of items, including garden tools to fix up our long, narrow backyard that backed up against a steep hill. I was grateful for the privacy but wondered about landslides.

I noticed that once again my chest was getting covered with those scaly, itchy white spots that started to appear before Peace Corps training. As a result, I decided to see the PC Doctor, Nick Fortesque, a recent graduate of Duke. He concluded, "I don't believe you have a fungus. I think it's a skin reaction to stress and your body producing too much adrenaline. I had to calm down and relax. As soon as I did, the spots disappeared. For the next several years, whenever a spot or two would reappear, I realized I had been under some extra stress. Some people got ulcers, I got spots.

Near the end of January, Marge and I talked to the teachers, the nurse, and the Mayor about the town's almost nonexistent water supply. Some families had their own well, but most others scooped it out of the creek that was now almost dried up. I soon realized, however, that the schoolteachers and the Mayor didn't get along, and we would have to talk with them separately. Then the newly arrived and enthusiastic School Director quit. I think she realized this wasn't the place for her.

A few days after that, Francisco Garcia, and I, along with several of his students, hiked up the hill over a mile away and saw the origin of the water supply. From a tiny spring, there was a two-inch steel pipe that carried just a dribble of water to the mayor's office. It was a sorry sight. This would not do.

Keni Kent, along with Bill Pearson, my roommate from Las Cruces, and Jay Jackson, another city volunteer, delivered our trunks of clothes, including my Bolex 16mm. movie camera, and a standard box of PC books. For Marge and me, it was better than Christmas. A couple days later, I returned to Guatemala City and bought two unfinished pine dressers, more chairs, two tables and a bookcase. This time, I knew enough to get it all loaded on one of the three buses that left San Pedro every morning and returned the same afternoon.

85. SAN PEDRO AYAMPUC'S FIESTA

FROM FEBRUARY 12-17, 1964, San Pedro Ayampuc held its annual fiesta. Several days early, people started camping out and building stalls in the plaza, where they sold a wide assortment of carnival trinkets, local handicrafts, hand-made fabric, wool blankets, food, and even cotton candy. By the 11th, the fiesta was already going full blast and the plaza was packed with people and Indians dressed in their traditional clothes. One four-man marimba and dance area were set up right in front of my bedroom window, while another was up by the school. The loud monotonous drumming and ruckus continued until 3:00 to 6:00 a.m. each morning. I was amazed at their stamina. They seldom took a break and when they did, it was noticeably short. During the daytime, there were horse races, various traditional dance groups, soccer games and a lot of drinking to excess.

The Bear Dance

At the end of the week, the Mayor invited Marge and me to the big dance. It was for the rich people, those who could afford the Q2 entrance fee. As soon as we arrived, I was kept busy dancing, first with Juana, the Sports Queen, then with Christina, Miss San Pedro Ayampuc, and next with some 14-year-old for the next ten dances because I didn't know how to excuse myself. The Mayor even requested that the professional marimba band from Guatemala City play the "twist" in our honor. I was amazed at the way drab looking girls could walk out of their dusty, stick and adobe houses looking as if they had just been to the spa. Finally, at 1:45 a.m., I was able to sneak home. The next day, dozens of stalls were removed, and the empty, dusty plaza was littered with junk, scraps of paper and corn husks that were wrapped around humitas, steamed corn cakes that were sold by the hundreds. That's when I received a love letter from the 14-year-old, who must have thought I felt the same after ten dances in a row.

Sanitary facilities were totally lacking for the hundreds of fairgoers, and the only water available was from the nearly dry creek. The Mayor had turned off the small trickle carried by the two-inch pipe that went to his office because, as he said later, "I didn't want outsiders to use it all up." With the influx of people, fleas were everywhere. For weeks after, I could feel them crawling on my ankles when I was reading in the evening. I'd roll back my white socks and crush them between my fingernails one at a time. I also bought flea powder, poured it between the sheets on my bed and then beat on my bed until it puffed up through the blankets. I also mopped our rooms with Pine-Sol hoping that would help. After a while, they mostly disappeared. I'm glad they never gave me the plague. I got that from other sources — on a regular basis.

When a little Indian girl knocked on my door and offered to wash my clothes, I was pleased. After all, hauling bucket after bucket of water and scrubbing my clothes with my bare knuckles was a hassle. When she returned a day later, I could see that they were clean and whiter than ever. After the beating they took on the river rocks, however, my new T-shirts and undies were so thin that they looked like I had worn them for years. On my next trip to Guatemala, I bought a small washboard and continued to do my own laundry. When the little girl returned a few days later, Marge showed her our new washboard. She had never seen one. I had — in antique stores.

During the first few months, I spent a lot of time cleaning up our house, painting, fixing up the backyard and digging a trench so rainwater running down the steep hill wouldn't flood our patio and bedrooms. I also planted a garden, made screens and doors for the kitchen and a lot of other improvements. In between, I continued to read and study Spanish several hours a day. I was getting a bit better and could carry on a simple conversation but had an awfully long way to go.

86. THE CARE LUNCH PROGRAM

WE CONTINUED TO GET MORE PEOPLE interested in starting a school lunch program. The school had received CARE food in years past, but I heard from Francisco Garcia that the teachers sold the milk in Guatemala City and the Mayor didn't seem to care. Every chance I could, I also mentioned the need to get a new village water supply, but the one teacher I knew the best, Francisco, suddenly left town for a different job. I began to wonder how much influence the teachers had. Two of them had already departed in less than two months.

On February 24th, Marge and I attended a meeting at the school to discuss the CARE school lunch program. It eventually degenerated into a long discussion about portion sizes and costs but at least the decision was made to proceed. The first supply of CARE food arrived the next day.

Then I learned that there was no water in the school to mix the milk or cook the beans. As we headed across the plaza to discuss this problem with the Mayor, Marge suggested, at the last minute, that it might be best for me to talk with him by myself. She felt he might accept suggestions better from me than from her. When I mentioned that the school didn't have any water and the toilets had been clogged up for days, he reluctantly agreed to walk next door and have a look. Upon seeing the terrible filthy conditions, he was appalled and relented. He asked Aristeo, the policeman, to dig down by the water pipe and turn on the spigot so a trickle of water once again flowed to the school. We carried buckets to clean up the mess and before long, with the help of a bunch of kids, the situation vastly improved. My first little victory was in the books. It was also when I became more aware of male chauvinism.

On Monday, March 2nd, I walked up to the school to see how preparations for the school lunch were proceeding. They weren't. The teachers had gone to Guatemala to pick up their checks. It was the same on Tuesday because there were still no pots and pans. I then told the Mayor that Marge and I were going to a conference in Guatemala City, where I hoped to be able to say that the program had started. Perhaps he took that as a threat because it started the next day.

By 10:00 a.m., they were mixing milk with sugar and boiling beans, while I cut up a 7-pound can of cheddar cheese, so each kid could eat a piece with their bread roll made by the bakery next door. It worked out exactly right. I could cut a can into 224 pieces. After just a few days, they were preparing the correct amounts of food for over 215 kids. The teachers prepared and served lunch and ate with the kids. For several weeks Marge and I worked with the teachers to make sure it got off to a proper start. The kids all seemed grateful for the lunch and knew who was responsible. When they saw me, they would smile and repeat over and over, "Goodbye," the only English word they knew.

Boiling Beans

Sleeping in San Pedro Ayampuc was a new experience. At one or two in the morning or anytime at night, a dog would bark. Then another, and another, followed by a rooster's cock-a-doodle-doo, and the loud braying of a donkey. After a couple minutes, every critter in town was howling and crowing their heads off. It was so loud I couldn't believe my ears and actually started to laugh. When the dogs and roosters realized there was nothing to howl or crow about, the ruckus slowly died down.

I wasn't doing very well staying healthy. Once again, I woke up sick with a temperature of 101 and a destroyed digestive track. Marge and I did our best to boil the water and follow all the rules but that wasn't enough. Many PCVs consumed Terramycin from their medical kits as if they were jellybeans. They could also buy all they wanted from any drug store where no prescriptions were needed. I never took Terramycin unless prescribed but after hearing their stories, wondered if I should have. Dehydration was always a concern, but Marge and I did manage to drink enough liquids which were often in the form of tea instead of lukewarm water from our 5-gallon Salvavidas water bottle. Fortunately, we had an ever-bearing lemon tree in our yard which all year long produced just enough lemons for our tea to keep us happy.

Every PCV in our group received a telegram from Keni Kent asking if we wanted to stay with a Guatemalan family during our upcoming March conference. I responded back positively but later learned that just about everyone else except me, Marcia Lang and Jim and Celeste Corzine, chose to stay in the hotel — to the dismay of our leaders who had spent a lot of effort making arrangements for all of us.

The following Saturday, most of us headed to Guatemala City, but first I went to see Bill Pearson, Jay Jackson, and Charlie Carreras out in Zone 7. Their house had running water, indoor plumbing, and electricity, but I would have been unhappy living in such a monotonous city environment. Before the conference on Monday, a cobbler resoled my shoes which had lasted just three months walking over the rough streets and paths of San Pedro Ayampuc. When I picked them up and paid Q3.50, I could read "BF Goodrich" on the bottom. Eighteen months later, the name was still legible. I guess it was worth it.

A bunch of us, including Tim Kraft, Nola Alberts, Marcia Lang, and Bryce Hamilton, went to the scenic Lake Amatitlán and spent the afternoon swimming. In the evening we saw Cleopatra, starring Liz Taylor, but by then I was so tired, it seemed as if I were suffering through the worst movie ever made. The night was topped off by sleeping in a grubby little flophouse in Zone 7, where people were coming and going all night long.

87. A LUXURIOUS INTERLUDE

SUNDAY NIGHT WAS A DRAMATIC IMPROVEMENT for me, Marcia, and Jim and Celeste Corzine as we were driven to our wealthy Guatemalan hosts in ritzy Zone 14. For the next nine nights I stayed with Mr. and Mrs. Eduardo Garcia Salas, the uncle and aunt of Olga Alvarado, the CARE-PC Secretary. My hosts had previously travelled 26,000 miles all around the U.S. and the world. Their adopted son, Eduardo, worked at a bank and when he came home, kissed his father on the forehead. That was new to me. We had a delicious, formal dinner served by their maid. The next morning, they drove me to the Universidad Popular where our group listened to lectures all day.

At dinner the next night, I was completely deceived. First the maid brought out a huge bowl of spaghetti. After seconds, when I thought we were done, she then brought out the main course of huge steaks, potatoes, asparagus, salads, and little pies for dessert. To be polite, I ate that too. By the end of the evening, I had no doubt impressed my hosts with my ability to consume an inordinate amount of food and drink as I went off to bed. After another big breakfast, they handed me a sack lunch as I walked out the door and asked why I hadn't asked them to prepare it. I guess I was too shy to ask.

Our group met at the Palace Hotel, then boarded a bus to San Juan Sacatepéquez where we worked in a school garden and found out how to grow papayas, a fruit that matured in just eight months. We next learned how to set up a school lunch program and how to prepare and serve the food, training that came too late for Marge and me. At noon, I was still so full that I gave my lunch away. For the rest of the week, at different locations, we had more lectures and classes.

One evening, a few of us had dinner at Mr. Crisostomo's, a USAID employee. There we had the first glimpse of our future PC Director, Andy Hernandez, who was then the PC Director in the Dominican Republic. He had been sick with Dengue Fever in Puerto Rico when our first month of training was cancelled. He seemed glad that our present CARE-PC bosses would eventually be replaced and said that he would demand more accountability. I thought that our monthly activity reports were all the oversight I needed or wanted.

At the end of the week, we had our first big dinner party at Keni Kent's house where we consumed three huge pots of chili plus several gallons of ice cream. Tony Duran asked me, "Is there any ice cream left?" I answered, "Yes, a lot of it." Tony said, "Good, I was worried for you." They were amazed at how much we consumed, which we laughed about years later. One of the CARE employees, Ron Baker, had said, "Never turn down a free drink" which I modified to mean, "Never turn down a free meal."

On Saturday, my host family drove us to Chulamar, on the Pacific coast, just 4 miles west of San José. We all went swimming and I enjoyed riding the huge 8'-10' waves which crashed down upon me when I got too far in front, flipping me upside down and every which way as I was washed up on shore like a pebble. Their ocean front home was in a more upper-class area where no banana peels wrapped around my ankles. For two days, we enjoyed walking along the endless black, volcanic-sand beach and soaking up too much sun. I had made a great decision when I agreed to stay with a local family.

88. SORTING OUT PROBLEMS

AFTER TEN DAYS AWAY from San Pedro Ayampuc, we tried to solve all kinds of new problems with the school lunch program: lack of water, poor record keeping, an unhappy cook, and lazy teachers. So much talking was exhausting as I tried to sort out what words to say and what tenses to use. In the middle of it all, Tony Duran stopped in for a visit and tried to help. The teachers just couldn't seem to tell the truth, but we made some progress. On top of it all, I was once again hit by the plague for the next four days. I wasn't the only one. Little Sonia Saso, the lively five-year old who lived across the street, was also sick. I suggested to her dad, Mr. Octavio Saso, that maybe it was because of all the flies. He took my advice, made a smudge fire, and smoked all the flies out of her bedroom. Days later, I noticed he had put poison in several saucers and had fly paper hanging from the ceiling that wiped out thousands more. Sonia was soon better but who knows why. I never smudged my bedroom and kitchen. The smart flies were across the street where the pickings were better.

89. EASTER VACATION

A WEEK BEFORE EASTER, I headed to Guatemala City, met Dr. Nick Fortesque, and arranged to get tested the next day for amoebas. That's when I got to see under a microscope just how the little boogers looked. In Biology class, they were just innocuous, one-celled organisms but now I was full of them and they were making me miserable. I also visited some of the city volunteers for three days before Dave Siebert, Doug Taber and I boarded a bus for Panajachel on the shores of Lake Atitlán.

On a cold Good Friday morning, as we walked down to the lakeshore, I was surprised to see several hungover Indians sleeping in the tall, wet grass with no blankets or covers. I think I would have frozen to death and wondered how they survived the night. Later in the day, we watched a religious procession. Rows of Indians struggled to carry several heavy statues of the Virgin Mary and a coffin of Christ as they walked along the streets. It all seemed a bit depressing.

After two nights, Dave, Doug and I checked out of the third-class Maya Azteca Hotel and hitched a ride back to Guatemala City with an Englishman who worked for the Bank of London and Montreal in San Salvador. He had the top down on his little red convertible and we almost froze but didn't want to admit we were cold. The Englishman, who was warmly dressed, finally got cold himself and put the top up. We sure didn't want to complain about our free ride in a sports car. He dropped us off at Mr. and Mrs. Crisostomo's where we stayed another two nights. Mrs. Jones, whose husband was helping train the Guatemalan Police Force, brought over a big turkey, while Mrs. Crisostomo baked eleven lemon pies for us poor PCVs to eat. What was she thinking? What kind of a reputation did we have? We even ate lemon pie for breakfast before we headed back to our villages.

Mr. and Mrs. Saso, my neighbors across the street, also had a daughter, Berta, who was about 20. He wanted me to teach her English and I thought maybe she could help me with Spanish. One afternoon she kept mispronouncing the word "it" (the "short "i" sound doesn't exist in Spanish) so I went and got my cassette tape recorder so she could listen to herself. Soon we were surrounded by a dozen kids who started singing songs and having a great time listening to themselves talk, while getting embarrassed at how they sounded.

90. EXPANDING THE LUNCH PROGRAM

IN EARLY APRIL, Marge and I hiked four miles over a miserable, steep, rocky trail to a small village, Petacá, with the goal of starting another CARE school lunch program. There we met two men, one of whom talked with Marge about starting a program, while the other showed me some hot springs over two miles down a steep hill into the river valley below. It was kind of him to show me the sights, or perhaps he felt honored to take a Gringo who would help with the lunch program. For 2 ½ hours, as we hiked along, I had an engaging conversation with him. He was easy to understand and I only asked him to repeat a few things. As it turned out, he was the president of the club that later organized the lunch program. It was a long, hot hike and by the time we returned, we were soaking wet and I had never been so thirsty. I drank four dusty bottles of the most insipid soda I ever tasted, which had probably been sitting on the shelf for several years. By the time we arrived back home, Marge had such a sore knee, I wasn't sure she would make it. People were surprised we had gone so far without a horse.

Shortly after I arrived in Guatemala, I noticed that I had at least fifty plantar warts on the bottom of my right foot and toes. They didn't bother me, but I thought they might worsen as time passed. Everyone seemed to have some remedy to get rid of them, but Paul sent me an article from one of his medical journals on what to do. It sounded simple. Heat up a pot of water to 105 degrees and soak your foot for 20 minutes every other day for three weeks. I bought a candy thermometer, heated up the water on my two-burner kerosene stove, but soon discovered that according to my thermometer 105 degrees was way too hot for my foot. I had to dip my toes in and out over and over until I could get used to it and by then the water was no longer hot enough. Once I could tolerate continuous heat, I had to keep adding more scoops of hot water to maintain the temperature for 20 minutes. This was such a hassle, I quit after three treatments. A month later, I noticed they were gone. The short version of the hot water cure worked.

One Saturday in early April, I travelled to tropical Guazacapán, near Escuintla, where I visited Dave Siebert, the surfer from La Jolla, California, Priscilla Takano, from Guam and Cathy DeMet, who were stationed together in a decent house with two flush toilets, three showers and electricity from 6:00 a.m. to 10:00 p.m. I thought they had a rather luxurious set up. Mr. Crisostomo showed up the next day and I was lucky to ride back with him to Guatemala City. He even took me all the way to the northern bus terminal after stopping at the meat market where each week I bought a big roast. Even without refrigeration, Marge and I had no problem keeping it from spoiling before the end of the week. We simply kept it covered in the same pan and heated it up every day. That worked for us. At least we thought it did.

Since CARE food had recently been delivered to most of the small villages around San Pedro Ayampuc, I needed to follow up and see how the lunch programs were progressing. On April 14th, I left at 6:00 a.m. for the village of Carrizal, just over six miles away. It took me 2 ¼ miserable hours, miserable because there were several forks along the way which, of course, I took, but then had to retrace my steps wasting time. I talked with the teacher in front of his class about preparing the food and paperwork. They had just started the program a day earlier, so he was glad for the help as we prepared lunch together. He and a small store owner even brought me three bottles of pop, but I have no idea why I never purchased a canteen for such hot days. As I was leaving, I was surprised to meet the doorman from the Palace Hotel in Guatemala City who was on vacation. Until then, I had no idea that I had just spent 2 ½ hours at a tourist destination.

From Carrizal, I hiked 3 miles down the hill to Los Achiotes, guided by one of the school kids, but unfortunately the teacher had gone to Guatemala City for the day. My student guide then walked with me back up the hill to Carrizal and onto a third village, El Tizate, where I met with the teacher and women who would prepare the food. The teacher then walked with me to a fourth village, Lo de Reyes, and again kept me from getting lost. After more discussions, I headed on to Lagunilla where I discovered that I had just missed the last bus back to San Pedro Ayampuc. After walking two more miles, I hitchhiked the last three just before dark. It was refreshing to clean up and rub my tired legs after walking over 21 miles up and down the dusty, rocky trails.

The next day, I unloaded a cart full of rocks, provided by Eduviges Montenegro, and finished off my rock garden. He was 74 years old and was the richest man in town. He owned 150 cows and one of the three buses. I was more impressed by the fact that he had 24 kids. I never did hear how many wives he had.

91. THE NATIONAL CENSUS

CARMEN, THE SCHOOL DIRECTOR, justified missing school because she had to get an injection. I don't know why so many people got injections or what they were for, but Ninfa, the teacher who went with her, blurted out that they had gone to a soccer game in Guatemala City. I guess they wanted to escape and do some errands before the National Census started on April 18th. Everyone in the cities had to stay home for two days and the people in the countryside were stuck for a week until the teachers finished counting everyone. I accompanied one of the teachers to several houses in town as he filled out the lengthy questionnaires. They wanted to know everything about you and what you owned. A couple months later we learned that San Pedro Ayampuc had 587 houses and 3,363 people. In the surrounding villages, there were 1,097 houses with 6,082 people.

While Marge and I were sitting on our doorstep one evening, two little Indian girls started crying because they had lost two pennies. Since it was quite dark, they had no chance of finding them in the dusty street, but we all helped look anyway. After a minute, I took a penny out of my pocket and yelled, "I found one." Then I gave another to Alvena Saso, who lived in front of us, and told her to say the same thing. The two little girls were overjoyed as they continued down the street.

Jose, Francisco, Mario,
Carmen, Ninfa, & Graciela

When the busses started running again after the census, Marge and I went to Guatemala City. She found out about teaching English and bought a stack of books. That evening, all the PCVs in the country attended a farewell party for a PC Representative, Brud Harper, at the American Club. Then we went to Dr. Nick's house for a beer blast until early in the morning. I still don't remember ever drinking one, which nobody could believe because they knew I was from Wisconsin.

Once again, Dave Siebert, Doug Taber and I stayed at the Crisostomo's, who I thought worked for USAID. That evening he had another guest as well, Andy Rogers. Somehow it slipped out that he was the CIA Chief. In retrospect, I was surprised at all the times several of us socialized with the Crisostomos because USAID and Embassy people were to stay away from PCVs to avoid accusations that we were CIA spies. That night he couldn't ask enough questions, but I couldn't imagine that what I knew would be useful to him. The next day, at the invitation of Mr. Rogers, we lounged around the pool at the luxurious Biltmore Hotel.

92. THE SCHOOL SUPERVISOR

WHILE RIDING THE BUS back to San Pedro Ayampuc, I sat next to the Provincial Supervisor of Education, Mr. Gilberto Rojas, who had an office in the CARE office. He had read one of my monthly activity reports that mentioned some of the problems we were having with the lunch program and was coming to see if some improvements could be made.

At school later that day, he talked about the program and of course the six "hard working" teachers made themselves sound great. Since Marge had gone to Mataquescuintla to visit Bryce Hamilton, Nola Alberts, and Marcia Lang, I invited the Supervisor to spend the night at our house. After serving him some delicious French toast, he went up to the school to observe some classes and the lunch program. Later he gave a rousing 90-minute speech exhorting the teachers and some 40 mothers to take full advantages of the CARE program. That was followed by a lengthy gripe session where everyone got in on the action and brought up old petty complaints about almost everyone. Nothing changed.

Mr. Rojas was sad that I had seen such a display of childish behavior because he feared I would return home and tell others that's how Guatemalans sometimes acted. Then to increase that possibility, he added, "Guatemalans are like dry corn husks. First they burn rapidly and then there is nothing." In other words, at first, they display a lot of enthusiasm and later, when the real work starts, they rapidly lose interest. Over the years, I have heard people talk about how different people are in different places, but I have observed they are much the same everywhere.

Since there were still three more villages around San Pedro Ayampuc where lunch programs could be started, I headed to San Antonio El Ángel, guided by a boy who came on horseback once a week to pick up the mail. As I walked behind him, I asked, "How long will it take to travel the six miles?" He said, "About 2 hours but since you don't have a horse, probably 3 1/2 hours." Next, I said, "Let me walk in front so I don't have to breathe all the dust kicked up by your horse." We arrived in 1 1/2 hours. Down steep rocky trails, horses walk slowly, and I frequently had to wait for him to catch up.

In San Antonio El Ángel, I talked with a half dozen men and discovered that the main problems were a lack of water and poor school attendance. We scheduled another meeting in May, as we did in the next village, Los Achiotes, where the only teacher taught 20 kids in first and second grade. The same thing happened in the third village, El Guapinol, where the teacher wanted to start a program for his 50 kids. Before I started my journey home, a kind and considerate woman prepared a fresh homemade drink just for me, but I tossed her scary concoction into the bushes when nobody was looking. For the last three legs of my journey, I was generously provided with both a guide and a horse. After riding nine miles on the underfed swaybacked creature, I arrived home with a sore rear and soon discovered that my dietary precautions had been in vain.

On Saturday, May 2, 1964, Marge and I headed to Guatemala City to attend the wedding of two PVCs, Mike Schwartz and Betsy Markland. I knew they were often together, but a wedding came as a surprise. We ran around town buying presents before the 7 p.m. service at the non-denominational Union Church. After the reception at Keni Kent's home, Mike and Betsy were whisked off to Lake Atitlán by Jerry's Tour Service, while all the rest of us enjoyed the food and seeing each other once again. At 2:30 a.m., the CARE Representative, Ron Baker, took a few of us out for one last drink but after driving around the Plaza de España three times, we were stopped by the police. After Ron dropped the name of some Colonel, we were soon on our way. Ron said he never felt quite right about getting off the hook just because he knew the name of some Colonel, but he wanted a ticket even less.

As Marge and I rode the bus back to San Pedro Ayampuc, which was so crowded we could hardly breathe, we came upon the earlier bus tipped over on its side after it had descended the first little hill on the edge of the city. While we waited a couple hours for a crane to tip it upright, we saw that its wheel had fallen off. None of the old school buses looked well-maintained although the drivers were a helpful, friendly crew. When one driver shifted into first gear to go down a steep hill, he turned the key off and on, which caused a terrifyingly loud backfire as we passed an Indian woman, heavily laden with a basket on her head. That caused everyone to laugh.

Descendants of the Mayan Indians made up more than half the population of Guatemala. They were mostly concentrated in the western highlands and each village had its own traditional dress. Throughout the country they were discriminated against and suffered horrific atrocities during the country's 36-year civil war that started in 1960. Living in San Pedro Ayampuc, however, I was mostly unaware of any overt discrimination or atrocities that I heard about years later.

For quite a few weeks, I continued taking long hikes to all the surrounding villages to follow up with scheduled meetings. I never did decide which was easier, walking or riding a horse. After five months, I finally borrowed a two-quart canteen from the PC office. That helped the most. Some lunch programs were going quite well while others suffered from a variety of problems. In San Antonio El Ángel, the irate parents wanted me to report the drunk teacher who had been in Guatemala City the entire previous week. He said he missed the week of school because he had been kicked by a horse. When I inquired what type of medicine he took, he said, "beer." A few minutes later, he fell over backwards during our meeting. There was just one problem with reporting him to the Supervisor of Education. The Supervisor was his brother.

Now that the spring rainy season had started, I continued to hand out a lot of Burpee vegetable seed packets. The people loved getting free stuff, but they did put them to good use. CARE had several barrels of the donated seeds and I had to write a few letters thanking the donors. The heavy afternoon rains sometimes flooded the plaza and poured down the hill behind our house. The drainage ditch I had dug, fortunately, worked perfectly. With the rains came bugs. One afternoon we were attacked by a hoard of flying termites. When their flimsy wings fell off, they kept crawling towards the kitchen and came in every crack, but Marge and I finally won the war. As we quietly read and studied in the evenings on our back patio, hunched over our books lighted by our dim kerosene lamps, huge black beetles, almost three inches long, would come zooming in and crash against the wall. Marge loved that.

93. A BIRTHDAY SURPRISE

I LEARNED that I had amoebic dysentery on May 16, 1964. Happy 24th birthday, John. At the PC office, I was congratulated, given a lot of impressive looking pills, and felt, well, not the best. Over the following three weeks, I popped 154 pills of Diiodoquin and Terramycin. A couple weeks later, Dr. Nick sent me a letter saying I should also take some extra doses of Aralen (Chloroquine), to kill any amoebas that might have migrated to my liver. We also took Aralen weekly to prevent malaria.

On Sunday afternoon, Marge and I were visited by one of the city PCVs, Norma Wilder. That, of course, caused somewhat of a sensation. Mr. Saso was convinced she was my girlfriend and later when the three of us went up to the school, Marge joked that I had a lot of girlfriends. Norma chimed in quickly and said, "Yes, too many." She left early the next morning, probably wondering how we could live in such a place, but she had enhanced my "macho" rating.

A couple hours later, Tony Duran arrived to help me initiate a water project in El Hato, one of the nearby villages. We were to be accompanied by the Director of Public Health and the villagers had even sent four horses for us to ride the three miles up the hill — but then we got a call from Keni Kent saying the Director was sick and couldn't come. We went anyway, talked with half the town, and learned more about the situation. It was always frustrating to plan big meetings with government officials and not have them show up.

A day after some heavy rains, I headed for Guatemala City. The road was in terrible condition and I wasn't sure we would make it out of town. The driver even put on chains, which I learned work as well in mud as in snow. All the men got out and walked so the bus could make it up one slippery hill. As we passed a couple of mules loaded with firewood, they bolted and started running alongside the bus knocking down a little Indian girl carrying a big basket on her head. She looked scared but didn't cry. Indian kids learned early that it didn't help to cry.

I went to see Dr. Nick at the PC office but first bumped into Andy Hernandez, our newly arrived PC Director. In a sentence, his 40-minute monologue consisted of telling me how we were going to set Guatemala on fire by organizing committees to circumvent the lazy mayors, teachers and other officials who would never do anything except collect a paycheck. Just a few days earlier, I had come to the same conclusion. This was further reinforced days later when I again talked to Eduviges Montenegro, the rich old man with 24 kids and former Mayor, about getting an adequate village water supply. He said the Mayor would never do anything. Since Eduviges had his own well, he probably didn't care either. I wondered if it would be up to me to achieve such a goal. In PC training, we learned that for a project to be successful, the idea had to come from and be supported by the local people. That is why I had been talking about such a project, almost from the first day I arrived with everyone I met. I hoped that by talking with everyone over a number of months that they would all start thinking it was a valuable idea and might even start believing they had always thought so.

I had my selfish reasons for wanting clean water. Boiling water for 20 minutes was a constant chore and took a lot of kerosene. Drinking warm water was nauseating, but tea and lemons off our tree helped make it more bearable.

That evening, Mr. Saso was steaming mad about the no-good teachers. He ranted and raved for several minutes and about the only thing I could understand was that he wanted me to teach his kids. I could envision all the problems that would cause and suggested we form a committee of influential persons who could make the teachers teach instead of spending half their time in the city. He didn't seem to see how that would work until I brought up the idea of a water project. He had heard of betterment committees. If we could start with just two or three people, we could probably find a few more. He quickly volunteered to talk with Eduviges Montenegro, who had been primed by my earlier conversation, and would talk with me later in the day. A couple days later, Mr. Saso proclaimed, "Now we have four."

The next day, Berta knocked on my door, barged past me saying, "Excuse me," and plopped down on one of our patio chairs. She was once again ready to start her English lesson. I wished I could have said, "I can't stand doing this every week because you never seem to learn anything," but I didn't. She seemed to think I was born to help her, and her dad was extremely interested in her progress which made it worse. They both thought that someday she was going to be a bilingual secretary. They were dreaming, but the truth is I did learn a few interesting tidbits from her. She said

Weaving a Huipil

the Mayor was her uncle by marriage. That made me extra careful not to make critical comments about anyone, as I would never begin to learn about all the family connections. Berta never seemed to learn much English but years later I heard that she was living in the U.S. Maybe she was doing better than I thought.

During the February fiesta, Marge and I were both amazed by the colorfully embroidered *huipiles* (blouses) and *fajas* (wide belts) that the Indian women wrapped around their waists. We thought the most colorful ones were from San José Nacahuil, a small hilltop village two

miles away that we could see from the plaza in San Pedro Ayampuc. Marge had asked one of the Indian women to make her one and in early June she appeared at our door. She wanted Q30 for the blouse and Q25 for the belt. The Q55 was too much for Marge so I took over and bargained. Finally, the lady and I agreed on Q37 for both. It took her three months to make each one, so I was happy with both the price and the quality which was far better than the ones for sale in Guatemala City's central market. She was pleased when I took her picture and gave it to her later.

One evening I was talking with Mrs. Saso and her daughter, Berta, about curiosity in cats. When Berta said, "Cats have seven lives," I responded, "That's interesting. In the U.S. they have nine lives." Mrs. Saso quickly replied, "That's because they eat more vitamins in the U.S." They laughed so loud I thought they would burst.

94. PLAGUED WITH FRUSTRATIONS

WHILE WE WERE TALKING, a new teacher, Mr. Mario, came to the door. Since I was busy, he talked with Marge, first about the lunch program but then asked to borrow Q5 because his family was sick. Marge said, "No," but when he asked for just Q2, she gave in. She eventually got Q.50 back and we learned he owed a lot of people money.

The school lunch program continued to be plagued by small frustrating problems. At 3:00 p.m., only an hour late, a big meeting began at the school, attended by the teachers and some 25 mothers, to discuss the future of the lunch program. Marge started the meeting by saying we have a lot of food but no money to pay the bills to prepare it. The meeting quickly degenerated into 30 minutes of chaos. Marge talked with two women who wanted to stop the program because they felt cheated after paying Q.20 but then their kids didn't get fed for the whole month because the teachers were often gone. Marge got angry when she found out they hadn't paid anything at all and walked out of the room. Then I walked out too and one teacher, Graciela, said they decided to stop the program. Then I entered the room again, walked up to the front, and started talking. At these meetings, I talked so seldomly that when I did, they all paid attention. When someone would try to interrupt, I just stared them down and asked that they wait until I finished. I told them that I had organized six lunch programs in the surrounding villages, and all were successful. I used the village of Tizate as an example and told about the seven groups of mothers who came each day to prepare the food. I finally said, "If you don't want the food, we will send it back to CARE." And we left. Since they knew I was serious, the School Director came running after Marge and me and asked us to wait a few more days. She was obviously worried that they might get in trouble. Nobody knew what powers we had and were a little bit afraid not to go along with what we said. They probably thought I was responsible for bringing out the Supervisor of Education a couple months earlier when he gave them that 90-minute pep talk. Since the Supervisor had read my monthly report, I guess I was responsible.

At 5:30 the next morning, I left with the local soccer team for Comalapa which was west of Guatemala City and about thirteen miles north of Chimaltenango. Along the road to Comalapa, there were dozens of soldiers, all toting machine guns, which didn't make me feel any safer. I was a little surprised to be invited by Francisco, the son of one of the teachers, but had an enjoyable time. We won the first game 5-0 but lost the second 2-0 after our goalie got a bit roughed up. It was an interesting day to travel with the local team and eat dinner with them at a player's house. I even took a swig of whisky to be one of the boys.

95. HEALTH WOES

ON THE WAY BACK, they dropped me off in the city and I went to visit Jay, Charlie, and Bill. Bill complained about suffering from both amoebas and whipworms and seemed to enjoy being a martyr — like we all did to a certain extent. Then they told us about Marcia Lang, whose health woes outdid even Bill's. A few days earlier, after arriving in the tiny village of Sampaquisoy, Marsha got a severe case of double-ended Montezuma's Revenge and became paralyzed from her toes to her jaw so she couldn't talk. When Dr. Nick received the emergency telegram, he immediately drove two hours to Mataquescuintla, hired a horse and guide, who proceeded to get lost on their all-night quest to find her. In the meantime, Keni Kent, called Col. Enrique Peralta, the Head of the Military Government, who provided a helicopter that flew to her aid.

By the time Dr. Nick and Keni arrived the next morning, Marcia was somewhat better, but they took her to Guatemala City for observation. Dr. Nick or Keni couldn't decide who was the biggest hero. Until then, they were simply scared. To Marsha's chagrin, Dr. Nick was not happy his trip seemed to be in vain.

Bob and Camille Gilkey, 58, the oldest couple in our group suffered from a chronic cough. They were also heavy smokers who pursed their lips to suck every last bit of tar and nicotine from each cigarette, to the point of almost singeing their fingertips. When they complained that the medicine wasn't helping, I suggested, "Why don't you just quit smoking?" Bob instantly set the record straight, "Why don't you mind your own business?" And that was that.

The next morning, I headed to the PC office to see Dr. Nick who gave me some salve for my scabby looking eyelid as well as my quarterly gamma globulin shot to prevent hepatitis. Compared to a few years later, we received a double dose which made us sore for several days. Dr. Nick had us drop our trousers, bend over the table next to the picture window alongside the driveway and then stuck us in our cheek. I said, "Doc, aren't you going to pull the shade?" "No," he replied. "We charge extra for that."

I also talked to the PC Director, Andy Hernandez, who gave me a copy of his Community Development Handbook. He said, "Read it because I'm coming to visit you tomorrow." That was the only problem living so close to the city. We were easy to visit. Sure enough, he showed up the next day and talked almost continuously, except for a brief lunch break, until 5:00 p.m. when he headed home.

Marge and I walked up to the school to see if any money had been collected for the lunch program. Since it hadn't and because we didn't want to return the food to CARE, we suggested a Father's Day dance. It was agreed. A couple weeks later the dance was held in the municipal building but since nobody had remembered to invite the girls, only a few showed up. That was new to me. We grossed Q9.00, paid the marimba band Q2.00 and had a profit of Q7, not enough to pay many bills.

On the longest day of the year, the Mayor called a meeting to decide whether to cut down the huge Ceiba tree in the plaza. They would need government permission to chop it down, because the Ceiba was the national tree. After a lot of discussion, they decided that the half-rotten tree should get the axe because it could possibly fall on the school. I told a few men they should just leave it alone — after all, it was too far away to smash into my house. They were amused by that. Months later, a few volunteer firemen sawed and chopped for several days before they felled the 100-foot tall tree with a 7-foot diameter trunk. Over the next year, it slowly disappeared as individuals chipped it away for firewood.

On these warm sunny days, Marge and I were beginning to smell something awful, probably a dead animal, when we were out in our yard. We soon learned it was coming from the medical dispensary next to our house after Ramiro, the nurse's husband, took off some roof tiles to see what he could find. With my garden rake, he lifted out, in pieces, a rotten cat that was trapped inside when they had built a new ceiling a few weeks earlier. Shortly thereafter, the nurse got a kerosene-powered refrigerator to store medicines. When I heard about that I wondered if it could be used for cold drinks. Sadly, it couldn't.

96. A NEW PRIEST

A NEW PRIEST WAS ASSIGNED to San Pedro Ayampuc, the third in the last six months. He appeared to be a go-getter and was surprised that San Pedro Ayampuc had been in existence for 400 years and still didn't have water for its inhabitants. When he learned we weren't Catholic, he showed us a book about Billy Graham but also gave us some magazines on the Maryknoll Fathers, who were the leaders of a movement to free the masses from social, political and economic oppression before they worried about people's salvation. This Latin American movement was later called Liberation Theology. At first the priest enthusiastically talked about doing all kinds of projects but after a few months he started spending most of his time in Guatemala City. In the meantime, we did get together several times for English and Spanish lessons. I think I got the most benefit. My Spanish was improving, and I could usually say what I wanted one way or another. It was always much easier to speak with an educated person. They were better able to understand me and were probably more adept at simplifying their speech so I could understand them better as well.

When the priest borrowed a few books from my PC collection, he looked at my wet cement bedroom floor, which attracted more moisture than a glass of ice water, and said, "I see you are living in luxury. Where else can a person sleep and take a shower at the same time?"

One evening an Indian couple across the street got into a screaming fight over her husband's affair. Soon there were quite a few spectators, almost more than there had been the night before to watch a small circus that came to town, but they scattered each time the raging wife slammed the shutters. I discreetly watched from my bedroom window but was getting concerned for their lives. A few weeks earlier, an Indian in San José Nacahuil cut off someone's hand with a machete in a drunken fight. That was not uncommon.

A few days later, a U.S. military helicopter landed in the plaza and created quite a dust storm. Out stepped two tall, handsome pilots, one American and a Guatemalan trainee. A week later, when they landed at a banana plantation near Puerto Barrios, they were both hacked to death by a bunch of machete-wielding thieves who thought they had the payroll of the United Fruit Company.

June 25th was Teacher's Day, June 29th was San Pedro and San Pablo's Day, and June 30th was Army Day, which meant there was no school. In the meantime, Keni Kent visited me three times and accompanied me to several villages to see the school lunch programs and to inquire about initiating water projects, especially in San Pedro Ayampuc. Once he even came with his wife, Neal, who brought us some groceries and a lemon pie. Our scheduled meetings with engineers from Guatemala City, however, didn't amount to anything because they didn't show up. We did, however, continue to generate more interest in starting a clean, continuous water supply.

97. THE SECOND SIX MONTHS

DURING THE NEXT SEVERAL WEEKS, I kept busy holding small meetings in San Pedro Ayampuc to get people interested in a water project. I also continued to meet with several different agencies in Guatemala City that could install village water systems. This was briefly interrupted when our entire PC group attended a short course about making latrines. We got several days of on-the-job training and I disseminated the information to the nurse and a number of interested families.

Finally, in the middle of July, we were visited by Engineer Ricardo Carrion from the National Institute of Agrarian Reform (INTA). After looking at our situation, he concluded that a 200' well should be drilled with 3000 gallons of storage capacity and be powered by a gasoline engine. The cost would be about Q2000. That is what I hoped he would say. When he talked to the Mayor and the village Treasurer-Postman, Don Rodolfo, he suggested we get a list of all the residents in favor of the project so he could present it to the Minister of Public Sanitation. When I suggested that the priest could request all the people in church to come to the meeting, Don Rodolfo poked fun by crossing himself in jest and said, "The people will work harder than slaves if the priest asks them." Several days later when we did get signatures, everyone got a kick out of the way I signed my name, left-handed, which to them looked like I was writing upside down. The Mayor, however, was such a coward at committing himself to anything, he wouldn't even sign the petition. He must have been worried he might lose his Q40 a month salary. I was surprised that the Secretary earned Q120 and the Treasurer Q80.

Two PCVs, Doug Taber and Dave Siebert, were planning to quit the PC. Doug never found it interesting and said he wanted to "go home and write sarcasm." Dave had already moved once from Guazacapán and probably wished he could be surfing in La Jolla. After Dave handed his resignation to Keni Kent, he asked me and Betsy Swartz to go with him to Quezaltepeque to pick up his stuff. I wanted to see more of the country and Betsy wanted to revisit her old site and see her former roommates while her new husband, Mike, was in New Orleans getting the series of 21 rabies shots after his dog bit him in the face. That's why the PC didn't want us to have pets. Others had dogs as well and unfortunately, he was just one of several who had to be sent to New Orleans. For a three-week vacation, they thought it was a worthwhile trade-off. Dave drove the CARE Jeep faster than a madman, first past Progreso and Zacapa, and then south through a desert region with large cacti, until we arrived three hours later. It was so hot, dusty, and bleak, I could see why he wanted to leave. Back in the city, however, Betsy and I finally convinced Dave not to quit, and Tony Duran assigned him to work temporarily on a vaccination program. He rented a decent two-bedroom apartment for Q50 and I volunteered to pay him Q10 per month so I could stay with him on my frequent trips to the city. That worked out great for both of us.

Before I returned to San Pedro Ayampuc, I stopped at a half dozen embassies, as I had done on many other trips, to see if they had any free books and magazines for the school library. Most embassies contributed and we accumulated quite a pile.

By early August, I had formed two groups that surveyed 153 houses and asked about their interest in getting a latrine and contributing towards a water project and electricity. Only nine houses had a latrine, and most people didn't care if they had one or not, but we did get pledges of Q285 towards a water project. We met a lot of extremely poor people, with blank faces and dull eyes, who, it seemed, never had a chance. Many of them wanted to progress about as much as a stone.

My next trip to Guatemala City to meet with the engineer and public sanitation was a bust as they still hadn't talked with each other. The days kept going by and it seemed the government was designed not to function. I had a lot of errands to complete, but while I was eating lunch with several other PCVs, our borrowed PC Jeep was broken into and robbed. I lost two jars of Skippy peanut butter (which caused everyone to groan when they learned it was crunchy), my gym bag, books, batteries, plus the list of signatures we had collected in support of the water project. At the bus terminal, I mentioned my misfortune to a new "rich" finca (big land) owner who had come from San Salvador. He bought me a bottle of pop, a cantaloupe and even paid for my bus ticket. We rode on top of the packed bus all the way to San Pedro Ayampuc. It was quite a ride. When we got off the bus a couple blocks down the street from my house, he then tried to buy me a beer at every little store we passed. Passing up warm beer was easy for me.

Because I had lost the list of signatures, we again had to survey the town but this time our pledges increased to Q367. In the evening, I started getting an ear infection so on Monday morning, I hitched a Jeep ride to the city and met with Dr. Nick. He sent me to a specialist who diagnosed an outer ear infection and gave me some ear drops. Back at the CARE-PC office, I was given the wrong pain pills which didn't work. After a third terrible day and night, I returned to the specialist who added Terramycin to my regimen and got stronger pain pills which saved the day. By the end of the week I was much better and paid the boys, Bill, Jay and Charlie, Q5 for staying with them while I mainly slept for most of the week. In the meantime, I heard from Dave Siebert that Tony Duran was going to Colombia on September 8th. Fine for him but lousy for us. Dave thought we should visit him over Christmas.

When the priest returned to San Pedro Ayampuc on Sunday, he led a big celebration as hundreds of people paraded to the church. After a mass, marimbas were played all night. There were also two funerals but that wasn't unusual. There were two or three every week, usually little babies.

Marge and I returned to the city, along with all the other PCVs in our group, for a health conference at the Nutritional Institute of Central America and Panama (INCAP) and learned about Incaparina, a low cost, high-protein food developed for infants. We listened to lectures all day long and then in one sitting got booster shots for tetanus, diphtheria, typhoid, and rabies. I wondered if we were getting overdosed.

At the conference, we heard about a restaurant that gave discounts to PCVs called "Bill's Braziers," owned by a Texan, that featured an "all you can eat" steak dinner. Since that sounded worth investigating, we went that very evening. The steaks proved to be big and delicious. So delicious in fact that Mike Schwartz requested a total of five steaks, I ordered four and Mike's wife,

Betsy, just three. Since Dave only had enough money for a salad, we fed him pieces of our ours until we were all sufficiently full. It was a great evening — until Mike asked for the 20% PC discount. Bill, the big Texan came over to our table and said, "… and don't ever come back." I don't know why there are some people that ruin it for all the rest.

98. COMING TOGETHER FOR PROGRESS

BACK IN SAN PEDRO AYAMPUC, things were starting to come together. We had a big meeting with about thirty men, including Marcial Cutzal Maxia from the National Indian Institute, who offered to pay up to Q4000 for the water project. That was great news. After a lot of talk, we decided that several of us should again meet with INTA, which I had done several times earlier, to confirm that the Q4000 would be forthcoming. Finally, after several more meetings and phone calls, it was confirmed that the well-drilling equipment from INTA would arrive on September 1, 1964. Drilling started the next day. It was an exciting time and the talk of the town.

While they continued drilling, all the PCVs in our Group III were again called into Guatemala City for a short conference on September 3rd. We discussed various projects and I led one discussion group but most everyone talked about raising chickens and rabbits. Then came the big news, the real reason why we were together. CARE-PC was coming to an end. Andy Hernandez would be taking over, Tony Duran would be transferred to Colombia to help with that CARE-PC program, and Dave Fledderjohn was going to Panama. None of us was happy.

A whole month later, after overcoming a number of problems, such as drilling through several layers of extremely hard rock and the 9"-diameter steel casing getting stuck, which forced the workers to start over, the 200-foot well was finished and the water started to flow. It was pumped by a 5-hp Wisconsin air-cooled, gasoline motor made in Milwaukee. That was a surprise. Best of all, I could walk across the plaza and fill up my five-gallon Salvavidas bottle with clean water! No more boiling and drinking warm water. Life in San Pedro Ayampuc was improving!

At the end of a long day, the INTA Engineer, Ricardo Carrion, who was the man responsible for doing the drilling, came over to my house with a bottle of aguardiente, the local whiskey, and a Pepsi so we could have a celebratory mixed drink. He told me he talked to the Mayor about what the PC was doing in Guatemala. The Mayor responded by saying, "Yes, he is causing us to do a lot of work." Mr. Carrion continued, "Yes, PCVs are doing good things." Then, while the two of us were sipping his terrible brew, the engineer confided, "What this town needs is a new Mayor." Then he shocked me by stating that beginning Monday, they would also be drilling two additional 4"-diameter wells, 120' deep. Sure enough, they started drilling again on Monday morning, lined them with less expensive PVC pipe, and finished in two weeks. The two extra wells were a surprise to all of us. After organizing and enduring dozens of frustrating meetings and delays, I never expected that would happen. While I was helping the well drillers, an old Indian man, blind in one eye, asked,

"How much longer will you be living in town?" "About a year," I answered. He then said, "You should stay longer because you are doing such good things." That was satisfying to hear.

Just three days after the main well was completed, I noticed that the Mayor was only running the pump two hours each day, instead of four, as the engineer had instructed in order to keep the water clean and from clogging up the well and pump. The Mayor complained, "The gasoline is too expensive." He had it turned on again after I explained why it was necessary, but he continued to need reminders. Later, I even bought a 54-gallon barrel of gasoline and had it delivered by the bus to keep the well running. Fortunately, I was reimbursed for the Q24.50. A year later, after dozens of meetings, we eventually got permission from the Treasury Secretary in Guatemala City to buy tax-free gasoline for Q0.15 instead of Q0.45 a gallon.

Engineer Ricardo Carrion and a Happy PCV Admiring the Newly Drilled Well

PCV Dave Siebert, partly because he spoke fluent Spanish, was given a PC Jeep and was now acting as a liaison between management and all the rest of us PCVs. In San Pedro Ayampuc, we had a productive overnight visit, I showed him the three wells, and we talked more about taking a trip together over Christmas. A few days later, I travelled with him and Ron Brousseau to see a chicken project in Patzún and then on to Chichicastenango with Carol Belamy and Elva Reeves, who gave a demonstration on how to prepare Incaparina, the nutritious baby food. It was always interesting to see other projects and convenient for me to stay in Dave's apartment which was located quite close to the northern bus terminal.

While in the city, I picked up the "Imparcial" newspaper and found an article about the water project in San Pedro Ayampuc. The Mayor and Aristeo, a policeman who was taking care of the pump, were pleased. So was Don Rodolfo, the Treasurer-Postman who, once again, was still on a three-week drinking binge. Eduviges Montenegro said that I would have a "Good remembrance of San Pedro Ayampuc because of my water project." I said, "Yes, but it is not my project, it is the town's."

99. INCAPARINA FOR SALE

WHILE MARGE WAS ON A THREE-WEEK VACATION in Bolivia where she had lived years earlier, I continued having meetings with various people about fixing the road, chicken projects, latrines, Incaparina, paving the basketball court and other ideas. From INCAP, I got 200 Incaparina posters depicting a chubby blonde baby (their ideal of exceptional health and good looks) and fastened them on the front of all the little shops and houses on the main street. They all loved the new posters. To follow up over the next several months, I also bought several hundred pounds of Incaparina packaged in small bags and sold it primarily to the shopkeepers, who in turn sold it to people with babies. It was a highly publicized regional project throughout Central American and Panama. I have no idea of its nutritional impact in San Pedro Ayampuc but could only hope some kids benefitted.

While selling Incaparina, I came across a mother with such a dirty little girl that she had gnats crawling all over her matted eyes and runny nose. I scolded her as much as I dared and she replied, "I wash her every three days, no more because she gets dirty too soon." I left, saying she should wash her three times a day. At another house, a young Indian mother came to the door without her blouse. She was a bit embarrassed but not necessarily because of a lack of clothes. Like almost everyone else, she bought a bag of Incaparina. I was surprised that everyone called me Don Juanito, or little John. I guess I was the Little John in Robin Hood.

Between all my conversations and daily tasks, I went weekly to the city to buy groceries, do various errands, and just have a change of scenery. With Dave Siebert, who had a CARE Jeep, we visited other PCVs and met various U.S. government employees, such as Charlie and Joan Connolly, who sometimes invited us for dinner after an afternoon playing touch football at the University Club. They seemed to enjoy our visits and we enjoyed their more elegant homes and delicious food.

The Basketball Team

Somehow, I got roped into helping coach the girls' basketball team. Even though I hadn't played since being a mediocre guard on my ninth-grade homeroom team, I became the local expert who wowed them by holding their undersized ball in one hand. I showed them how to pass the ball and explained what I could, but the most I can say is that they had a lively time. However, we did succeed in leveling off the area in front of the school and covering the entire court with small stones. After that it was possible to dribble. They later inaugurated the court and sang the Nacional Hymn.

When Marge returned from Bolivia, Julio, and Graciela, the fourth and sixth grade teachers, invited us to the sixth-grade graduation. The kids sang songs, recited poetry, and gave speeches with all the appropriate hand motions and gestures. They were quite adept at speaking and performing. I couldn't imagine myself doing as well.

On Sunday evening, November 15th, as Dave Siebert and I were leaving the Palace Hotel, a big, tough-looking, American insisted we have a drink with him. As soon as I heard his name, Lee Maye, I knew he was a Milwaukee Braves baseball player who was touring Central America with an all-star team. As he drank one beer after another telling us about his exploits, we didn't dare leave. Finally, two hours later, we managed to skip out when he left to call his wife.

Carmen and the 6th grade graduates

The next morning, I attended a meeting at INTA to resolve the fact that we were not getting pumps for the two smaller wells. At INCAP I picked up another 100 posters and 200 pounds of Incaparina, and at the PC office I told them of my vacation plans. Dave Siebert and I then made plane reservations to visit all the Central American capitals, Panama, and Colombia. We both thought, "When will we ever be able to go there again?"

I was surprised to receive a telegram from the U.S. Ambassador, John Bell, inviting me to his home for Thanksgiving dinner. I also got a letter from the Wisconsin Historical Society wanting me to write a diary so that future historians would have a record of what the earliest PCVs from Wisconsin accomplished. I wrote back saying I would, but when I later received a tiny, leather diary with little space to write, I never filled it out. Besides, it came a year too late.

Next, Marge and I started to introduce Incaparina to the surrounding villages. I rented a horse, Marge rented a mule and we headed off to Petacá, two hours away. There we put up 30 posters and sold a few packages to almost everyone we met, including small quantities to a few tiny stores. The mule saved Marge's knees, but the horse didn't do anything for my posterior. Alone I could walk the distance in half the time. One man whom I had seen before said, "I am waiting for God to bring us water." I replied, "God will help those who help themselves." At the time, I hope I didn't believe that because it sure isn't in the Bible.

100. A LONG TIME COMING

I DID TAKE TIME, finally, to write Donna a letter. Because so much time, over a year, had elapsed without any communication, I made the letter somewhat impersonal, signing off as "Your friend," because I had no idea how she might feel about me now. Could she even be married? I didn't know it, but a month later in December she was just getting home after traveling in Europe for four months with Sandy, a nursing classmate of her sister June. On the way home from the airport, her mother handed her my letter. When Donna finished reading it, she was so angry that her mother thought "Donna must still love him." I wish I had known that. Since I didn't, I continued to write more impersonal letters during the next year. She did too.

Marge and I were invited by the boys' soccer team to a match in Siquinala, a town halfway towards the Pacific coast, just west of Escuintla. We were told to be ready at 4:30 a.m. which seemed too early to me. To make sure we weren't being played, I asked a few others if the time was correct. Everyone confirmed it was, but I still didn't believe them, set my alarm for 5:00 and went to bed. After Marge and I finished breakfast at 5:20, I walked up to the bus and asked the driver, "What time are we leaving?" "6:00," he answered. At 5:30 the bus roared up to our door, picked us up and many others as we drove down the street. For once, I had figured them out. The day before, they had no trouble agreeing to 4:30 a.m., but when the time came, the pain was too great to follow through. An hour late was close to the standard deviation.

We all wandered around Siquinala for a few hours before the 4:30 p.m. game, which we lost 4-1. To cool off, we all took a bath in the river and waved at the girls as they walked past. Back in Escuintla, there was a big fiesta with a huge Ferris wheel called the "Wheel of Chicago" and a few of us decided to go for a ride. I was told that this was the same Ferris wheel built for the first World's Fair in Chicago that finally opened May 1, 1893, to commemorate the 400th anniversary of Columbus. When we were up 264' in the air, however, it started tilting from side to side and I was scared it would tip over and ruin my day. The view was fantastic, but I was relieved when it was over. That was my last Ferris wheel ride. A late rain made the steep, downhill road into San Pedro Ayampuc so muddy that the bus almost slid off the road. Everyone got off the bus and walked the last mile in the dark and we arrived at midnight.

101. THANKSGIVING AT THE AMBASSADOR'S

ON THANKSGIVING DAY, 1964, after a hard workout at the University Club with Dave Siebert and Stan Tulson, another California surfer from Group IV, several of us, including Ozella Long, Linda Sanderford, Nola Aalberts, Ginny Moran, two couples from Groups II and IV, and two Fulbright scholars showed up at Ambassador John Bell's house. The formal table was beautifully set, the turkey dinner delicious, and we were on our best behavior, carefully observing which fork or spoon to use next. We enjoyed pie for dessert and when asked, "Who would like a second piece?" I nodded, "Sure." The others were apparently too bashful. We then played a little golf and croquet in their backyard and had some political conversations. They were exceedingly kind to invite such a low-income group, which we all appreciated.

That evening we watched the freshmen of Louisiana State University whip the University of San Carlos basketball team 70-35. Many flagrant fouls committed by the much shorter and inferior local team were not called and it was evident the visiting team was under strict orders not to react. That was followed by a party at Jay, Charlie, and Bill's house, and by 4:00 a.m. I was back at Dave's apartment. Luckily, Dave had set up the cot for me. The next four days were spent driving with Dave to Guazacapán, visiting PCVs, swimming in tropical Escuintla, shopping, cashing my check which included an unexpected Q100 clothing allowance, getting tested again for amoebas, more shots, liver X-rays, a physical, going to the movies and getting more lab tests. Milk of Magnesia and Polymagma were saving the day. One evening, as several of us PCVs sat around the fireplace at Charlie and Joan Connolly's, listening to music and eating ribs, I almost forgot that my little village even existed. Charlie worked for the Regional Office of Central America and Panama (ROCAP), a USAID-funded program to promote the area's common market. They enjoyed the finer things in life that we couldn't afford. They had a pair of beautiful German Shepherds which I couldn't tell apart for weeks until I got to know them better. During the day they mostly loafed around the house but when we went to the beach at San José, they ran up and down the shoreline, in and out of the water all day long. For several days after each trip to the beach, they were so sore and stiff they could hardly move.

Once back in San Pedro Ayampuc, I rode around town in the CARE-Public Health Mobile Unit, with loudspeakers blaring, announcing that movies would be shown at 6:30 p.m. on the church wall. Hundreds showed up to watch the films about the U.S., Canada, Hawaii, and basketball. During the breaks, they plugged Incaparina and mentioned Marge and me, "Dona Margarita" and "Don Juan." At the end, they showed four rolls of my movies taken during the February fiesta. When the crowd saw themselves and their friends on the big white wall, they hollered and cheered.

In early December, a couple of local carpenters started building a small shed to protect the Wisconsin engine from the weather and possible vandalism. Soon after, we received the instruction manual, which I helped translate, so the engine could be properly maintained. The National Indian Institute also brought us plans to build a platform to support six 500-gallon water storage tanks. They also sent plans for a *pila*, which is a concrete water tank with clothes washing stations around the outside, so about 15 women could do their washing at once. The Treasurer also started to collect some of the pledges that were promised earlier.

December 7th was the Day of the Virgin's Conception. After dark, everyone celebrated by making a fire in front of their house to chase the devil away. However, since the devil was cleverer than any or all of them, they never could quite get him. That was probably a good thing, or they wouldn't have been able to burn all their junk in the street every year. After the fires died down, hundreds of people proceeded up the street to the church behind the Priest and a statue of the Virgin Mary. They were accompanied by church bells and plenty of firecrackers before and after the mass.

The next morning, our committee met with Romeo Hidalgo, a representative from Public Sanitation who came with exciting news. Starting in January, they were going to start a latrine project. The plan was to construct 50 latrines each month. Later in the day, Marge and I invited Romeo, as well as Rodolfo, our town treasurer, to dinner. They even taught us a few Guatemalan idioms as we talked all evening in our kitchen. The weather was getting cooler at night and our kerosene lamps helped keep us warm. Once in bed, I needed both red wool blankets that I had bought at the fiesta almost a year earlier.

After a long weekend, which included a great day body surfing at the beach in Chulamar, I returned home and was surprised to find Elva Reeves, a PCV in our group who was working with INCAP, giving a demonstration on nutrition. Earlier in the day, her little dog had fallen into our latrine, about 8' down into the goop below, but somehow they fished him out. That was another reason why PCVs shouldn't have pets. It was also a fortuitous time for me to be away from home.

102. CHRISTMAS VACATION

ON DECEMBER 19, 1964, Dave Siebert and I left on vacation. First, we flew to San Salvador, the capital of El Salvador, where we wandered around until we landed at the Hotel Nuevo Mundo. Our room had a panoramic view of the city, but there didn't seem to be too much of interest. Then we went on to the capital of Honduras, Tegucigalpa, a quaint little town. When we got back to the Hotel Astoria after 10:00 p.m., the Manager wasn't too happy when we woke him up to unlock the door. After watching Burl Ives and Tony Randall in "The Brass Bottle," I guess we shouldn't have gone out to eat. The next day, I bought a hand-carved, round mahogany table and a jewelry box which the shop mailed home to Wisconsin. We then flew off to Managua, Nicaragua, a pleasant place, as was the Hotel Estrella. We even watched some USAID officials present nine tractors and two trucks to Nicaragua through the Alliance for Progress. The downtown area was busy with nightlife.

In San José, Costa Rica, Dave and I were pleased that the nearby volcano, Irazú, was no longer belching black, greasy ash, which a year earlier had required snow removal trucks to clear the streets. In the evening, hundreds of young people walked the streets throwing confetti as we walked by. For two days we almost walked ourselves to death as we explored the capital and the suburbs. We saw much less poverty in Costa Rica. Later it became a favorite retirement destination.

On Christmas Eve we flew to Panama on a big four-engine plane with just one other passenger. As we disembarked, the stewardess handed each of us a bottle of champagne and said, "Have a Merry Christmas." Going through customs was always a breeze, thanks to our courtesy visas that were normally issued to high profile people and entertainers. Since PCVs were going to change the world, we were special too.

We headed straight to the Lux Hotel, the "official" PC hotel. For $3 per night, we lived in luxury in a big, modern air-conditioned room. The next day, we crossed over the Bridge of the Americas, past the American Zone, and enjoyed the day at Vera Cruz beach. We met a lot of eccentric Americans, including one, who I believe, had been drunk for quite some time. He recounted how his first wife was from frigid Duluth, but the next five were better. Next, we headed to the Peace Corps office, reconnected with Dave Fledderjohn, confirmed our reservations to Cali, Colombia, wandered around the duty-free stores downtown and bought some *molas*. *Molas* were made in pairs by the Kuna Indian women in the San Blas Caribbean islands, to decorate the front and back of their blouses. I enjoyed bargaining with one shop owner for 20 minutes before he agreed to lower the price on a double *mola* from $40 to $10. Back at the hotel, we met a lot of PCVs from Panama and talked for hours, finding out where to stay and what to do in Colombia.

Three days later, we flew to Cali, a beautiful tropical city of about 800,000 people. We stayed in a small hotel for one night, met a lot of PCVs, went to a party and saw much of the city. Later the next day we boarded a plane back to Bogota on Avianca, the Colombian airline. We sat in the bulkhead with plenty of room to stretch our legs. Even before we took off, Dave squashed a big cockroach with his foot as it ran up the wall. Before long, we had a contest. I think the score was 9-8 but I can't remember who won. Our old family friends from Madison, Vance and Dorothy Austin, picked us up at the airport. Before being whisked off to a farewell party where we met about fifteen USAID couples for a big turkey dinner, Dave realized that one of his expensive wingtip shoes was missing from his suitcase. We concluded that he must have left it in the hotel back in Cali — but who packs just one shoe?

Bogota was a big, busy city, 8500' high, and full of expert pick-pockets and thieves. We constantly had to be alert and aware of our surroundings. While driving, our windows were up, and the doors locked so teams of thieves wouldn't steal our watches or worse. We visited Mr. Austin's office at USAID where he was promoting cooperatives, the PC office where we met our old boss, Tony Duran, as well as another PCV, Anne Cartwright, our group's champion traveler. We went shopping and bought a couple *Ruanas* (heavy wool capes to keep women warm in the cool evenings) and several pigskin gym bags which I used for years. We lived in luxury at the Austins who fed us, provided excellent accommodations, and took us out for beef fondue, which was the first time I had ever heard of it. It was a great way to prolong dinner and promote conversation. Thanks to our PC, CARE and USAID connections, we were invited to a lot of dinner parties and a great New Year's Eve party with dancing and elegant cuisine. We even tried to dance the "Cumbia," a Colombian dance whose rhythm I never could get.

Everywhere we went, we heard stories of pickpockets, robberies and worse. On two consecutive nights, a six and then a ten-story office building were completely stripped by thieves who removed every desk, chair and plumbing fixture. Dave and I almost got in on the action one night when we walked back to the Austin's home from a movie. Just two blocks from their house in the golden ghetto, we suddenly heard two pistol shots as two teenagers sprinted past us. Seconds later, two men waving pistols followed them and asked, "Which way did they go?" We pointed up the street and kept walking. Then we heard more shots.

After we had enjoyed the posh life for a week, Tony Duran volunteered to drive us to the airport. When he didn't arrive on time, we were worried and almost missed our flight. Tony explained that he had locked himself in his house and had to wait until his maid returned to open the door. Security was a huge issue. Everyone had steel bars on their doors and windows.

103. A NEW YEAR

BACK IN GUATEMALA on January 3, 1965, we were met at the airport by PCVs Pat Smits and Dave and Sally Snyder. They gave us the latest news that Mike and Betsy had a baby boy. During training, we were told that anyone having a baby would be sent home, but that never happened. In fact, those who had babies, like Dave and Pat Smits, thought they became more effective.

The PC Director, Andy Hernandez, and I briefly discussed various possible actions I could take to avoid more delays in completing the water project. Then I had lunch with Ron Baker and Millard Burr, both CARE employees and alumni of The American Institute for Foreign Trade (AIFT), located in Glendale, Arizona. At Ron's house, we talked about the school and its three-part curriculum of language, area studies and business. He said he would help me write a letter and would write a recommendation. That was something to think about. In previous months, I had also written to a half dozen other schools, but the truth was, my search was haphazard and not focused. I still had no idea what I wanted to do.

Although I intended to return to San Pedro Ayampuc, the last bus, piloted by Don Chevo, had

Unloading Don Chevo's bus

broken down. Back at Dave's, we visited Betsy and her new baby, Chris, in the hospital. They were doing fine. I knew she would be. Betsy was tough. When she was about eight months pregnant, she kicked a football almost 40 yards and Mike yelled, "Betsy, what are you doing?"

In the new year, the Peace Corps started taking over more of CARE's duties. Besides the new PC Director, they hired a new Assistant, Joe Sklar, who had just completed his two-year PC assignment in Peru. Since he was from New York City, he had never even learned to drive a car and we found him to be an inadequate replacement. At 22 years of age, he took some driving lessons, got his license but soon rolled his Jeep and hurt a couple of his passengers, including the PC Secretary who gashed her arm. We learned that the PC Director wanted to form a committee, with one PCV from each district, so we could more effectively let him know about our gripes. Since our new Director Hernandez had been making a lot of pronouncements, I guess there was a lot of griping. That was one thing we were good at. We used to joke, "If we couldn't complain, we'd quit." None of it was serious even though a few PVCs occasionally went to the airport just to watch the planes come and go. Hernandez, however, thought our group was already "lost" and he knew we didn't appreciate the administrative changes that were made when CARE was pushed aside. We had made that clear to the PC Latin American Regional Director Frank Mankiewicz, who came from Washington, D.C. to assuage our group. I was "impressed" that he answered our questions without saying anything. As a result, our new Director never got too demanding with our group. Since we were spread all over the country doing whatever we wanted, how could he? It is true that we had a lot of freedom to do whatever we wanted, which we heard from the very beginning in training. In later years, PC groups became homogenous with everyone trained and focused to do just one activity like forestry projects or teaching English. Everyone in our group was different. We were "generalists" which meant we knew a little about a lot of things but not very much about anything.

One morning a sergeant from the Guatemalan army was trying to teach a squad of young Indian men how to march in the central plaza. He wasn't having a lot of success and was being watched by several Ladinos, Guatemalans of Spanish-Indian descent, who were taunting and laughing at their ineptness. Somehow, these Ladinos had enough pull or connections not to get drafted. Just then Dr. Nick Fortesque and his wife, Ann, showed up with a picnic lunch. So, Marge and I drove off with them in his little white Jeep to a nearby waterfall where we enjoyed chicken, potato salad and cake. Nick had wanted to find the place where he heard there was petrified wood, but our quest ended up being a wild goose chase.

Back in town, the priest and I had a short basketball game against nine girls. We held them even. I wowed them by dunking the ball, which I could do with our somewhat lower basketball hoop. The priest then asked Marge and me to attend the Sunday, 7:00 p.m. mass on January 17, 1965. As we entered the church, I sat on the left with the men and Marge on the right. We were soon kneeling, but I didn't fit in the space provided. It was almost more than I could bear as I tried to scrunch down, unsuccessfully, so I wouldn't stick up so high. My legs almost went to sleep before we could sit again. Then came the big announcement. From now on, the service would be in Spanish, instead of Latin, so the people could understand. That was one positive thing, he said, that the Protestants did 400 years earlier. Next, he chastised the young men for not serving in the military like the Indians. Finally, he admonished everyone to do things for themselves instead of waiting for gifts from the Americans and Europeans. After a few more ups and downs, the bells rang, and we departed. Progress was coming to the church.

After a busy weekend in the city, I accompanied Dave Siebert on a trip to the eastern part of the country. We dropped off Stan Tulson in San José Pinula, then Steve Haas in Juliapa, which was a miserable place to live all alone. When we left, we felt we were abandoning him on a desert island. In Yupiltepeque, we met Al and Claire Sumner on horseback as they were returning from a nearby village. Next, we met Bob and Sue Hetzel in Quesada, who were two of the seven UW graduates in our group. I was grateful I wasn't posted in the dry, eastern part of Guatemala. The roads were terrible, bumpier than a washboard, and so dusty it was impossible to pass another vehicle. If you got close enough to pass, you couldn't see the road or anything else. I had planned to take some movies, but there was nothing to see.

Back in the city, I saw an ad for a big Yamaha motorcycle that I thought might be a great way to travel after leaving the PC. Just 30 minutes before I arrived, however, it was sold. In retrospect, that was extremely fortunate. I didn't know anything about riding a motorcycle and that's why I'm still alive.

On George Washington's birthday, Ron Baker and his wife invited me to climb the volcano, Agua, which was close to Antigua. On the way, we picked up PCVs Bernie Engel, Tim Kraft, Mike and Betsy Schwartz and their little baby boy. We drove quite a way up but hiked the last two hours. I made it to the crater first, thinking that they would never make it. On my way down, however, we met up again and then we all made it. I ended up carrying their baby most of the way up and back as I ran down the steep trail to the car. That night, we all enjoyed grilled steaks at the Baker's as we talked until early in the morning.

Back in San Pedro Ayampuc, I rented Eduviges Montenegro's white stallion, the only decent horse in town, and took off for the villages of El Hato, Buena Vista and Petacá where I discussed the possibility of digging wells. On this trip, I decided to ride a bit farther and came upon some hot springs in a canyon that reminded me of Parfrey's Glen near Devil's Lake in Wisconsin. I took off my shoes and was enjoying the peace and quiet when an Indian and his two boys came by. Before long, they invited me to their house. There I met his wife, who was washing clothes in the river, along with the wife of one of the boys and a younger girl about nine, who covered her mouth, embarrassed by some sores on her lips. They invited me to share their lunch of black beans, freshly ground corn tortillas, a hardboiled egg and lemonade. I scooped up the beans with my tortilla, as best I could, and we talked and talked in front of their adobe house. They were fortunate to live next to a river, so close to water. It seemed that most of the villages were perched on top of hills which forced the women to walk for at least an hour just to bring back a jug of water on their heads. After conversing for the next four hours, the nine-year old no longer remembered to cover her face and was sad to see me go. On the way, they first had to show me a rock formation that they thought looked like the Virgin Mary about 100' up on the side of a cliff. I couldn't visualize it, but they hoped they could make some money showing it to people. Unfortunately, that scenic tour was a 45-minute walk from Petacá, which was in the middle of nowhere. We had a distracting afternoon conversing and looking at birds through my binoculars, the same ones I had bought with my snow shoveling money when I was eleven.

104. DRUNKS AND FLEAS

SAN PEDRO'S ANNUAL FIESTA was again in full swing. The marimbas were back in front of my bedroom window, booths packed the plaza and the drunks and fleas were making a comeback. This year there were some new events, including a race, which started somewhere this side of Guatemala City. About eight runners completed the race and were wildly cheered as they ran up the main street to the finish line in the plaza. The winner had a time of 49 minutes, earning the grand prize of Q3. The second-place finisher won Q2 and the third Q1. What would the winner do, I wondered, with three whole dollars? Another new event was climbing a 30-foot pole. Whoever climbed to the top won the Q10 bill on top. The pole was waxed and slippery which made the task much more difficult, but it wasn't long before some kid picked off the bill.

I should have known that just like last year, this would be the time when the Mayor would do his devilish best to turn off the water supply to the fairgoers. The well pump ran out of gas, lost its prime and we couldn't get it restarted. So, off to Guatemala City I went to talk with the engineer who told me what to do. He also wrote the Mayor a letter, at my request, with instructions for the future. Back with five gallons of gasoline, the fairgoers once again had clean water and I started to wonder what would happen to the well once I left. I certainly couldn't count on the Mayor to do the right thing. His main objective was to save gasoline which was a constant source of irritation.

The recently elected Queen of San Pedro Ayampuc's Fiesta, Floridalma Montenegro, and her sister, knocked on our door and invited Marge and me to walk past the edge of town to watch the harvesting and processing of sugarcane. It proved to be quite a process. Two Indians fed the long stalks of sugarcane through a big grinder powered by two mules plodding around in a circle, which crushed the cane and caused the sugary juice to dribble into a huge iron bowl about 6' in diameter. The sugary juice was then boiled over a wood fire. As it thickened, the kids dipped in pieces of sugarcane and ate it like taffy. When the juice became thicker, it was poured into molds until it hardened into half-sphere, brown sugar cakes. Two halves were then tied together and sold as a pair. It sure wasn't an easy way to make a living.

The National Indian Institute provided money to build a road from San Pedro Ayampuc to the village of Petacá. Fifteen men were hired, given picks and shovels, and paid the grand sum of Q0.50 a day. If they ate only corn tortillas, black beans, and an occasional egg, I guess they could survive.

105. GRADUATE SCHOOL PLANS

A YEAR BEFORE MY PEACE CORPS STINT was scheduled to end, I started thinking more about where I would go to graduate school. Because my whole life had been aimed towards some biological field, I thought about going to the University of Florida in Marine Biology. I applied and was quickly accepted. If you think that seemed easy, well, it was. At the time, the country was still bombarded with government ads promoting the PC and saying how great PCVs had to be. Thanks to the Wisconsin Project, the UW was providing more PCVs than any other school. I also inquired about North Carolina, Illinois, and even Dartmouth which wanted to see the results of my Graduate Records Exam, which I finally took just after Easter.

Then, Ron Baker, the CARE representative, again suggested that I consider the American Institute for Foreign Trade (AIFT) in Glendale, Arizona. As I mentioned earlier, he had gone there and said it was a steppingstone to getting a job overseas. Working abroad sounded more adventurous, and I thought I could always return to Wisconsin and teach if nothing else worked out. I wondered, would all my years preparing for a career in Biology be just an interesting side show? A job like Ron's,

Talking with the Queen, Floridalma, and the Kids Eating Sugar Cane Taffy

however, sounded way more interesting than my memory of practice teaching those five ninth-grade classes. When Ron told me about a Peace Corps scholarship, I applied and got it. That put me over the edge. My first semester would be covered, and I decided to start in January 1966. Would that $700 tuition scholarship change my life's direction?

On March 22nd, the fifth priest arrived in town. He was from Belgium and bragged that he spoke eleven languages. His first pronouncement was, "I can't live in this place," and he was gone in minutes.

106. OFF TO MEXICO

I WAS ALSO MAKING PLANS TO LEAVE — to meet Mom and Dad in northern Mexico. Although Dad was always busy and found it hard to take more than just a few days off, they both decided now was the ideal time to take a trip to Mexico and Guatemala. With their own personal guide to show them the highlights, they wouldn't even have to worry about not speaking Spanish. Since they had never left the U.S., however, it was still quite an adventure just crossing the border into Mexico.

My vacation started with a spur-of-the-moment afternoon trip to Guatemala City when I hitched a ride with an ice cream vendor in his loudspeaker van. Along the way, I listened to his 45 rpm records at least three hundred times, ate 13 ice cream cones and plenty of dust. After cleaning up at Dave's apartment, I met Jay Jackson for dinner followed by a movie, "Kiss Me, Stupid" with Dean Martin and Kim Novak. Many other movies we had seen were not very memorable, but really we looked forward to the James Bond movies, "From Russia with Love" and "Goldfinger." In the next two days, I got my plane tickets, traveler's checks, found out I was again suffering from amoebas, got more medicine, partied with some PCVs, and flew to Mexico City on March 27th.

As I wandered around Mexico City for two days locating the highlights, I bumped into PCVs Ginny Moran and then Charlie Carreras. After fifteen months in Guatemala, volunteers in our group seemed to be travelling everywhere. That evening, after walking for hours, I sat down on a park bench next to an old man. As we relaxed and watched the people walk past, he began to reminisce about all the beautiful girls from his youth. "Yes," he said, "The most beautiful girls in the world live in Lebanon."

On the flight to Ciudad Victoria in Northeast Mexico, south of Brownsville, Texas, I met an engineer and managed to hitch the twenty-mile ride with him into the city. I was getting to be quite adept at saving money. I guess some people just felt obligated to help poor volunteers. I checked into a hotel, and as I walked up the street at 4:30 that afternoon, hoping to meet Mom and Dad as we had planned, there they were, driving towards me in their mud-covered 1958 VW Beetle. We were relieved and happy to see each other after more than a year. Just as I had requested, they even brought me a box of Hershey candy bars. A year later I laughed my head off when I read that craving chocolate was a symptom of culture shock.

The next morning, we headed south, a day's drive to Zimapán. As we chugged through the mountains up a twisting, narrow two-lane highway, there was a sheer rock wall on the left and a 300-foot drop-off on the right. The scenery was beautiful, and we could see for miles. Suddenly, two S-curves ahead, I saw two huge semi-trucks passing two others, racing down the mountain at breakneck speed. There was no room for me. Just as suddenly, there was a break between the guardrails, and I pulled over as far as I dared. As Dad looked over the cliff he yelled, "Don't go over any farther." A second later, the four trucks roared past, missing us by at least ten inches. In a bigger car, we would have been twice-ground hamburger.

On April Fool's day, we cut across to San Juan del Rio, checked out Querétaro and drove on to San Miguel de Allende, a beautiful Spanish colonial city with cobblestone streets, which later became a world heritage site. Mom especially enjoyed walking around for a few hours, as her legs were still aching from the long car trip. Later that night, we arrived in rainy Mexico City. It was a wild ride as we sped around the edge of the city while I desperately searched for any recognizable street sign or landmark. Suddenly all the lights blacked out in our section of town just as I realized we were at the Zócalo, the main plaza, right where I wanted to be. Now I knew exactly where we were, just a few blocks from the Hotel Jena. For the next three days we saw the sights, including the cathedral, the university, the castle in Chapultepec Park, the market of San Juan de Letran, the National Museum of Anthropology, many shops, and a show at the Ballet Folklórico.

Our trip to Acapulco was a slow seven-hour drive in our underpowered Beetle, which struggled along with a shimmy and a heater we couldn't turn off. Once we arrived, however, Mom and Dad loved walking along the famous Acapulco beach and swimming at Pie de la Cuesta — until we saw a big shark. There we met Wisconsin PCVs, Dave and Pat Smits and went deep sea diving and fishing with them. Like all tourists, we also watched the famous divers at Quebrada leap off the 136-foot cliff into the shallow water below.

Dad, Mom and John in Taxco

On our way back to Mexico City, we stopped in Taxco, hired a guide who showed us many small shops where they made silver jewelry and of course we all bought a few small pieces. From Mexico City, it was a ten-hour drive past Puebla through the desert to Oaxaca, a city that had beautiful shiny, black pottery. From Oaxaca, it was another twelve-hour drive to the border town of Tapachula. Leaving Mexico was easy but entering Guatemala was a hassle. According to the customs officials, it was always lunch hour or break time, which required us to pay a total of $13 at nine different locations — unless we wanted to wait who knows how long. Part of the cost was for a pair of Guatemalan tourist license plates which were installed over our Wisconsin plates. From there, we took the southern route to Mazatenango and on to Escuintla so Mom and Dad could see the tropical side of Guatemala.

107. THE BIG BANG

TWENTY MILES BEFORE REACHING GUATEMALA CITY, we were chugging up a long hill when we met an old school bus going down. As it passed us, it made a loud backfire boom, just as Don Chevo and the other drivers going to San Pedro Ayampuc liked to make, simply by turning the key off and on in order to terrify the Indian women walking by. We quickly discovered it was our trusty Beetle that had made the big bang as we coasted to a stop. Now what? It was Palm Sunday afternoon and much of the country was already shut down for Holy Week.

I walked down the hill a few hundred yards and turned into the center of Palin, a small town where I found a group of men conversing in the shade of a huge Ceiba tree. Its lower branches spread out over 180' from side to side and was one of the grandest trees in the country. As they watched a strange gringo walk into their midst, I soon had the opportunity to explain what happened. They looked around at each other and one man, who just happened to be a mechanic, said, "I can help." So, on a Sunday afternoon, for just Q20, he towed us to Guatemala City where we left our dead Beetle parked outside the new VW garage. For Q2 extra, he then drove us to Dave's apartment, the Palace Hotel and finally to Olga Delgado's house, the PC Secretary, where I called Dr. Nick. He

Ruins at Tikal

lent me his Jeep so I could return to the VW garage and unload the VW. By 7:30, we were eating dinner at the Palace Hotel and could relax.

On Monday morning, I returned to the garage to check the car in for repairs, which would take at least two weeks, bought tickets so we could fly to Flores in El Petén, rented a car, and made arrangements to transfer ownership of the VW to me, so Dad and Mom could fly back home. We next dropped off our excess belongings in San Pedro Ayampuc and returned the same evening to catch an early Tuesday morning flight to Flores, the largest city in northern Guatemala, near the Mayan ruins at Tikal. On the plane, we met PCV Tim Kraft, who, along with Carol Bellamy, was stationed in Flores. We also bumped into PCVs Norma Wilder and Bernie Engel. With only four months remaining, PCVs were travelling everywhere. We had an informational trip through the ruins and could now appreciate how unbelievably difficult it was to cut down and remove the dense jungle growth of thick twisted vines and huge trees that grew into and buried the pyramids. Later that night we returned for a moonlight tour of pyramids #1 and #2. Dad especially, enjoyed such trips, and he always seemed to know more about what we were seeing than anyone else. Perhaps the best part for Dad was that he could relax because he had a trusted guide who made all the arrangements.

Back in Guatemala City for the day, Mom and Dad enjoyed wandering through the big Central Market near the National Palace and the Cathedral, which was loaded with local handicrafts. That's where Mom bought several tablecloths which she used for many years. Early the next morning we left San Pedro Ayampuc, this time with Marge, for a quick trip to see the famous Indian market in Chichicastenango. Three hours

Sawdust Carpets

later, however, we discovered that we had missed the market which was held a day early because of Holy Week. A more experienced guide, perhaps, would have known that, but we did see the cathedral and were able to buy a few strongly woven, wool Chichi bags that I used on all my hikes and shopping trips. As Mom and Dad walked around the plaza, even Mom looked big compared to

Carrying His Cross

the little Indian ladies. Most of them barely came up to Dad's waist. From there, we drove to Sololá, down the hill to Panajachel, met yet another PCV, Priscilla Takano, but the weather was so foggy I was disappointed that Mom and Dad couldn't even see the volcanoes across the beautiful Lake Atitlán before we returned to the capital.

The Good Friday celebration in Antigua was a big deal. For several days, the downtown cobblestone streets had been blocked off as the people spent hours covering them with intricate floral designs mostly made with brightly colored sawdust. To see all the amazing street carpets, we had to be there early in the morning because by 9:00 a.m., the religious procession started. It consisted of about twenty extremely heavy statues, some of the Virgin Mary and others of various Saints and Apostles. Over 3000 Indians, dressed in purple robes and hoods, each paid Q3 for the privilege of carrying one a few yards through the streets, over the newly finished carpets, before they were relieved by a new batch of men. The biggest "float" depicted Jesus carrying his cross, as 25 men on each side struggled to carry it down the street.

Later in the day, Mom and Dad flew back to Madison where they had been living for less than a year in their new house. When they made their plans to drive to and from Guatemala, they overlooked how much farther it was than Ciudad Victoria where we had met. Their trip home would have been over 3000 miles one way and well over 50 hours of driving time. Blown pistons on the VW was a fortuitous occurrence.

I spent Easter weekend playing football, swimming at the American School, going to the movies and socializing with various PCVs and other American government employees. Still using my rental car, a red VW Beetle, I returned to San Pedro Ayampuc for the day to wash a ton of clothes. Since the well hadn't been used much during my absence and wouldn't start, I returned to the city and talked with the three men who had drilled it. They gladly returned with me and got it started once again. In the meantime, the nurse mentioned that there were five new cases of typhoid. I'm glad Dad didn't know that because he hadn't gotten a typhoid shot before the trip. Mom hadn't either but she had had typhoid when she was little.

Back in the city, I returned the rental car, checked on my old VW, bought four months of car insurance for Q82.90, and asked the insurance man to call the garage to see if they could give me a break on the repair costs. The bill, thanks to his call, was lowered by Q50 to Q227.40, which was almost two months' salary. They completely rebuilt the engine with new pistons, and all was fine. With great caution, I used it for a few days and even made a quick trip to San Pedro Ayampuc to test it out.

At the PC office, one of the PC secretaries, Kay Menke, told me the Director knew I had a car, which was against PC regulations, and wanted to talk to me about it on Monday. I was surprised. How did they get that information so fast? From Customs or when we changed over the title? At any rate, I had to act fast and find a place to park it, so that if necessary, I could occasionally use it. Charlie Connolly came to my rescue and volunteered his garage. The PC Director seemed to think that was okay, but Joe Sklar, that pesky new PC Representative from New York, the same Joe that had just rolled his own Jeep a few weeks earlier, wanted me to park it at the PC office. I suggested, instead, that I would give him the tourist license plates, which placated Joe, and would store it at Connolly's. We were now both happy. He never noticed that most tourists from the U.S. were never issued tourist plates.

108. MAUNDY THURSDAY AT THE BALLET

DURING OUR IMPROMPTU FOOTBALL GAMES that we usually played at the University Club, I met Doug McMillan, who worked for the United States Information Service (USIS). Just a couple days after Easter, he let me preview my five recent rolls of movies and splice them together on one reel, which I appreciated. He then suggested, "Why don't we get a date, go out to eat and see the National Ballet tonight?" That sounded interesting but whom would I ask? Perhaps I could ask the secretary at the Italian Insurance Agency where I had just bought four months of insurance for the VW. After all, her boss had just saved me Q50 and she seemed friendly and, I hoped, single. I told Doug, "I'll let you know," and drove off to the Agency in my reconditioned VW. She said, "Yes, I'd like to go but I'll have to ask my dad." That's when I found out her name was Maria de la Luz Gonzales. After another visit and a phone call, it still seemed that her dad intended to come with us. I wondered, "Could she be only 17?" I never asked but I did find out that her dad was a custom's official and my next step was to meet him at work and explain what we were going to do. I must have made a favorable impression because he said, "Yes." After all that, Doug found out his date was going to eat somewhere else so I would have to pick them up later. It might have been because they weren't in the car with me when I picked Maria up for dinner, daddy came along with her. This was a first for me. It was also the first and last date I ever had with daddy watching every bite. I was a gentleman, paid the Q8 tab at "Las Tablitas," which was one of the better restaurants in the city, dropped off her dad at home, picked up Doug and his date, and off we went to the National Theatre. At the end of the evening, well before midnight, her dutiful dad was sitting on the front steps, waiting.

109. THE LAST FOUR MONTHS

SUDDENLY, ON APRIL 26, 1965, my home-away-from-home roommate, Dave Siebert, got fired from the PC. We all knew that he did whatever he wanted, visiting PCVs and enjoying himself, but I had never heard of anyone getting fired. Five others had quit for various reasons, but this seemed to be a power play by Joe Sklar and Hooper, another new PC Representative. A week later, after a lot of farewell parties, Dave showed up for his final appearance at the PC office, driving Doug McMillan's black Jaguar. It was a grand exit which convinced Joe and Hooper he was just a party boy. Off he flew, first to Mexico before returning to La Jolla and the Big Sur where he surfed and taught high school for years.

On the weekends in the city, we continued to stay at Dave's apartment. I don't remember if we were squatters, highly unlikely, or if he paid in advance until the end of August, which was even more unlikely. Late one Saturday evening at 3:00 a.m., the two CARE Field Representatives, Millard Burr and Ron Baker, knocked on the door, barged in and played the guitar and sang for an hour. The next night, at the Bakers and with a bigger crowd, we did the same thing. They knew how to party.

In early May, a little Indian girl came to our door selling white navy beans, the same kind that CARE provided to the school lunch program. Yes, I was surprised so I asked, "Where did you find these beans?" As I suspected, she had bought two 100-pound bags from the School Director for Q9 each." A few days later, Millard Burr showed up from CARE to investigate the problem.

110. BEYOND COBÁN

WHILE MILLARD AND I WERE TALKING, he mentioned that he was being transferred to Colombia but first wanted to see more of Guatemala. He asked me if I wanted to go with him, along with his driver, Norberto, to Cobán, a medium-sized city where the artisans made a lot of delicately woven silver jewelry. Of course, I would go. I would never turn down a free trip.

On Monday, May 9, 1965, we took one of CARE's little blue Jeeps, drove past Progreso and Calama, and after six hours spent the first night in Cobán at a little hotel called the Monja Blanca, or the White Nun. First thing in the morning, instead of looking around Cobán, Millard decided to continue north to see how far we could go. The roads soon deteriorated and became mere tracks in the jungle as we headed 65 miles north until we came to a place, five hours later, named Sebal. From there we learned that we could take a boat to Sayaxche, Southwest of Flores, but since it would take two days, Millard decided not to take the risk. Instead, we continued past San Luis where we frequently saw small, noisy flocks of brightly colored parrots and macaws fly overhead as we drove. We also saw deer and an animal I thought was a Coati. A few times we even had to move logs so we could proceed. When we passed through small villages, which consisted of several stick houses, we'd inquire, "Is it possible to go farther?" The answers were always "yes" so on we went to Tuila, where we crossed from the state of Alta Verapaz into El Petén. A few miles later, after bouncing along in our little army-style Jeep all day for almost 140 miles in ten hours, we arrived in Poptún. At our little hotel, we celebrated our great feat of going where no roads were shown on our Esso gas station map. Poptún, we learned, had three Aviateca flights a week.

North of Poptún conditions quickly improved, as there were a lot of machines and soldiers working on the road. Finally, in three more hours, we made it all the way to the city of Flores. We soon found Tim Kraft and Carol Bellamy at the Economic Development Office of El Petén, and then went with Tim to his house on the shore of Lake Flores.

Tim was shocked to see us. He had wanted to be the first man to drive to Flores. Now he wasn't. I can't be sure we were either, but we did have quite an adventure. Since we were now in the lowland jungle and it was hot and muggy, we went swimming in front of Tim's house. It was great until Millard gashed his foot on a broken Coke bottle. After we finally stopped the bleeding, Millard decided he should call the CARE office and let them know where he was. The immediate response of the CARE Director, Waldo Tibbetts, was "What the blank are you doing up there? Get back immediately." So, the next morning Millard and his driver headed back. Their return trip was way worse and downright terrifying as they almost got trapped in a forest fire. It was so rough, as they bounced along through the burning jungle, that one of the Jeep's doors almost fell off by the time they arrived back at the office.

After seeing some of the few Mayan pyramids that had been uncovered from the dense jungle, Tim and I took a free military flight back to Guatemala City. It was an unusually bumpy flight in the old DC-3 and someone behind me was gagging into a paper bag with every breath. Listening to this wretched soul for 20 minutes, made me wonder if I would be next. Tim and I got to know each other a bit better and discovered both of us hoped to travel around South America after the PC.

From time to time, I used my VW to do errands, such as taking it to the garage for its 300-mile checkup, as well as for mini-vacations, as I did on my birthday, when Doug McMillan, Stan Tulson and I drove to Chulamar for a day at the beach. I was also happy Dad and Mom sent me $160 to help defray the cost of the VW's repair and Paul sent me $41 for two months of insurance. I even got another letter from Donna. Of course, I replied.

The unfinished water project remained my main concern. Until the storage tanks were installed, nobody could have access to clean water unless the pump was running — which was not often. For the last few months, therefore, I was continually meeting with different Guatemalan officials and engineers every time I was in the city. In San Pedro Ayampuc, some of us even collected and carried rocks to the site which were used later when construction of the storage platform started. Marge and I also worked on several other little projects including a school library for which we collected books for over a year. I also helped many families start their own vegetable gardens and was working with a big landowner to start a fishpond. Both of us had also been teaching English to several different kids, some of whom were doing quite well.

111. UNEXPECTED VISITORS

ON THE LONGEST DAY OF THE YEAR, Nancy and her mom flew to Guatemala City, went to the Palace Hotel and then tracked me down at Dave's old apartment. I was shocked to see them as I had no idea they were coming. After talking for a few minutes, we went to the north terminal and took the bus to San Pedro Ayampuc. After the heavy rain, the bus was soon covered in mud and Mrs. Bredendick had a fit as it slid all over the road. The next day we walked around town, looked at the water project and the water storage tank platform that was under construction, and headed back on the early morning bus for breakfast at the Palace Hotel.

Since the Assistant CARE Director in Panama, David Fledderjohn, had borrowed my car, I first had to track him down and retrieve it before the three of us could drive anywhere. The weather was rainy as we visited the ruins in Antigua, before driving west to Panajachel on Lake Atitlán. We stayed at the Rancho Grande and met PCVs Nola Alberts, Marcia Lang, and Carolyn Plage. Thursday morning was sunny as we drove up to Sololá and on to Chichicastenango, where the Indian market was packed with people, vegetables, and handicrafts.

Negotiating

Back in Guatemala City, Nancy and I had what turned out to be our farewell dinner at Las Tablitas. It was just like any other date with no talk about future plans or intentions. I wasn't ready for such a talk, but for all I knew, that's what she was hoping to have. The year after I graduated from Wisconsin and went to the PC, Nancy and my sister Mary became roommates as they continued their studies. They also had another roommate, Eduardo, a Sociology student from Spain. According to Mary, some 50 years later, he was a "nice" fellow and soon started going out with Nancy. I never guessed, but in retrospect I wondered if Nancy's mom was trying to breathe new life into our relationship or if she was just along for moral support. All I know for sure is that eventually everything turned out for the best.

The next day we all shopped at the Central Market, had lunch at the Palace Hotel, and at 5:00 p.m. I watched them fly off to Mexico. And that was the end of that. When I met Marge later in the day, she handed me a letter from Donna. A coincidence? Maybe. Maybe not.

112. THE END OF CARE-PC

THE NEXT NIGHT ALL THE PCVS in our Group III attended a farewell party for our well-liked and excellent leader, Keni Kent and his wife Neal, who were headed for Malaysia where he became the CARE Director. Even Tony Duran came from Colombia and we talked and danced until early in the morning. We were sad to see them go because we all had a lot of complaints about the new PC Representatives. The Snyders and Jay Jackson, for example, wanted to leave a month early to attend graduate school. Joe Sklar's answer was "No." They would have to quit and pay for their plane tickets home. We thought that was unreasonable. Keni's wife, Neal, told how she waved and honked at Joe while following him to the PC office. When she stopped alongside him and said, "Hi, Joe," he responded, "But I don't even know you." They had met four times in the previous two weeks. Keni said, "Good ol' dingbat Joe."

Back in San Pedro Ayampuc, we finally received all six 500-gallon water storage tanks and construction progressed on the ten-foot platform. Work was sporadic as the workers ran out of cement every few days, but I started to believe the project might even be finished during my tour of duty.

To celebrate July 4th, about ten of us visited the PCVs in Barberena, Evelyn Brubaker and Linda Sanderford, where we had a party with a Piñata of Uncle Sam. On the way back to Guatemala, the bus was so packed that there were 18 people standing in front of me in the front seat. A couple of them, of course, were hanging out the door, which never concerned anyone.

113. CLOSE CALLS

I WAS GETTING BOLDER about driving the VW as our time shortened. Well aware there could be severe consequences if I got caught, I was constantly on the lookout for those little, blue PC Jeeps and any other signs of danger. I always did my best to leave an escape route. One day while sitting at a stoplight on a two-lane, one-way, busy downtown street, it started to rain when I looked in my rearview mirror and saw a big bus barreling down the street behind me. I thought, "It's not going to be able to stop," as I quickly moved over to the right lane and up ahead several cars. Smash! The bus crashed into the car that had been in front of me and careened sideways and crunched some parked cars on the left. Guatemala is where I learned to be a defensive driver.

Rumors of my car being seen outside of Charlie Connolly's garage possibly reached the ears of Joe Sklar or why else would he come to visit me in San Pedro Ayampuc, which by pure chance, was the same day that Marge and I decided to drive to the city. As I was heading down some S-curves, I could see a little, blue PC Jeep coming up the hill. I had no escape. My best hope was to lower the plastic sunshade, speed up and roar past so fast he wouldn't be able to recognize me. As I flew by, Joe was hunched forward, tightly gripping the wheel with terror written on his face. In my haste, I almost went off the road myself as Marge firmly gripped the door handle. I don't know what Joe found out in San Pedro Ayampuc. All I know is that he never said a word to me. He was soon sent to Venezuela.

Two days later, I drove to the beach with Steve Haas, Orie Reich and Ginny Moran. It was a beautiful day; the waves were big and crashing down at our feet as we walked along the black sand beach. A little later, Steve and I swam out past the breakers and enjoyed floating in the warm ocean water. After a half hour, Steve suggested, "Maybe we better head back," as I too realized how far we had drifted. No need to panic. I was swimming alongside an experienced Californian.

114. NEARING THE END

AT THE END OF JULY, we were tested for our Spanish language proficiency. An American from the State Department, who didn't speak much Spanish, and a local Guatemalan conducted our verbal exams. The American asked me a question and I'd answer in Spanish. Then he'd ask the Guatemalan if what I said was correct. "Yes" he would say, "That's the way we say it here." He said that so many times I began to wonder if they said it the same way anywhere else. Anyway, I got a 3+ on a 1-5 scale, which was probably generous. Since I had been in the sixth of the eight language groups in training, several PCVs were surprised I had done so well. I was pleased and glad that I had studied Spanish on my own as much as I did, which I did to survive. I hated not being able to speak correctly.

Two PC employees from Washington, D.C. had us all fill out a ten-page, unsigned questionnaire where we expressed our opinions about our experiences. The main complaint, of course, was that none of us were pleased when our CARE bosses got pushed aside and replaced by new inexperienced PC employees. After two more sessions the next day, everyone headed over to Ron and Cecil Baker's house for a big surprise farewell party, as they were soon to be transferred to Santiago, Chile. A party with Ron never ended before 3:00 a.m. and this one didn't either.

The biggest party by far was held several nights in a row and hosted by the departing U.S. Ambassador, John Bell, who invited every known American in the country. When I started to introduce myself, he quickly interrupted and said, "Oh, I know who you are, John. You're the one who had the second piece of pie." "And it was good, too," I said, "And thank you again for that delicious Thanksgiving Day dinner." We both laughed, but I began to wonder if I had committed a faux pas. Every Embassy employee that I joked with about the event assured me I had not.

During July and August, we went from one social event to another. We saw movies, including "Zorba the Greek," had many get-togethers, went swimming, played football games, and joined in on any other entertainment we could find. We visited several other PCVs at their sites, wandered through various Indian markets, made several more trips to the beach at Chulamar, water skied at Lake Amatitlán, visited Quetzaltenango where Bernie Engel, Marsha Lang and I stayed with some Presbyterian missionaries, Don and Anna Sibley. It was exhausting as we stayed up all hours of the night telling stories and talking about our future plans. I also had a physical and X-rays, packed my belongings and got the VW's shimmy, wipers, broken windshield, and tire repaired for Q57.82. That's when I realized I had driven the VW for 3000 miles. I was broke and could only pay Q30 of the car expense until I picked up Dave Siebert's Q82 refund from Aviateca airlines. When I received my salary a few days later, I mailed Dave his money.

115. FINISHING UP

WHILE IN GUATEMALA CITY, I met Tim Kraft and drove him to San Pedro Ayampuc where he saw my humble abode and the almost completed water project. I was pleased to see that the workers were continually making progress even when I wasn't there. The new water tank platform was finished, and work was almost completed on the pila, a large concrete water tank about 3' high with fifteen clothes-washing stations where women could stand and scrub their clothes. It was a huge improvement over the filthy creek that meandered down through town where that little Indian girl had almost destroyed my new shirts and undies over a year earlier. When the well pump was running, the storage tanks filled up and water was available all day long for everyone. This was the highlight of my PC accomplishments. I was happy and relieved it was almost finished.

On Saturday, August 21st, I drove to and from Guatemala City with my closest neighbor, Mr. Saso, where we picked up several cases of pop and ice that his wife had ordered for our farewell party. Marge and I had cleaned the house and sold our last few pieces of furniture before the marimba arrived at 7:30 p.m. Our house, patio and the street in front were soon packed with hundreds of people who danced, drank, and cried the evening away trying to say good-bye. It was a great send off. Hugo Rosales, one of the teachers, gave a rousing "thank-you" speech as we were cheered and applauded. As Marge and I drove off down the dark, rutted street and out of town, we had mixed emotions about leaving the place where we had lived for twenty months — a place where we both had spent so many hours talking to people, trying to instill ideas into their heads to improve their health and living conditions. We both knew we had done what we could, and I was happy that my major effort — to get clean water — was 99% complete. I told everyone I would be back in late November.

The last few days before we left Guatemala, all of us PCVs didn't have much to do except a bunch of errands such as making plane reservations. To kill some time, Tim Kraft, Bernie Engel and I stopped to see Norma Wilder, Elva Reeves, Mary Hammond and Anne Cartwright at their house in Zone 5. When we arrived, they were frosting and dying each other's hair. I had never seen those plastic caps that had hundreds of little holes so a few hairs could be pulled through each one and dyed. To get in on the action, I asked Norma Wilder if she could dye mine just a little blonder. She would try. So, she mixed up a dose, rubbed it into my hair and waited. After she repeated this several times, I noticed that my hair didn't turn from dark brown to a lighter shade, but over the next hour, went through several different color changes. Finally, she could do no more. I now had a head of bright yellow-blond hair that seemed to glow in the dark that night in the movie theater. Those Guatemalan theater goers had never seen a gringo like me.

First thing in the morning, I went over to Ron Baker's house with the desperate hope that his wife, Cecil, could bail me out. After laughing hysterically, she fortunately had some brown dye and agreed to help. I couldn't thank her enough. I was almost back to normal.

Our last official day in the Peace Corps was Wednesday, August 25, 1965. When I checked out, I received $162.85 for my flight home, and $570 which was about one-third of my readjustment pay. Combined with $300 that I received from home, I went to the bank and bought $1000 in Traveler's Checks. After being temporarily in debt just a few days earlier, I felt rich. I then said good-bye to just about all the departing 52 PCVs and was ready to start a new adventure.

Six 500-Gallon Water Tanks

PART VI: 1965

OUR LATIN AMERICAN ODYSSEY

The Blue VW Beetle with John, Bryce and Tim

AS WE HAD PLANNED, Tim Kraft and I both were getting ready to see the rest of Central and South America — just as I had dreamed of doing with Steve Martin almost three years earlier. I had already seen quite a bit of Mexico, some of Central America, Panama, and Colombia, but there was still much to see. And now I was so close and could even speak some Spanish. After all, I might never get the chance to come back again. When Tim and I heard that Bryce Hamilton also wanted to go, we said "Great." It would be more fun to travel together. There would never be a better time. We were in our mid-twenties, had money and absolutely no responsibilities.

The next day, on August 26, 1965, bright and early, Tim, Bryce and I packed up the Beetle and were soon on our way. Tim sat in the front and Bryce squeezed in the back. We all took way too much stuff and poor Bryce could hardly move or even be seen as we headed out of Guatemala City on the familiar road to Escuintla. From there we turned east and by 9:30 a.m. arrived at the El Salvador border. That's when Bryce discovered the U.S. Consulate had failed to put his visa into his new passport. Tim and I drove on while Bryce returned by bus to correct the mistake. We would meet up later, somewhere.

In San Salvador, Tim and I found the PC office, talked to the Assistant Director and the doctor who gave me HCl nose drops and Terramycin for my miserably sore ear that I had suffered from months earlier. Tim had the "Aztec Two Step" but nothing that Polymagma couldn't cure. Our first day was off to a shaky start but we were on our way. After some PCVs gave us a key to their apartment where we stayed the first night, things were looking up. Free was good, better than cheap or inexpensive. On such a long trip, we knew we had to save when we could.

The next morning, we left the capital and soon were admiring beautiful Lake Ilopango and the volcanoes before driving on to San Miguel and Santa Rosa de Lima. From there we took the north branch instead of the Pan American Highway. That proved to be a bumpy mistake, but we still arrived in Tegucigalpa, Honduras, in time for supper. By then the PC office was closed but we did meet two Mennonite missionaries from Pennsylvania who lived next door. They invited us to stay the night and even served us hot chocolate and cookies before bedtime.

We were surprised to see PCVs Jim and Celeste Corzine at La Vitrina, where I bought a lamp, hand carved out of Honduran Mahogany, too match the table and lamp I had bought on my previous trip with Dave Siebert. Tim and I then drove to Managua, Nicaragua, where we arrived after dark at the Hotel Colón. After a morning swim in Lake Nicaragua, the big lake with two volcanoes in the middle and even freshwater sharks, we headed to the Pacific coastal town of San Juan del Sur and found a gorgeous horseshoe bay and beach. There were so many bugs at our $1.15 a night open air Hotel Estrella that we were almost eaten alive. Luckily, I had an ample supply of antihistamines in my PC medical kit that I kept tucked under the car seat.

When we arrived in Costa Rica, we found Bryce at the border where he had slept the night hoping we would come by. We then climbed the impressive Irazú volcano and peered into the rumbling, bubbling and belching abyss. We also enjoyed a relaxing day at Ojo de Agua, an area with natural hot springs and swimming pools. Back in the capital, San José, we watched "El Padrecito," starring Cantinflas, the famous Mexican comedian. We probably missed half the jokes, but we still laughed our heads off.

Peering into the Abyss

From San José, the capital of Costa Rica, we continued east on the Pan American Highway to San Isidro and met a couple PCVs who taught English at a luxurious high school — at least compared to what I was used to seeing in Guatemala. We met some of the teachers and even got a big free lunch. About 5:00 p.m., we stopped at a small bridge and asked a couple fellows how far it was to Villa Neilly, the next town where we hoped to spend the night. One chap on his bicycle replied, "About six hours." The other more astute observer, who perceived we had a car interrupted and said, "No, it is about two hours." Our car was a little faster than the bus and we arrived ninety minutes later despite the terrible gravel road that was pitted with potholes. The little Beetle took a beating as I drove way too fast to miss them all. We soon found a motel with little cubby holes for rooms that were hot and stuffy. As people paraded by and opened and slammed doors all night long, we were the only ones, I believe, who stayed the whole night. Eight hours of sleep, for the price of one, was a real bargain.

After bouncing along the Pan American Highway for a couple days with Bryce still crammed in the back seat, he finally inquired, "Why do I always have to sit in the back seat?" He didn't. From then on, he traded seats with Tim and became an equal partner.

117. PANAMA

BRYCE KILLED some time nonchalantly by tossing a few stones, while the three of us waited to go through customs on Friday, September 3rd. The Costa Rican custom's official, however, thought he was stoning the flag. Bryce quickly apologized and the offense was soon overlooked when they concluded that Bryce was just a clean-cut American kid who didn't realize it was a flagpole. Both Tim and I, however, let Bryce know that after all our PC training, we were disappointed to be travelling with an ugly American.

The Panama Canal

We soon met some local PCVs, who steered us to San Carlos on the Pacific where we encountered a beautiful white sand beach without a soul in sight. We ate our sandwiches, watched the sun set, went swimming without even getting our suits wet, and slept on the beach. The weather was perfect.

By noon the next day we pulled into Panama City and met our friend, Dave Fledderjohn, the Assistant CARE Director in Panama, who had been transferred from Guatemala about a year earlier. We also talked with some local PCVs that had just returned from Colombia and Peru and soaked up all the information and money-saving tips we could get.

The next morning, Tim, Bryce, and I drove around Balboa, a city in Panama's American zone. There we met a few of the 32,000 zonites, those sometimes-ugly Americans that lived in and sometimes never left the American controlled Zone, where the schools, salaries and living conditions were far better than in the rest of Panama. At Balboa High School, where they had the "flag incident" on January 9, 1964, we saw where 28 students had been killed arguing over flying the American flag. That eventually led to a new U.S. treaty with Panama, signed by President Jimmy Carter in 1977. That ended the American Zone in 1979 and gave complete control over the canal to Panama in 2000. It took ten years to finish the canal in 1914, an incredible engineering feat, but it was designed at a time when most ships were much smaller than just a few years later. Yes, I was expecting the locks to be much wider as we rode the train along the length of the canal to Colón.

After hitting all those potholes, I took the VW to the garage for an alignment. They also pounded out some dents, fixed the back window and welded on the back bumper which was coming loose. In the evenings, we saw some floor shows at the Palladium and at Maxims next to the Hilton and even saw the Chilean Beatles, who were surprisingly good. One night the U.S. Military Police, who assumed we might be soldiers breaking curfew, even checked our passports.

118. COLOMBIA

AFTER TEN DAYS IN PANAMA, Tim and I left the VW at the house of Bryce's friend, Carlos Kiamco, and hoped it would still be there upon our return from South America. Fortunately, his dad drove us to the airport in a blinding tropical rainstorm or we would have missed our $30 flight to Medellin, Colombia. This Avianca flight was much better than the cockroach-killing contest that Dave Siebert and I had just after the previous Christmas. We even had a gourmet meal with a glass of wine and creme de menthe. As we studied the map, we realized the equator was a long way off. We had to pick up the pace. A taxi took us to the Hotel Residencia Gladys where we stayed in a room for less than $2. Hot water would have been a plus.

Medellin was a big city of about one million, well-known for its serious, hard-working population. According to Dave Luria, the local CARE Field Representative, they also had a well-run lottery which generously financed the local CARE program. After a brief look around the very Catholic provincial city, we flew Aerocondor to Cartagena the next day. There we met Millard Burr and Tony Duran at the Hotel Bahia on the Caribbean coast, where they were attending a CARE-PC conference. Tim and I met up once again with Bryce who had decided to skip Medellin. He left the next day for Santa Marta.

Tim and I stayed at a small hotel on the beach, visited the cathedral, the old walled city, and the huge Fort of San Felipe with its many underground passages. Before Tim and I flew to Bogota, Ron Burkhard, a CARE Field Representative, took us up to Cartagena's highest point where we had a fantastic view of the city and coastline.

In Bogota, which was cold at 8500 feet, I called our family friends, Vance and Dorothy Austin, but

John, Bryce, and Tim

their maid, Anna Maria, who was extremely security conscious for many reasons, had her doubts about us staying there until the Austins returned the next day from Uruguay. When we showed up at their house, she relented and we had a luxurious place to stay in the golden ghetto, as we called it. On our way out to eat, we stopped at a drugstore where I asked, "Where is the nearest restaurant?" The clerk responded by giving me a pack of cigarettes. We both laughed as Tim made a crack about my defective Spanish. When Tim asked the same question, using his own impeccable Spanish, the clerk gave him a stick of deodorant. Bryce showed up the next day and the three of us travelled together again.

On one of our visits to the PC office, we met a PCV, who had just finished his tour, reading a letter from home. He looked stunned as he read, "Get home quickly. You've been drafted." I felt awful that he couldn't enjoy a great trip like ours. My deferment was valid until January 31, 1966, when I would once again be in school. When I turned 26 the following May, my draft board sent me a letter that said I was no longer eligible for the draft. That was fine with me as the Vietnam war was beginning to heat up. I knew several people from high school and university who didn't make it back.

We passed through some great scenery as we headed south on the Pan American Highway through Ibague, Armenia and Buga. We crossed over the "highest" bridge in Colombia and through land that grew four crops a year, thanks to the ideal climate. In Cali, our driver dropped us off at the Casa del Viajero, the traveler's house. The owner asked if we were PCVs and charged us $0.85 each. We were at the right place. After checking out various modes of transportation, we ended up taking a bus to Popayan, a four-hour ride, that took six because of road construction. The next day, we endured a 170-mile bus ride on a pitted gravel road to Pasto in southern Colombia. The mountain scenery, however, was beautiful as we drove across a canyon on a bridge that was much higher than the "highest" bridge we passed earlier.

119. ECUADOR

ON SEPTEMBER 24TH, we left Pasto for Ipiales on the frontier and then on to Tulcán in Ecuador. From Tulcán, we wanted to take a TAME flight to Quito, but the pilot said they were overweight, even though there were four empty seats. We learned too late that if we had paid a small bribe, we could have had a quick and easy trip. Instead we bounced along in the back of a pickup for eight hours. The bus drivers were crazy as they passed on blind corners near cliffs. One bus plowed into the bank while others missed pedestrians by inches. When we were high up, it was cold, and we needed our jackets. In the valleys, it was hot. At 9400' Quito was cool. We soon found the PC hotel, the Residencia Lutecia, where we needed a hot shower and a comfortable bed. After travelling for thirty days, we finally crossed the equator, and after our harrowing ride in the open pick-up, had sunburned noses to prove it. From Wisconsin, Tim, Bryce, and I were now halfway to our southernmost destination.

Quito was a picturesque, hilly capital city with a refreshing climate and plenty of sunny days that varied in length by no more than 15 minutes from one season to the next. A newly arrived PCV, who was in a group of electricians and engineers and knew where he was going, accompanied us as we visited Independence Plaza and the old Spanish San Francisco Cathedral. The huge gold-covered altar was a fantastic sight to behold. The Spaniards had come to find gold and this place got its share. We did some shopping, changed some traveler's checks into sucres and got visas for Peru. Just as we had done before arriving in Colombia and Ecuador, we had the local PC office write a letter to the Peruvian Embassy requesting that we be issued a visa without having to buy a round-trip ticket. They always obliged.

We left early for Guayaquil on the Autoferro, a 22-passenger school bus outfitted with train wheels that traversed down the steep hills to the coast. We dropped 10,000' in just 50 miles and when we came to one particular switchback, we actually went backwards. The 14-hour trip was a bit disappointing because of the rain and fog, but we did meet four interesting Ph.Ds. who were going on a 30-day boat ride to study the Humboldt — the cold current that flowed north from the Antarctic up the west coast of South America.

By ferry we crossed the Guayas River into Guayaquil, a muggy, grubby port city and the biggest in Ecuador. After a quick taxi ride, we arrived at the Hotel Helbig which cost 20 Sucres, a little less than $2. Guayaquil was more alive than Quito with more people bustling about in the streets. They were called monos, or monkeys, by the people in Quito.

We investigated going to the Galapagos Islands, but the schedules were so irregular and unreliable that we turned down the idea even though the prices were reasonable. At Chinos, a sidewalk cafe and PC hangout, we were accosted by a variety of entrepreneurs selling whiskey, cigars, cigarettes, lottery tickets, jewelry, socks, undies, and drugs, as well as watches and dirty pictures which they kept inside their shirts.

Shoeshine boys, of course, were ubiquitous. We talked the evening away with several PCVs. Two of them, dressed in boots and black T-shirts, had each purchased BMW motorcycles to drive back to the states. Months earlier, I had the same idea but luckily it didn't work out.

The next day we met PCV Jim Semilyan from Tim's alma mater, Dartmouth, who showed us the slums where flimsy bamboo houses were built above the mud flats and connected to each other by rickety bamboo board walks. Falling off into the muck was not an option as we tiptoed from one house to another. When the monthly tide came in, voila, all the garbage and waste washed out to sea. Close by, a paved road led to a new $25,000 church financed by Cardinal Cushing, Archbishop of Boston. At that moment, after witnessing such extreme poverty, it seemed the money could have been put to better use.

After seeing the ugliest side of Guayaquil, we had dinner with Jim and his wife, Cecelia, and headed to Pier #9. There we bought first class tickets on a big ferry boat, the "Don Antonio," which travelled daily across the Gulf of Guayaquil to Puerto Bolívar, close to the Peruvian border. We were under the assumption that our expensive $1 tickets would provide us with more comfortable conditions for the night voyage, but we were wrong. It was first-come, first-serve and crowded everywhere. Hammocks were inches above cots that were tightly packed together. After a couple hours, I was so sick of looking at rear ends just above my head, I traded my cot for a hammock, which would have been fine had I been 4' tall. Six hours later, at 2:30 a.m., we arrived in Puerto Bolivar. This boat trip did, at least, save us a long road-trip back through the highlands of Ecuador. Two hours later, our bus departed for the frontier.

120. PERU

WHILE WE WAITED FOR CUSTOMS TO OPEN, we met a couple teenagers from Quito whose father worked in the Consulate. Luis and Fernando took our passports and got us checked through in a hurry and we were soon on our way to Tumbes, Peru.

Northern Peru

In Tumbes, customs got ridiculous. We were stopped three times before we went 100 yards. Each time we all got out of the bus and handed over our passports for inspection while they looked at our luggage. And it didn't improve much farther down the highway. Altogether, we were stopped 18 times for inspections. According to the two kids, it was because of communist infiltration. That was partially true, but it was mostly because Ecuador and Peru had a long-standing territorial dispute and weren't getting along all that well.

As we continued our 25-hour bus ride south to Lima, which cost just 211 Soles or $8, the dry, sandy scenery was spectacular mile after mile. The hazy Pacific was on our right as we hugged the huge, sandy hills that were devoid of any vegetation. When the road dropped down to sea level, we could see thousands of dead seabirds strewn along the shoreline, starved by overfishing the anchovies. Or perhaps it was because this was an "El Niño" year when the eastern Pacific warmed more than usual, which reduced the upwelling of the nutrient rich Humboldt current. In any case, with less food, there were fewer anchovies and more starved sea birds. This was the first time I had ever heard of El Niño which occurred every seven years.

On Saturday afternoon we pulled into Lima and finally found a vacant hotel. It wasn't even up to our low standards, so we moved Sunday morning to the Hotel Americano which included breakfast. After wandering the streets, we encountered a man who recommended that we eat at "Jardin Rosita Rios." It was quite a long ride on bus #22 but just when we thought we might be lost, the driver pointed it out. It was a big, crowded restaurant with four open dining rooms. At first Tim and I weren't too sure if we wanted to stay, but just a minute later some strolling musicians started playing guitars and singing, while several lovely girls started dancing the "Marinera." Without asking, the waiter brought us each a "*Pisco Sour*," the local cocktail. Next came "*Ceviche de Corvina*," raw, pickled fish with onions and "*Ceviche de Choros*," a brownish mussel. That was followed by "*Tamales*" and "*Sangresita*," which is chicken liver and blood that looks similar to cottage cheese. "*Chicharrones*," or deep-fried pork rinds came next, before "*Cau-Cau*," a goulash of meat, intestines, and potatoes, and "*Patitas*," another kind of goulash. As we continued to eat everything in front of us, we started to fill up and wondered what could be next. It was "*Anticuchos*," bite-sized chunks of roasted cow heart served on bamboo sticks. Sections of "*Choclo*," or corn on the cob, were followed by "*Cara Pulcra*," whatever that was. We were still drinking from two pitchers, one filled with "*Chicha de Lora*," some alcoholic drink that tasted like raisins, and from another filled with "*Chicha de Morada*," a raspberry-flavored alcoholic beverage that was our favorite. When the waiter asked if we were now ready for the main course, we said, "Yes," but weren't sure why. So, then he brought us "*Chupe de Camarones*," a milky soup with shrimp in the shell. That was followed by a big plate of chicken with rice. Our final dish, before coffee, was "*Picarones*," corn fritters with syrup. It all added up to 17 different items, which just might have been all the typical Peruvian dishes in existence. Our tab for dinner was 160 sols, or $3.20 each, a bargain because it saved us from buying supper and breakfast.

We met a lot of people in Lima, visited the Museum of Anthropology where the pottery and artifacts weren't even labeled, looked at a lot of shops, got visas for Bolivia, bought plane tickets to Cusco (the bus would have taken four days), visited the site of a PC girl who had no idea what to do or where to begin in a terrible slum with no electricity or water (she needed another assignment and a partner), bought AAA maps, and after two days we left for the airport at 4:20 a.m. The 90-minute LANSA flight to Cusco, a city of 90,000 nestled in a valley at 11,000 feet, was fantastic. The snow-capped Andes mountains made the Rockies look like hills. Cusco was a pleasant surprise after cloudy, dreary Lima where the sun rarely shines. We checked in at the Hotel Ollanta and spent the next two days seeing the sights, including La Compañía Cathedral on the Plaza de las Armas, which had the best collection of colonial art in Peru. We walked everywhere around town and talked to PCVs that were easy to pick out of a crowd.

The *autovagón,* another name for a bus with train wheels, travelled alongside the Urubamba River which fed the Amazon. With snow-covered mountains on both sides, it was a beautiful ride down the valley towards Machu Picchu. Just over three hours later, we arrived at the base of the mountain. Here a bus was waiting to take us up eight switchbacks to the Incan ruins set in a saddle between the mountains of Machu Picchu and Huayna Picchu. The physical setting was remarkable. The steep mountains looked almost like upside down cones, an ideal place for a hidden city that never was discovered by the Spanish. The buildings and houses were probably built in the 1400s, so they said, out of big rocks that fit so tightly together there was no space for even a drop of mortar. I couldn't imagine how the stonemasons cut the huge angular rocks and fit them in place like a puzzle. We had four hours to wander around the site, eat our sandwiches and enjoy the surroundings and the perfect sunny day before descending the switchbacks and back to Cusco. The entire day cost about $8 to see one of the most fantastic places in South America. That is no longer true. In 2020, 55 years later, the entrance fee into Machu Picchu was $45. With our PC discount, our fees were each reduced from $1.10 to $0.30. Best of all, we didn't have to put up with hordes of tourists.

Just Talking

Travelling Over the Altiplano
Bryce Hamilton & John McLeod

Early the next morning, we boarded the train to Puno, about 240 miles south on the west end of Lake Titicaca, the world's highest navigable lake. We travelled second class for $3, instead of $6 for first class, and it was another trip to remember. As we rattled along over the altiplano, we reached elevations as high as 12,556 feet. As the cold wind blew in the windows, we needed our light winter jackets, but the little Indian boys wore just a sweatshirt. They didn't seem to feel the cold as they sat their bare butts down on the freezing leather seats. Meanwhile, their mothers chewed on coca leaves which turned their lips and mouths a slimy green. It was a cold and desolate place to live but the coca no doubt eased their misery. The flat land was filled with llamas, sheep, oxen, and women who seemed to be breaking up clods of dirt with pickaxes. Just as in all the other third-world countries we visited, it seemed as if the women did at least 70% of the work.

The train stopped in a tiny place called Sicuani where Tim and I each bought a colorful, Santa Claus-style wool hat. Farther down the tracks at Juliaca, we got off the train and hitched a ride in the back of a large truck, standing room only. We had to hang on to the wooden slat siding, but because the road was too narrow for two vehicles to pass each other, we had to quickly pull our hands off the slats to keep from losing our fingers. In the small town of Puno, we stayed at the Hotel Tito, a miserable little place that claimed to have hot water. We ate dinner with a couple of French travelers, which guaranteed we all complained about the horrible food. It was so inedible they even refused to pay for dinner. Fortunately, there were plenty of blankets on the bed.

On Sunday morning, we bought some Alpaca rugs and then hitched a truck ride to Ilave where we heard there was an Indian market. Unfortunately, it was mediocre because there weren't many local handicrafts, so we hitched another truck ride to Juli, a small town on the Southwest side of Lake Titicaca. Some kids showed us where the PCVs lived who seemed to be doing well. Tim, Bryce, and I watched them prepare lunch at a community center they organized. They also started a library and had collected a large number of books. After conversing for a while, we returned to the Hotel Florida. We were pooped.

In Juli, at 13,000 feet, we waited several hours in the plaza hoping for any kind of transportation. Eventually we hitched a ride to Yunguyo, another town by Lake Titicaca. This proved to be a horrible place, but by local standards was very *alegre* (happy) when we arrived because a big fiesta, the Day of San Francisco, was in progress. The people were dancing in ornate, bizarre costumes, bands were playing and almost everyone was drunk, staggering, yelling, and fighting. Both plazas were packed, the streets were filthy and smelled of urine. Thousands of drunk Indians were everywhere.

We definitely had made a poor decision when we decided not to take the boat from Puno across Lake Titicaca directly to the Bolivian border town of Desaguadero. Instead, two days later, we were still struggling to find any kind of transportation to get there. Finally, Tim, Bryce, and I, along with exactly 30 others of various sizes, squeezed into the back of a pick-up. Bryce was hunched over the top of the cab holding onto our suitcases as we sped along the dirt road. Tim and I were on each side helping to support Bryce, who almost froze to death. Near the end of the 90-minute trip, Tim's little army fatigue hat blew off in the wind, causing him to frantically pound on the roof so the driver would stop. He quickly hit the brakes, probably thinking someone had fallen out, as Tim ran back and picked up his hat. The driver, who never would have stopped for just an old hat, shook his head in disbelief but Tim was happy as a clam.

121. BOLIVIA

BY 11:00 A.M. WE PASSED THROUGH customs, boarded a packed bus to La Paz, the capital of Bolivia, which was 73 miles straight east past the south edge of Lake Titicaca. Every so often we had to stop for 45 minutes while the police checked for contraband. They never found any because the Indian women

had already given their marshmallows, candy, liquor, and plastic articles to the driver who kept it all hidden. For five hours, the driver never got over 25 mph and we constantly had someone's rear or elbow in our face. Yes, this segment of our trip was a hassle, but at least it only cost $1.15. On our left, we could see the snowcapped mountains across the lake. That was some consolation.

La Paz, at 11,975 feet, is the highest capital in the world. We weren't bothered by the altitude since we had been even higher for more than a week. The Hotel Neumann was an oasis. They did laundry and even took ours. We spent quite a bit of time shopping and bought some more Alpaca rugs, which we shipped home. I also bought a heavy, brown Alpaca sweater that I wore for years. While I was buying stamps at the post office for my collection, a man said,

Rural Bolivians

"You can't get any decent stamps here." We hopped in a cab for a five-block ride and I waited until he came out of his house with a stamp book. He picked out about 25 different, more collectible stamps and said, "I want you to have something to remember from Bolivia." As we travelled farther south and west, people seemed to be getting friendlier, just like in the U.S.

Taking a Break

That evening, the PC Secretary, Susie, and another PCV, drove Tim, Bryce, and me to the semi-finals of the South American tennis championship. There were plenty of disputed line calls among the players, the linesmen, and the crowd. The Brazilian, who barely beat an Ecuadorian from the Guayaquil Tennis Club, was so frustrated that he hit one ball to kingdom come. We almost froze to death as the match dragged on. Back at the Hotel Neumann, our room key was missing. The dim-eyed doorman said, "What can we do?" Finally, the bar manager took some action and broke the lock with a crowbar and hammer.

The next morning, Bryce and I talked with the AFS student who had spent a year in Tipton, Iowa, where Bryce went to high school. We then met the President of the Mercantile Bank, Sr. Mariaca P., who was Marge Bradbury's old friend from years earlier when her husband was a mining engineer. Marge was happy to hear he was doing well.

In the evening we left La Paz on another *autovagón*. It was an all-night ride, via Oruro, to the more tropical city of Cochabamba at 8500 feet. It was called the city of eternal spring, and was the same as Guatemala's national slogan. After being above 11,500' for over a week, we were pleased to see lush vegetation. We checked into the Hotel Ambassador and spent the day looking for treasures in the

The Traffic was Ridiculous

market where we bought even more Alpaca rugs and some ponchos which we mailed to some of the PCVs that had given us shopping requests. On Sunday we relaxed at a high-class swimming pool which kept the riffraff away with a $0.35 cent entrance fee. In the cabaña, I was impressed by the size of an anaconda snakeskin which stretched around the inside walls for about 25 feet.

On October 18th, Tim, Bryce, and I boarded the early morning autovagón for the ten-hour ride, mainly through a valley with interesting rock formations, back up to Oruro, which at 12,250 feet was a cold and dreary place to live. There we bought $10 "first class" train tickets and immediately headed towards the coastal city of Antofagasta, Chile, a 30-hour trip. We squeezed in with two old ladies to keep warm under their blankets. Both were petty smugglers who later paid off the border agents with some of their small toys. We soon were rumbling past the huge salt flats of Lake Poopó. It was the most desolate landscape I could imagine.

Llamas Eeking out a Living

In the dining car that evening, we met two young Americans, Bob and Andy, who were headed to Santiago, where they would study to be priests. Several other priests continued to imbibe, gradually becoming much more jovial, and by the end of the evening, just plain drunk. That's when they invited us to stay with them the next night at the Rectory in Antofagasta. Back in our seats, we soon wished that the train's dormitory rooms had been available as we tried in vain to get comfortable on our hard benches.

Early the next morning, we were still rumbling along at over 14,000 feet. We first passed deposits of white borax, then nitrate mines and some of the biggest copper mines in the world. It was desolate, windy, and cold, which we experienced when the train stopped a few times so we could get out and stretch our legs. We spent most of the day in the dining car conversing with several interesting people. One couple, Joe from Switzerland, and his wife, Doris from England, lived in Antofagasta, as did a big Scotsman, Graham Sommerville, who invited the whole group of us to his house the next day.

122. CHILE

AS WE CHUGGED CLOSER to our destination, we wondered, "Should we accept the drunken priest's invitation to stay at the rectory?" We decided to give it a try. After all, those two young student priests had even called ahead from Calama to say we would be coming. That night at the rectory we each had our own private room and a restful night's sleep. Bob and Andy woke us up late and the three of us ate breakfast alone. One priest kindly picked up our airline tickets to Santiago while we talked, ate lunch, and walked on the beautiful beach. That evening, the big Scotsman and his wife entertained all ten of us train travelers. Dinner started with sea urchins and fish eggs and ended with wine, cognac and pisco sours, all firsts for me, except the pisco sours which we had tried in Lima.

Our $13 DC-3 flight to Santiago first headed northeast back to Calama, then south to Potrerillo, a tiny copper mining village in the desert, before arriving in Santiago five hours later. The friendly pilots gave us a blow-by-blow account as we flew, pointing out all the mountains and sites. The flight saved us a two-day bus trip through the desert, but I felt sick, stuffy and had the chills. By the time we reached the little Hotel Moneda in Santiago, my temperature was 102 degrees. While I stayed in bed the next day, the owner frequently brought me hot lemonade and food. So far everyone we met did what they could to help us out. The second morning, I swallowed a pile of pills and we walked to the top of Santa Lucia and had a scenic view of the city.

Bryce and I then left Santiago in the front seat of a new Mercedes bus and headed south through Rancagua, San Fernando, and Talca down the central valley. The new concrete highway was something we hadn't seen in a long time. We passed huge vineyards, rows of Lombardy Poplar, Eucalyptus and Weeping Willow trees. It was a pleasant change from the desolate altiplano and the sandy mountains of the north. As we drove south, we saw snow-capped mountains on our left and enjoyed the perfect weather. It was a pleasant nine-hour ride to Concepción on the coast. When we got off the bus, I started talking with an older lady, who was a teacher, and her daughter. When they found out we were PCVs, they squeezed us into their tiny Fiat 600 and gave us a tour around the city. They even found out there was going to be a PC party that night and took us. Then they were gone. That's when I vowed to be more helpful to foreign students but I'm not sure I ever was. Along with a bunch of PCVs and their students, all of whom hoped to get scholarships to the U.S., we ate hot dogs and potato salad, went out dancing to real live music, and strangely ate peanut butter and drank coffee before crashing at 2:00 a.m. on some PCV's apartment floor.

At 8:30 the next morning, we boarded another luxurious bus for the eleven-hour trip to the small town of Puerto Varas, located on the shore of Lake Llanquihue, the biggest lake in Chile. Along the way we talked politics with a couple of men who thought the moderate President Eduardo Frei was all talk and not much action. They thought the only reason he won was because the other candidate, Salvador Allende, was a communist — which is probably why most

Americans were happy with Frei's election. The men were happy with the Alliance for Progress, started by President Kennedy in 1961, because new schools were being built all over the country. When I asked if they had teachers for all the schools, the man said, "Yes, and that is our responsibility." I was glad to hear they were taking ownership. As we travelled from country to country, we saw hundreds of signs pointing out projects financed by the Alliance. Streets, parks, schools and even suburbs all over Latin America were named after the immensely popular President Kennedy. If he hadn't promoted and signed the PC legislation, I probably would have been teaching Biology somewhere in southern Wisconsin.

We checked into the Hotel Bella Vista in Puerto Varas, where I enjoyed soaking in a big tub of hot water. Before Bryce and I got to the dining room, we met a fellow who insisted on driving us to the top of the hill where we had a tremendous view of the town and Lake Llanquihue. It seemed every Chilean we met was under orders to be kind to us. The best thing about this big, wooden hotel was the honey mixed with butter which we thickly spread on our breakfast toast. It was delicious and I never could replicate it.

Petrohué Falls, Chile

After admiring the scenery, we took a bus to the nearby port city of Puerto Montt, located at the southern tip of the famed Pan American Highway. This was as far south as we would go. While we unsuccessfully tried to call the PC office, a girl in the bus station — instead of just telling us where it was — called a friend who sent two boys to take us. On the way, Bryce and I saw Tim, who had flown from Santiago by himself, standing on the corner with some local PCVs. We continued to the PC office, dropped off our bags and eventually spent the night there. If it was free, that's where we headed. That night we all had dinner with the PC Doctor, Andy Horvath and his wife, both UW graduates. Once again, we didn't get to bed until 2:00 a.m. which was another reason I had a hard time getting over my cold. The following night wasn't any different. A Mr. Harry Nelson from Wieser, Idaho, invited us out for dinner to help celebrate the marriage of his PC son to a Chilean girl.

Early the next morning, we barely got to the bus station on time for our ride back to Puerto Varas. I felt half sick, Tim had a hangover, and Bryce had a sore foot. Before long we all improved as we rode to Petrohué Falls, a beautiful spot on the raging Petrohué River, and on to the shore of

Todos los Santos or All Saints Lake, one of the most scenic places on earth with the Puntiagudo volcano and mountains in the background. After two rainy days in Puerto Montt, we enjoyed perfect weather as we crossed the lake to Peulla, Chile, a beautiful place to spend the evening.

123. ARGENTINA

ON OCTOBER 29TH we continued by bus across the border to Puerto Frias, Argentina, boated across a small lake to Puerto Blest, followed by a short bus ride to another big lake, Nahuel Huapi, where we boarded another boat for the long cruise to San Carlos de Bariloche. The scenery was fantastic, and the weather stayed sunny. There we again met the father of the groom, the man from Idaho, who once again bought us dinner. He apparently liked our company, and even better, we enjoyed a free meal in a first-class hotel.

Bariloche seemed to be the ski sweater capital of Argentina. In the summer months, the women knitted sweaters and sold them by the thousands during the June-July ski season. I bought one but never wore it much. During our two day stay, we walked throughout the town, where the shops stayed open until 11:30 p.m., visited nearby Llao-Llao where we discovered those big, juicy steaks, and learned that the average Argentinian consumed over a half pound of beef every day. In the evening we boarded the train and headed east across the endless, flat, grassy pampa where there wasn't much to see except cattle and a few gauchos, Argentine cowboys. When we reached Carmen de Patagones on the Atlantic, we headed northeast to Bahia Blanca and the big capital city of Buenos Aires. This two-night, 40-hour, 900-mile trip, cost $14 which included a dormitory room with beds. It was worth it.

Looking Back: Fresh Snow on Puntiagudo, Chile

At noon, we checked into the Hotel Adriatica and devoured another big steak dinner for $1.25, served with a fried egg on top, at the Palace of French Fries. We wandered all over the downtown area for two days and visited government buildings, the Casa Rosada, fancy shops, the botanical garden and zoo. In the evening, Bryce and I had our first cultural night as we splurged $2.50 on tickets to "Lulu," a German opera, at the world's largest opera house, the "Colón." We sat on the right side in the fifth of seven balconies. It was an elaborate and beautiful theatre but since we couldn't understand a word, nor could we appreciate the dissonant atonal music, we left at intermission. Other richer and more cultured patrons spent up to $35 for the best seats but ours were surprisingly good.

124. URUGUAY

BRIGHT AND EARLY, Tim, Bryce and I boarded the new hydrofoil, a big ferry on skis, that roared 30 miles over the muddy River Plata estuary in less than an hour to Colonia, Uruguay. Customs was a breeze before we boarded a new bus to Montevideo, the capital of Uruguay. Because Tim still had a nasty sore throat, the sweats and chills, we took him to the Embassy, and they took him to the Hospital Británico where he stayed for two nights.

Bryce and I met the Assistant PC Director, Arnie Baker, who had been a PCV in Guatemala before us. He drove us to the comfortable PC Hotel Los Ángeles, where we talked about Uruguay's welfare state that was busting the national bank. They were losing millions just subsidizing public buses which charged only $0.015 for a ride. Back in Guatemala, buses cost Q0.05 but the government didn't increase the price for at least the next 50 years to keep the workers from rioting — as they periodically did at the mere mention of a possible increase. Montevideo was picturesque and loaded with antique European cars, which economically was not a positive sign. The country was so short of foreign exchange that they only imported a few essential items. On Friday, Saturday and Sunday, beef sales were banned so more could be exported.

Tim informed us the next morning that the hospital was run by the three stooges. When he asked a nurse for a bar of soap, he had to wait until they could find someone to sell it to him. From there Bryce and I went shopping. While I was picking up a few stamps, a girl suggested we mail our letters at the Pan American office. She then took us to check out bus schedules and to the Brazilian Consulate where we got visas. By now we knew her name, Alicia, and she next took us to her home where she sang and played the guitar. Her mother then took us to a guitar factory where Alicia's guitar teacher sold Bryce a guitar for 1200 pesos, or $20. The next day, I picked up Tim from the hospital, which cost him $16, and met Bryce at a shop where we each bought a suede sport coat. When Sunday came, Tim slept, while Bryce and I left for Alicia's house where we met her mom and dad, brother Alex, his girlfriend, another friend named Alicia and even a couple of AFS students. They gave us a tour of the city, took us to a museum and soon we were eating pizza while Alicia again played and sang.

On Monday, the three of us packed our bags, bought bus tickets to Porto Alegre, Brazil, and were invited to dinner by Arnie Baker and his wife who barely got us to the bus station by 10:00 p.m. Alicia and her mother were there too to see us off. Before I even got home, Mom and Dad had received a letter from her parents saying that I had been an excellent ambassador of goodwill. Mom and Dad were so proud that they gave a copy to their Methodist Pastor, Rev. Kalas, who wrote a column about it in "The Chimes," the church news bulletin. Were there such friendly people in the U.S? Everywhere we went, people helped make our trip easier and more interesting.

125. BRAZIL

AT 3:30 A.M. WE CROSSED THE BRAZILIAN BORDER. When the sun came up, we saw rolling hills, cattle, a few wild Rheas, which resembled Ostriches, and other strange birds. At Porto Alegre, customs officials helped us get through quickly so we could catch another bus to Rio de Janeiro. We had some rough moments understanding Portuguese and were glad that we had had it so easy as we passed through the first 13 countries of our trip. Before noon, we got our first glimpse of the huge city and skyscrapers of Sao Paulo. Seven hours later we arrived in Rio, and checked into the annex of the Hotel Florida, near Flamingo Beach, on Wednesday, November 10th. We had been riding buses for 44 hours.

After breakfast, we headed to the famed Copacabana beach which was well-populated with gorgeous girls in skimpy bikinis. There was no topless swimming in Rio but sometimes it was hard to tell. Before we knew it, maybe we were distracted, Tim and I looked around and said, "Where's Bryce?" Seconds later, we saw him being hauled out of the water, looking half drowned. Thanks to Art, a PCV we had met in Cochabamba, assisted by a couple of Brazilians, there was a happy ending. We hadn't even thought about riptides at such a famous beach.

One day, in between our swimming and tanning sessions at Copacabana and Ipanema, we saw a parade for the King and Queen of Belgium as they drove by in a Rolls Royce. A day later, we met Tim's Senator from Indiana, Birch Bayh, and Senator Fred Harris from Oklahoma, who were here to learn more about the issues and problems of Brazil. We accompanied over twenty Brazilian PCVs to their ritzy hotel, listened to them speak, followed by a question and answer session. Sen. Harris didn't think the Watts riots in Los Angeles were a result of racial problems, but it sure seemed they were to us. It was all interesting, but far less memorable than what followed much later that evening.

With eight other PCVs, we ate dinner at a sidewalk restaurant across from Copacabana. After Bryce finished his frog legs, Tim and I presented him with a cake to celebrate his November 13th birthday. We then followed two of the local PCVs, Dave and Jim, to Rio's largest favela, which were terrible slums where shacks were crammed together on the steep hillsides. As we wove our way up the steep, twisting narrow path, we came to the dance floor that was also used as an outdoor ñbasketball court. It was filled with a circle of girls dancing the Samba accompanied by a twenty-man band playing mostly drums and shaking instruments. I had never seen such fantastic dancing, costumes, or rhythm. With each dance, the pace picked up until it was a wild frenzy. This was, after all, a practice session in preparation for the famous Carnival in Rio, still two months away, when they would compete against many other clubs. We were served beer, shrimp and chicken and our presence was announced over the loudspeaker as they presented us with small pennants of their club. Off we went, following our PCV guides, Dave and Jim, to another club where the queen asked me to dance. It was fun, but rhythmically, I was hopelessly out of my league. At 4:30 a.m., our guides Dave and Jim crashed on our hotel floor.

One night while Bryce and I were sleeping, Tim came in late, climbed into bed, put on his little army fatigue hat, the same one he almost lost in southern Peru, and continued to sit there with the light still shining. After a couple minutes, I asked, "Aren't you going to lie down and turn off the light?" Tim replied, "I can't because I have the twerlies." I asked, "What are the twerlies?" "You mean you went to the University of Wisconsin and never heard of the twerlies?" He had to explain, "If I lie down while I'm still dizzy, I'll throw up." Now I knew.

In a small tourist shop on Rio Branco, where I bought some little thank-you gifts and a small, wood tray covered with blue butterfly wings, I met Maura. She spoke fluent English, after being an AFS student, and I asked her out. First, however, I had to ask her dad's permission which went well. Much better than my first such experience in Guatemala. Over the next several days we did quite a few things together — swimming, going out to eat, seeing "The Sound of Music, " visiting the top of Sugarloaf Mountain, that huge round rock in all the pictures of Rio, and attending a soccer game in the biggest stadium in the world which held 200,000 screaming fans.

126. HEADING BACK TO GUATEMALA

ON NOVEMBER 20TH, after ten full days in Rio de Janeiro, Tim, Bryce, and I headed to the airport for our five-hour Peruvian Airlines flight across the continent to Lima. Sure enough, Maura came to see me off. As we waved goodbye, I thought how easy it would be to fall for one of those cute Latin girls. But I had other plans. At least I hoped I did.

The "Golden Age of Aviation" was just beginning, when airlines served a hot meal and freely gave away hotel vouchers. We were happy to participate in this new era as we took a taxi to the first-class Hotel Riviera in downtown Lima.

The next day in the Bogota airport, we again said "Hello" to Senators Birch Bayh and Fred Harris, then went to the Austin's house and gave their maid, Anna Maria, a gift from that little shop in Rio. The next night at Tony Duran's in Panama, we watched the Cassius Clay-Floyd Patterson boxing match on satellite TV. Millard Burr, the CARE Representative in Guatemala, was there too but had just been fired from CARE for punching a PCV. You may remember that Millard took me to Cobán and Flores before he gashed his foot on a coke bottle.

In Panama, I picked up the VW and could see that Carlos, the custodian of my VW, had almost driven it to death in our absence. First gear hardly worked, and the wheel bearings were making a racket. We dropped it off at the garage, picked up our mail at the PC office, bought some Guayabera shirts and car insurance, and a day later were off and running.

At 4:00 p.m. on November 24th, we headed west and drove all night until we arrived in San José, Costa Rica the next afternoon. We were exhausted. Early the next morning we set out again. First came Nicaragua, then Honduras and El Salvador. We drove steadily, all day and night until we got to the Guatemalan border at 7:00 a.m. Finally, our 95-day odyssey through Central and South America had come to an end. We had seen more, for less money, than anyone else on earth. We were convinced of that.

Back in Guatemala City for the weekend, we kept busy greeting and eating with old friends, and doing a lot of errands, including buying our airline tickets home. Before leaving, however, I had to make one last trip to San Pedro Ayampuc. What would I find?

On Monday morning, I drove up the street as people waved and smiled. The first person I met was Graciela's husband, Pablo. He was drunk and wanted Q0.30 for a drink. My neighbor, Octavio Saso, and his wife each gave me a big hug and a quart of black beans. Their chubby daughter, Berta, to whom I had tried to teach English, was now thin. Mark Antonio had run off with last year's fiesta sport's queen, Juana. Aristeo sold me his machete. The basketball court was completely paved and posts for volleyball were installed. The water project was finished! The well-house had a chimney. The pila had a roof to shade the women from the hot sun, and all was working. Now that they could buy tax-free gasoline for just Q0.15 a gallon, they had only run out of gas a few times. There were even water pipes to the school and to the municipal offices. I talked to dozens of people, gave them an update on Marge, and after a few hours drove off feeling much better about my twenty-month effort.

Chugging Home

Back in Guatemala City, I decided to sell the old Beetle which was in rough shape. It survived the 1800-mile trip from Panama, needed at least $300 in repairs, had over 130,000 miles and many of those had been brutal. The Pan American Highway might sound great but much of it was gravel, peppered with nasty potholes, and I had hit a lot of them. With help from the PC Secretary, I soon found a buyer, a lawyer, and we agreed on the price of $225. The only part of the sale that made me unhappy was that I forgot my Peace Corps Medical Kit underneath the front seat. It was a small aluminum suitcase and had a lot of medicines in it. Like I heard and repeated many times, "You gotta' expect losses."

Over the last three months, the brown dye started to fade and turned my shaggy hair a bit blotchy, but a short haircut before my flight home solved the problem.

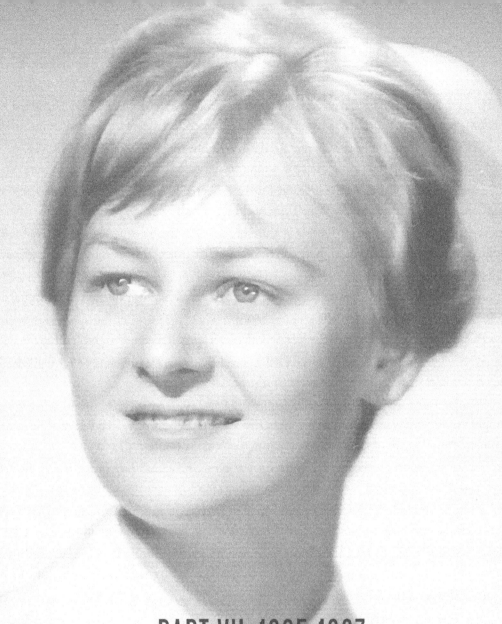

PART VII. 1965-1967

AT THE INFIRMARY

127. AN EVENTFUL REUNION IN MADISON

IT WAS NOW DECEMBER 1, 1965, and I was almost home. Dad and Mom picked me up at the new Dane County Regional Airport in Madison. The main entrance and the new terminal, unbeknownst to me, were moved from the east side along Highway 51 to the west side of the airport. As we departed, I said to Dad, "Aren't you going the wrong way?" A few miles later, when we were on the beltline closer to home, I was on the lookout for the Gilbert Road exit. Everything was new and different as we turned onto Whitney Way. I was glad I wasn't driving.

On Sunday, I was hoping to see Donna at church, so I sat in the balcony to have an overview of the congregation. I looked down and there she was on the left aisle. As soon as the service was over, I quickly ran down the stairs, but she was gone. How was that possible? Once again, I had to make some phone calls to see when she worked. Later in the day, I drove over to the UW Hospital and found her at the student infirmary. She seemed happy to see me. The other nurses quickly realized what was happening. They had heard the story about how I had ditched her and run off to the Peace Corps, so they let her off several hours early. They knew she wouldn't be much use after that anyway. We then drove to my house where we talked for the next few hours.

For the next three weeks, Donna and I kept seeing each other whenever she wasn't working. Every night we would stay up late and every night she wouldn't get enough sleep. Meanwhile I wasn't doing much of anything except sleeping and loafing around the house.

After a week, Mom started urging me to get a job. "You could bag groceries at the A&P grocery store," she suggested more than once. But I stood firm. I wasn't even going to look. "Mom," I responded in jest, "I haven't been home in two years and now you don't want to see me? And who would hire me for less than two weeks?" Since she knew I had to be at AIFT in Glendale, Arizona, in early January 1966, she finally relented. Donna and I continued to see each other at every possible moment and by the time I flew off to the sunny Southwest, she was so run down she got a terrible cold.

128. GRADUATE SCHOOL

GLENDALE, ARIZONA WAS A SMALL RURAL OUTPOST on the edge of Phoenix. Nothing much was there so I spent most of my time on the small campus. It had been the site of a WWII airbase called Thunderbird Field No. 1, which opened in 1941. The swimming pool was in the center of a rectangular grassy area surrounded by buildings and classrooms. The dorms were just beyond but close to the dining hall and classrooms. The campus was surrounded by desert.

The school was chartered in 1946 and 98% of the first students were on the G.I. Bill. It was the first graduate school to train students in global business. When I attended, the school only offered a bachelor's degree which they said was equivalent to a Masters. During my second semester, they began to implement a true master's degree program, which later required a second year of classes. By 1975, nine years after I left, they only offered a Master's. The school's name has since changed several times and is now the Thunderbird School of Global Management. In 2013 big changes were made. It was relocated from Glendale to downtown Phoenix and became a unit of Arizona State University.

I signed in, paid my fees of just $445, and thanks to my Peace Corps Scholarship, saved $765. There were four of us in a good-sized room and we each had a desk in an adjoining room. The bathroom had two showers and four sinks.

The three-part curriculum consisted of language training, business, and area studies. I took 18 credits the first semester, including 9 credits of Spanish (conversation, grammar, and commercial correspondence), Latin American area studies and a variety of business, marketing, and accounting classes. The second semester, I switched to Portuguese, but that proved to be a waste of effort as I never heard or spoke it again. In one business class, we spent quite a bit of time learning about Bills of Lading, a shipping document, and all its legalities. All the business teachers came from the business world and were not academics. The school seemed proud of that.

All 350 students were male except for a few spouses and two single girls. There were quite a few students from Latin America and one of them, Blas Caceres, was a Cuban who had been in the Bay of Pigs invasion. After that botched attempt to overthrow Fidel Castro, he absolutely hated President Kennedy, who had promised them air support but then withdrew it at the most inopportune time. After being in the Peace Corps, where almost everyone except me joined because of their love for President Kennedy, this was a totally different view. Kennedy eventually apologized over his Cuban miscalculation.

The old asphalt runways out back were covered with weeds and grass about 3' high and were ideal habitat for jack rabbits. For our night entertainment, using Joe Thompson's white, convertible Impala, we drove through the weeds, with lights on bright, until we kicked up a rabbit. Then the fun started as we twisted and turned trying to follow those sneaky hares as they zig-zagged and leaped high in the air trying to escape. We never caught one. It was the chase that mattered.

Throughout the semester, Donna and I regularly talked on the phone. I'd call collect, of course, because otherwise I'd spend too much time plugging a pile of quarters into the pay phone every few minutes. One night I called just before her mom and dad left for a Sunday night church service and when they got home, we were still talking. That was over the top and Donna got stuck with the $200 phone bill. Maybe her dad thought Donna should pay because he feared she would eventually marry someone who he thought believed in evolution. He knew I had been a Biology major.

One of my roommates, Joe Thompson, lived in Champaign, Illinois, and was kind enough to drive me home to Wisconsin at the end of the semester. On the way, we stopped at RMBL, just north of Crested Butte, where you'll recall, I spent the summer in 1961. RMBL and Gothic still looked about the same, except now there was an outside staircase to get to the second floor of our old abode. As Joe tried to drive across a stream, just past the biological station, his big Impala got stuck. I was worried. It seemed unlikely any cars would come by at 4:00 in the afternoon because we were at the end of the road. What would we do? After a few minutes, while we were pondering our situation, I could hear a truck heading down the road toward civilization. I ran out and flagged down the driver. No problem. He pulled us out in no time, and we were soon on our way back toward Crested Butte and civilization.

129. GETTING SERIOUS

I GOT A CONSTRUCTION JOB during the summer of 1966 building the foundation of the new Wisconsin State Taxation building out on University Avenue near Segoe Road. It was a hot, tough job, and I earned union wages. I stayed at Dad and Mom's new house at 6007 Schroeder Road, later changed to 80 White Oaks, and was able to drive Donna's Honda 50 motorcycle to and from work. Donna was still an RN at the UW hospital student infirmary and we saw each other as much as possible.

On the last Saturday morning in June, Donna and I picked strawberries. While driving home and knowing that Mom and Dad loved fresh strawberry shortcake, we decided, on the spur of the moment, to tell them that we had just gotten engaged in the strawberry patch. What could be more romantic? Of course, getting a ring never occurred to me. I had never seen any TV ads showing engagement rings. Donna didn't mention it either, but a month later when we decided to get married, she was much more insistent. Maybe she thought a ring would tie me down after my two-year escapade.

After we decided to get married, Donna and her mom had just one month to plan the wedding. It was to be on September 2, 1966, just five days before I had to be back at AIFT. A few days later, Dad asked me, "What's your hurry to get married?" I had heard this kind of comment before, so I asked, "Dad, how old were you when you got married?" Dad was 24. I was now 26.

Almost 25

Mom and Dad had been hoping that I would make an excellent choice. And I did. It might not have always been obvious, but I did know what kind of wife I wanted. Mom and Dad, by their comments over the years, made sure I had thought of that. I even had a written list of my own requirements. How romantic was that? Mom, however, had another suggestion which shocked us all. "If you really want to find out how your future wife will be, take her camping." That went against everything I had ever been taught and believed was the right thing to do. I never was sure if she meant it.

Donna and I decided to have our wedding rings made by a local artist, recommended by Mary, who had a small shop on State Street in downtown Madison. In the meantime, I was still working construction, now helping to build a school in McFarland. Just a few days before our fingers were to be measured, I had the job of carrying 44-pound cement blocks, two at a time, to the masons who were standing on scaffolding making a school wall. After carrying blocks almost all morning, I began to wonder how long I could keep it up. I made it to lunch as we sat under a tree, hot and tired, eating our sandwiches. One of the full-time laborers said to me, "How come so many flies are buzzing around you?" I quickly replied, "That's because they think I smell like a flower." After a minute went by, he said, "Awh, flies don't like flowers." By the time lunch was over, my shoulders, arms, wrists, and fingers started swelling up and I started turning into "the incredible hulk." Later in the day, I could hold the blocks above my head to show off. That was the only day I lugged cement blocks, but I stayed puffed up for several weeks. When my ring finger was measured, the artist said, "I have never made a ring this large." Six months later, however, it was almost falling off my finger and I had to return and have him cut out a chunk of the valuable white gold.

In the meantime, Donna had thought about making a wedding dress but finally ended up at Yosts, a fancy women's store on State Street. She tried on several dresses before spotting one in the display window. Just what she wanted, and it fit perfectly — for $25.

Brother Paul was my best man and Tim Kraft, one of my Peace Corps travelling companions, agreed to be my groomsman. I was all set for the wedding rehearsal on Friday night at the First Reformed Church in Friesland, Wisconsin. On the way, Tim and I made a quick stop to pick a handful of flowers from a nearby neighbor's front yard as we proceeded on to the church. I'm sure those neighbors never saw me, but Donna was a little shocked and probably noticed that I had arrived in body only. I was nervous and acted a bit silly. Anyway, I somehow got through the rehearsal and would need a day to calm down. After that experience, I highly recommend a run through before the big day.

When the wedding day arrived, the weather was beautiful but then suddenly at 5:00 p.m. a wild and wooly rainstorm came blasting over the corn fields. It quickly passed, and before 7:00, it was sunny again. Jay Jackson, another PCV from our group, showed up, so I enlisted him as an usher. The church was filled with over 150 guests and the service was conducted by Rev. Pyle. Paul, Tim, and I entered from the side and waited. I had on my old black suit, Paul wore his dark blue suit and Tim had a dark brown suit. Nobody noticed. I didn't either until I saw the photos. Next, sister June, who was Donna's bridesmaid, walked down the aisle followed by Ruth Householder, her Maid of Honor and nursing school classmate. Then Mendelssohn's "Wedding March" started and Donna came into view. Everyone was standing and Donna was beautiful and radiant with a huge smile as she walked up the aisle with her dad. Aunt Ruth De Young sang a solo, we said our vows, I kissed the bride, turned around and we joyfully walked down the aisle. My dad said he had never seen a happier bride. The only person I missed was my sister Mary, who was confined to the sanitarium in Madison recovering from tuberculosis, which she had probably contracted during her second year in Germany.

The reception followed immediately in the church basement and was prepared by the church ladies. Ham sandwiches, 24-hour grape salad, and potato salad were some of the staples. Tim had wanted to spike the punch, but I talked him out of it a day earlier, explaining that there would be way too many church ladies around. When there weren't, Tim fretted "I could have done it." Donna would have been horrified.

At the end of the reception, Donna broke a long-standing church tradition. Until this day, the church ladies opened all the wedding gifts and spread them out on a table in front of all the guests. Some attendees, no doubt, were surprised or maybe even disappointed that they couldn't compare what they had given to all the others. Donna, however, was relieved as we drove off to the nearby town of Columbus where we spent the night.

The Big Day, September 2, 1966

The next day at Mom and Dad's house, we packed Donna's 4-cylinder, 1967 Corvair, which according to Ralph Nader, was "Unsafe at any Speed." It suited us and was a sleek-looking car. It could even go 80 mph. After I tied Donna's Honda 50 motorcycle to the top of the car, we were ready to start our 2000-mile trip. To save money, I planned to camp along the way. At 5:30 in the morning, I'd say, "Let's hurry, it's already 6:30." That way we could get things going on time. Cooking bacon and eggs over a fire was just too much trouble, especially with a new bride who had never camped before in her life. To make matters worse, after four long days, we spent the night in a dumpy $6 motel. Although that was more than I was accustomed to pay, it was a bit later when I first heard her dad's motto, "It only costs a little more to go first class." I didn't know it then but have been reminded of it many times since. In fact, I have even started saying it myself.

130. GLENDALE, ARIZONA

AFTER WE ARRIVED AT AIFT, Donna got a job as an RN in a Phoenix hospital for $4.78 per hour. That was the going rate and was enough, along with my summer's savings, to get through my final semester. School was going well, we lived in a new motel-style dormitory and Donna and I got along great. One night, however, was an exception. Joe Thompson and I went out to play pool in a local bar and we didn't get back until after midnight, a half hour after Donna.

Since she didn't have a key, she was not a happy camper. Luckily for me, her dad had given her some excellent advice. Before we left for Arizona, he said, "Donna, come home whenever you want but make sure John comes with you."

During my second semester, everyone who would graduate in January was busy writing their resumes, interviewing when company representatives came to campus, and deciding where and what they wanted to do. Naturally, I was doing the same thing, although I didn't have any interest in working for some company. I interviewed with one, but it soon became obvious that neither one of us had any interest in the other. I was only considering CARE and the Peace Corps and CARE was my first choice. I knew quite a bit about what they did and admired the people who had worked in Guatemala. I had a bunch of resumes printed but only mailed two of them, one to CARE headquarters in New York City and one to Peace Corps in Washington, D.C.

131. OUR CALIFORNIA HONEYMOON

DONNA AND I HAD OUR FIRST VACATION, or as I call it, our honeymoon over our two-week Christmas break, We first drove to San Diego, California, where we visited one of Donna's nursing school classmates, Carol Gehl, and her husband Jerry who was doing a residency in psychiatry. In the harbor, we saw a huge aircraft carrier before we headed up the coast to visit former PCV Dave Siebert, who had traveled with me to Colombia, the same Dave who lost his wingtip shoe in Cali. He was married, taught school in La Jolla and loved to surf. We had a great time reminiscing before heading up Highway 1 to the Hearst Castle and finally to San Francisco. There we met two more PCVs from our Guatemala III group, Steve Haas, and his bride, Orie Reich. We crossed the Golden Gate Bridge, drove on to Napa Valley, visited a winery and even bought a couple half bottles for the first time in our lives. We then drove past Sacramento on a beautiful new highway that wound through the mountains to Lake Tahoe where we spent Christmas Eve in a hotel overlooking the lake. Since the heat was turned off, they gave us a small heater for the room. I was going to hang up my stocking but discovered my new bride had never done that. Really? No Santa Claus? As kids, we loved hanging up our stockings over the fireplace. Donna would have been in church with her family. Instead I took a can of shaving cream and drew a Christmas tree on the big picture window overlooking the lake. It soon started to sag but we enjoyed the evening. Maybe we even had a little sip of that Napa Valley wine.

We then headed south to Yosemite National Park. Since most everything was closed for the winter, we continued driving toward the Park just as it started snowing. By the time we got near the entrance, it was dark, and the snow was coming down hard. With no rangers on duty, we drove straight past the toll booth. After a couple miles, we could barely see where we were going as the snow was getting heavier. Concerned that we might drive off the edge and roll down the steep hillside, we turned around and headed back to the entrance where there were lighted and open bathrooms.

Our 1967 Corvair had a back seat that folded down into a small bed. After reassuring Donna that we weren't going to freeze to death, we ate some snacks, crawled into our sleeping bags and had a decent night's sleep. The next morning about six, we were awakened by a snowplow as it drove past the toll booth and into the park. It was a beautiful sunny day with four inches of pristine white snow covering the glistening pines. Deer stood silently watching us pass by.

In Yosemite Valley, we were surprised to see more people than we expected. As we drove slowly past a campground, a black bear wandered down the path right behind a little girl who looked about three years old. When she turned around and screamed, the bear ran off to our relief. We admired El Capitan and visited the gift shop where we purchased an original, signed, black and white photo taken by Ansel Adams. It was a perfect picture of the snow-covered landscape that we had just seen.

We continued to Sequoia National Park and marveled at the huge trees. At Lake Mead we camped next to Dave Siebert, and then drove on to Hoover Dam and Las Vegas, where we won $2.40 at the slot machines — just enough to call home. After that, we drove on to Socorro, New Mexico, and visited Marge Bradbury, who you'll remember was my Peace Corps partner in San Pedro Ayampuc. She lived in a small adobe home not so different from the ones in San Pedro Ayampuc. Sadly, she died in 1972 at the age of 73.

Back at AIFT, I was still waiting for a response from CARE-NY and was getting worried I would be a graduate without a job. I called Waldo Tibbetts, who was now in the CARE New York office after serving as the CARE Director in Guatemala when I was there. I explained that I had sent in my resume, but so far had not received a response. It felt as if we had an argument on the phone, and I certainly had no idea that CARE was receiving almost 200 resumes a week from people wanting to work overseas. Mr. Tibbetts promised he would call back.

In an unbelievable coincidence of perfect timing, Keni Kent, my CARE-Peace Corps boss in Guatemala, just happened to be in the New York office the same week I called. I had no idea, until many years later, that he had left Malaysia and was in the process of resigning from CARE. Fortunately, Keni said some sufficiently favorable words about me, so Mr. Tibbetts called back and hired me over the phone. I was to join a new training class of about ten new recruits in early January 1967. That meant I would have to leave AIFT a few days before the graduation ceremony but that was no problem. Things were now moving fast. I finished my exams, Donna quit her nursing job, we packed our bags, tied the Honda 50 on top of the Corvair and headed to Wisconsin.

132. NEW YORK, NY

WE FLEW TO NEW YORK, took a taxi to the Tudor hotel at 42nd and 2nd, and walked to the CARE headquarters at 660 First Avenue. Nine out of ten of us in the class were former PCVs, including Jay Jackson, who had attended our wedding. For three weeks we studied CARE's, administrative and accounting manuals, and learned the importance of spending every dollar wisely. CARE's money was all donated and not even a pencil was ever to be wasted. Just 3% was used for administration.

CARE started in 1945 to send food relief to Europe after WWII. The first CARE Package was delivered in Le Havre, France on May 11, 1946, one of 15,000 packages that were surplus "10-in-1" food parcels which provided one meal for ten soldiers. Soon CARE began to assemble their own $10 packages, which usually contained powdered milk, flour, sugar, coffee, macaroni, soap, diapers, toothpaste, school supplies, medicine, even fabric, and thread and needles to mend clothes.

In the early years, CARE received over 40 million dollars per year in small cash donations. Dozens of employees counted the bills, stacked them on windowsills, or wherever there was space. As the Cold War ignited, CARE also came to the rescue of the West Berliners in 1948, by providing over 250,000 packages, airlifted during the Soviet blockade. The program quickly expanded to Latin America and Asia in the 1950s. Years later I occasionally met Europeans who had received some of the 100 million packages. Their stories were sometimes tear-jerking, and they were all extremely grateful. They felt the packages had saved their lives.

At the end of our training class, the Head of Overseas Operations, Bert Smucker, handed out our country assignments. I was assigned to Colombia, where they just suffered through an earthquake. I was pleased. It sounded better than Bangladesh, India, or Liberia.

PART VIII, 1967-1985

WHERE WE WERE WHEN

133. OFF TO COLOMBIA

AFTER THREE WEEKS IN NEW YORK CITY, where the January weather was sunny and up to 69 degrees, Donna and I flew to Madison, just missing a 10-inch snowfall that blasted New York. We packed our wedding gifts and belongings, ordered appliances and before long the Mayflower Moving Company shipped them to Colombia.

In the meantime, Donna had transferred the title of the Corvair into my name, which seemed totally unnecessary to me. When I asked, "Why didn't you transfer the Honda motorcycle to me at the same time?" she replied, "No, that's mine." Before we left, she sold it to a farmer in Friesland and my dad bought the car.

After a tearful goodbye at the airport, we boarded our first flight to Chicago. Somewhere over Kentucky, Donna finally recovered from her goodbyes as we flew to Miami and then Panama for the night. We arrived in Bogota, the big, busy capital city of Colombia, on February 20, 1967.

The Assistant CARE Director, Ron Burkhard, and Vance Austin, our family friend from Madison, who now worked for USAID promoting agricultural cooperatives, met us at the airport. Mr. Austin also knew some of the bigwigs on the CARE Board of Directors and had written a letter on my behalf before I got the job with CARE, so we were elated to see him and his wife Dorothy. We then met the Director, Allen Turnbull, and had a short day of orientation. We'd be living in Ibague, a city of over 100,000 and the capital of Tolima, Southwest of Bogota. I'd also be responsible for the office in Neiva in the province of Huila, 200 miles south of Ibague. Next, Donna and I took a taxi to Ibague. It was a wild four-hour, 138-mile drive down a twisting, two-lane paved road from cool Bogota to the more tropical lowland, before rising a little to Ibague. We first went to the CARE-Ibague office and adjoining warehouse.

The local employees were all very friendly and the secretary could even speak excellent English. I noticed that the huge stacks of flour were full of little beetles and there was ample evidence of rodents. In fact, while we were standing there talking, a rat ran across the floor and I chased it into the bathroom where it jumped up into the toilet bowl and disappeared down the hole. That was a new experience. I knew I had a problem.

Just Relaxing

Three hours after arriving in Ibague, John Rutten, whom I replaced, drove us to Neiva for a three-day stay. It was a scary ride as we drove along the narrow road at 70 mph, missing pedestrians and sometimes pigs, by just a few feet. Nobody flinched or moved over as we roared past. I couldn't believe it but must admit, within a few weeks I was driving the same crazy way. We met the staff of three, did a physical inventory of the stacks of food, met the Governor of Huila, and attended the local Lions Club farewell dinner for my predecessor while we were welcomed to town.

As we drove around, it was evident that the whole area had been irreparably damaged by the January earthquake. One night we went to a movie, "The Battle of the Bulge," and sat in silence during two brief electrical outages. During the last noisy battle scenes, however, everyone suddenly panicked and bolted from the theater. The few people remaining ducked down in their seats while Donna and I just stood there, at first unaware there had even been an earthquake. We then looked up at the high ceiling, wondered if it would fall on our heads, and slowly walked out past the windows the other patrons had broken in their rush to get out.

Back in Ibague I visited some schools that received bread rolls made from the buggy flour. When one kid broke open his roll, I counted five beetles. He just nonchalantly picked them out and that was that. Yes, I was surprised that the kids didn't seem to mind a bit and I thought maybe we wouldn't have to sift all the flour after all. I also visited some health and childcare centers for orphans. The rooms were filled with malnourished kids who were so small they appeared to be babies, but many were several years old. They just lay in their cribs, dirty, wet, and pathetic looking. Some kids looked like little old men with distended bellies and wrinkled faces. When we walked by the older kids, they called us "mama" and "papa" and clung to our legs. It was depressing.

Beauty in the Rubble

We spent the next five days in Bogota for orientation and training and stayed with our old family friends, Vance and Dorothy Austin. They still lived in the "golden ghetto" and treated us royally.

For the next couple months, things at work were going smoothly as I traveled back and forth between the Ibague and Neiva offices. In Neiva, I was able to get a new 15-month contract signed with the Department of Huila and collected 96,000 pesos, with the balance of 96,000 to be paid in July. We also met some interesting people, such as a German coffee buyer, who informed us that the best coffee was exported to Europe because the Americans wouldn't pay top dollar. Our favorite outdoor restaurant roasted whole chickens on a spit. We'd call ahead and a delicious meal would be waiting for us.

My assigned vehicle was an old beat-up Jeep Wagoneer that had a lot of problems. When I mentioned this to the bosses, they were surprised and said no accident reports had ever been filled out. I then found out that on several occasions, my predecessor had paid for the repairs himself to cover up his alcohol induced accidents.

We rented a small two-bedroom apartment on the fifth floor of a nine-story building in downtown Ibague. Our rent was $66 per month, paid in pesos, which was inexpensive considering that my daily per diem was $18 per day, also paid in local currency. A loaf of bread cost $0.12, two lemons $0.01, a huge avocado $0.04, a restaurant meal cost $0.60 to $1.50, and a haircut $0.25. My dollar salary, paid by CARE in New York, was $3500 per year. It wasn't much but Social Security taxes were not taken out of salaries above that amount. In total I received $10,400, which was one of the highest salaries of anyone who graduated from AIFT. I felt rich.

From our balcony we not only had a beautiful view of the valley but could also see the effects of the recent earthquake. Huge cracks, several inches wide, were visible up and down the concrete sides of many of the taller downtown buildings. Although it looked dangerous to me, they were all still occupied as if nothing had happened. Several of the old colonial churches had completely collapsed. We rented some basic furniture and bought some cheap dorm-style mattresses, which we put on the floor until our personal belongings arrived. We soon discovered that they were full of bedbugs and did our unsuccessful best to get rid of them. Another issue was cockroaches. They were everywhere, in the oven, on the counters, even inside a plastic bag that Donna had supposedly sealed. I even saw the antennas of one poking through an electrical outlet. Although we killed at least a dozen of them every night, it was obvious the infestation would never end because everyone dumped their garbage down an open chute from the top floor to the first. I put up some screens, puttied over some cracks and continued to use insecticides which made some difference, but since our front door was open above to the outside hall, they could enter at will. Fortunately, the weather was great. We weren't too far north of the equator.

The beautiful weather, however, didn't make Donna's life a whole lot better. People pointed and stared as she seemed to be the only blonde in town. Nobody seemed to speak any English, and there were no grocery stores where she could pick out what she wanted. Instead she had to point at every item, over the counter, using her rudimentary Spanish, and hope the clerk would give her what she wanted. She used a little English-Spanish dictionary, but since it was from Spain the names of many vegetables and fruits were different.

Donna met some PCVs who asked her to help give smallpox vaccinations at a clinic. Over a two-day period, she scratched the arms of over 200 children who looked dirty, poor, and starved. Like the newly arrived PCVs, she didn't know enough Spanish to keep the kids in line, but she was learning more every day listening to tapes. She was now on lesson six from my class at Thunderbird in Arizona.

We joined the local country club, and a few times enjoyed the pool, tennis courts, and bowling. The first time I bowled, I got a 95 and a 172. That was almost the last time I ever bowled.

One weekend Donna and I drove to Popayan, near the Ecuadorian border and ordered a dining room table, eight chairs and a buffet, as we looked forward to a better day in a different house. From the road to Neiva, we headed west on a two-rut road that resembled a farmer's driveway, across the mountains from Neiva to Cali, a trip that would be impossibly dangerous a few years later because of the drug trade. It was a real adventure as we drove for miles without seeing any other vehicles. In Cali we stayed in the same little hotel where Dave Siebert and I had resided just over three years earlier in 1964 when he lost one of his expensive wingtip shoes. Before we left, I checked my suitcase to make sure that none of mine were missing. It was! I wondered, how many shoes the maid must have by now? I searched the room and found it hidden inside the bedside cabinet and off we went. I should have asked to see her right-shoe collection.

Another time, Vance and Dorothy Austin invited Donna and me to Giradot, a town between Ibague and Bogota. Since we wanted to do some shopping in Bogota, we thought we could do both. In Giradot, we also met up with Director Allen Turnbull and Wally Campbell, Vance's friend, who was on the CARE Board of Directors in New York. Unbeknownst to me, Mr. Turnbull and Vance were having some differences and he was not happy that Vance had also asked us along. Since we were there, Mr. Turnbull felt obligated to invite us to his cocktail party that evening in honor of Wally Campbell. Until then, I had never met Mr. Campbell, but the CARE Director probably preferred to invite only the bigwigs to his party, or maybe he just didn't get along with the Austins. It was a strained affair. A few weeks later, Vance's contract ended, and they returned home.

By the end of my fourth month in Ibague, my accountant and I had some confusion about how to do the monthly petty cash report. Unbeknownst to me, that was the last straw. I had "complained" about the bugs, the rats, the beat-up Jeep and now the petty cash report. A week or so later, I received a letter from Bert Smucker in New York and was shocked to read that I was fired. I had apparently become a troublemaker. No word from my local bosses in Bogota. It was easier to fire the new guy.

Now we had to get rid of a lot of food in our refrigerator. The best way to do that was to invite a bunch of PCVs to dinner. Donna prepared a huge meal, and they ate and ate, just like we used to do in Guatemala when there was free food. We were all so stuffed that Donna wanted to serve dessert a little later, but I knew better. I joked, "No, don't do that because they'll get a second wind and will want to start eating all over again." We then cranked a gallon of ice cream and soon it was all gone. Upon departing, one PCV said, "That was really good. I hope we can do it again sometime." We never did.

We said farewell to our staff, packed our suitcases, drove to Bogota, and said goodbye to Allen Turnbull and Ron Burkhard. The boss said, "You had a bad deal" and "It was a communications breakdown" and they actually seemed sorry I was leaving. Are you kidding me? Now I had no choice. I'd have to go to New York after I got home. At 5:15 p.m. we boarded the plane to Panama. Our order of furniture from Popayan would be shipped later and our shipment from the U.S. would be diverted back home. Donna was probably happy. I never asked her.

For the next ten days we flew to Guatemala and Mexico where we had a great vacation visiting many of the places I had seen as a PCV. Soon we were home.

134. NOW WHAT?

WE HAD A JOYFUL REUNION in Madison with our parents, brothers, sisters and their kids. But after a week or so at home, I became more and more irritated with how my firing had transpired. Vera Neff, a friend of my parents from church, reinforced my earlier idea by suggesting I write a report stating, "what I had found upon my arrival and what I did to solve the problems." She said I should then tell

David, Jennifer, Eric, Elaine & Paul McLeod, August 1967

them that I still want to work for CARE. So, I did. I wrote a three-page report that detailed all I had done, such as getting rid of insects and rats, starting a new inventory system, and collecting money owed to CARE by the provincial governments. Then I flew to New York, made my case to Mr. Smucker, the Director of Overseas Operations, and was rehired. Easy as that. A month later we would be on our way to Chile. Donna was not overjoyed that she first heard about our new overseas assignment from her mother-in-law, but she was a dutiful wife.

In the meantime, three of us, all former Wisconsin wrestlers, decided to take our wives on a week-long canoe trip to the Canadian boundary waters. We would follow the same route that four of us wrestlers had taken in 1960 when we were led by Coach George Martin. It would be great. And we had a proven easy way to traverse the fifty miles across Rainey Lake. We'd use the same wooden frame to hold two of the three canoes together and Coach Martin's 10HP outboard would do the paddling.

We had all the supplies, dried and canned food, the equipment we needed, and headed north in two full cars. Early the next day at the south end of the lake, we connected two canoes together, dragged the third, and away we went. In just a few hours, our outboard companion pushed us to our first portage. We hid the wooden frame and boat motor in the bushes and proceeded to carry all our gear and canoes over the first rough and overgrown trail. We then reloaded the canoes and started paddling. We still had a long way to go on the second portage when we realized that two wives were suffering from a common monthly condition. Then Steve's wife got stung by a wasp and her lips and cheeks instantly started to swell. It looked serious. I gave her a couple of antihistamine pills that I had kept out of my long-lost Peace Corps medical kit, which quickly reduced her swelling. As we encountered more wasps on the trail, the girls caused quite a ruckus each time. By the end of the fourth portage, which was almost a mile long, they were frazzled, and we still had to paddle to our island destination, make dinner and set up camp. It was grueling — not that easy for a bunch of ex-wrestlers let alone for our wives. We had bitten off more than the girls wanted, but we made it into our tents before the mosquitoes attacked. The woods hummed with them.

The next few days were much better as we caught plenty of Walleyes and Northern Pike and enjoyed the swimming and sunbathing, but all too soon we faced the long trip back. At least a lot of the heavy canned food was gone. We made it, of course, and I even had one antihistamine pill left over. We had a great trip, but it was the last time Donna and I ever went on a real camping trip.

Three years later, Coach Martin, who led our original trip, died on July 11, 1970 in a canoe accident somewhere on the Little Jackfish River near James Bay. His canoe tipped up on end, got sucked into a whirlpool and disappeared. The canoe was later recovered, but sadly, George was never seen again. Coach had given me a lot of confidence which enabled me to make a lot of decisions I might not have otherwise made.

135. STARTING OVER IN CHILE: 1967-1971

OUR LONG TRIP TO SANTIAGO, Chile was now upon us. At the end of August, 1967, we said our goodbyes at the airport and flew to Chicago. Donna cried most of the way because she wouldn't be seeing her family for over two years and didn't know what to expect. By our next flight to Miami, Donna had recovered and started conversing with an older lady across the aisle who asked, "Where are you going?" Donna answered, "To Chile." She replied, "Oh my, that is a long way from home." Yes, it was. To be exact, it was twelve hours in the air and Donna cried all the way to southern Georgia. After Miami, our direct Braniff Airlines flight to Santiago went more peacefully. I was hoping that she would be able to see the gorgeous Andes mountains and the huge snow-covered volcanoes in Chile, but it was cloudy the whole way. That surprise would have to come later.

In 1967, Santiago was a big city of about 700,000, surrounded by snow-capped peaks. It enjoyed a great climate with only 11 inches of rain a year. Chile was over 2600 miles long and no more than 110 miles wide. The northern Atacama Desert hadn't seen rain in over 400 years, the central valley was a rich fruit and wine producing area, the south was filled with beautiful lakes and trout-filled rivers, and the extreme south was rugged and wild all the way to the Straits of Magellan. The Pacific coast had many beautiful beaches but the cold Humboldt current that flowed up from Antarctica discouraged most swimmers. There were even a lot of German blondes and no one could ever tell that we were Americans by just looking. Best of all, especially for Donna, they had huge, modern, well-stocked Almac supermarkets.

The office address, 42 Orego Circle, was on a small cul-de-sac in the area called "Providencia" and was about a ten-minute drive downtown. Director Allan Kline had a Ph.D. in English and the Assistant Director was my old friend, Ron Baker, from Guatemala — the same person who said AIFT was the best school to attend if you wanted a job overseas.

The first few nights we were entertained by the bosses, first Ron and Cecil Baker. Their oldest son, Scott, who was now six, even remembered me. When he was about four, he and Ron visited me in San Pedro Ayampuc and was soon surrounded by about 30 kids, who had never seen a little blond kid. He quickly became the center of attention and soon realized that he must be incredibly special as they surrounded him and touched his hair and skin. After a couple minutes, he started to run around the grassy plaza followed by a mob of his older admirers, which made Ron and me laugh in amazement. This little incident made me think about how the Mexican Aztecs had immediately concluded that Hernando Cortés must be a god when he arrived in 1519. Unbeknownst to Cortés, his arrival coincided with an important Aztec prophecy. The Aztec god, Quetzalcoatl, whom they credited with the creation of humans, was soon expected to return to earth. Cortés was greeted with great honor and the little Baker kid, with great curiosity.

Allan Kline, who had previously taught at Lawrence College in Appleton, Wisconsin was a no-nonsense Director, a bit pompous, fussy and opinionated. A lot of people didn't appreciate his style, but we got along well, and I learned a lot at the same time.

After just three days, the boss wanted me to fly south 660 miles to Puerto Montt, at the end of the Pan American Highway, to audit one of the local Juntas (School Assistance and Scholarship Councils) responsible for distributing CARE food to the schools. There I met one of CARE's school supervisors, José Contreras, who accompanied me. After we completed our first day's work, we went to a restaurant, split a bottle of wine and had some snacks. When we finished, we went to another restaurant, ordered our meal of Congrio, an eel that looked and tasted like fish, plus another bottle of Chilean Cabernet. By the end of dinner, José looked at me and said his first words in English, "I think I'm drunk." Since I was bigger and apparently had a healthier liver, I was fine, even though I had drunk more wine that day than in all my first 27 years.

136. A TWO-PAGE REPORT

MY FIRST OFFICE TASK was to write the Discursive Report which described what had happened the previous six months. Discursive Reports were distributed to all the other CARE countries to keep everyone up to date. I was to talk with everyone, discover what had been accomplished, and write a two-page report. This sounded simple but without any idea of what had happened, it proved to be difficult. Getting information from busy people was more difficult than pulling teeth. After a couple days, I handed my report to Ron. He read it and then completely rewrote it before sending it off to New York for distribution. I had flunked. Six months later the task was much easier when I knew what had happened. After a few years, I realized that I could sit down at the typewriter and write two, well-written pages, in less than a couple hours. This no doubt was partly due to Dr. Allan Kline, the Professor, as he was called. He made us write all the letters to government officials as well as all the letters and reports to CARE-NY. He would then correct them and show us what he had done. When they were just right, he signed them with his fancy ink pen, and they were sent on their way. It reminded me of being in a freshman English class every day.

For the first two months, Donna and I stayed in a furnished third-floor apartment owned by an 86-year-old Scottish lady whom we never met. At $140 per month it was a lot cheaper than the hotel. It was full of formal, English furniture and was quite comfortable, but several mornings we were awakened by earthquakes. They started slowly but kept increasing for a minute or so, until the joints of the building started creaking and the chandeliers were swinging back and forth. One was even a 5.5 on the Richter scale. Just when I started to get concerned, they would stop. This was a common occurrence.

We arrived at the end of summer, which in Chile was the end of winter. It was chilly at night and we even used our sleeping bags for an extra blanket. Each morning I got up an hour early to light a kerosene heater, which I put in the bathroom to warm it up. This worked quite well until one morning when a big cloud of greasy smoke billowed out into the apartment, covering everything with black flecks of soot. I went off to work and Donna got stuck cleaning up the mess. She worked all day and had barely completed her task late in the afternoon when the doorbell rang. It was the landlady's daughter who wanted to see how we were doing. All was in perfect order and I was much more careful lighting the wick the next morning.

On the weekend, Donna and I drove to La Parva, 25 miles or 90 minutes up the mountain. It was the closest ski resort but with the snow gone, it was closed for the season. Just before reaching the first chalets, a stone got kicked up which bent the fan and cut the radiator. It made a terrible noise and steam came pouring out. I thought we were in a real fix but a few minutes later, a man came by and towed us to a garage. There a mechanic bent the fan blade back in shape and plugged the radiator with a bar of "Chilean Soap" so it wouldn't leak so fast. He asked me if I were an American and then said, "I sure don't know how this could have happened." He was from Peru, had married a girl from Massachusetts, and invited us for dinner in their ritzy chalet. On this first exploratory trip, we didn't see much of the resort, but we did meet some great people.

I was sent to Chile to replace another Field Representative, Fred Schields, who was resigning to run a bookstore in Pasco, Washington. I thought that was quite a change. He must like to read. He had married an 18-year-old Chilean girl, Maria Inez, who was taking a driver education class to make it easier for her to get a license in the U.S. One day she asked, "Fred, why are there white lines on the road?" Poor Fred. Did she really not know? That's when I got the best overseas-living advice I ever heard, "Don't assume anything."

137. SOUTHERN CHILE

FOR THE NEXT TWO YEARS it was my job to supervise the school feeding program south of Santiago. In each province I visited the local Junta offices, which were in charge of storing the PL 480 products, such as powdered milk, bulgur wheat, corn-soymilk (CSM) blend, and soy oil, which they then delivered to the schools. I knew how much food they received, subtracted the amounts sent to hundreds of schools and verified all their records. I'd then visit as many schools as I could to check their inventories and records — which luckily were almost always in order. It was a well-run program and we were quite efficient in our supervision.

As part of my management auditing duties, I also travelled to the seaport of Valparaiso, straight west of Santiago. There I met our shipment expediter, Leonard Loxley, an Anglo-Chilean who showed me the ropes. We boarded the cargo ship, the Gulf Banker, owned by Grace Lines, while they were unloading several thousand bags of cornmeal and cases of soy oil. For the first time, some of my classroom studies at AIFT came to life. There I had learned all about Bills of Lading, the main shipping document, which came in handy. At the nearby port of San Antonio we also watched them destroy 2649 bags of flour, unfortunately contaminated by a detergent spill on the ship.

138. MEETING NEW PEOPLE

DONNA WAS INVITED to attend the American Women's Club held at the United Nations building on the first Monday in October 1967. She heard an interesting talk about improving living standards and met some new friends. The Women's Club became a major source of many social activities.

Since joining the PC, going to Guatemala, graduate school and to Colombia, I had only been in church a few times. Shortly after we arrived in Santiago, however, we began attending the Union Church, which was non-denominational and had both English and Spanish services. The English-speaking pastor, Rev. James Thoburn (Toby) Legg, was a short, bearded American about 70, whose father had been a Methodist minister before him. We joined as Associate Members on December 3, 1967. I didn't want to attend every Sunday or get too involved, because I feared someone might ask me

When We Were Young

to do something which might interfere with our weekend travels and activities. After just nine months, however, Pastor Toby asked if I would be interested in serving as an associate deacon. I wasn't.

We soon met a lot of people who worked for USAID and the U.S. Embassy, plus many more expatriates from all over. We had them over frequently for dinners and they did the same. Our friends became our family as we were all in the same boat. We had a busy social life which involved a lot of cooking, eating, and dancing. There were also many superb restaurants where they served all kinds of delicious food, including steaks, chicken with cognac, and all kinds of fresh seafood, such as sea urchins, clams, fish, oysters, shrimp and even shells that could have been barnacles.

At church we met one Embassy couple, Drake and Evie Reid. Evie had even taught at Schenk School in Madison, just as I had with those five ninth-grade biology classes five years earlier. Drake had also gone to summer school at the UW and they had even lived in Colombia, where they met the Austins before being transferred to Chile. They soon became our loyal friends and we were pleased that they offered to import some basic Craftsman hand tools from Sears. At a cocktail party one night, there was an awkward moment when someone asked Evie if Donna was her daughter. She did have several blonde girls.

In the big Almac supermarket, Donna met an English girl, Mary Clark, who invited us over for high tea. We didn't know what that entailed and almost didn't go. Fortunately, we did and discovered that it was a big deal, as Mary had prepared all kinds of fancy foods. Her husband, Roger, worked for Cable West Coast, and was also a ham radio operator. He connected us several times by phone patch to our families who hadn't heard our voices for months. To make the connection, he scanned his radio frequencies until he found another ham operator in the U.S., who in turn located yet another who lived close enough to make a local or collect phone call to Mom and Dad. It was somewhat time consuming and awkward to say much with several people listening in — but it was free. Roger knew a lot about electronics and assembled his own radios from kits. Once he re-assembled our Hamilton Beach blender which I had tried to fix but couldn't put back together. Those little springy carbons just wouldn't stay in place.

John and Lucy Carlson were another young couple who became intimate friends. John worked at the U.S. Embassy and they had three little kids. One day they decided to have dinner for their maid and all the people that depended on her. They were surprised when 23 people showed up and were even more amazed that for just $35 a month, they were supporting so many people.

139. GETTING SETTLED

WE RENTED A SMALL, THREE-BEDROOM HOUSE on Cristina Barros 549 in Las Condes, Santiago, for the reasonable price of $140 that was less than fifteen minutes from the office. It had a small front yard with a ten-foot Blue Spruce and a short wood fence next to the sidewalk. A long row of roses that bloomed all year lined the driveway. We enjoyed our back patio which was great for entertaining since the weather was almost perfect most of the year.

A small dairy at the end of the block provided us with fresh, raw milk. My two-gallon milk pasteurizer kept it tasting fresh for at least ten days. The only downside was seeing a wee bit of manure when we poured out the last glass.

After two months, our shipments of new furniture from Colombia and personal effects and appliances from the U.S. arrived at just the right time. Since the electricity was 220V, we also needed a lot of heavy transformers so our appliances wouldn't burn up. We also bought all new light fixtures since rental houses never included them. That was a surprise, but it was great to be in our own house after living out of suitcases for almost a year. Now we could start entertaining all the people who had been making our first months so enjoyable.

Then we were robbed. As we drove into our driveway, I noticed a sheet of paper on the front lawn that I had left in our bedroom. I walked around to the half-opened back bedroom door and discovered that Donna's jewelry box, which contained a lot of silver jewelry, mostly from Mexico, was gone. Just a few hundred dollars lost. Ron Baker always said, "When you live overseas, you gotta' expect losses." We soon put new locks on the door.

140. DELIVERING DONATIONS

CARE RECEIVED A SHIPMENT of orthopedic medical equipment before Christmas, which I presented to a local hospital where I met Dr. Jorge Tapia. As we sat and talked, I discovered that Dr. Tapia had done his orthopedic residency at the University of Iowa, where I was born. He had even lived in Coralville and gave me an Iowa decal for my car which I never used because I was a Wisconsin Badger fan. He specialized in scoliosis, showed us some X-Rays and his stainless-steel carpentry tools and rods he used in his surgeries. That was something I didn't want to get. We were sometimes invited to their private family club and its beautifully landscaped swimming pool. They even had a bowling alley, a pool table, and a great view of the snow-capped mountains surrounding Santiago.

This was a fortuitous meeting because Donna, by her next birthday on September 7, 1968, had developed a herniated disc which Dr. Tapia treated. He put her in traction at home for about three weeks and visited us several times to see how she was doing. During Donna's convalescence, I had to do all the cooking. I even baked her a birthday cake (from a box) and made chocolate frosting from scratch with Hershey bars, flour, water, butter, and I don't know what else. It took me a long time to get rid of the lumps, but it was tasty.

In early February 1968, Donna and I hopped in my new Chevy II station wagon and drove 575 miles south to deliver a lensometer, donated by the Lion's clubs in Idaho, to the Osorno Lion's Club. Lions clubs in the U.S. collected used eyeglasses and frames which were then sent by CARE to countries around the world. The local Lions used the lensometers to classify the lenses so they could be donated to people who couldn't afford new glasses. Until that moment, I had never heard of this program, but it helped a lot of people.

As we drove south, the weather was perfect. Donna got her first bouquet of Copihues, the national flower of Chile, and for the first time admired the snow-capped mountains and volcanoes that lined the east side of the Pan American Highway. It was a smooth concrete road all the way, and in no way resembled the miserable gravel roads in Costa Rica and Panama.

Selling Copihues, the National Flower of Chile

At the Lion's Club, we presented the lensometer at a formal meeting with members and their wives. It was the first time I ever had to give a short presentation speech in Spanish and of course our pictures were on the front page of the newspaper. Donna also did her best to communicate and I was impressed that she could always find someone who spoke English. Just stand around, be blonde and pretty, and someone will come to your rescue. In this case, several ladies did.

The next day, the eye doctor gave us a tour of the old hospital. It was depressing to see the poor, dirty conditions, and some malnourished kids. Bed sheets were spread on the grass to dry because the clothes dryer had broken and there was a lack of modern equipment. To our delight, the doctor took us out to eat and we had a delicious seafood dinner of clams, crabs, oysters, barnacles and things we had never seen. The Chileans we met were always extremely helpful and friendly.

A month later I presented another lensometer to the Lions Club in Concepción, about a seven-hour drive south. At least I knew more about the program than I had the first time in Osorno. The president of the club was impressed with my speech and pronunciation which, I did not confess, was mostly written by the CARE secretary. It was rewarding to visit the eye clinic where Donna and I placed new, free glasses on the faces of about 75 kids. As soon as they realized how much better they could see, they broke out in huge smiles.

After meeting one of the Lion's Club members at his optical shop, we were invited out to dinner by another member, Mr. Sweet, and his wife. He was the U.S. Consul and they had been living in Chile for forty years. This was followed by another delicious seafood dinner with five other couples. We met a lot of great people who were grateful for the help they received through CARE.

On this two-week trip, I also did a lot of regular inspection work at the Junta offices and schools, where I reviewed the books listing the amounts of CARE food received and distributed. Donna and I both loved to take such trips and explore the beautiful southern half of the country. There we had time to see the picturesque lakes and volcanoes that I had seen two years earlier on my post-Peace Corps adventure.

Unloading the Fishing Boats in Puerto Montt

In Puerto Montt, Donna and I walked down to the seashore early one morning when the fishing boats were unloading to sell their catches. As I took a movie of one vendor selling *picorocos*, which looked like long barnacles, he offered one to Donna. She couldn't refuse. With fear and trepidation, she took hold of its beak, pushed it down to break it free from its cone-shaped shell, and lifted out a five-inch glob of pure white meat. Taking a bite, the expression on her face turned to a broad smile as she tasted the delicious, fresh delicacy. I would try some later in a restaurant. I was glad she had gone first.

When travelling even to the rural areas, on orders from the boss, I always wore a sport coat and tie. Dr. Kline insisted we had to "look the part." This was no problem on the paved highways, but the side roads were another story. With months of no rain, the gravel and dirt roads were covered with an inch or two of powdered dust. We had to keep the windows closed but then we cooked from the heat. I finally learned to open the front air vents, which increased the air pressure inside the car. That helped keep out some of the dust but with no air conditioning, it was miserable, and the back window was coated with a half inch of dust. Luckily, there was a new National Hotel chain (HONSA) in all the bigger towns so we usually had great places to stay and eat.

141. TV, A KITTEN AND WINE

BEFORE LONG, WE GOT A SMALL BLACK AND WHITE TV. Most of the programming came from the U.S., dubbed in Spanish except for Dean Martin and the Three Stooges. After watching the soaps for a few months, Donna could understand quite a bit. I was amazed. Understanding the plot of those local soaps was more than I could do. She wasn't afraid to make mistakes like I was and got along quite well despite her unusual grammar.

Cranking Ice Cream with Mom and Samantha

After seven months in Chile, Donna found a Siamese kitten, which she had wanted ever since we arrived. We had to choose carefully because the breeding stock was so isolated and inbred, many of them had stubby tails. The one we bought for $27 was fine but I thought we were crazy to pay such an exorbitant sum for a cat. I was amazed that our new kitten, Samantha, was so quick that she could trap flies with her paw against the glass windows. The little geckos that got in the house never had a chance either. In Thailand, Siamese cats were used as watch dogs, a behavior I once observed when our cat clawed at the window trying to get at our new gardener as he walked around the side of the house. Samantha loved to tear down the hall, leap up on top of our new leather easy chair and dig in her claws to keep from smashing into the front window. We later reupholstered the chair with vinyl, partly because the maroon dye used on the leather rubbed off on our clothes.

Chile was well-known for its high-quality wines and it was always interesting to visit the huge wineries. One of the biggest and closest to Santiago was the "Concha y Toro" winery. The wine was stored in huge 25,000-gallon barrels lined up in the cellar, where they had about 7,000,000 gallons in storage. We also visited an even higher-quality winery, "Macul," which was preferred by our rich Chilean friends, the Tapias. It cost about $1.00 for a bottle. Chile also exported a lot of bulk wine to France, which was a big surprise to me. The French would then label the wine as their own which greatly irritated the Chileans.

After Martin Luther King was killed on April 4, 1968, we attended a memorial service and listened to U.S. Ambassador Edward Korry give a eulogy. He spoke in general terms, almost without mentioning MLK, and we weren't too impressed. Just two months later, Robert F. Kennedy was killed. The Chileans asked, "What is wrong with Americans?"

Our only source of news was Time Magazine and the Miami Herald Tribune, which arrived daily. Back then the news didn't seem so biased, but every time I had first-hand knowledge of a story,

I found that the news reporting was wrong or incomplete. Before long I even began to cheer for quarterback Dan Marino and the Miami Dolphins. That's how biased it was.

142. FEELING SECURE

IT DIDN'T TAKE LONG for us to be thoroughly acclimated to Chile. Donna canned over two bushels of tomatoes, 14 quarts of peaches and 31 pints of pickles. I guess she thought my job was secure. I dug up the whole backyard, planted grass and a lot of flowers we got from the Bakers, who had been transferred to Costa Rica. I would miss my friend, Ron, who was replaced by Russ Christianson. Our busy social life included dinners, movies, and dances, while my constant travelling schedule seemed in many ways to be a vacation. Donna always went with me and our trips often lasted over two weeks. When travelling, we ate in restaurants, which was more expensive but we still managed to save a few hundred dollars every month when we didn't buy too much for the house — such as a kerosene space heater to fend off the cold winter evenings.

143. GOING ON VACATION

IN THE MIDDLE OF WINTER, at the end of July, Allan Kline signed a new annual agreement with the Chilean government so we wouldn't be unemployed. He also told me I could leave on a two-week vacation to Lima, Cusco, Machu Picchu and La Paz, as I was looking forward to showing Donna some of the sights, I had seen on my PC adventure. After scrambling to get visas and tickets, we flew to Lima. When we checked into the hotel, I was surprised when the clerk asked, "How long have you lived in Chile?" I guess I had a Chilean accent. That seemed way better than having a gringo accent.

We wandered around Lima for three days seeing the sights and then flew east to Cusco, that

Stocking Up on Fresh Fruit & Vegetables

very picturesque Spanish city at an elevation of 11,500 feet. I never was bothered by high-elevation headaches, but Donna woke up with a doozie and didn't want to take the train to Machu Picchu. She agreed to go only after I told her Machu Picchu was 3000' lower. As we rumbled down the train tracks, sure enough, her headache dissipated. When we arrived at the station below the ruins, a taxi took us up the switchbacks to the top. Just as

I had done at my first sight of Machu Picchu, Donna marveled at the huge rocks that fit together so tightly, it seemed impossible for humans to have done the work. This was a trip everyone should take in their lifetime and I was happy to see it for the second time.

From Cusco we took the train south to Lake Titicaca and then crossed it by boat. In La Paz, we met some friends-of-friends and enjoyed dinner at their house. Afterwards Donna excused herself, but then we found her 20 minutes later lying on the tile floor, recovering from too big a dinner combined with the extreme elevation. She was okay and we were relieved. The next day we enjoyed a day trip by taxi down to the jungle where breathing was much easier. With the help of friends, we explored La Paz before flying back to Santiago. We purchased jewelry, alpaca sweaters and alpaca and vicuña rugs, as well as a piece of tooled Peruvian leather for a coffee tabletop that we later had made in Santiago.

During these few months, Donna's brother-in-law, Fred Vorlop, got a job as Principal of Delavan high school. Another brother-in-law, Chuck Dykstra, was cutting hair at his Cambria barber shop. Margie had her first daughter, Kristin. Mary's husband, Louis Barbash, got a job in Austin, Texas, with the Federal Equal Employment Opportunity Commission, while Mary continued teaching German and ballet at St. Edward's University. Paul was an OB/GYN doctor at Jackson Clinic in Madison. Dad got another big CUNA job, kept busy landscaping around their new house, while Mom was hooking a 10'x14' rug for their living room.

144. MOUNTAIN OYSTERS

ON NOVEMBER 26, 1968, Donna and I departed on a three-week work trip to the far south of Chile. First, we drove 660 miles to Puerto Montt and then took the ferry to and from Chiloe, the big island just south of Puerto Montt. From there, we flew to several small, isolated outposts including Chile Chico, Aysen, and Coyhaique. The Junta employees were quite surprised to see me so far from home, but I found the school feeding program to be well run.

In Chile Chico, we met a sheep rancher who invited us to his ranch. He had thousands of sheep and on this day had a team of men organized to castrate 700 lambs. It was quite a process. One man, called the "technician," was the only one who did the deed. He had a small knife to cut the sack, next pulled out the testicles, then buried his face between its hind legs and stripped the vas deferens with his teeth which reduced bleeding. After several hours had passed, his face was completely caked with blood and sheep excrement, and the whites of his eyes and teeth were the only parts of his face you could see. He was, however, clearly admired for his speed and skill. That evening, there was a feast of roast lamb and plenty of mountain oysters. Nobody noticed that I avoided this once-a-year delicacy. That technician had quite a job. Back in high school, nobody ever told me about such job opportunities.

Towards the end of our trip to Coyhaique, I met the burly fisherman whose photo was on all the tourist posters holding up a string of huge trout. We started to talk about fishing together when he asked, "How many yards of line do you have on your reel?" I said, "About 100." He responded, "That's not enough. What are you going to do if a 44-pound trout runs for 150 yards?" I wasn't prepared for that question and declined the invite because I still had too much work to do. I also knew we were getting low on money and couldn't afford to delay our trip. A credit card would have been useful, but I didn't have one and never met anyone who did. Not fishing that day was an opportunity lost, but for being so conscientious about the work I had yet to do on that trip, it's no wonder I got an encouraging evaluation afterwards. I must admit, however, the boss had more to say: It boiled down to, "Act seriously." To be a heavyweight you must act seriously but that is something I never was able to sustain. I worked hard, got others to do the same, but I couldn't walk around looking serious. Luckily, my position and being an American overseas enabled me to maintain authority.

After another day of work, we boarded a DC 3 and headed back to Puerto Montt. After 20 minutes of climbing, my eyes flashed to the right as I thought something flew past the window. It was the right propeller. The pilot instantly did a U-turn and headed back to the small runway. Without deicer's, he didn't dare risk going over the mountains with only one prop. With the delay, my money situation was getting more serious and I wondered, "How long will we be stuck here?" To save a little money that night, we bought a loaf of bread and some cheese and ate dinner in our room. Then about 9:00 p.m., the hotel bellboy knocked on our door holding up a big trout and asked, "Your fishing guide wants to know if you'd like this for supper?" "Yes," I said. We quickly changed out of our pajamas and ate the most delicious baked trout we ever had. No charge. And with the two-day delay, I could easily have finished my work and gone fishing.

1968 was the driest year in Chile in 102 years. No snow fell in the ski resorts, over 300,000 cows and 75,000 sheep had to be slaughtered and many more transported to the southern part of the country where there was always rain. About 120,000 farmers were in financial trouble and we were all asked to cut down on our electricity and water consumption. One day in the middle of December, the lights went off without warning from breakfast until midnight, as well as on several Tuesday afternoons. The weather, however, was wonderful — because spring lasted all winter.

Donna with Dad and Mom, 1968

145. THE STRAITS OF MAGELLAN

FOR SEVERAL MONTHS we had been asking Mom and Dad to come for a visit. We had given them long lists of items to bring and plenty of suggestions for getting visas, shots (such as smallpox, typhoid, and gamma globulin), and what clothes to pack. Finally, on December 30, 1968, Paul's wife, Elaine, drove them to the airport in Madison. Dad wrote home saying, "We were put on a North Central plane to Chicago because Northwest was so late. In Chicago we had to walk the full length of the airport to get to Northwest. Our bags didn't arrive in Miami on time, so we filed a claim and headed for Chile, a smooth uneventful trip via Panama, Lima, and La Paz. No trouble in customs but filed a claim there and our cases came the next day. Again, no trouble with customs."

Picnicking along the Way in Our Chevy II Station Wagon

When we were still in the airport getting their bags, Dad started to tell me that he had our set of "Old Colonial" sterling silver in his little blue gym bag with a false bottom. I couldn't believe it. If the customs officials had cared to look, it might have been more than just a tad *embarrassing. This* was totally out of character. Dad was scrupulously honest and always followed the letter of the law and even the spirit of the law as he thought it was intended.

Dad continued his letter to Paul and Elaine, "Starting on Saturday, January 4, 1969, we drove south a few hundred miles and stopped at a beautiful waterfall, Salto del Laja, with deluxe accommodations and a view of the falls. We drove on to Puerto Montt, the farthest point south that John reached on his Peace Corps trip. The following day, we took a boat trip to the Argentine border and back. There were beautiful snow-capped volcanoes all around. On January 7th, we flew to Punta Arenas on the Straits of Magellan and prowled around the town while John worked at

Heading to Torres del Paine

the Junta. I gather from John that he accomplished a lot. We went out for seafood dinners each night — some quite unusual."

"Thursday, we took the bumpiest, dustiest bus ride I ever hope to experience, 150 miles and 6 hours north to Puerto Natales where John continued his work. From there, we squeezed into the back of a pick-up with four Chileans from the Junta who took us 45 miles farther north to a beautiful area called Torres del Paine (now a National Park). There we had a picnic of grilled lamb and marveled at the fantastic scenery. On the way back, we saw several Rheas and Black Necked Swans as we drove through the vast Patagonian grasslands — nothing but endless grass, sky and sheep and the always present clouds and wind. In Punta Arenas we asked a cab driver if he had ever seen a day in his life without some clouds. He laughed and said, 'Never.' The days and scenery seem to be going by like a

Mom & Dad McLeod at Torres del Paine

kaleidoscope." Dad continued writing in his letter, "We flew back on a Lan Chile Airlines jet over the mountains to Puerto Montt, had clear skies for the last part of the flight and took pictures of the beautiful peaks. We could see the Pacific on one side and the mountains in Argentina on the other."

146. REGULAR OYSTERS

BACK IN PUERTO MONTT, Donna and I were excited to take Mom and Dad to my all-time favorite seafood restaurant that we discovered on an earlier trip. It was a few miles north of town with a beautiful view of the Pacific. I was eager to once again order "*Curanto,*" which was a huge basket of various clams, shrimp, lobster, sea urchins, *picorocos*, fish and more than I can name. There was also a bowl of soup containing chorizo, potatoes, chicken and some other ingredients that I thought I'd never forget. I was sure Mom would be thrilled with the seafood because when I was in grade school, she told us that oyster stew, which we ate just once a year on Christmas Eve, was a great delicacy. At the time, I hated the warm milk and I didn't much care for the squishy oysters either. Every year I put up a big fuss to no avail. Now it was my turn to treat Mom and Dad to some good, fresh seafood. Dad ordered *Curanto*, Donna and I ordered *Curanto*, but Mom ordered a steak. What? "Mom," I said, "I thought you loved oysters and seafood?' She replied, "No, I never ate any oysters. You were so busy fussing and complaining that you never noticed." I was appalled. For the first 28 years of my life I had been hoodwinked by a clever mom who got me to eat everything she served. When I was little, she just waited until I was starving and then gave it to me first.

A couple nights later in Valdivia, we went to another excellent restaurant. I ordered a bottle of wine and Dad gladly had a glass or two. Growing up, however, we never had any alcoholic beverages in the house and I never saw him take a drink. When my brother, Paul, asked him why Jesus and his disciples could drink wine, Dad said, "Because they didn't have any clean water." That satisfied Paul, but now that Dad was 65 and a long way from home, I guess he decided to try some. After the bottle was finished, I quietly signaled for another. When the waiter came and opened the bottle, Dad said indignantly, "Who ordered another bottle?" I responded, "Dad, they just bring it to you." I didn't order a third. Mom never had more than a fraction of an ounce. All she had to do was smell wine to feel funny. Like her dad, she might have been allergic to alcohol.

Back in Santiago on January 20, 1969, we watched, via satellite, the inauguration of President Jimmy Carter. The next week Mom and Dad travelled around town with Donna as their tour guide and returned home to Madison on January 29th.

By February, I had finished CARE's 55-page self-audit of the feeding program which was submitted to USAID. I was happy it was finished so I could continue my regular schedule.

A new Field Representative, Wally Chastain, arrived to work in the northern half of Chile. His wife, Sally, had just had a baby with a heart defect and pneumonia so she stayed behind in Houston. Sadly, the little baby died ten weeks later. Wally replaced Jim Coberly who had been a PCV in Colombia and was also in my training group back in New York. Now he was leaving a great post with ten days' notice and going to Pakistan. I bought his excellent Canon reflex camera and custom ski boots.

Wally was a tough, cowboy kind of guy who would almost tear his clothes apart as he walked. In fact, he did. He had a couple suits made by a local tailor and after a few days had to take one back to repair some seams. He and Sally both loved skiing and he would even hike up into the mountains to ski down the slopes before the resorts were open. A little snow between the rocks was enough for him. He always seemed to want to get physical but since he knew I wrestled for Wisconsin, he always shied away. That was fine with me.

Good news from CARE-New York. I got a $300 salary increase. Dad wrote back, "Is that $300 per month?" I answered, "No, it's per year."

One morning I woke up with a small crick in my lower neck. A few hours later, while driving back to the office after a meeting downtown with our Chilean counterparts, my neck was getting so stiff I could barely turn my head. I soon decided I'd better drive home while I still could. I lay down in bed and was fine unless I made the slightest movement. When I did, I felt I had been stuck with a knife. I took a couple of Darvon pain pills and after a few hours, Wally Chastain came over and drove Donna and me to the hospital. Then Dr. Jorge Tapia, gave me a cortisone shot with a needle so long Wally said, "I thought Donna was going to pass out." I could feel he hit the exact spot and instantly I was much better, but I did stay home the next three days.

We continued to make many new friends, including quite a few Canadians, most of whom worked for the Canadian International Development Agency. One couple we got to know best was Bob and Anita Anderson. When we learned that Anita was a U.S. citizen, Donna asked, "Where are you

from?" "From Louisiana." she replied. A few years later, after we knew them much better, Anita mentioned that she had thought Donna was trying to find out where she was from just to see if she might be black. To be that sensitive, I guess she must have been "a little bit black" but such a thought never entered Donna's mind.

Carving Moai   *Starving Art*

We also met a local artisan who carved Easter Island "Moai" statues of various sizes and styles. We bought several little ones and three much bigger ones about 4' and 5' high. Since we were undoubtedly his best customers, his wife asked us to be godparents to their sixth baby. They must have thought we were rich.

Donna decided I should have a big 29th birthday party on May 16, 1969. After all, I was approaching the end of my youth. We decided to have an Indian, any kind of Indian costume party. Donna made me a big headdress of turkey feathers. For some reason, she decided to cover her dress with white chicken feathers. Sewing on hundreds of little clumps of feathers took hours and as we hob-nobbed with our twenty guests crowded into our little living and dining room, feathers were soon all over the house. We had a great time.

147. NORTHERN CHILE

I HAD KEPT BUSY AT WORK travelling all over southern Chile for the first two years but in June 1969, I traded jobs with Wally and was now in charge of the north half of the country. It was the same job with different scenery. I continued to inspect our counterpart's records so that we would be satisfied that the millions of dollars of food aid we administered was being effectively use. Donna continued to travel with me.

Our Country Director, Dr. Kline, was transferred to the Philippines and replaced by Bill Salas a day before we headed north on a 24-day work trip. First, we stopped in La Serena, then Antofagasta, which was one of my favorite destinations. There we watched millions of seabirds swimming and diving for Anchovies in the cold, nutrient-rich Humboldt Current as it flowed up the coast. It was quite a sight to see. From Antofagasta, we drove east back up the steep hill to the Pan American Highway where we encountered a big truck tipped over on its side in the center of the road. In the middle of nowhere, with no other vehicles in sight, the lonely driver was bent over picking up some of the thousands of chicken eggs that were strewn all over the highway. I couldn't imagine how the accident occurred or how he was going to remedy his situation before losing all his cargo. In the pre-cell phone era, he probably had a long wait before any real help would pass by. On the 22-hour, 1265-mile trip from Santiago to Arica, many overloaded trucks had breakdowns.

From there we went on to Tocopilla, Calama, Chuquicamata, San Pedro de Atacama, Iquique, La Tirana, Arica (at the northern tip of Chile) and then to Tacna, Peru for a day of vacation. The scenery was vastly different. Instead of lush green valleys with fruit trees, vineyards, cattle and sheep, and trout streams with snow-capped volcanoes in the distance, we now travelled through the desert. The cities seemed isolated by miles of huge, dry, barren hills.

On July 16, 1969, Neil Armstrong, Edwin (Buzz) Aldrin and Michael Collins, blasted off on Apollo 11 for the moon. Four days later, the first two landed their "Eagle" lunar module on the

The Arch at Antofagasta Covered with Cormorants

moon, walked around for three hours doing experiments, picked up moon rocks, and planted the American flag. They then joined Collins, back in the "Columbia" command module, who had been circling the moon. From the time they entered the atmosphere at 12:25 just after lunch on July 24, 1969, several of us at the office were excitedly listening to the radio until they safely splashed down just 15 miles from the recovery ship, the USS Hornet. After decontamination, they went through customs in Hawaii and declared moon rocks among their items. This all happened just 65 years after the Wright brothers achieved their first airplane flight of 12 seconds travelling 120' at Kitty Hawk, North Carolina.

148. SKIING IN THE ANDES

WE RENTED A SKI LODGE up at La Parva with Wally and Sally, along with Steve and Linda Smith. Steve was the Director of a non-governmental organization (NGO) like CARE and they played the guitar and sang. We rented a spacious cabin for the grand sum of $1000, a bargain for the season. We drove the 25 miles up the steep, curvy, snow-covered switchbacks, which Donna absolutely dreaded. When Wally and I talked about making it, we meant with or without chains. Donna simply heard we might not make it at all and end up at the bottom of the mountain. Each morning we had a beautiful view of Santiago down the valley but the big buildings in the center of town were always hidden by a dense layer of smog. As the day progressed, the smog dispersed and almost reached our cabin. Each weekend we'd drive up with all our food and equipment and have a great time. I was lucky to be the recipient of Jim Coberly's custom ski boots. Then I bought some decent used Head skis and poles and for Donna new skis, boots and poles. We were all set. All we had to do was learn how to ski. Periodically I took lessons from some of the Colorado ski bums, quickly learned how to snowplow, and after the first day could maneuver myself down the baby slope. Donna was more cautious and skied mainly on the easier slopes near the cabin because she didn't want to risk hurting her back. I always skied faster than my ability just trying to keep up with someone. Dr. Tapia assured me he'd fix up any broken bones.

After a few weekends of practice, Wally told Donna, "I'm gonna' take the starch out of John." First, we went up a T-bar lift with Wally on the left and me on the right. I struggled to keep my skis together, but Wally kept me on the straight-and-narrow. We made it to the top of the lift but by then I was frazzled after five minutes of what was for me a full-body isometric exercise. From there we had no place to go but up another long lift. This chair lift was more relaxing but now I was already a long way up. As I contemplated my plight, Wally took off down the hill. I had to follow. I went part way, then fell. I went a little farther, then fell again. I was always out of control trying to catch up. On one fall, I ended up sitting straight up with my feet spread out in front of me. I'm not sure how long I had been sitting there before I realized that one ski was stuck in the snow straight up next to me and the other was lying across my lap. Nobody was around but someone must have gathered up my skis to be in that position. Finally, I reached Wally. No, he didn't wait for me to catch my breath. He took off again. And again. And again, until I made it all the way down. I was almost starch-free.

La Parva was a great place with terrific weather and at 9400 feet, not too high. There were a lot of different slopes and ski lifts and after a few months I had gone down all of them. I never earned any style points but had a great time. The lines were usually short, and we could sometimes get in fifteen runs a day. Best of all, our season lift tickets cost just $15.

149. A BIG INVESTOR

DURING THIS TIME, quite a number of older, long-term CARE overseas employees had been inquiring if there were any way they could invest their money. Since they were all spread around the world without connections, they had never done anything about this until a former CARE Director resigned and started an investment firm. He then sent a letter to all of us overseas employees inquiring if we would be interested in investing a minimum of $1000 into a CARE Overseas Employee Fund. I dug up $1000 and sent off a check. At the time, the Dow Jones was at 4000, but soon dropped to 1000. After another three years, the fund had done so poorly that it was disbanded, and I ended up with $850. That was my last attempt at investing for the next twenty years.

150. HOME LEAVE

WE LEFT SANTIAGO in May 1969, for six weeks of home leave. First, we spent a week in New York where I was debriefed by the CARE-NY department heads and given a physical exam. Instead of taking an expensive taxi straight up First Avenue past the United Nations to my exam, I decided to take a bus. A block before I was to get off, I stood up, walked to the door, and waited for it to open just as it did when I was a little kid in Madison. When it didn't open, I noticed a sign, "If the door doesn't open, push the buzzer." As soon as I pushed the buzzer, the driver turned around and yelled, "Push it, buddy, push it." So, I pushed the door open and walked the last half block. No need to feel stupid. Nobody knew me in New York. That was just one of many "culture shock" episodes. I also bought two new suits and two sport coats in the garment district in lower Manhattan where everyone jabbered in Yiddish.

At home in Wisconsin, we moved back and forth between Friesland and Madison about a week at a time, to lessen the burden on our parents. It was great seeing all our siblings and friends.

But after living in Chile, I realized that my driving habits had taken a turn for the worse. While driving south from Baraboo on Highway 12, I wanted to turn left up the hill to Sky High Orchard, but instead of signaling and waiting in my lane for an oncoming car to pass, I just pulled over to the left gravel shoulder and kept going. When I turned left, the lady in the oncoming car looked terrified as Donna screamed, "You can't do that. You're in the United States now."

Donna, 1969

Just before our flight back, I turned off the beltline onto Fish Hatchery Road towards town. As I drove over the little hill, going 42 in a 35 zone, the whole line of cars, including mine, got pulled over and fined $10 for speeding. It seemed more unjust than a small-town sheriff's speed trap. I was, however, relieved. On many other occasions, I deserved much worse.

On this first home leave, we had a long shopping list and ended up spending all the money that we had saved the previous 30 months. To squeeze all our new purchases into our suitcases, we removed all the packaging and left no space unfilled. We took the stress off the zippers on our big, cloth suitcases by cinching up a strap around each one.

On the way back, we stopped in Austin, Texas to visit Mary and Louis in their first house on five acres out in the country. Mary was enjoying the nine-foot grand piano she had just gotten for her birthday, but I got chiggers walking around outside which drove me crazy for a week. We also stopped a couple days in Bogota. Donna mainly relaxed while I took some trips with Jay Jackson, who, you may remember, was a PCV in Guatemala, had attended our wedding, and later was in my CARE-NY training class.

I had some Braniff Airlines overweight slips which came in handy on our flight from Miami. I then tried to get some more from Air France for our flight to Santiago, but the boss, Mr. Castellanos, said, "No." When we checked in later at the Air France desk, the attendant said, "You have some overweight bags." I quickly replied, "Mr. Castellanos said it wouldn't be a problem since we only have three of them." He hesitated but let me through. After all, I was only 122 pounds over the 88-pound limit. I saved $90.

151. BACK TO CHILE

BEFORE HOME LEAVE, I had written a project proposal to equip 80 rural school kitchens and dining rooms around Temuco with $50,000 worth of pots, pans, and utensils to facilitate preparation of the school breakfasts and lunches. After I spent two weeks in Temuco overseeing the project, the CARE Director, Bill Salas, and one of my local school inspectors came to help inaugurate this experimental program. We were interviewed and got our pictures in the paper; publicity is the part that Bill liked best. It also gave him the chance to talk about CARE's countrywide school breakfast and lunch programs, which fed over 1.2 million kids every day, and our cookie program that provided 2500 metric tons of high-protein cookies to 700,000 kids.

After we inaugurated the school kitchen program, Donna and I drove south to Villarrica, a resort town by a beautiful snow-capped volcano, where we arranged to go on a fishing trip down the river. Donna and I were in separate row boats, each captained by a young kid who rowed upstream as we floated down the rapids. We were not prepared for the cold rain that started to fall and after three hours we were almost frozen. We caught eleven trout between us, which were delicious — suitable compensation for our discomfort.

152. CHILEAN POLITICS

CAMPAIGNING FOR THE UPCOMING PRESIDENTIAL ELECTIONS had begun in earnest by early 1970. A socialist-Marxist, Dr. Salvador Allende, was running for president for the fourth time against two other candidates, a conservative and a centrist. So many businessmen were panicked about the possibility that Allende might win and nationalize their companies that the country virtually came to a standstill the last six months before the November election. Dozens of buildings under construction, such as the Sheraton Hotel, came to a screeching halt. As a result of the uncertainty, inflation was becoming a huge problem for the average person. In 1963, one Escudo was worth a dollar. Four years later when we arrived in Chile, it was E5.96. Currently it was E14 but on the black market the rate was E25 to U.S. $1.00. That's why our season ski lift tickets up at La Parva were so

Our New House

inexpensive. While my rent was getting cheaper each month, prices for the locals were rising higher. One Chilean girl made a bet that she would swim nude in one of the pools along a busy street in downtown Santiago if her debt were forgiven. When she did, people got so excited that they jumped in the fountain with her, including one man who took off his clothes and almost drowned the poor girl. She had to be carried off by the police to a medical post — but she was debt free.

Dr. Jorge Tapia's brother-in-law was one of those worried millionaires. He owned a copper mine, which would soon be nationalized, as well as a new house he had never occupied just a block from their family club and pool. To prevent squatters from moving in, he asked me if I would rent it. He knew I worked for CARE so he said, "Would $100 per month rent, to be paid in dollars, be too much?" It sure wasn't and at the end of September we moved into his much bigger and better home. It had four bedrooms, four baths, two maid's bedrooms, and big living and dining rooms with huge windows and doors that faced the interior patio. Now we needed more furniture. We ordered a new bedroom set, a stereo cabinet with copper artwork on the doors, and a hand-carved credenza which was a copy of a medieval French credenza. I also rebuilt an old antique bellows into a coffee table. We tried to buy only sturdy wood furniture that would last a long time. We still have it all.

My new landlord's maid, a Mapuche Indian lady named Zulema, came along with the house. Until then we never had a maid, but Donna continued to do the cooking. That was until the Tapias told us that Zulema could do everything. Then we quickly discovered just how well-trained she was. She cut string beans French-style and could peel a pear without even touching it. She finally said, "Don't you have a bell (to call me)?" We didn't but soon bought one. Ringing the bell for service the first time, however, took more courage than we expected. Donna wouldn't do it. Finally, with some trepidation, I did, meekly. It was easier the next time. From then on, Donna's life was much easier.

When Allende won with 36.2% of the vote, 1.3 points more than the conservative candidate, many wealthy Chileans left the country. I heard later that one out of eighteen Chileans departed for Ecuador, Brazil, Argentina, Switzerland, and many other countries. Dr. Jorge Tapia, and his brother, my new landlord, were two of them. Jorge went to Geneva, Switzerland, and his brother to Rio de Janeiro. Many rich Chileans regularly sent money back to fund the opposition.

Steve and Linda Smith drove us up to Portillo, a beautiful ski resort high up in the mountains where the 1966 Ski Olympics had been held. Steve and I skied for half a day and had a great time. It was the end of the season, so we were just about the only ones there.

Donna and I celebrated our fourth anniversary on September 2, 1970, by going out to eat with Drake and Evie Reid, who were being transferred to Washington, D.C. Five days later we went out to eat again, this time with John and Lucy Carlson, to celebrate Donna's 29th birthday.

153. EXCITING NEWS

JIM AND WENDY ETZEL, both teachers at the American School, were two friends whom we saw quite often. They taught us to play pinochle, husbands against wives, and it was always amazingly even. Late one afternoon back in June 1970, they stopped over to tell us their exciting news. Wendy was pregnant. Then Donna said, "I might be too." So, with the name of Wendy's doctor, we headed right over to his office to find out. Donna tested positive! We were ready. I had just turned 30 and Donna was 29.

This was a time when a lot of people were worried about the world's rapid population growth. People were starving in India where CARE was distributing thousands of tons of food and the green revolution wasn't yet in sight. Nevertheless, we were happy and let everyone know in our 1970 Christmas letter that Donna was expecting in February. All our relatives were happy, but one friend, Jeff Dean, replied, "I cannot sincerely congratulate you on the expectant arrival as we are upset about the population problem. I hope you think about limiting your family to two."

This is the same Jeff who had the lead in our school play, "Naughty Marietta" and whose grandfather started Dean Clinic in Madison. Once Jeff had even arranged for the two of us to drive to

Janesville where we went on a double date. I have absolutely no idea how that turned out, but I do remember showing Jeff how the cruise control worked on our 1959 Chrysler Windsor. On a country road, I dialed the speed up to 105 mph and soon noticed a cop coming up behind me. Coming from a side road, he had no idea how fast I had gone but knew it was over 55 mph. He issued me a $10 ticket for going 10 over the limit. Jeff gave me $5 to help and nobody else ever heard a thing about it.

Jim and Wendy had gone several times to the casino at Viña del Mar straight west on the Pacific coast. They played roulette, red-and-black, or odd-and-even. They thought they had a fool-proof method to make money. If red came up three times in a row, they would make a small bet on black, and would continue to double their money on black until they won. They thought this would ensure they would always make money. They couldn't lose and their system had already worked on two previous occasions. I knew perfectly well, after taking a probability math class at the UW, that this didn't make sense, but we decided to go with them anyway. It would be fun. Only Jim and I betted as Donna and Wendy were by now so pregnant that they didn't want to be on their feet for long. This time Jim and I waited until an even number showed up three times. Then we bet on the odds. We lost. No worries. We doubled our money and bet on the odds again. Then again. And again. Our small bets were getting bigger as we each continued to bet on odd numbers about ten times in a row until we each were losing just over $100. We had to quit. We still had to pay our hotel bill and didn't have any more money. Then we stayed and watched. Finally, after a total of sixteen even numbers, an odd number appeared. What a great system. It was fool proof. If we had had $6500 more, it would have been.

During Christmas vacation, we went to the Santiago airport and met a couple and their daughter from Beaver Dam, Wisconsin, who came to visit their Chilean AFS student. Donna's sister, Sharon, and the girl's mother were both nurses and the daughter, who had taken four years of high school Spanish was, she said, bilingual. When Donna was driving them around the next day, she discovered the girl couldn't understand anything anyone said, and Donna became their translator. I was amazed. Donna was now a translator.

The office sold our Chevy II station wagons and now we each had new Ford Torino station wagons that came equipped with air conditioning. CARE had finally relented and responded positively to our numerous requests. A couple days later, as I returned from playing tennis at a nearby club that we had joined, I was broadsided by a little Fiat 600 at an intersection. I hardly felt the impact but the girl in the little Fiat spun around, cut her knee and even fell out of her car. We both decided that it was nobody's fault and drove off.

In some ways, December was a sad month. While Donna was getting bigger and bigger each day, several of our close friends departed for the U.S. Donna missed her family back in Friesland, and the beautiful, sunny weather in Santiago just didn't seem like Christmas. In other ways, all was well. We both were healthy, and Donna could still do her 50 sit-ups as she had been doing her entire pregnancy. We also kept busy hosting Canadian house guests for almost a whole month before they were transferred.

Being pregnant didn't stop Donna from entertaining. She hosted a farewell party for an English couple, Ian, and Kathleen Faichney, who were going to Kenya. They provided the guest list of 18 people, mostly strangers to us, and we served BBQ ribs, baked tomatoes, beans, cinnamon rolls, various salads, and string beans. For dessert, each received a half melon with a scoop of ice cream topped with raspberries. Nobody ever went home hungry when Donna was in charge. Donna was worried that she might go into labor during the party because several friends had just had their babies and some had arrived early. It did help to have a maid who was a great cook and who worked half the night cleaning up.

I'll always remember Ian, a little Englishman in his mid-fifties, who also did a bit of skiing. One sunny afternoon at La Parva, an out of control teenager went flying past and fell with a loud snap right in front of him. He was so unnerved by the kid's broken leg, just three days before he was to take a three-month vacation across the U.S., that he stopped, took off his skis and walked down the long hill to his cabin. It was a prudent course of action.

About a month before Donna's due date, she had her suitcase packed and ready to go. This was important because the hospital didn't provide any baby items, clothes, diapers, soap, towels, cotton nightgown, blankets or anything. I was expected to take the cloth diapers home and wash them every night. Donna's pregnancy, however, didn't keep us from attending a big dance put on by the American Society. As Donna mostly sat on the sidelines, feeling fat and wearing a dress she thought was too short, she noticed that the English girl I was dancing with reached up and gave me a kiss. And yes, I will admit that I was insufficiently solicitous to Donna under the circumstances. When we got home, Donna was so angry that she started packing a suitcase to go home to Wisconsin, while I was removing stuff as fast as she was packing. I reminded her what her dad had said, "Come home anytime you want as long as you bring John." I also reminded her that she needed my permission to leave the country — which didn't exactly help the situation — but she eventually calmed down. When the English couple got home, they discovered half their belongings were outside in their backyard. They had arrived just in time to scare off the bandits.

During these last few weeks, the boss was a pain in the neck. He hadn't wanted me to take my inspection trips earlier, but just a couple weeks before our baby was due, he thought I should. He drove me crazy with his last-minute changes of mind. Being a native speaker was his best attribute.

154. OUR NEW ARRIVAL

ON FEBRUARY 15, 1971, I wanted to take some movies of downtown Santiago. Donna went with me as I filmed various government buildings and other points of interest. By now Donna was very pregnant and due any day so she waited in the car and watched. After lunch, we went swimming at the nearby club owned by my landlord and our friends, the Tapias. As we sat in the sun, Donna started having contractions. We soon called the midwife, Sylvia, who came right over and told us to meet her at the hospital at 3:00 o'clock. I said, "Do you mean today?" "Yes, today," she replied. By now Donna's contractions were every seven minutes. This was really happening.

We arrived at the hospital on time and briefly met with Sylvia before Donna was escorted to the delivery room. Then I waited. I had even remembered my Canon camera that I had set out a week earlier. At 6:00 p.m., the nurse walked into the waiting room and handed me our new son. At 7 pounds and 8 ounces, he looked healthy and hungry, loudly smacking his lips together as if to say, "Feed me. Feed me now." The next afternoon, we all left the hospital together. When I went to develop the film, I discovered the camera was empty. Doctor Noriega, who had been trained in the states, and his wife, Sylvia, who had been an obstetrics nurse for eight years in the states, together with the hospital, charged a total of $100. I made a $100 profit since CARE automatically paid us $200 when we had a baby.

We decided his name was going to be Shawn Andrew McLeod. Shawn was an Irish name, not Scottish as we had thought, and Andrew was the name of Donna's paternal grandfather. When I called home, I told Dad how his name would be spelled and then started to fill out the birth announcements — but I couldn't write "Shawn." I filled out two cards before I got a sheet of paper and wrote it over and over, but even with a little practice, I still couldn't write his name quickly. The letters just didn't go together. That did it. We decided his name would be Sean. Sean was easy to write and that's the way it should have been spelled in the beginning. It was still an Irish name, but it was also Sean Connery's name, perhaps the most famous Scotsman of our time. And I still looked forward to the James Bond movies I had first seen in the PC.

Before we left the hospital the next day, the midwife suggested we put him on a schedule and feed him every four hours. That sounded great but schedules were completely out of the question. Sean was so hungry, and Donna had so much milk that sometimes I thought he would drown. Fortunately, our friend, Lucy Carlson, who had three little kids, helped Donna get through the first few most difficult days. She gave us a lot of baby items and clothes, as had Dr. Jorge Tapia's wife, Maria Antonieta, or "Toni," as we called her.

155. MOM AND DAD DE YOUNG'S VISIT

WHEN SEAN WAS JUST TWELVE DAYS OLD, Donna's dad and mom, Walter and Dorothy De Young, visited for almost a month. The weather in Wisconsin had been terribly cold and snowy and Wally arrived with his long underwear, top and bottom, underneath his wool suit and tie. He wasn't prepared for the hot, sunny summer day in Santiago. By the time we finished driving through traffic for an hour at noon, he was thoroughly cooked. Those first days we stayed close to home and took Sean for walks around the neighborhood in our proper English pram which we bought from our English friends, Roger and Mary Clark.

Dad wrote a poem to commemorate Sean's birth:

Spread the news to every clime
Get Gramps and Grandma on the line
Mother, Father doing fine
In Santiago.

Joy abounds all around
Cherubs chant the happy sound
Sean Andrew has come to town
In Santiago.

Healthy, bouncing, cooing, crowing
Seven pounds eight ounces showing
Twenty inches long and growing
In Santiago.

Sean and John, 1971

A glorious day to celebrate
February 15th is the date
Because of what has taken place
In Santiago.

Mother Donna, Daddy John
Now they've added baby Sean
A family's what they've started on
In Santiago.

Hearing of the bless'd event
Of the gift that's "Heaven sent"
Grand folks Walt and Dorothy went
To Santiago.

Safety pins and pacifiers
Bassinets and dripping diapers
Will greet them when they both arrive
In Santiago.

May Sean strong and handsome grow
Learn all things worthy to know
But let's hope he'll soon come home
From Santiago.

So join the fun and play the game
See the boy of great, if local, fame
All you do is hop a plane
For Santiago.

After the first week, Doctor Noriega and his wife, Sylvia, came over to see how things were going. Thanks to Zulema, we didn't have to do anything except look at baby Sean. She prepared all the meals and did all the washing, ironing and cleaning. Anytime we wanted something, we just pushed the bell and she came running. Donna wrote, "John is holding him now and he is trying to hold his head up. I think this week is about the most exciting week I've ever had."

On March 7th, Sean was baptized in the Union Church. He wore a long, 100-year-old Scottish dress borrowed from Mrs. Russel, an old Scottish lady in Donna's Red Cross sewing group that made diapers for new babies. Sean behaved perfectly and then slept quietly through the whole service while we listened to two sermons, one in Spanish and one in English. So many people were leaving Chile that the two services had been combined. There was even talk about joining with the Anglican Church and selling one of them. President Allende's new Marxist government had been busy nationalizing private schools and many businesses while trying to control the rampant inflation that his policies caused. I could have bought some beautiful houses for just $3000 but wasn't in a position to do so. Some PCVs, however, who had married Chilean girls, did take advantage of the situation.

With Donna's mom and dad, we drove two hours north to La Ligua where they bought a half dozen ponchos for the grandkids. Then we headed to Zapallar where we had a picnic overlooking the Pacific and on to Viña del Mar. I carried Sean everywhere in a padded, blue carrying case. He was a cheerful traveler, nursing and sleeping much of the day, but by supper time, he was usually a bit fussy for an hour while Wally carried him around, but then stayed awake for several hours. He loved his pacifier and clutched a second one in his hand for added comfort.

With Donna's mom and dad, we drove two hours north to La Ligua where they bought a half dozen ponchos for the grandkids. Then we headed to Zapallar where we had a picnic overlooking the Pacific and on to Viña del Mar. I carried Sean everywhere in a padded, blue carrying case. He was a cheerful traveler, nursing and sleeping much of the day, but by supper time, he was usually a bit fussy for an hour while Wally carried him around, but then stayed awake for several hours. He loved his pacifier and clutched a second one in his hand for added comfort.

Just before the Ides of March 1971, we all headed south. In Villarrica, Wally and I took another one of those fishing trips, with the boatmen rowing against the current as we trolled ahead of the boat while floating down the River Toltén. This time the weather was beautiful, and Wally caught nine trout, one more than I did. Wally loved it and was happy he had brought some of his fishing gear. We then drove to Puerto Montt and the island of Chiloe where it was almost impossible not to see at least one beautiful, darkly colored rainbow. Along the way, Wally was intrigued by seeing the old-style farm machinery he had operated as a kid. When Wally could hardly believe his eyes, he'd say, "That's interesting." He never uttered a critical word. We all had a wonderful trip and enjoyed our time together. We were grateful we could share our overseas living experience with them.

156. EASTER ISLAND

Backs to the Ocean

DAD AND MOM ARRIVED a few days after Donna's parents returned to Friesland, were excited to see baby Sean, and came loaded with Pampers, which we saved for trips.

First, we had to get an identification card and Chilean passport for Sean. Even though Lucho, our office boy, arrived an hour before the office opened to save us a place in line, there were at least 25 people ahead of us. When the officials saw

Dad Amongst the Moai

Sean, however, we were ushered to the front. They quickly took his photo and footprint and we were done in no time. He also got a U.S. Passport through the Embassy and had dual citizenship.

Now that we all had proper documents, we were ready to fly to Easter Island, located over 2300 miles west of Santiago. Fortunately for Mom and Dad, I had been able to buy their round-trip tickets from Madison, including Easter Island, for just $900. It was a bit complicated to arrange accommodations for the five of us because Easter Island was not yet a popular tourist destination. Since there was no hotel, we stayed with a local family for three nights until the next LAN-Chile flight returned. Accommodations were rustic and water and food were at a premium.

In a pick-up, we were driven all over the 63-square-mile island. Donna held Sean in the front seat while Mom, Dad and I rode in the open box. The weather was warm and the roads dusty. One minute there would be a sprinkle of rain, then the sun would come out and plaster the reddish-brown dust to our skin. If more than a dribble of water had come out of the shower, that wouldn't have been a problem. After just one day, not even Donna and Sean were spared. All our white towels were badly stained.

We saw everything there was to see. Inside the volcano, we walked around the huge Moais, the monolithic human figures carved by the Rapa Nui people between 1250 and 1500. Some were still uncut from the rock below and it must have taken a lot of muscle and skill to carry them out from inside the old volcano to the seashore. Several sites had been reconstructed where the huge statues were lined up in a row with their backs to the sea. We also looked inside the man-made caves where the inhabitants later tried to hide from slave traders. It was an interesting trip and we were practically the only tourists on the island.

Back in Santiago, we visited a little shop where they did extraordinary copper work. That's when we discovered that many months earlier, the Sheraton Hotel had commissioned them to make a copper globe light fixture to hang in the lobby. It was about 20 inches in diameter, with cut-out stars so the light would shine through. It was a beautiful creation that took over 200 hours to hammer out. After Allende was elected, the Sheraton cancelled the order before they were nationalized. At just the right time, we entered the shop

Sean and Grandpa, Art McLeod

with Mom and Dad who bought it for just $240. Luckily, the Hotel had made the down payment. A day later they flew home carrying the big globe. It looked great in their new house where it hung for the next 34 years.

157. A LONG ROAD NORTH

A Lone Cactus

DONNA AND I, along with Sean, soon departed on another work trip once again to the north half of Chile. It was a long drive, about 1500 miles each way, and I visited all the junta offices and many schools along the way.

The national "HONSA" hotels were all quite good, but in Calama, a small town in the high desert, we had to stay in a very mediocre place without heat or hot water. The rooms were so small that I had to stay in one while Donna and Sean squeezed into another. It was cold. Through the wall, I could hear Donna waking up to feed Sean and I don't know how they didn't freeze half to death. In the morning there was a foot-long icicle hanging off the roof.

The next night was much better. In Chuquicamata, we stayed in luxury at the American Anaconda Copper Company Hotel and visited the largest open-pit copper mine in the world. They welcomed visiting Americans and offered us free lodging and meals. The mine was an amazing operation. The pit was about a mile long and over half a mile deep, and the trucks, which each carried 150 tons of ore, appeared to be toys from our vantage point. We visited just in time. It was nationalized a week later.

On this trip, we had to leave the country again to renew our visas at the Chilean Consulate in Tacna, Peru. On our way back to Santiago, which took over three days, we stopped at La Serena. Hoping to leave early, we were shocked to find out we would have to wait seven hours because of a "Citroën" car race from Santiago to La Serena. Chile was full of those bouncy, flimsy, French cars with canvas lawn-chair seats. When the race was over and we were finally able to leave, I looked over at Sean, who sat between us in his car seat, and noticed he suddenly looked sick. I said, "Donna, quick get the bucket." Luckily, it was at Donna's feet, since earlier we'd been at the beach. She quickly

Too Cold Above the Knees

responded and Sean immediately vomited into it, saving us from a disastrous mess on a hot day. When we got home, he slept for the next four days.

When we arrived back in Santiago, we were greeted the next morning by our first Chilean snowfall. Several inches fell, schools were cancelled, and we made a four-ball snowman in our front yard. It didn't last long, but there was plenty of snow up at La Parva.

158. THE END IN SIGHT

THE BOSS, BILL SALAS, returned from New York and our office boy, Lucho, met him at the airport. He had arranged for Bill to go through customs without a problem but was ignored by Bill who saw one of his own friends. This "friend" then confiscated his $200 Zenith transoceanic shortwave radio, forcing Bill to spend a lot of time and effort to get it back. Bill continued driving us all crazy. He would ask us to urgently prepare some letter or report and then a few hours later would say, "I don't need it after all."

Wally Chastain had a neighbor who was a LAN-Chile Pilot. After much time and effort, the pilot had arranged for Wally to fly in the cockpit with him to Punta Arenas. Then, just the day before he was to go, Bill told Wally he couldn't go because Bill wanted him to do something else. Wally was furious as he told me the story. Just then, Bill walked into our office and I was primed and ready to respond inappropriately. I said, "I'm sick and tired of taking all your crap." Bill quickly turned around and went back to his office. That night I composed a letter to CARE-NY requesting a transfer because "I had already been in Chile for a long time." After Bill read my letter, we had a sincere talk and got along better, but the die was cast. The head of Overseas Operations in New York could read between the lines.

Bill Salas, finally at the last moment, agreed to let us take the week of June 3, 1971, for our local vacation. We flew to Asuncion, the capital of Paraguay, and then on to Iguazu Falls on the border of Paraguay, Argentina and Brazil. After some heavy rains, a tremendous amount of water was pouring over the falls, dwarfing Niagara Falls. With Sean firmly fastened to my chest in his little baby carrier designed by a PCV in Africa, I carried him down to the end of the catwalk that crossed the raging rapids in the middle of the falls. When I recently saw a postcard of Iguazu and that catwalk, I wondered, "What was I thinking?"

Little blond Sean, who was almost four months old, was often the center of an adoring crowd. A group of about eight Brazilian ladies grabbed Sean right out of my arms and quickly passed him from one to

Sean Flying to Paraguay

another until they could all give him a hug, kiss his hands, and feel his blond hair.

In August 1971, I was informed by CARE-NY that I was being transferred to Guayaquil, Ecuador. When I told the head of Grace Lines, he said, "Oh my God. What did you do wrong?" We had an uproarious laugh, but I knew that being posted in Santiago was as good as it gets, especially when compared to Guayaquil, the hot, muggy port city. I had visited the terrible slums over the tidal flats where the outgoing tide carried away the waste and garbage below the rickety houses built on bamboo stilts and connected by boardwalks. On our three-month adventure through Central and South America in 1965, Tim, Bryce and I had seen both wealth and squalor.

We had just a couple weeks to pack, pay all our bills, say "Goodbye" and leave. The packers were excellent. I was amazed at the way they could, in just seconds, wrap up a wine glass using a half sheet of newspaper, and throw it in the corner to be boxed up later. Nothing arrived broken.

We spent our last weekend in Chile in our cabin at La Parva. The snow was gone but it was a relaxing two days. An hour before we headed back down the mountain, someone knocked on our door and warned us, "Don't drink the water. It's been contaminated by sewage."

159. OFF TO ECUADOR: 1971-1974

I FLEW TO GUAYAQUIL on September 1, 1971, while Donna and Sean flew home to Wisconsin. After a few days in Friesland, she got sick, went to the hospital, and was diagnosed with hepatitis. The doctors wanted to keep her in the hospital but instead Mom insisted she would take care of her at home. Donna occupied a basement bedroom, isolated for three weeks, while Sean stayed upstairs in the bedroom next to Mom and Dad. When I got the news, I quickly got a gamma globulin

Donna, Mom, Sister Margie with Husband Bob Buege, Daughter Kristin & Dad

shot, as did everyone else who had contact with Donna during the previous week. This was a tough time for Donna. When she heard Sean crying, she was frustrated that she couldn't do anything about it. Once again, however, Mom did a great job caring for Donna and Sean, just as she had done for me years earlier on numerous occasions.

In Guayaquil, I spent a day meeting my office manager, Walter Moran, and all the staff, saw the port and thousands of bags of food, looked at the crummy office, got oriented and flew to the main office in Quito. My new boss, Charles Niemann, had been in Guatemala and then Panama before Ecuador. He had also gone to AIFT. His wife, Ingrid, was a blonde Swede and they had an 18-month-old girl, Erica, and a 3-month-old boy, Eric. Charles treated everyone as equals and was well-liked. The next day we drove south from Quito about two hours to Ambato to inaugurate a carpentry and auto mechanics' workshop.

Back in Guayaquil, I met some of our Canadian friends from Santiago, Bob and Anita Anderson and Murry and Lise Esselmont. In addition, Steve and Linda Smith, who shared our ski lodge at La Parva, now lived in Cuenca. In the meantime, I stayed at the Majestic Hotel and even before Donna returned, I rented a 2-story house with five bedrooms, four baths, a modern kitchen, and a small yard for $220 per month. I also hired a maid, Jesus, and an older wash lady, Juana. Both had worked for Myron Tomasi, a CARE Assistant Director, whom I had worked with in Chile. Bob Anderson introduced me to the Guayaquil Tennis Club which I soon joined and started playing every day at noon for two hours. The club had about six clay tennis courts, a couple of covered indoor concrete courts, and a big swimming pool. I met a lot of people, including a photographer and the Director, Jack Parker, of the United States Information Service (USIS). They put me on TV and said a lot of complimentary things about me: "Although young in age (31), he has plenty of experience in Latin American affairs," so said the opening line in an article that they placed in the newspaper. I soon met the Mayor of Guayaquil and the head of the Port Authority, who both proved to be a big help. After a month in the hotel and getting to know the downtown area, which had been cleaned up considerably since I had passed through six years earlier, I moved in with the Andersons while I waited for improvements to be made on our "new" house. The Andersons had stayed with us in Chile just before Sean was born.

160. TOGETHER AGAIN

DONNA WAS MOSTLY RECOVERED from Hepatitis after two months and had her ticket to Guayaquil. Her flight was late, so every little while I'd call the airport and ask when it would arrive. Since the Andersons lived barely five minutes from the airport, we could get there quickly and meet Donna and Sean even if the plane landed before we left. Every time we called, it still hadn't arrived, so we kept waiting and calling. Then I got an unexpected call from a stranger who said my wife and baby were waiting for me at the airport. We were shocked and tore out of the house as fast as we could. We found Donna exhausted and upset, wondering if she was even in the right country. If she could have returned to Wisconsin at that moment, she would have.

We stayed almost a month at the Andersons and enjoyed their hospitality. Sean loved bouncing up and down in his Jolly Jumper and having ferocious tug-of-wars with the Anderson's feisty Rat Terrier. Sean would hang onto the end of a hand towel while the terrier would growl furiously and pull Sean way off center before Sean would let go, swing back and forth and laugh.

On November 27, 1973, our belongings arrived from Chile and we moved into our new house. Our address was Calle Primera 613 y Las Monjas, La Urdessa, Guayaquil. After three months, we no longer lived out of suitcases. We also got our Siamese cat, Samantha, back from my secretary. For almost three months, the cat was confined to an upper bunk bed to keep away from their big dog. By the time we got her back, I think she suffered from PTSD.

On December 13, 1971, we sent "First Day Issue" cards with the new CARE stamp, celebrating CARE's 25th Anniversary since its founding in 1946, to a lot of our Ecuadorian counterparts. Then we enjoyed a big Chóristmas Party at the Niemann's house for about sixty people that was catered by the Colón Hotel. Whenever we went to Quito, that's where we stayed. Unlike some other CARE Directors, Charles Niemann always wanted us to stay in a comfortable hotel when we were away from home. We also saw the Russian Circus headlined by a famous clown. The juggling was incredible, as were the acrobatics and animal tricks. Back in Guayaquil, we saw it a second time.

In a letter home I wrote, "Sean is addicted to his pacifier which he flips upside down. He loves to wave his arms in the air and beat his spoons on his highchair. He pulls himself up into a standing position and crawls, but sometimes tips over on his head." Just a couple weeks later he was doing much better and could crawl down the hall in record time. Except for his first cold at Christmas, he was extremely healthy.

On January 9, 1972, we found a church. There were about 25 people, including all the kids, and the minister was a layman whose father was the first protestant missionary in Ecuador. He once told me that he used to get terrible migraine headaches, but after acupuncture he never had another. That was the first time I had heard of acupuncture.

Our family friends, Vance, and Dorothy Austin, came to Ecuador and stayed with us for a couple days. We enjoyed their visit and showed them the town. They next visited the boss, Charles Niemann, in Quito, and told him about my work and our hospitality. In a letter to Mom and Dad, Dorothy wrote that "The CARE Director was very complimentary about John's work. We would expect this, but it was reassuring to hear." It was great having a cheerleader.

161. TENNIS AND WORK

DURING ALMOST EVERY TWO-HOUR LUNCH BREAK, I played tennis at the Guayaquil Tennis Club. If I couldn't find a partner, I'd take a half hour lesson from one of the tennis pros. In the beginning, I would get so out of breath dashing from one corner to the other that sometimes I'd have to sit down and suck air for a few minutes. After a few weeks, however, I was in great shape and enough better that I didn't have to play only in the corners. On most Saturdays, I played for several hours. Donna also took some lessons and played a little but spent most of her time in the pool with Sean.

Work was going great and I was busy. Our large food shipments for the country-wide school feeding program were being efficiently moved from the port to all around the country. We had a crew of about ten laborers who manually loaded the trucks and filled our warehouses in Guayaquil. They had a hard job unloading and stacking the 50- and 100-pound bags, which they carried on their backs three or four at a time. When bags arrived damaged, they were reconstituted in new paper bags and claims were made against the shipping lines.

In Guayaquil, 150,000 school kids received a bread roll every day made by a local bakery. For me it was interesting to see just how they could make so many each day. Mom used to make rolls but it took her several minutes to form each one and put it onto the baking sheet. The young men in the bakery, however, could make a perfectly sized roll in seconds. I could hardly believe my eyes. I wish Mom could have seen it.

One day while I was in the port warehouses, I noticed a huge stack of 50-pound bags of DDT. I thought it had been banned after Rachael Carson wrote "Silent Spring" in 1962. It was finally banned in the U.S. ten years later in 1972, but not overseas until 2001. As late as 1980, beef imports from some Guatemalan processing plants were halted by the FDA because of the high DDT content. Way back in 1963, my wildlife ecology professor, Joe Hickey, said he wouldn't give his kids cod liver oil because too much DDT was concentrated in the fat of cod and other oily fish. Back then, even penguins in the Antarctic had 4 ppm in their fat. I wish Mom had known about that before she gave it to me. DDT is still being used around the world, especially in household sprays. Although it has saved millions of lives from insect borne diseases, it should have been replaced years ago.

One day I was visited by the Secretary of Education for the province of Guayas. As we discussed the school feeding program, he cleared his throat, turned around and spit on the cement floor of my admittedly tacky looking office. I was shocked to say the least but didn't respond. That's when I decided to upgrade the location and decor.

Over Easter, Donna and I flew to Cuenca, a beautiful, old Spanish city about 8400' high, to visit Steve and Linda Smith. Steve and I, of course, played a few sets of tennis. During the first set, I felt energetic, but I huffed and puffed like I was about to die. After 30 minutes, I suddenly adapted and breathed normally as I did at sea level. The weather was perfect, less humid than Guayaquil.

162. AN R&R WORK TRIP

GUAYAQUIL WAS A REST AND REHABILITATION (R&R) post because of the muggy climate and perhaps because of the general messiness of the city. That meant we could take an extra vacation out of the country. For six days in April 1972, we flew to Bogota, Colombia and visited both the

Carlsons and their three kids, our friends from Chile, and Jay Jackson from the Peace Corps who a year earlier had married another PCV in our group, Marsha Lang. The R&R, however, turned out to be a semi-business trip. My big boss in CARE-NY, Bert Smucker from Overseas Operations, arrived in Bogota, then coincidentally flew with us to Quito and Guayaquil. Every night in Bogota and Quito, we went to a party for Bert, and when we arrived back home in Guayaquil, Donna and I had dinner for him that night as well. Bert Smucker, you may remember, was the man who fired and rehired me after Colombia. When Bert visited my office, all was in order and Charles Niemann had given me a glowing evaluation. Among other things, I asked Bert what my future was with CARE. He said, "Don't worry about your experience in Colombia and you can expect to be promoted to Assistant Director in the near future." A month later, our shipment arrived from New York consisting of a stove, freezer, radio, TV, air conditioners, fan and somehow two floor polishers. Things were looking up and I was soon promoted to Assistant Director.

Keeping Cool

One day after a heavy rain, as I drove my big ugly Chevy Carry-all down to the port, I noticed that the driver in a new sedan next to me was chauffeuring two elegantly dressed ladies. At that moment, I hit a big, water-filled pothole and a huge wave of muddy water poured in through their wide-open rear window soaking the ladies. Since I couldn't do anything about it, I just kept going.

Sean started walking everywhere at 13 months and two months later spun in circles like a ballet dancer. He enjoyed taking walks, going shopping in the stroller and was very affectionate with everyone including all the little kids in a playgroup that Donna organized. This gave the five mothers a chance to drink tea and eat cookies. Donna was also happy to be elected membership chairwoman of the British-American Women's Club. Now she could meet even more people.

Donna kept busy entertaining a lot of friends and in turn we were invited out often. One evening, Curt and Linda Ferber came for dinner. He was starting a new business buying local handicrafts and exporting them to the states. Donna made corned beef which had to be cured with saltpeter for three weeks in the refrigerator. Saltpeter could only be purchased in a drugstore, and since it was an ingredient to make explosives, she had to give them her name and address. I wasn't too sure about eating saltpeter either because of the rumors I had heard. The next night Jack Parker, the Director of USIS, and his wife Carol, invited us over for a Mexican meal. Jack drank, often to excess, and one night many of their guests took off their outer garments and jumped in the pool. I was way too sober to follow — but I did think about it.

In June and July 1972, the three of us flew home to Wisconsin for about six weeks of home leave. We had a great time seeing everyone and of course went on a bit of a buying spree.

A couple years earlier in 1970, the Physics building, Sterling Hall, on the UW campus was bombed and the anti-Vietnam war protests continued. On our home leave, I went to Paul's church to a debate on the war. The church was packed but no minds were changed. I just heard a lot of angry people yelling at the others. Dad had written a full-page anti-war editorial that was published in The Capital Times, Madison's afternoon newspaper, which showed a map of Madison, including the lakes, covered with dots. Each one represented a 500-pound bomb and showed how devastated Madison would be based on the tons of bombs dropped in Vietnam. The country was divided.

Donna, Sean and John, July 1972

Back in Guayaquil for Christmas and New Year's, we attended a bundle of cocktail parties. Our order from Sears Roebuck, which included a 6' Canadian Pine Christmas tree, arrived just in time. Sean got a lot of toys including a Fisher Price Airport and a talking Bugs Bunny. He mostly threw his toys and we were fortunate that we had relatively indestructible, solid wood furniture. Donna felt better after we learned from Paul that I used to do the same thing. Mom thought I was a perfect kid and couldn't remember such behavior although she did briefly mention it in my baby book. Paul, however, remembered because he was on the receiving end of my cast iron toys. I was born in the iron age.

We ordered a 10'x13' wool carpet with a pattern of squares filled with Aztec designs from a shop in Ambato, a town south of Quito. At my request, it was made an extra half inch thick so we could have a wrestling mat. It was hand-made with 60,000 knots per square meter, similar to a Persian carpet. It completely changed the appearance of our living room which now looked more comfortable with some of the terrazzo floors covered up. The first thing that Sean did was climb up on the bellows coffee table, jump down and roll over on the carpet, thus giving our purchase his seal of approval.

In January 1973, the rainy season started with a bang. The streets downtown flooded, covering up all the potholes, and people would take off their shoes to get to their cars. Then the *grillos*, or crickets, would cover the sidewalks and streets by the millions making popping sounds when we drove over them. Every seventh year, when the plague was the worst, the roads and bridges became slippery with several inches of squashed *grillos*. Luckily, we missed the worst of it.

I somehow became the Program Chairman of the American Society. My first job was to organize the Valentine's Day Party. It turned out to be a big success as over 150 people attended. Everyone sent their $8-dollar entrance fee to me. As I was counting the heaps of money with another American who worked for a big U.S. accounting firm, he looked at me and said, "It sure is lucky we are honest."

163. AN EMERGENCY AND A SURPRISE

ONE NIGHT ABOUT 11:30 P.M., just after we fell into a deep sleep, we got a phone call from a stranger asking if Donna, being an RN, could immediately accompany him and his four-month-old baby boy, Voepke, to New York for an emergency operation. Voepke had recently had surgery for a bowel obstruction and the local doctors didn't want to risk another. We quickly agreed, got dressed, grabbed Donna's passport, an almost empty suitcase, and rushed to the airport where the authorities were waiting to escort Donna to the idling Braniff jet. Seconds later the plane took off and she found little Voepke hooked up to an intravenous tube clogged with blood. As the jet roared down the runway, she frantically tried to get it flowing again. She asked if there was a doctor on the plane. There was but he was drunk. For the next several hours, Donna sat crossways in the seat, checking the baby's temperature, and monitoring how he was doing. Meanwhile, Voepke's Dutch father was seated several rows behind while his mother was stuck in a Guayaquil hospital with hepatitis. Shortly before the plane stopped in Miami, Donna decided another long flight to New York might be too much for little Voepke, so arrangements were made for him to be taken to a Miami hospital as soon as they landed. Disembarking in Miami turned out to be the right decision because as the plane descended, Voepke's intestines became "unobstructed" which meant additional surgery would probably not be needed. All three quickly sped off in a waiting ambulance to the hospital where Voepke recuperated.

Tsáchila (Colorado) Indians

Donna enjoyed a week's vacation in Wisconsin before meeting up with Voepke and his dad in Miami for their return flight to Guayaquil. This was a whirlwind trip and Donna felt nauseated much of the time. There was a reason why. Donna was pregnant.

In April 1973, Mom and Dad flew to Ecuador for a month. On the way to Quito we briefly visited some of the few remaining Tsáchila (Colorado) Indians who mostly live in the rainforest around Santo Domingo. The men shave the sides of their heads, cut their hair to look like a cap, and dye it red with achiote seeds which they mix with grease. The women normally went topless and they both wore striped skirts. We then continued up the steep highway and headed north to the Indian market in Otavalo and Ibarra, famous for its wood carvings. We next showed them Quito before heading home to Guayaquil.

164. EXPLORING THE GALAPAGOS

THE HIGHLIGHT OF THEIR TRIP to Ecuador, was a week-long trip to the Galapagos Islands. From Guayaquil, we flew straight west for 600 miles and landed on little Baltra Island using the same runway that American servicemen built during World War II.

The Lina A

A bus carried us to the "Lina A," a 1000-ton Greek ship that held 60 passengers comfortably. The schedule was well-planned with breakfast sometimes as early as 6:00 a.m. We made 2-5 stops per day, mostly wet landings, which meant we waded the last few yards to shore holding our cameras, socks, and shoes. We were divided into four groups of 15 people, each with an excellent guide. During the hot noon hour, we stayed on board and after an afternoon stop, we had happy hour at 5:30, dinner at 7:30 and briefings for the next day's adventure at 8:45. All our long rides, from one big island to the next, were at night.

When we crossed the Equator, we had a special call to the lounge by Davy Jones and were told to get on our knees. Then Father Neptune came raging in, dressed in an outfit replete with a gold crown, trident, a skin-diving outfit, and a sheet for a mantle. He carried a large fish on a meat hook and then castigated us for polluting his domain, dropping film wrappers, chasing the iguanas, and pestering the sea lions. To expiate our many sins, we had to kiss the fish. It was a good icebreaker.

Back at the UW I had read "Darwin's Finches" and knew about the endemic bird and animal life. There were 13 "different" finches that all built nests with roofs, laid 4 white eggs splotched with pink, made similar unmusical sounds, yet had different shaped beaks depending on the food source available on the island where each lived. Some had beaks for eating seeds, others for catching insects, one pecked blood from the tail of the White Booby and one even broke off cactus spines to probe grubs out of holes. This differentiation of beaks caused by the different availability of foods on each island intrigued Charles Darwin on his 1835 voyage and led to his theory of evolution. To me, these behavioral changes and beak modifications were no different than those caused by breeding dogs. The finches were still finches, and all the sizes and shapes of dogs were still dogs. One species didn't turn into another.

Whalers and pirates exploited the tame fur seals and giant tortoises, which weighed up to 500 pounds. The tortoises, stacked in the ship's hold, provided them with fresh meat for more than a year. Of the 15 species of tortoises, four are now extinct. The introduced goats, pigs, donkeys, dogs, cats, and rats have destroyed some islands. On one island, three goats multiplied to 30,000 in 15 years. Sea Lions were the most common animals lounging on the beaches and the big bulls outweighed the cows by seven times. We saw a lot of Marine Iguanas, Land Iguanas, Galapagos Penguins, Sally Lightfoot Crabs, Swallow-tailed Gulls, Lava Gulls, Waved Albatrosses, Lava Lizards, Galapagos Snakes, Galapagos Hawks, Flightless Cormorants, Galapagos Doves, Galapagos Ducks, Fur Seals and Galapagos Tortoises. We also saw many birds that could be seen in other places including Magnificent Frigate Birds, Flamingoes, and the Blue-footed, Red-footed and White Boobies. For me, it was the trip of a lifetime.

165. A NEW OFFICE

I HIRED A NEW SECRETARY to replace the one who thought I was too fussy. Finally, my letters were typed without a lot of mistakes. My new secretary was just 18 years old, had gone to school for six months in Los Angeles, and could speak and write well in English. When I told Donna that she was even good looking, Donna replied, "And I bet she calls you Mister." I was almost 33 and Donna was right. I also hired two new inspectors, and a new warehouse man with two assistants. In addition, I rented a new office, ordered new office furniture, carpets and even hung pictures on the wall. I thought that if the Provincial Director of Education visits me again, he would now behave more appropriately. On July 6, 1973, I had an open house celebrating my new office, with catered snacks. A lot of important people came, about 40 in all, including the Mayor of Guayaquil, the Director of the Ecuadorian-North American Center, our counterparts, the CARE Director and a new Field Representative, Ginny Ubik, who was stationed in Quito.

The new office furniture was made by an American of Russian descent, Dimitri Voronek, who

Blue Eyes

quite often traveled north of Guayaquil to Manta and Bahia de Caraquez, where he bought Pre-Columbian pottery that the locals dug up. He then sold it to the tourist shops in Quito for 25 times more than he paid. I went with him several times and bought about 30 smaller pots and bowls for about $600. Most of it was from the Manteño Period (600 to 1534) and some from the Bahia (300 BC to 500 AD), the last of the Inca civilization in Ecuador. Someday, I thought, I could make some money for my retirement.

Donna continued to be active in the British-American Women's Club and was elected Second VP. She loved all the social activities and we never did slow down having dinners, parties, and dances. Being pregnant again didn't slow her down a bit. It appeared too that Sean was growing up. He was mostly potty trained, wasn't throwing things anymore, only took one nap a week, and once when Donna asked him to put an empty milk carton in the garbage, he actually did it. He understood a lot more Spanish than English and watched Sesame Street on TV, but on our recent home leave, he wouldn't watch it in English. By the time our second baby would arrive in October, we had hopes that our firstborn would be nothing less than a well-behaved little gentleman.

In June, Donna and I were invited to meet a young local artist, Jaime Villa, who was having a private exhibition of his oil paintings at the home of one of our acquaintances. I fell in love with one 3'x4.5' painting, very typical of Ecuador, with seven kids, a chicken, and a cat. For years it was displayed above Mom and Dad's fireplace at their home in Madison.

Although it might seem hard to imagine for everyone who knows me merely as the husband of Mrs. Hospitality, I continued to be the Program Chairman of the American Society. Believe it or not, I organized activities, such as the July 4th celebration at the American School where we had donkey and train rides, games, baseball, a raffle and even some fireworks, and a few months later, a wine and cheese fondue party.

Our Swedish neighbors, Björn and Hannelore Edstav, took care of a tiny Ecuadorian baby that was being adopted by their friends back in Sweden. The baby was severely malnourished, lethargic, and weighed just six pounds even though she was almost seven months old. They had to wake her up every few hours to eat because she had learned that no one would respond when she cried. By the time the paperwork was completed, and her new parents arrived, little Helena had turned into a happy, chubby baby. We provided Helena with some elegant outfits that the Tapias, back in Chile, had given us before Sean was born.

A year before Björn and Hannelore arrived, it had been interesting to watch their future house being built. The workers first poured the concrete walls and then chiseled out the openings for the windows. One day as we left the house, we saw a dead rat that the workmen had tossed into the street. I said to Donna, "When you see one rat, there are ten more." Sure enough, when we returned late in the day, there were ten dead rats lying in the street. Another morning, just as I was about to leave for work, Hannelore called me in a panic, "Could you please come over right away and kill the rat in my bathtub?" I killed it with a broom handle. It had come into the house up through the toilet, jumped into the tub and couldn't get out. I'd seen that before and it did give you something to think about.

Donna was into macramé in a big way. Once she taught herself how to tie the many kinds of knots, she started covering bottles and Japanese fishing-net floats and made various items such as purses, key chains, and wall hangings. Soon she was teaching classes and had up to 26 women in our house at a time. In the market she could buy various thicknesses of high quality cotton cord which all had to be rewound to get them untwisted. Cords were all over the house.

In addition to my duties supervising the various school and maternal child feeding programs, I was also involved with a project in Cuenca where we built small village water systems. The water sources were often high on hillsides above the villages, which we first protected from contamination before the water was piped down the hill. The program benefited a lot of rural people and I was amused that the first three times I went to Cuenca, my picture appeared on the front page of the newspaper. At the inauguration of one project, they served the local delicacy, guinea pig, and a full glass of warm local whisky. The guinea pig was rather sweet and quite tasty but most of my warm scotch was used to water a nearby plant. I often wondered if it would kill a potted plant since I did this on more than one special occasion.

In Ecuador, unlike Chile, I occasionally found schools with rodent-infested storerooms full of old, damaged bags of food. Those School Directors either had little interest in the program or, to put it more charitably, had no money to hire someone to prepare it. CARE provided food to all the public schools, while Catholic Relief Services (CRS) supplied the much smaller number of Catholic schools. A few times, however, I encountered Catholic schools that received CARE commodities. This situation was usually a big headache because the priests in charge were accustomed to doing whatever they wanted, were never questioned by the people, and often didn't follow the guidelines of the program. All we required was that they store the commodities in a clean, dry room and prepare them for the kids on a regular basis. One day when I visited a parochial school, the bags of food were chewed open by rodents and the storeroom was so filthy I suspended it on the spot. As soon as we departed, my school inspector and I quickly drove to the other nearby Catholic school, which had obviously received a call from the first. As we approached the school's entrance, we watched a column of students quickly carrying bags of powdered milk across the open courtyard to a classroom. After they had finished, we entered the school and talked to the Director who showed us the almost empty but messy storeroom. Then I asked about the bags that the kids had just removed — and CRS got another school to manage. I was glad not to be the Director of CRS who had to deal with the untouchable priests.

In early October 1973, the Embassy announced that the Thunderbirds, The Air Force's precision flying team of F-4E Phantoms, were coming to Guayaquil. At 11:00 a.m., the exact moment they were scheduled to arrive, I almost jumped out of my seat as they roared directly over my office. Later, along with hundreds of other people, we drove to the airport where we stood on the runway no more than 50 yards from the jets as they took off. They soon disappeared but after a minute we could see them all silently coming right at us, each from a different direction before they all crossed just feet above our heads. The noise was deafening. It was a great show as they performed various formations and flew straight up and out of sight. The next day in Bolivia, they broke the sound barrier and the sonic boom knocked over 80 shacks on the edge of La Paz. I don't know who paid for that.

166. OUR NEW BABY GIRL

AFTER DONNA WAS ABOUT SIX WEEKS from her delivery date, her outings with Sean always included a stroller. If he broke free, it was getting too difficult for Donna to catch him. Then, just one day before her due date, the boss, Charles Niemann and Ginny Ubik, came to Guayaquil for a

Sarah Elizabeth McLeod

day of relaxation. Even though Donna was due any moment, we all went on a power boat ride with some friends and almost got dumped in the water when the steering cable snapped, spinning the boat around in a sharp circle. Charles and Ginny then stayed for dinner and the night since all the hotels were full. After dinner, Donna started having regular contractions. By 2:00 a.m., we called the doctor and woke up the boss to grab the packed suitcase and tell him we were leaving — but "We might be back."

At the clinic, Donna continued having contractions for the next four hours. Some moronic intern came in and even pushed hard with his knuckles on the top of her stomach hoping to push the baby out. Donna said, "There has to be an easier way." Finally, Dr. Medardo Blum arrived about 6:30 a.m., and after an additional hour of pushing, he decided to do a C-section since the baby's heart rate had increased too much with each push. That's when I left the room.

At 8:30 a.m., on October 10, 1973, Sarah Elizabeth was born. Donna was relieved and happy when she saw her healthy, baby girl who weighed 7 pounds, 9 ounces. The whole ordeal had not been as quick or relatively easy as her first, but she was perfect. We named her after Donna's Grandmother Sarah and her Aunt Sarah and after my Aunt Elizabeth and her daughter, my cousin, Mary Elizabeth. After all that had happened, plus six days in the clinic, it still cost less than $200 to have a baby in Ecuador.

Sarah was not very hungry and took her time nursing. Halfway through, she would fall asleep or get the hiccups. She had small hands and feet and was a very feminine little girl. Sean always wanted to hold her but when she started to cry, he quickly handed her off to the nearest person. After six days at the Clínica Hill, I took Donna and Sarah home. We had decided that two kids would be our limit and I was the lucky one who avoided the operation. As a result of our actions, we were worried that night when Sarah had a fever. When the doctor said she was just a little dehydrated, we were relieved.

Sarah was a happy, healthy, cute little baby, with a more tranquil temperament than Sean who travelled thousands of miles all over Chile, Ecuador, and to Wisconsin within months of being born. After 60 days, Sarah had gained 50 ounces and was doing well.

Rev. & Mrs. Alan Reid who baptized Sarah with Donna & John

Meanwhile, Sean turned into Dennis the Menace. He loved to tie his train, a Fisher-Price airplane and two noisy toys behind his tricycle and race around the table making a lot of noise. He stayed on the go all day long, almost never took a nap and wouldn't go to sleep until he went outside and looked at the moon and stars. When the maid next door told Sean that she was going to take Sarah home, Sean ran over to Sarah, gave her a hug, and said, "No." Another time, Sean was unrolling the toilet paper when I said, "No, it costs a lot of money and I don't have a lot of money, so please don't waste it." Sean said, "Plata," which meant money in Spanish, and stopped doing it. At almost three years, after jabbering all day with the maids, he understood much more Spanish than English.

We continued going to a lot of farewell parties, Christmas parties, New Year's parties, all kinds of parties, including one at the home of the CEO of the Standard Fruit Company. They lived in a grandiose house paid for by millions of stalks of bananas. With two little kids, Donna was starting to get tired of parties and preparing so much food.

For the previous three months I had coached wrestling every noon to some junior high kids at the American School. It had been eleven years since I wrestled, and it was fun to do it again. I weighed 180 pounds, just a few more than my in-between-match wrestling weight. The school even paid me $5 per hour which covered my Tennis Club dues. Tennis was keeping me trim.

The American Consul appointed me to be on the Board of Directors of the Ecuadorian-North American Binational Center. I was also on the Board of Directors of the American Society and our church.

Dad wrote a poem for our new baby girl:

"The Belle of Guayaquil"

There is a special place on earth
Round which the equator reels,
And if you go there you will find
The Belle of Guayaquil.

October 10th of Seventy-Three
A big event revealed.
That's when the stork delivered
The Belle of Guayaquil.

There was Donna, John, and Sean, but
For a family ideal,
Along came Sarah Elizabeth
The Belle of Guayaquil.

She's a cutie in pink booties
With tremendous sex appeal,
And to her Dad and Mom she is
The Belle of Guayaquil.

She's a "Bless'd Event" and "Heaven Sent"
A fact you can't conceal,
We'll count the days 'till we can see
The Belle of Guayaquil.

167. TRANSFER NEWS

IN JANUARY 1974, CARE-NY wrote that I would soon be transferred to Islamabad, the new capital of Pakistan. The city was designed by a Greek architectural firm in 1959 and the first people started living and working there in 1965. We started to empty out the freezer, but then my transfer was delayed because the Director of Overseas Operations "had to study the chessboard a little longer." Moving people around was a complicated process and it wasn't easy matching people with new countries, but it did irritate Donna, who felt she was an uprooted pawn. In the meantime, my boss, Charles Niemann, got transferred to Jordan on April 5th and the new Director, Jim Puccetti, visited for a few days from Nicaragua. Until he arrived three months later in July, I was the Acting Country Director and had to fly to Quito several days each week.

News of our upcoming transfer threw a wrench into the gears of Donna's contentment. She wrote, "I'm tired of Guayaquil and being involved with too many projects. Next things are making Easter baskets, arranging Easter breakfast at Church, and then a farewell party at our house for our Swedish neighbors, the Edstavs. I'm also in charge of the food for a charity BBQ for 130 people. I'll be glad when it is May." For that party, we grilled 70 pounds of filet mignon with all the fixings, baked pies and churned ice cream and made over $500, much more than we had expected." Filet mignon cost the same as hamburger so you can guess what we always ate.

Meanwhile, I kept busy flying back and forth between Quito at 9400' and Guayaquil at 4' above sea level. In Quito I signed a new Maternal-Child Feeding Program contract with the Minister of Agriculture, and the next day in Cuenca, a $90,000 contract to construct gravity-flow water systems

Sharp Dressers: John, Ginny Ubik & Jim Puccetti

in two rural villages. I also played a lot of tennis whenever I got the chance, and in retrospect I'm sure Donna would have been happier if I'd been around home more. We did enjoy a couple weekends at the beach in Salinas. Sean loved the beach and ran and ran. On the way home he went to sleep in the car at 4:00 p.m. and didn't wake up until the next morning.

Donna continued, "Sean still goes to nursery school each morning and loves to play with the other kids. He says a few more words but still doesn't express himself well. Physically he is continually active. It is hard to explain how active unless you see him in action." I wrote home saying, "Sarah is cute and has light brown hair. She gets up on her hands and feet and does push-ups and rocks back and forth. She doesn't crawl on her hands and knees, but she covers a lot of ground on all fours. She almost sits up by herself and is strong and alert." A month later in May, "She was standing up and crawling all over the house. Sean loves her, and when she smiles at him, he lights up." He also started swimming lessons, jumps in and struggles a couple yards to the edge of the pool."

168. LOANS TO FRIENDS

CURT AND LINDA FERBER, two of our friends, had a business exporting local handicrafts to the States a year earlier, Curt explained he had a cash flow problem and made a proposal to me — I would loan him $3000 and he would pay me back in short order with a sizeable profit. I agreed and withdrew the money from my Chase Manhattan account. After a couple months, I didn't receive the promised payment, but Curt assured me he would pay me soon. Because it didn't come, he tried to pacify me by giving me several onyx bowls and other items which were hand crafted. Then I was surprised to learn that Curt had received at least a half dozen much more sizable loans from other Americans and Canadians, who I thought should have been sophisticated enough to have declined his offer. He finally paid back a couple hundred, but my time was running out and I had to think of something before my upcoming transfer to Pakistan. Then I learned that a person who wrote a bad check could be imprisoned, so I persuaded him to write me some post-dated checks for the full amount. He agreed, probably because he was sure I would be transferred before the dates on the checks. CARE, however, for the only time in my career, was slow to act. During the next three months, I was able to cash the checks and recover my money. From then on, I have only loaned money that I was willing to lose, money that I didn't expect to get back. Better yet, be anonymous if you can, because expectations are resentments waiting to happen.

169. A SORE BACK AND FRUSTRATIONS

ONCE OUR TRANSFER TO PAKISTAN WAS FINALIZED, Donna, Sean and Sarah flew home to Friesland on June 22, 1974. Donna needed a vacation and was feeling a bit frustrated with life. She had been living a long way from home and had missed her family and her sisters. Her back was sore and bothering her again as it had in Chile, partly from lugging all those suitcases and kids on her trip home, and she was even being influenced by the women's liberation movement. I was doing what I wanted but Donna was left with the kids and the maids and didn't have her nursing job for self-esteem. She had been covering up her frustrations by being overloaded with social activities. When she arrived in Friesland, it was obvious to her sisters, Sharon, and June, that she needed to be "born again."

Both Donna and I had always gone to church, and we attended regularly in Ecuador as well, but except for Sunday morning, our lives weren't reflecting our stated beliefs. We had been living like everyone else, working, eating, drinking, and making merry. At the time, everything seemed fine to me and I thought it was the same for Donna. Her sisters, however, could see that she was somewhat overwhelmed keeping up with Sean and Sarah and couldn't even stand up straight because of her sore back. To make matters a bit worse, Sean came down with impetigo, a highly contagious skin infection that caused red sores on his face. Sharon's husband, Chuck, also talked to her about being born again one afternoon in his fishing boat where Donna and Sean were a captive audience. Donna had never heard of being born again and she thought they were all a little wacky.

Sharon and June loaded her down with books on the Holy Spirit along with a little pamphlet called, "Have you Made the Wonderful Discovery of the Spirit-Filled Life." Her whole family knew that Donna needed prayer.

Just before leaving Ecuador, I did my best to get tennis out of my system. From 8 a.m. to 5 p.m., I played 23 sets. I was pleased to find that the Tennis Club had a masseuse who I thought was going to pull my toes off.

After a turnover with the new CARE-Ecuador Director, I flew to Wisconsin on the last day of July — after visiting Mary and Louis in Austin and having an interview in San Francisco with Dole, the banana company. I wasn't all that interested but thought I'd investigate the possibility. After a short stay in Madison, about eight months after we first heard about our upcoming transfer to Pakistan, all four of us headed to New York on August 12, 1974. For three days, once again, we all stayed in one of those tiny rooms at the Hotel Tudor where we met up with Ruthie Householder, Donna's maid of honor, and our former pastor, Toby Legg, from Chile.

While Donna, Sean and Sarah waited patiently in the hotel lobby until we departed for our 7:56 p.m. flight to Frankfurt, I was informed that we would not be going to Islamabad, where the Director was stationed, but to Lahore, the capital city of the Punjab. There I would be the Assistant Country Director in charge of the sub-office with two American Field Representatives. That was a big surprise but fine with me. The old city of Lahore, I thought, would be a more interesting place to live than in the newly built capital city.

170. PAKISTAN - A DIFFERENT SORT OF PLACE: 1974-1976

AFTER AN ALL-NIGHT FLIGHT, we arrived in Frankfurt, where we shopped and toured around the city. For the final leg of our journey, which was ten time zones east of New York, I thought we had plenty of cash. Lufthansa Airlines, however, relieved me of $583 for our overweight suitcases. As I counted out my cash, I wondered, "Do I have enough?" I had $15 left but found out minutes later that Donna had $20 of mad money that her dad had given her. We were fine. The next morning at 7:20 a.m., August 18, 1974, we landed in Rawalpindi, the old city next to Islamabad, where the Director, Joe Steele met us at the airport. He handed me an envelope of Rupees, the local currency and took us to the Hotel Intercontinental Rawalpindi. Three days later, we flew to Lahore. Within a week, I met an American who worked for American Express. He quickly got me an American Express card and I no longer worried about such unexpected travel expenses.

My first week was a bit of a whirlwind. I was not only suffering from jet lag, but all the names and places were completely different. My Spanish and much of what I knew was, of course, useless, and now I had to get used to the Pakistani accents and the completely different Islamic customs. I realized I was asking the same questions several times and Mike Viola, whom I was replacing, said at the end of the week, "At first, I was beginning to wonder about you." So was I. After a few weeks, it got easier to remember names and places. I found it interesting that the busiest main street in Lahore, and in other cities as well, was McLeod Road, named after Donald McLeod, who became the Judicial Commissioner of the Punjab in 1854. Whenever I said my name, they all knew how to spell and pronounce it.

During those first few days I didn't even try to drive my car but instead observed what everyone was doing. I thought that since the steering wheel was on the right side, that would make it somewhat easier to drive on the left side of the road. When I first ventured out on my own, however, I ended up on the wrong side after the very first corner. After a few days, I got the hang of it.

171. A CHANGE OF HEART

FOR THE FIRST THREE WEEKS IN LAHORE, we stayed at the Intercontinental Hotel which had a big pool and international food. It was very pleasant, and the kids loved swimming. Sarah, at 10 months, floated around with arm bands and Sean, now 2 ½, could dog paddle across the pool. Sarah's crib fit in the closet, and while the kids were napping, Donna started reading the books and the tiny pamphlet that her sisters had given her.

It was the pamphlet that first caught her attention. It talked about natural, spiritual and carnal man. A natural man, she read, doesn't accept the things of the Spirit of God because they seem foolish. Such a man sits on his throne and does what he wants, which often results in discord and frustration. A spiritual man listens to and does what God wants for his life. Christ sits on his throne and directs him, which results in harmony with God's plan. The carnal man is one who has received Christ but who lives in defeat because he trusts in his own efforts to live the Christian life. He is on his throne and he directs his interests, which again results in discord and frustration.

Donna realized that even after all these years, she was living as a carnal Christian. She could see that she had many traits of such a person including jealousy, worry, guilt, discouragement, and a critical spirit. She wanted what she wanted and was frustrated with the way her life was turning out. Several verses started making sense. "I am the vine, you are the branches; he who abides in Me, and I in him, he bears much fruit; for apart from Me you can do nothing." John 15:5. "But the fruit of the Spirit is love, joy, peace, patience, kindness, goodness, faithfulness, gentleness, self-control; against such things there is no law." Galatians 5:22, 23. "But you shall receive power when the Holy Spirit has come upon you; and you shall be My witnesses both in Jerusalem, and in all Judea and Samaria, and even to the remotest part of the earth." Acts 1:8. She realized she didn't know God in a personal way, so in her hotel room, while I was at work, Donna prayed to be filled with the Holy Spirit — and she was. Her entire attitude towards me, Sean and Sarah suddenly changed. She was now happier, more content and satisfied.

Soon after arriving, we discovered that a church service was held at Forman Christian College. The college, founded in 1864, was administered by the Presbyterian Church and had been attended by many notable Pakistanis. The minister, Al Scholorholtz, had been an Iowa farmer, attended Princeton Theological Seminary, and with his wife, Peggy, were missionaries in Pakistan for 25 years before going to Nepal for ten more. He taught English at the college and we soon got to know him well, along with many others who attended church. There we met several people who were definitely different from all the others. When you met a real Christian, it was evident in the way they talked and acted. It made an impression on me but when people asked me how Donna had changed, I would joke and say, "She's now a little bit grumpier." That kept the conversation trivial. I still had a long way to go and didn't even know it.

172. SETTLING DOWN

AFTER JUST ELEVEN DAYS, we rented a big, three-bedroom, three-bath ranch house at 3 Gulberg III on a one-acre lot surrounded by a brick wall. It had a half-circle driveway with a garage and two gates, a big, flat backyard, servants' quarters on the end of the house, big open living and dining rooms, plus a large screened porch and brick patio. With many recommendations, we soon accumulated the required number of maids and servants. We hired 1) a cook who shopped, baked bread and prepared the meals ($25 per month), 2) a bearer, who served the food and cleaned except for the bathrooms ($20), 3) a nanny to take care of Sean and Sarah ($20), 4) a gardener who mowed the grass and cared for the landscaping, 5) a sweeper who worked about 2 hours cleaning up around the outside and also cleaned the toilets ($4), 6) a night watchman who walked around the house all night to keep us safe ($19), and 7) a washer man who came several times a week to wash and iron our clothes ($6). It was a lot to supervise but probably sounded heavenly to people back home. For us, there were too many social distinctions. We certainly were, however, helping to support a lot of people for less than $150 per month. After just a week, we thought one of them stole Donna's Chilean gold coin broach that we purchased in Tacna, Peru when we renewed our visas. This caused Donna to walk around with a bunch of keys, opening and closing cabinets, to keep everyone honest. On our next home leave, we discovered Donna's long-lost pin in the little top dresser drawer at her mom's house in Friesland.

Until our shipment arrived from Ecuador, we rented a refrigerator and some furniture to make camping out in our house more comfortable. At first, I thought it pretentious that people kept their refrigerator in the dining room, but soon discovered that our kitchen was so warm, often 105 degrees, that it wouldn't make ice. That's when I pushed ours into the dining room as well. After our air conditioners were installed, we had 36,000 BTUs in our living-dining rooms and they barely kept us cool. Each bedroom had a 20,000-BTU air conditioner as well. We also rented beds, but Sarah's bed had to sit on four saucers filled with soapy water to keep the ants from attacking her and her baby bottle. Big black ants were everywhere. Surrounding our patio, columns of ants crawled up and down the trees. The exterminators dug a trench around each tree, poured in a gallon of ant poison and covered it up. The next day our entire brick patio, which was about 25'x30', was covered with ants that I swept up in piles and dumped in the garbage.

We also rented an ironing board that arrived broken and wouldn't stand up. The washer man didn't care because he just squatted alongside as he ironed the clothes. While waiting for a bus, most Pakistanis squatted flat-footed. You had to be thin and flexible to do that or your stomach would push you over backwards. At age 34, I was surprised how easy it was to squat.

At sunset, the night watchman kneeled on a white sheet and prayed towards Mecca for about fifteen minutes. The rest of the night, he walked around the house, stomping his staff on the brick walkways which let everyone know where he was.

Sarah Exploring the Backyard, Lahore

173. A NEW OFFICE

I RENTED A NEW BIGGER OFFICE located just down the street from our house and my two main local employees were an accountant, Hafeez, and a secretary named Gilani. Both were hard workers, but it did seem strange to dictate letters to a big, burly man. His shorthand was fast, and my predecessor said he had even typed 80 pages one day. We also had ten other local office employees. There were two American Field Representatives, Brian Walker, a big 6'6" former PCV in India and Randy Trudelle, an architect who wrote and illustrated a handbook on how to build soil-cement houses. Most recently, he had been in Timbuktu, Mali. Everyone was busy supervising a construction project of 100 houses.

The 10'x30' houses were simple and consisted of two rooms with two windows and two doors. The 4"x6"x10" blocks were made by compressing a mixture of sifted dirt, sand and 7-10% cement in a Cinva-Ram machine. The roofs were made with concrete tiles which were supported by reinforced concrete beams covered with several inches of dirt and dung. Each house cost about $350 and the new owners were responsible for preparing the soil and making the 4000 blocks needed for each house.

I worked on a new 2200-house project, financed by USAID, at a cost of $620,000 in the war-affected area called Bajwat near the city of Sialkot. In 1971, India and Pakistan had gone to war, a nasty border skirmish, and when the Indians retreated from the area called Bajwat, they carried off everything of value leaving the Pakistanis with nothing. Because the U.S. supported Pakistan in this instance, Americans were very welcome, which facilitated our negotiations and relations. All the older people in Pakistan and many of the young spoke English because it had been part of India, a British colony, until 1947, just 27 years earlier.

In addition to the USAID financed project, we signed another agreement with the Canadian International Development Agency (CIDA) for 3000 more houses costing $1,000,000. Now we had plenty of work on our plates. When the CIDA contract was signed, a third Field Representative, Brian Wolf, arrived from Canada to help manage the program. CARE provided the materials, supervision, and training. Pakistan exempted CARE from taxes and purchased 4000 Cinva-Ram block-making machines. We hired 150 construction supervisors and were managing one of the largest construction companies in Pakistan.

Early on, I decided that I would try to make a 16mm movie of the housing project. As I learned more and more about the project, I added to my outline all the shots I would need. Since CARE-NY was always on the lookout for fundraising photos, they agreed to purchase the sound film. After I filmed several rolls, I mailed them to NY where they were developed and copied. They sent back the copies and commented on the results. This went on for more than a year.

Life was busy for Donna who was struggling to adapt to managing seven servants and learning about a vastly different culture. We purchased 69 yards of heavy cotton material which she sewed into curtains, as every room had big floor-to-ceiling windows and doors that opened to the back patio and yard. The tile floors were all cleaned by several workers using diesel-powered grinders

Sean & Sarah with the Nanny, Rosalie, & her three kids

which made a huge, smelly mess for days. If you didn't pay close attention, the workers often stopped. We had to fire our first cook and then the nanny who followed Donna around like an imprinted chicken. Finally, we found a faithful nanny named Rosalie who lived in the end of our house with her husband and three little kids. She was kind and loving but couldn't be firm with Sean, whom she called "the little master." Sean was over in their quarters much of the time and was getting quite adept at eating curry and naan with his fingers with all the Pakistani hand motions. I was stunned He could understand the gardener speaking in Punjabi, but He still didn't say much in English.

174. HOME IMPROVEMENT

AT CHURCH, THE NURSERY WAS CLOSED one Sunday, and Sean sat through the entire service without a peep. Sarah was a little cutie and at 13 months walked all over the house and yard. Everyone we met touched her light brown hair as if it brought them good luck.

Sean & the Gardner

In November 1974, we received two of our three boxes from New York including our new refrigerator, a stereo and a recliner chair that had a vibrator and heating pad in the back. On cold days, it was a great way to warm up and the vibrator quickly took away any headaches after a frustrating day. The new refrigerator made Donna happy because she no longer had to prop the door shut with a can. The kids loved the new swing set and Sean his big wheel.

For Thanksgiving, the U.S. Consul, Bill Spengler, invited 170 Americans over to his grandiose house for a potluck dinner. If you ever visit Lahore, remember that the weather in November and March is almost perfect. Our personal effects arrived from Ecuador before Christmas and even though one of the lift vans arrived upside down, very few things were broken. Best of all, I traded the big wooden boxes for a 4'x6' Pakistani carpet. At the same time, we bought an inexpensive 10'x14' rug that we put under our dining room table. It dressed up the room but one morning, just before we headed to church, we found Sean sitting under the table eating from a pint jar of honey. When we asked him to come out, he poured it on his head and all over the rug. By the time we left Pakistan, we decided to leave the rug behind. It wasn't worth cleaning.

175. CHRISTMAS IN LAHORE

ALL THE AMERICANS IN LAHORE were again invited to a big Christmas party at the Consul's house. There were games for the kids and even a snake charmer who played his flute, while the cobra and the hundred kids followed his every move. When he was done, he tucked the snake back into its round wicker basket and flipped the lid shut. During the entire show, 14-month-old Sarah wandered through the crowd as she pleased but as soon as the cobra was placed back in its basket, she ran over and started to lift the lid. Nobody moved to stop her except Donna who sprinted across the lawn just in time to close the lid. Donna didn't know if the cobra was de-fanged but minutes later learned that in Pakistan, Santa arrived on a camel.

At 15 months, Sarah was imitating everything. When we said, "No," she would smile and repeat "No." Sometimes she showed her temper by lying down on the floor crying but would soon stop if we didn't pay any attention. She often changed her clothes and danced whenever she heard music. We thought she was very precocious.

Donna and I took Urdu lessons for a couple months. We learned a few useless phrases but could see it would never amount to anything. Everyone we met spoke English, and the locals, I found out, spoke Punjabi. Besides that, there was no way for Donna to act normal around the male teacher who would take every gesture or direct look the wrong way.

Buying meat, which was mainly goat and water buffalo, was an interesting experience. At the outdoor market, the butcher sat inside a screened enclosure surrounded by big chunks of meat hanging from hooks. As he squatted on the floor, he held a long knife between his toes and would then draw the meat over the knife and cut off the amount we wanted. Sarah liked to go shopping too, but since she had an extra keen sense of smell, she would gag if she got too close. Donna had to leave her in the car with the driver.

176. THREE GIRLS IN AFGHANISTAN

ON JANUARY 22, 1975, Donna, along with two other girls, Nancy De Young and an Indian girl married to an American, took a week-long trip to Afghanistan and India. They first flew to the border town of Peshawar where they stayed the first night in an old hotel. Donna was surprised that the Indian girl, so accustomed to being surrounded by hordes of people, actually paid a hotel employee to sleep outside her hotel room door all night.

All Dressed Up

The next morning, they were served bed tea in their rooms before departing for the bus station. It was an all-day trip on an old school bus which switched at the border to the left side of the road before continuing over the Khyber Pass to Kabul, the capital. The scenery consisted of desolate rock-covered hills with occasional small compounds or towns surrounded by high adobe walls for protection. While in Kabul they stayed at the USAID guest house and one night enjoyed an American movie at the American Embassy. On their way back to the guest house, the taxi driver kept reaching back to grab their legs, but they kept slapping his hands away and survived the ride.

Shopping in the bazaar, which was full of handmade rifles, clothing, silver jewelry and semi-precious stones such as lapis lazuli, was most interesting. They flew to New Delhi on Afghan Airlines, best known for its "two frights per week," and enjoyed all the pungent curries and Indian foods before flying back to the border city of Amritsar where I picked them up. Knowing what I soon learned about Afghanistan, I never would have let Donna go on such a trip with two other girls. For Donna, however, it was a real adventure. This all happened just four years before the Russians invaded Afghanistan in 1979 and occupied the country for ten years, losing 15,000 soldiers and millions of dollars of planes and equipment. While Donna was gone, the American Women's Club elected her Membership Chairman. She wasn't too happy, but it was the easiest job. Donna was still "entertained out" after Ecuador.

While Donna was gone, I wrote Mom and Dad a letter saying that "Sean is talking a bit more, not always too clearly but is a sweet little kid. Sarah could be a bit stubborn but most of the time is a perfect little doll. She dances to the stereo, acts coy, plays very well by herself and even looks at books for 10 to 15 minutes by herself. She started crying at dinner tonight and I couldn't figure out why. I finally handed her a bottle which she promptly threw on the floor. Sean said, "She wants her bottle." He got out of his chair, picked it up, held it for her, and she drank and was quiet. I'm glad someone was observant. Sean was almost four years old.

177. TEN HOUSES PER DAY

WORK WAS GETTING BUSY at our Bajwat building site, a three-hour drive Northeast of Lahore to Sialkot and up to four more hours by Jeep or horseback.

I had three Field Representatives working on the 2200-house project aided by 150 local employees. Some worked in the central casting yard, where they made the roofing tiles and reinforced concrete beams and lintels. Others supervised the delivery of materials from the closest

Loaded Camels and our Jeep Crossing the Tavi River into Bajwat

city of Sialkot to the building site on the other side of the Tavi River, while still others trained the future homeowners to prepare their homesites and make the blocks.

In one week, I purchased 116,000 bags of cement for $110,000, steel reinforcing rods for $65,000, a stone crusher to make gravel for $5000 and 10,000 gallons of sodium silicate to help waterproof the blocks. All these materials were carried across the river by camels. It took a lot of delivery orders to keep track of the 150 camels that plodded back and forth several miles each way. One big camel carried 900 pounds of cement. If it were dry in Kashmir and the river was low, we could drive across the river by Jeep, or if not, we used a small raft just big enough for the Jeep and a few people. It was always risky and sometimes we'd have to take the engines apart to dry them out.

I don't believe there was ever a project where the people worked harder. This wasn't true, however, in the beginning. At first, the people had a hard time believing that a compressed-soil cement block could hold up against the torrential downpours and flooding that occurred every

Sifting Soil for Making Cinva Ram Blocks

Unloading Cement

rainy season. As a result, the project got off to a slow start. The severe flooding that came a few months later, which submerged the stacks of blocks for several weeks, was the turning point.

A Christian group, sponsored by the World Council of Churches, planned to build 200 houses but ended up completing only 70 before their money ran out. They had suggested that CARE take their money since we were far more efficient. CARE benefitted from a basic agreement with the government, while they were forced to spend half their time and energy doing menial tasks just to stay alive. Being a missionary was often frustrating without the benefits we had.

A House Nearing Completion

178. WILD BOAR HUNTING

IN THE MIDDLE OF JANUARY 1975, I went along on a nighttime wild boar hunting trip near our Bajwat project site. Our open Jeep was filled with six rifle-toting Pakistanis who all helped supervise the housing project. We bounced over the lumpy fields hanging on for dear life looking for boars.

The slaughter started as soon as we found herds of 15 to 25, some big and a lot of little ones. Everyone was shooting wildly, and the driver ran over and squashed as many as he could. This massacre went on for several hours and I soon lost count of the number killed and maimed. Being Muslims, they hated pigs with a passion and wouldn't even touch them. About 2:00 a.m., we stopped at a stranger's house, knocked on the door, and when the man finally answered, the driver asked if he could give us some hot tea and something to eat. To my surprise, he agreed. Pakistanis, especially in this case, were beyond hospitable. Maybe it was because everyone was toting a rifle except me. By then I was almost frozen and was glad to step out of the Jeep.

Near the end of our hunt, I was asked if I wanted a pig to take home. Not worrying about being culturally sensitive, I said "Yes." Before long they shot a choice 60-pounder which I stuffed in a big plastic bag. Back at the project, I put it in my Jeep and started home the next morning. That night, after dark, I started to gut the day-old carcass. For a while, my butchering project was going quite well, and I had a couple chunks of meat removed. After all, I had dissected animals in comparative anatomy class and knew where the various parts were located. I even had a refresher course during our Peace Corps training, but despite this classroom knowledge, I proceeded to nick the boar's intestine which quickly and totally ruined my project. I carefully stuffed the smelly mess back into the plastic bag, put it in the car and Donna and I looked for an uninhabited spot to dump it. Everywhere we went that night, there were people. In fact, so many people lived in the old city that if everyone came out of their houses at the same time, there wouldn't be room on the streets for all of them. Every time we thought we had found a spot, someone appeared. After consuming a half gallon of gas, Donna jumped out, quickly opened the back door, pulled out the bag and we sped off into the darkness. Knowing how hated pigs were, I always wondered who got the job of removing it from the gutter. No doubt it was a Christian sweeper.

In 1975, when relations between the U.S. and Pakistan were at their best, I never felt any tension from my Muslim co-workers which they harbored against their hated Indian Hindu neighbors. Tension was stirred up years later by Islamic fundamentalists who took the Koran, the Haditha, and the sayings of Mohammad literally. With 75,000 Madrases currently in Pakistan, which teach hate and death to infidels, I wouldn't want to return. Any religion that depends on force to obtain followers proves it's not based on truth.

179. SEAN'S FOURTH BIRTHDAY

WE RENTED A SHAMIANA (an 18'x18' canopy), to shield us from the sun for Sean's fourth birthday. In no time at all, the man who brought it had it up and firmly secured at all four corners. The colorful Shamianas greatly added to the party atmosphere and were used at all Pakistani celebrations. In addition, we had a man-powered merry-go-round so six kids could twirl around at once. Four donkeys also gave rides to the 13 kids. We even hired a snake charmer who played his flute while the cobra swayed back and forth following his movements. He then had a little sparrow fly around and pick pennies off the foreheads of the kids. It was a great party with plenty of cake and ice cream and Sean enjoyed getting all the birthday cards.

180. HOME LEAVE

Back: Elaine, Paul, Donna, Sarah, Eric, David & John
Middle: Jennifer, Esther Jane, Art, Margie and Mary
Front: Sean, Karin and Kristin

OUR NEXT HOME LEAVE was now set from May 23rd to July 24, 1975. We flew to Karachi, Athens, Frankfurt, and Geneva where we met Jorge and Toni Tapia, our doctor friends from Santiago. Donna was in the market for a watch, but after Jorge suggested an Omega with some diamonds that cost a mere $3000, we decided to postpone our purchase rather than look like the poor cousins we were. Next, we flew to Copenhagen and Stockholm and spent the week visiting our Swedish neighbors in Guayaquil, Björn and Hannelore Edstav. Houses in Sweden were very modern, but everything was in miniature and close together. On May 31st, we returned to Frankfurt and Donna, Sean and Sarah flew to Madison. Before joining them, I flew to New York for the week where I was debriefed by all the CARE Department heads.

In Madison we enjoyed staying at Mom and Dad's where I was able to rip out dozens of honeysuckle bushes and cut down dead trees from their 4.3-acre lot. At Paul, Elaine, David, Jennifer, and Eric's house, we loved the meals and all the ice cream. We appreciated seeing Margie, Bob, Kristin, and Karin in their new house in Greenfield, and Mary, who came from Austin.

When people say, "You don't choose your family," they usually mean "Make the best of the miserable hand you've been dealt. If I could pick mine, I'd gladly choose what I was given.

When Donna's Mom and Dad heard that Charles and Frances Hunter, known around the world as two of the "most anointed and energetic evangelists on earth," were coming to Minneapolis on June 26th, they wanted to go and took Donna along. At the end of the service, the Hunters prayed for Donna. That day she learned that there was power in the Holy Spirit.

Dorothy & Walter De Young
with June, Sharon, Mark & Donna

We also spent time in Friesland and Delavan visiting Donna's relatives. Of course, we went to the Tuesday night band concerts in Friesland for pie and ice cream which were a regular feature since 1914. Some of the original band members were still playing.

With Donna's sister June, her husband Fred, their three kids, Gretchen, Betsy and Fritz, along with Donna's other sister, Sharon, her husband Chuck and two of their kids, Linda and Amy, and the four of us went to Moon Beach Camp at St. Germaine in northern Wisconsin. All thirteen of us stayed in one big cabin and we had a great time swimming and enjoying all the kids and games.

181. BACK TO PAKISTAN

Horse Taxi

AFTER TWO MONTHS IN WISCONSIN, we landed in Karachi at midnight and were met by Scott and Linda Law, our friends who had just moved from Lahore. They took us to and from the hotel and we had a joyful reunion until our flight the next day to Lahore. When we arrived, the weather was perfect, but two days later it was over 100 degrees. Jet lag hit us all again and messed up our sleeping schedule for several days.

I spent a week in Islamabad attending a USAID seminar on how to write project proposals. It was interesting since CARE had just revamped the way we wrote and evaluated projects. Meanwhile, heavy rain slowed work at our project site and the river was high, forcing us to cross by boat. Every time I went to Bajwat, I continued filming the scenes I needed. My detailed outline of each step in the process was getting filled with film and I now had about 90 minutes of developed film on 30 three-minute rolls. I was pleased that I consistently exposed the film correctly and that it was steady because I always used a tripod. Donna's sister June wrote, saying she had seen my film in a CARE commercial on TV. When I wrote to CARE-NY, they confessed that the "eagle eyes of my sister-in-law had indeed seen my film." I was surprised they hadn't told me in advance. A thank-you note would have been a thoughtful gesture. At least they sent me a copy of the ad.

While I was away, Donna went down to the Delhi Gate in the old walled city of Lahore. It was one of thirteen gates or entrances to the old city named because it faced the Mughal Capital of Delhi, now called New Delhi, the capital of India. Pakistan, both East and West, broke away from India and became independent from British rule in 1947. Pakistan was formed for the Muslims while India remained majority Hindu. East Pakistan, which was separated from the West by 1000 miles, became independent in 1971 and is now called Bangladesh. The buildings around the Delhi Gate were used by the British for administrative offices.

Sean and Sarah Clowining Around

Donna was accompanied by Mrs. Shaw, whose husband Laverne worked for USAID. Once they arrived by taxi at the little Presbyterian Clinic supported by Forman Christian College, Donna helped dispense medicines to the poor people. She also folded paper into little packets so people could carry their pills home safely. They continued doing this for several months. The clinic was also close to the old-clothes bazaar, where you could buy anything imaginable, including old prom dresses used by American teenagers years earlier. For a costume party, Donna bought a majorette outfit and a clown suit for Sean. One man who attended the party wearing a pink bunny suit arrived late because he had been delayed when his car temporarily died at an intersection. The clothes had probably been collected by churches and sent overseas to needy people and ended up in the bazaar. Once Donna and Mrs. Shaw finished dispensing medicine, they sometimes rode home in a horse-drawn carriage.

On September 1, 1975, Sean started attending Nursery School each morning and soon had a girlfriend, Kathie. They enjoyed swimming in the pool, the classroom's pet mouse, and the day when the whole class went to the market to buy some finches. Once a week after school, Donna taught a macramé class like she did in Guayaquil. When Kathie's mother brought her along one afternoon, Sean gave her a kiss and a hug.

In October, before the hottest days of summer came to an end, we had a pleasant five-day vacation at the Hill Station, Murree, in the mountains of northern Pakistan. We traveled with another couple, Mr. and Mrs. Kubilay Saleh, Director of the World Food Program, who was from Cyprus. We stayed in a small hotel with a beautiful view down the valley and could see the second tallest mountain peak in Pakistan, K2, which was 26,400' high. We enjoyed the cooler weather, hiking and horseback rides. On our drive home, we were passed several times by a speeding Mercedes Benz that barely slowed down around the steep, blind curves. Every time we caught up and drove past them, their little girl was vomiting on the side of the road.

182. DONNA MEETS A RICH GIRL

MONTHS EARLIER, A WEALTHY PAKISTANI GIRL, Belum, chaperoned by her brother, had car problems in front of our house. She knocked on our door and Donna invited her in to make a phone call. Over the next few months, they became better acquainted and Belum even attended some macramé classes. Belum was from a very political family and her mother was the head of the Women's Pakistani Peoples Party (PPP). Belum confided in Donna about her upcoming arranged marriage, which was upsetting to her because her future husband was in the military and they would be living near the unruly Afghanistan border. When the time came, she invited Donna to the Mehndi, for women only, on a Wednesday evening where they painted designs on her hands with the red-orange dye from the mehndi plant (also called henna) for good luck.

On Friday we both were invited to the big wedding. We didn't need directions because we could see the sky glow from the thousands of colored lights that were draped over the huge two-story house. A big diesel generator inside a semi-truck provided the power. When we arrived, Donna went to the right with all the women and I went to the left with the men. We stood and talked under at least a dozen Shamianas, those colorful canopies, that covered most of the yard. There were several different kinds of delicious curries to taste and everyone was dressed in their finest. On Donna's side, she felt seriously unadorned and had never seen so much gold jewelry, so many gold bangles up and down the women's arms, or so many exquisite saris. Belum, of course, was the center of attention, and was loaded with gold necklaces, rings, and bangles up to her armpits. The climax of the evening was when former Prime Minister Zulfikar Ali Bhutto entered with his wife. Just four years later, when he was again the head of the PPP (which he had founded in 1959), he was deposed in a military coup and hanged.

Our Bearer, Lazarus, asked to take off three days because his mother was sick but then he didn't show up again as promised. Three weeks went by, then three months. Finally, Lazarus reappeared from the dead. His excuse was one we didn't expect. He had gotten in a fight and spent three months in jail. At least his mother hadn't died for the third time, an excuse that some had tried. Donna was glad to have his help once again and he did work hard, but by the end of the year, he disappeared again, this time for good.

183. A GAME OF SQUASH

AN AMERICAN FRIEND INTRODUCED ME to the game of squash, which is similar to paddle ball but played with a half-sized tennis racket and a small rubber ball about as big as a golf ball. My friend, who now weighed some 350 pounds, down 200 after several "removal" operations, soon tired after a few games. That's when he introduced me to a little Pakistani named Gogi, and suggested I play a game with him. Gogi agreed although he wasn't dressed to play, wearing bell-bottomed trousers, a tight long-sleeved shirt, and leather shoes. Near the end of the game, while I whacked the ball with my big tennis swing, I thought "If only I were in better shape, I could beat this guy." Near the end of our 9-3 game, Gogi hit that little rubber ball with a flick of his wrist so hard, I thought it would go right through the concrete wall. That's when I realized that getting in better shape wasn't the answer. My friend then mentioned that Gogi was the third-ranked squash player in the world. A few months later, at the world championships in Karachi, where Pakistan International Airlines constructed a new squash complex, Gogi won it all and became the world's top player.

184. LEATHER LUNGS

ONE OF THE MAIN SOURCES OF FUEL in the homes of poorer people was water buffalo dung. While it was fresh, the women shaped it into patties and slapped it onto the side of their houses to dry. In the winter months, dung fires caused a lot of air pollution and made it difficult for me to breathe. I felt like

A Charming Hotel at Bentoto

my lungs were made of leather and I had to consciously breathe deeply to get enough air. The doctor prescribed several different pills, including Valium, which helped by making me a bit more relaxed. Fortunately, we had a two-week vacation scheduled in Sri Lanka, formerly known as Ceylon, where the warm, moist ocean air near the equator was just what the doctor ordered.

On December 4, 1975, we met my PC friends, Jay and Marsha Jackson in Colombo, the capital of Sri Lanka, and vacationed with them down the west coast. We stayed at the luxury tourist hotels in Bentota and Tangalle Bay for about $20 per night. The beaches were beautiful and the weather balmy as we drove all the way south to Yala, the game preserve. There, a big elephant stood just inches in front of my rented Datsun "160," and didn't budge for twenty minutes. Sean and Sarah,

Taking His Time

ages 2 and 5, were getting antsy, and we were anxious that the big bull might sit on our hood. As the elephant ambled off the road, it literally disappeared after taking just a few steps into the brush. There were also huge crocodiles, deer, elk, monkeys, a leopard, storks, peacocks, hornbills and other strange birds.

At the museum, they had replicas of the largest Indian and African elephant tusks. The Indian tusk was about 7' long while the huge African tusk was about 15' and three times thicker. We also rode on an elephant near Kandy where we saw the Botanical Gardens and the Temple of the Sacred Tooth, which houses the relic of the tooth of the Buddha. It was a great vacation and I felt much better by the time we returned.

185. HEALTH CARE IN PAKISTAN

IN KARACHI WE EXPECTED to be met again by Scott and Linda Law, but they weren't anywhere to be found. A few days later we heard that Linda had died. They were playing frisbee in their yard when the wall fell on Linda and broke her ribs. After a couple of days in the hospital, her lungs started filling up with liquid. Then the prescribed medicine caused a convulsion. The next medicine stopped her heart. Unbelievable and sad. They were some of our favorite friends and still in their twenties.

The United Christian Hospital in Lahore, which was built and operated for years by missionary doctors, was also in decline. The missionary doctors had been asked to leave a few years before we arrived, and the hospital was now run by Pakistanis. I went there once to get a urine test and when I walked down the hall with my little plastic cup, I noticed that it was leaking. I hope the lab tested it quickly.

186. OUR VERY OWN SHAMIANA

AFTER SEEING SO MANY CANOPIES or Shamianas, we decided to purchase one for just $700. Shamianas were 18'x18' sunshades, which came with four 10' bamboo corner poles, and four sides about 7' high to keep the wind out. During the month when the Shamiana was being fabricated, we went to see how they were made. It was quite a production. We found six men working in a hot, sunny, concrete courtyard, all squatting down in front of old Singer machines, sewing one layer of colored cotton material on top of another making fairly intricate symmetrical designs that were repeated on the different panels. I couldn't believe how well it turned out. It obviously wasn't the first one they had made.

187. VISITORS FROM HOME

Welcome to Lahore

MOM AND DAD FLEW TO LAHORE on February 23, 1976, for a month-long visit. Donna, Sean, and Sarah met them at the airport along with my office staff who presented them with leis of flowers which they put around their necks. I arrived from Islamabad later in the day. Shortly after they arrived, we started getting ready for Sean's delayed fifth birthday party. We now had our very own *Shamiana* and we again hired the same three men to operate a merry-go-round, the cobra and sparrow show, and donkey rides. Donna baked a big train-shaped cake and we had plenty of ice cream for the 60 guests and kids. It was a great birthday party and Mom and Dad were amazed at the organized chaos. Every morning, the driver chauffeured Donna, Mom and Dad all over Lahore seeing the sights and sounds. They were intrigued by all the water buffalo, goats, dogs, gypsies, rickshaws, horse drawn carts, cars, bicycles, and huge numbers of people everywhere.

188. TRAVELLING ON THE GRAND TRUNK ROAD

Downtown Kabul

WE FLEW TO PESHAWAR, close to the Afghan border on March 13th, leaving little Sarah behind with our friends, Bill and Kathy Reisen. Bill was doing research on mosquitoes, along with his boss, Richard Baker, who lived across the street. Richard and his wife Anita had ingratiated themselves with Sean by lending him the video game, "Pong,"

Tough Negotiators

which in 1972 was just the second video game ever released. The Reisens had a couple of little kids who loved having Sarah with them while we were off on our ten-day trip.

The next day, we boarded an old bus and headed for Kabul, Afghanistan on the Grand Trunk Road, built in the third century. It started in Chittagong, Bangladesh, and passed through Calcutta, New Delhi, Amritsar, Lahore, and Peshawar, until it ended 1600 miles later in Kabul. We passed through several towns where groups of young teenagers were sitting around with their homemade rifles. Their targets were any bird that moved but there didn't seem to be many in sight. I couldn't figure out where their food was produced. All we saw on the all-day ride were big, barren hills covered with boulders. Everything was gray or brown. We also saw a lot of 1955 of Chevys completely loaded with baggage chugging over the rough gravel road. When we got to Jalalabad, several inches of snow were on the ground, the first Sean had ever seen. He enjoyed making snowballs.

Late in the day, we took a taxi to the USAID Guest House, but not before an Afghani, who carried my suitcase about 10' before I took it to the cab, became very angry because his tip wasn't large enough. As I got in the taxi and shut the door, he jerked the door open and the door handle I was holding fell off. It was a tense moment.

Overloaded, Overheated, and Overdecorated on the Khyber Pass

Moving Right Along

We found the next four days to be extremely interesting. Dad commented on how big the Afghans were because in Sri Lanka and southern India, the people were quite short and thin. Closer to Afghanistan, they got much bigger and stronger. The doorman at the Intercontinental Hotel was at least 6'10" and there were a lot of men bigger than Dad who was 6'4." They were handsome men,

The 6'10" Hotel Doorman

but we didn't know what the women looked like, since they were completely covered with black burqas. They could only see the outside world through a small mesh window. One man with a staff walked behind his wife swatting the backs of her legs as he angrily kept her moving along. It was not a safe place to be a woman.

The bazaars were amazing. There were hundreds of homemade guns for sale with beautiful inlay work on the stocks. It appeared everyone could make their own rifles. Donna bought several Afghan dresses adorned with tiny mirrors and embroidery and several old rings and pins. At a dinner party a few weeks later in Lahore, Donna looked absolutely gorgeous when she wore her new Afghan dress and jewelry. If I hadn't been there, my 6'6" Field Representative, Brian Walker, might have tried to run off with her.

From Kabul, we made an unscheduled stop in Kandahar, where U.S. forces built an air base after the September 11, 2001 attacks. Flying once again on Afghan Airlines (two frights a week) I thought, "What are we doing here?" When I read about people dying in airplane crashes in remote third-world places, I thought, "What did they expect?" Now I was doing the same thing with the people I loved most.

Look at Me!

Next, we visited New Delhi, a busy city swarming with people, bicycles, rickshaws, scooters, and cars. Donna and I loved the shopping and the food, but it was way too spicy for Mom and Dad. Mom almost stopped eating and Dad thought that his meal of spaghetti had more hot spices than would be needed "by all the people in southern Wisconsin." Until we were transferred to Lahore, it is true that the hottest food I had ever had, with one exception in Aldama, Mexico, was sharp cheddar cheese. After we left Pakistan, however, we missed the "hot" food.

We visited all the major tourist spots, including several huge forts and the Taj Mahal in Agra. When we went through customs in Amritsar, we noticed that the Indian officials had confiscated one of several bundles of peacock feathers from a young American couple who passed through in front of us. When we came through, the Indian officials served us chai tea and for the next fifteen minutes, we had a pleasant conversation with them. Little blond Sean was the center of attention and was given a present — the bundle of peacock feathers. A bit later, the couple noticed Sean with a bundle of feathers, but they were now ours and they decorated our houses for several years.

Back in Lahore, on our big back screen porch, we had a swimming pool 4' high and 10' wide. The kids loved it now that the weather was getting hot. Mom and Dad also enjoyed the pool the last week before heading back to Wisconsin. Then disaster struck. While Dad was walking down the five terrazzo steps to the brick patio in his swimming suit, his wet feet slipped out from under him and he landed hard on the tile steps. I thought he killed himself, but he got up and seemed to be okay. His lower back, however, was severely bruised and oozing in places. Dad, who was almost 68, didn't let it bother him and they departed the next day for Wisconsin. We were sad to see them go but they had a good, on-time trip.

Several months earlier, we had organized a dinner club with eight other couples. We each took turns preparing typical meals from the different countries where we had lived. We hosted the first one, a Chilean dinner, and I showed the movie I had made of Chile. Every couple went all out, relishing our time talking and eating. The dinner club gave us one more excuse to go out for the evening and Mom and Dad attended one of them, a Philippine dinner. Every night that we went out and left the kids with the nanny, we paid her an extra ten rupees or $1. For the month Mom and Dad were in town, we paid for 18 nights, which seemed excessive.

189. KEEP YOUR EYES ON THE SKY

RIGHT AFTER MOM AND DAD FLEW HOME, we hosted a Persian meal. We had our driveway lit up with about 100 small oil lamps which directed everyone to our backyard. The Shamiana was up and all our Pakistani and Afghan carpets and pillows covered the ground. We were all set for an elegant dinner when Bill Reisen looked up at the sky and said, "A sandstorm is coming." I had never seen one, but the sky did look ominous. Everyone, all 15 of us, quickly started carrying all the dishes, carpets, and everything back into the house. As soon as we finished, the wind started to blow, the sky darkened, and we were in the middle of a sandstorm. Someone then said, "Now the lights will probably go out." As soon as he said it, all went dark and the air conditioning with it. We lit the candles, washed all the dishes, set the table, and had our most memorable, delicious dinner. The next morning, we vacuumed up the inch-high sand dunes just under all the doors and windows.

190. CELEBRATING IN BAJWAT

AT THE END OF MAY, we got a cable from CARE-NY advising us that we would soon be transferred to Colombo, Sri Lanka. This was exciting news, since we knew that it was a beautiful tropical island and we would be missing the hot season in Pakistan. At the same time, we were planning to celebrate the nearly completed 2200 house project in Bajwat. I joined over 30 rolls of unedited film end to end onto two big 45-minute reels, so we could show them to the 150 workers and to the hundreds of new homeowners and their families.

Sprucing Up for the Show

Brian Walker plastered and whitewashed the side of a house to make a big movie screen, rented a generator for my projector and even hired some "dancing girls" from Lahore to provide a little entertainment. When Donna and I arrived on June 3rd, everything was ready. You might think that watching 90 minutes of raw footage would be boring, but it sure wasn't to the people who had never before seen themselves or any movie at all on the big screen. The evening was a great success and helped inspire everyone to keep working hard.

191. THE ISLAND OF SRI LANKA: 1976-1980

WE WERE PACKED UP AND READY TO GO less than a month later. Our personal effects were sent to Karachi, and on June 25th, Donna flew home, 11 time zones west, to Friesland with Sean and Sarah. I flew straight to Colombo on July 6, 1976, and stayed in the Cinnamon Garden's Inn, a small family-style hotel near the office. My room cost 50 Rupees a day including breakfast. I soon learned there were two exchange rates, Rs. 8.50 for the locals, and a better rate to encourage tourism of Rs. 14.50. Luckily, I could buy traveler's checks with my American Express Card and then get the higher rate at any bank.

Gathering Coconuts

Sri Lanka, formerly called Ceylon until it gained independence from the British in 1947, is an island just off the southern tip of India. Ports on the south and west coasts were visited by the silk and spice traders from the Orient in the 12th and 13th centuries. About the time of Columbus, the Portuguese arrived and ruled the country for 150 years. They were then followed by the Dutch and English successively, who each ruled about 150 years.

It is about half as big as Wisconsin but had 14 million people, compared to Wisconsin's four million at the time. The predominant religion was Buddhism, with smaller numbers of Hindus, Muslims, and Christians. The women dressed as they wanted, often in saris. Sri Lanka is just a bit north of the equator and the temperature hovers around a humid 85 degrees all year. For me it was perfect, way better than the dry, dusty, and sometimes smoggy Pakistan.

When I arrived, Sri Lanka was getting ready to host the Non-Aligned Nations' Conference held from August 16-25, 1976. They had a new building, constructed and paid for by the Chinese, who used only Chinese building materials and labor. Sri Lanka also painted their government buildings, resurfaced some streets, including the terrible road from the airport, all to showcase the country in a more positive light. During this time, no tourists were permitted to enter the country, presumably to eliminate demonstrations. Even the Buddhist Perahera, the big parade with 100 elephants held in Kandy, was postponed so that the leaders of some 84 countries would have a chance to see it during the conference.

Our Sri Lankan Home

After a month, I was able to rent a large house which took my new landlord, Ruan Ratnatunga, several more weeks to plaster and paint. One of his workers, while standing on a corner talking with friends, almost got picked up by the police as a vagrant. All unemployed people, or those who were just standing around, were taken to a camp until the end of the conference. It didn't look prosperous to have homeless people cluttering up the streets.

Donna and the kids arrived August 30, 1976 after stopping in Amsterdam for the weekend to visit Tony and Alicia Bradburn, our English friends from Ecuador, and Scott Law from Pakistan whose lovely wife, Linda, you may remember, had died in Pakistan. From Amsterdam, Donna and the kids had been on the plane for 18 hours when I met them on the tarmac at 6:30 a.m. They soon saw our house, which was still a mess with a dozen workers plastering, re-wiring, installing new faucets, water heaters and a lot more. Donna was concerned that the house was too big, but I held firm. It only cost $200 per month and was worth the wait. When you visit Sri Lanka someday, go see it at 3 Queens Avenue, just a few blocks from the office which was at 27 Alfred Place, Colombo 3. One thing I learned again about living in a big house is that it costs a lot more. You entertain more and tend to spend more on servants, utilities, parties, and everything else.

The Dolphin House School Kids in Colombo, 1979
Sarah (in white) and Sean (behind)

Earlier I had enrolled Sean in a small one-room school, The Dolphin House, located on the grounds of the Colombo Swimming Club which overlooked the ocean. The teacher, Miss Perera, had a dozen students, aged 4-8, from several countries, including Holland and Iran. Sean was the only student who supposedly spoke English, but he was still trying to sort out Spanish, English and Punjabi. I could see that Miss Perera would have quite a time just getting her diverse students to speak English. By Christmas we witnessed a miracle. The kids put on a 90-minute program, all in English, where they sang songs and recited poems. Sean recited "Little Boy Blue" and I was impressed. Of course, each one had that sing-songy English-Ceylonese accent which I recorded on a cassette tape, the latest technology that was replacing reel-to-reel tapes. Sean liked school but complained about having to sit so long writing letters between the lines.

We spent some of our weekends at the Neptune Hotel at Bentota, swimming at the beach. Donna had purchased snorkeling masks, inflatable life vests and flippers which we soon tried out. At first Sean was hesitant but when I said "Goodbye," he quickly changed his mind and joined me. Instantly, he turned into a little fish and we loved looking at all the tropical sea creatures.

192. MOVING IN

ON SATURDAY, SEPTEMBER 25, 1976, we finally moved into our house after living out of suitcases for three months. Upstairs our house had three big bedrooms, two baths, a sitting room over the carport and a big, open center area. Downstairs was another bedroom, bath, the kitchen, maid's quarters, and big living and dining rooms looking out to the tropical foliage and flowering temple trees. We parked our car in the open carport surrounded by pillars. By Saturday noon, our six lift vans were delivered, and we started unpacking, and by Sunday evening everyone from the office brought over a potluck dinner. It was hectic getting ready and setting the table but a lot of fun. At first a lot of little things didn't work but after our experiences in Pakistan, it all seemed minor. We hired a cleaning lady (Soma), a nanny (Rita), and a cook (John), who did an amazing job using a kerosene burner until our range got hooked up. Donna soon started remaking curtains using our 69 yards of curtains from Lahore and it wasn't long before we were thoroughly settled and back to a busy work and social routine.

193. BEING CONVICTED

DONNA STARTED LOOKING FOR A CHURCH by asking friends and looking in the newspaper. My single requirement was that it wouldn't put me to sleep. Finally, she found one that she thought would fill the bill. The concrete church was under construction on a busy street with parking space for 2-3 cars — but mine was the only one. Donna and I sat in the back row while Sean and Sarah were ushered up to the balcony with the kids. Little blond Sean soon realized that he was the center of attention and started singing "Jingle Bells" in his outdoor voice. Donna and I thought it couldn't be possible, but it was.

As people walked by the side of the church, they would stop and peer in the windows. When trucks or buses passed, it was hard to hear, although the preacher made it interesting with a rousing sermon and plenty of singing. At the end of the service, he asked me to give the benediction, but I couldn't believe I had heard him correctly as I looked at Donna for confirmation. I remained silent and he gave it a second later. At the end of the service, when he introduced himself and his wife, Lloyd and Roshini Perera, he said, "I thought you were missionaries."

The church was "The Colombo Gospel Tabernacle." In the following weeks, it seemed as if the pastor had talked to everyone I knew and then wrote his sermons just for me — which kept me awake. Yes, I was being convicted by the Holy Spirit whether I knew it or not. We became friends and when Christmas came, I was Santa Claus for the kid's program. Sean and Sarah suspected it was me from the shape of my nose but fortunately kept quiet.

194. DENGUE FEVER

DENGUE FEVER, YOU MAY REMEMBER, was the mosquito-borne illness that forced the cancellation of our first month of PC training in Puerto Rico. That's when our future PC boss hurt so acutely that a nurse had to lift his arms off his chest because he couldn't do it himself. Getting break bone fever wasn't funny.

Next it was Donna's turn. Shortly after we arrived, Donna came down with a non-stop, splitting headache and felt rotten. When she got up and opened the second-story bedroom window, she felt she could just fall out and wouldn't care. Back in bed, she couldn't even pray, so she asked me to pray for her. After a week, we went to the doctor who informed her that she was starting to get better, but that depression was a side effect. The doctor's parting words were, "You can get this again." Once Donna started feeling somewhat more normal, both Sean and Sarah came down with a milder version but were much better after a week in bed. A month later, an American couple's little girl got sick when they were on vacation in Nuwara Eliya and died from Hemorrhagic Dengue Fever, a more severe version, before they could get back to Colombo. After that, everyone was in a panic and no longer looked at mosquitoes as a harmless nuisance. We soon hung big mosquito nets from the ceiling that covered all our beds. Tucking the nets in became a nightly ritual.

After this scare, Donna became much more concerned for the kids' health. Weeks later, Sarah caught some intestinal bug, had a fever and was limp as a rag lying across Donna's lap at the doctor's office. With tears in her eye, Donna prayed and was filled with peace when she realized that Jesus loved her even more. Feeling peace at such a time was a real blessing from God.

194. AT THE OFFICE

CARE HAD SEVERAL PROGRAMS all aimed at improving the nutrition of infants, nursing mothers and school kids. The school feeding program provided eight high-protein cookies daily to about 1,000,000 kids in grades 1-5. Wheat-Soy blend (WSB), a PL 480 product, donated by the USAID program through CARE, was the major ingredient.

The Thriposha Program was another CARE effort aimed at infants and lactating mothers. We originally distributed repacked PL 480 Wheat-Soy Blend (WSB), but we soon started to use Instant Corn-Soy-Milk Blend (ICSM) because it was easier for the mothers to prepare. The corn and soy could also be locally grown, so we could eventually phase out the donated U.S. products. About 800,000 750-gram packets were distributed monthly at the Ministry of Health clinics.

It was my job to write a project proposal to coordinate a new soybean development program that was funded jointly by CARE and UNICEF. Each donated $227,000 to support soybean production, processing, and information to promote the program.

The cultivation of soybeans was assisted by the International Soybean Program of the University of Illinois (INTSOY), and Dr. Carl Hittle was the agronomist who consulted with the Department of Agriculture in their efforts to grow it successfully. He and his wife, Grace, lived in Kandy and became our friends and working partners.

Processing soybeans was the second part of the program. Because the diet of the average Sri Lankan lacked sufficient protein, it was CARE's goal to develop inexpensive soy-fortified foods and incorporate them into people's diets. In addition to Thriposha, we developed soy-fortified cereals with help from our consultant, Ron Tribelhorn from Colorado State University in Fort Collins. Using an extruder, which he set up and then trained our factory workers to use, we produced a variety of soy-corn-rice flakes and full-fat soy flour. Another consultant, Dr. Jim Spata, was the INTSOY Food Technologist who helped develop many other soy-fortified foods, including soy milk. These foods were produced in the new soybean processing plant that we built in Gannoruwa on the outskirts of Kandy. To develop all the new soy foods, we needed a variety of medium-sized industrial equipment which Jim ordered and installed. He then supervised the training and research.

Besides growing soybeans and developing new soy-fortified foods, the third part of the program was the dissemination of information to coordinate all the various activities and educate the populace to eat the more nutritional soy foods that we continued to develop. To accomplish this last goal, I chose to publish a newsletter. During the intervening months, I kept busy getting the proposal approved while continually adding new people and organizations to my future subscription list. Getting all the UNICEF and government officials to agree with the wording of every sentence in the proposal was quite a chore. These officials were quite concerned with contributing their two cents and could endlessly discuss the wording of a sentence even though the meaning was perfectly clear before they started. After one meeting, Jim Spata asked, "How can you stand all the picky and unnecessary suggestions?" My wife would have been proud of my patience.

195. VISITORS FROM HOME

JUST SIX MONTHS AFTER I ARRIVED in Sri Lanka, we were visited again by Mom and Dad. They arrived in early March 1977, for a six-week visit. We travelled all over the southern half of the island and visited all the beaches south of Colombo to the game park in Yala. Next, we toured the tea country beyond Kandy, visited the botanical gardens, climbed the 600' high rock called Sigiriya, and stayed at the Sea Angler's Club in Trincomalee on the opposite side of the island. Since we were members of the Royal Colombo Yacht Club, where we did a little sailing from time to time, we could

Natural Benches

stay at the sister club in Trincomalee. Mom and Dad enjoyed the beaches, always before 9:00 a.m. and after 4:00 p.m., so Dad's flour white skin wouldn't get sunburned. Surrounded by the shorter, slender, dark-skinned locals, Dad reminded me of a great white whale. Fortunately, the warm, salty ocean water cured the frostbite damage to his toes that had resulted from working too long repairing his cold workshop. He had been worried that his toes might have to be amputated.

On our trip we saw dozens of girls making batiks, people bathing wherever there was a lake or stream, dozens of Buddhist Stupas, men gathering coconuts and using the husks to make coir mattresses, huge fruit-eating fox bats as big as crows hanging by the hundreds in trees, monkeys, 6-foot monitor lizards and 12-foot pythons crossing the road. We even rode an elephant. Mom had a hard time trying to get up so high on the kneeling giant until I hoisted her up. She finally

Riding High

got situated but was sore for several days after straddling the huge, hairy beast. We stayed in a bungalow that served as General Mountbatten's headquarters in WWII. It overlooked the river where "The Bridge on the River Kwai" was partially filmed.

Our servant problems didn't end the day we left Pakistan. After the six of us returned from Yala, we learned that our nanny, Rita, was missing. The new cook, Raj, said she had gone to Jay Jackson's house where her brother worked. He also said that she was going to bring her boyfriend over to rob the house, but Raj had protested. When we called the Jacksons, Rita said Raj had tried to rape her. At that point I got an interpreter to understand the cook's story. He noticed that Raj's face was scratched and later that Rita's lip was bruised. Rita said Raj had started by bumping her in the kitchen and when she objected, he said, "Why do you object? People bump against you on the bus and you don't object." Rita was 28 and had a child and Raj was married but only saw his wife

every six months. In summary, Raj got fired.

Several days later, we told Rita we were going to the Swimming Club, but at the last moment went to buy a few tropical fish and came back 30 minutes later, much sooner than expected. When we entered the house, Rita was upstairs with her boyfriend. We knew just what to do. Kick her out. When we searched her bags, she had bars of soap, sugar, detergent and even some of Sarah's undies. We then hired an older lady for a short time before finally hiring another nanny, Seetha. We also hired Mary Ann who cooked and cleaned. Dad wrote, "Days go by in sort of a dream. Exercising either muscle or brain seems uncalled for. You cannot open or shut a door without a servant at hand. If you do, you are taking their jobs away."

Donna continued teaching macramé and had 17 students who each paid $10 to help cover materials. She was able to buy quality cotton cord in the market, and one day came home with 70 pounds. Meanwhile, in my spare time at home, I was busy editing my Pakistan Housing Project film and finally cut it down from 90 to about 20 minutes. The more I cut out, the harder it was to throw away useable film. Tough editing, of course, speeded up the film, eliminated the slow spots and made it more interesting. Then I timed each scene and wrote a narration to go with it. It all took a lot of time and I had bits and strips of film all over the bedroom.

Home leave was coming up again after another 30 months. Donna, Sean and Sarah left for Wisconsin on September 22nd and I arrived November 4, 1977, after a week in CARE-NY. When I got home, we once again shuffled back and forth between our parents' homes in Madison and Friesland. This time we were able to spend Christmas at home with snow for the first time in 12 years. However, after Sarah got pneumonia for a couple weeks, we decided that leaving a hot climate for a Wisconsin winter wasn't a great decision.

196. NEW LANDOWNERS

WE BOUGHT 74 ACRES of land while we were home along Highway 22, just north of Pardeeville and Highway 33. I paid the seller, Jack Wynn, on a five-year land contract at 9%. A bit later, we also bought 10 adjoining acres on Military Road from David and Lois Bradley. Our 84 acres now had access on the west side of Highway 22 and the southside of Military Road. Both parcels closed several months later when we were in Sri Lanka.

Each September, we'd suddenly realize we hadn't saved much toward our annual December payment, so we scrimped and saved for the rest of the year until we had enough. Someday, we thought, we would build a house on the property. In the meantime, the land was used for hunting.

We spent our last week of vacation visiting SeaWorld and Disney World. We were met at the Orlando airport by Donna's mom and dad and her Aunt Sarah and Uncle Harold Pautzke. They each had an Oldsmobile 98 which we filled up with all our luggage. We all had a great time although Donna's mom tripped in the motel parking lot and broke her nose and glasses. Three weeks later, on the last day of January while driving in Cambria, she was in a car accident and broke her collarbone, not an auspicious start to the New Year.

197. UNDER STRESS

I DEPARTED FOR NEW YORK a day before Donna and the kids because I was scheduled to narrate my Pakistani Bajwat Housing Project film in a New York sound studio. Because of time constraints, it was the most stressful three hours of work in my life, as I read and added and subtracted comments from my "prepared" script. Sometimes my voice would trail off a bit at the end of a sentence and then I'd be asked to repeat it. I finally finished at 3:00 p.m., just in time to meet Donna and the kids at JFK airport. Amazingly, our separate taxis both arrived at the same time and we all boarded our Swissair flight to Zurich on January 13, 1978. After another day, we were back in Lahore.

198. OFF TO SINGAPORE

TEN DAYS LATER, we flew to Singapore to attend a Soybean Foods Protein Conference along with Jim and Rita Spata, the Food Technologist who helped us develop all the soy-fortified foods. We were warned not to travel with chewing gum, which was strictly prohibited in the neat, clean city-state of Singapore. Those who were caught with gum could expect a stay in jail. Instead, we stayed at the luxurious Mandarin Singapore Hotel and dined in the Neptune Theatre Restaurant, where Donna met some exhibitors from DeKalb, the world's biggest corn and soybean seed producers. Donna's father was a District Sales manager for DeKalb and at the end of the conference and exposition, they gave her eight models of tractors and other farm machinery used in the production of soybeans, as they were "too bulky" to carry home. We had plenty of room since we left Sri Lanka with an empty suitcase.

It was an interesting conference, but at the airport our return flight was overbooked, and I was about to be bumped when smooth talking Jim Spata came to the rescue. He explained that I was the U.S. Ambassador to Sri Lanka and had to be back in Colombo for an important meeting. It worked. Anytime we wanted to get past an obstacle, like airport security to meet someone on the tarmac, we could always get through simply by being bold and acting authoritatively like we knew what we were doing. The poorly paid guards always assumed it must be okay as they certainly didn't want to risk getting into trouble by interfering with some important foreigners — who they assumed must surely have an authorized reason for being there.

During our trip to Singapore, Sean and Sarah stayed home with Noel Barrett, a big, burly teacher at the American School. I'm sure he enjoyed our air-conditioned house with servants to fix his meals. We knew they had fun making and sailing paper airplanes which we found for days under every piece of furniture we owned. They were all fine and so were all the tropical fish in Donna's 20-gallon tanks. Donna even brought home a few fish from Singapore which she carried in a water-filled plastic bag. A few days later, however, they all mysteriously died.

199. SNORKELING IN THE MALDIVES

IN FEBRUARY 1978, we flew to the Maldives, a country of 2000 islands surrounded by coral reefs, about 400 miles southwest of Sri Lanka. From Male, the capital, a boat ferried us to the small island of Bandos. It contained only a hotel, surrounded by a beautiful beach that we could walk around in

The Three Snorkelers

20 minutes. The crystal-clear water around the island was shallow, just a few feet deep, with a huge variety of beautiful, tropical fish, scary Moray Eels and other strange creatures that darted in and out of the coral. There were also Scorpionfish and plenty of nervous looking Barracudas watching our every move. What unnerved Donna, however, was a Stingray she floated right over. I couldn't imagine any place where the snorkeling could be better. Sean loved to snorkel while four-year old Sarah rode on my back. Next came a big surprise. About 200' from shore, we reached the edge of the reef. As we looked over the cliff that dropped off over 100' below us, we felt we would fall right off. Below was a huge Goliath Grouper which made me wonder if I could be its next meal.

The hotel was filled with European tourists anxious to get away from the long, dark winter nights. I couldn't believe how they sunbathed much of the day, even after they were burned and blistered. Throwing modesty aside, most were topless as they sunbathed or swam by. One blonde German girl and her boyfriend who worked for a tourist magazine, borrowed Sean and Sarah for a photo shoot, which later appeared in their magazine. They splashed and played with the kids at the water's edge and pretended to fly an inflatable Lufthansa jet as the topless photographer kept busy shooting. I guess they were the ideal-looking family.

200. BACK IN COLOMBO

SEAN SOON TURNED SEVEN and was getting taller and more grown-up. His birthday cake had seven baby chicks inside and 17 kids helped him celebrate. Sarah had continuous tea parties in her playroom and she constantly raided the refrigerator for food supplies. She also started school at the Dolphin House and loved it.

After work, I played squash a couple times a week at the nearby Gymkhana Cricket Club, mostly with Joe Breckweg, a German fellow who was organizing auto mechanics programs. Joe and his wife Carol also had young kids and we became friends whom we've seen a few times over the years. I also started jogging with a USAID employee who had been the Southwest Colorado mile champion in his high school days. He encouraged me to run slowly so I could talk normally at the same time. That was great advice, but the first few days were still torture. My lower back ached, and I'd have to stop every few minutes to bend over or do a few sit-ups to feel better. After a few weeks, however, my sore back disappeared, my speed increased, and I was soon running about five to six miles several times each week. No longer did I get those miserable side aches like I did during high school cross-country practice. I actually became addicted, and soon was running better than my mentor, who just happened to be a smoker.

Donna was taking piano lessons, batik lessons, a gemology class, yoga and even Japanese Ikebana flower arranging. At the end of the Ikebana class, they had a big show where dozens of people competed to make the best flower arrangement. The show was held in a school gym and some of the arrangements occupied several square yards and were very elaborate. Donna, however, arrived a bit late and had little time to put her simple but elegant creation together. When it was announced that "The winner of the Blue Ribbon is Donna McLeod," she was shocked and amazed. She did, however, spend a lot of time picking out her orchids and she did have some interesting sun-bleached, curly sticks that we had brought back from the Maldives. That's when we overheard another passenger ask, "Why is that lady bringing back firewood?" Her arrangement was simple and elegant. As I walked around the gym looking at all the other more complicated arrangements, I wasn't surprised she had won.

In March 1978, we bought a little Lhasa Apso puppy, Tashi, from the U.S. Consul in Colombo. The kids loved her. That part was good. Mrs. Neff, a friend of my parents, wrote "Soon Tashi will become a part of your family." That was the same Mrs. Neff who paid the vet $150 to watch her dying dog all night back in 1954 when I was 14. I was so flabbergasted that anyone could spend such a fortune that I asked, "Why didn't you just kill it?" That was definitely the wrong thing to say. I had it coming even though she had to wait 24 years to say it.

Donna was the leader of a small women's Bible study, but sometimes found it hard to keep them on track because it was too easy to talk about other things. She followed an Aglow study guide, started reading Watchman Nee's book, The Spiritual Man, and was pleased that it fit well with her Aglow guide. She wrote to her mom "I'm so thankful that God has made our family more loving. We love the kids and enjoy them more, especially when we look at each other with eyes of His love. Next month I have to demonstrate macramé and give my testimony at a different Bible study." Her testimony to the 35 women went fine. She wasn't too nervous. I was glad no one ever asked me to give my testimony. I didn't have one.

201. SAVING A LIFE

ONE OF THE LADIES in her group was Elaine Rader, whose husband also worked for the British Salvation Army. Their salaries were so low I couldn't imagine how they survived. One day Donna noticed that their little 18-month-old girl had a red line going up the vein in her forearm. Donna, being an RN, quickly realized she immediately needed antibiotics and drove them all to the hospital where the little girl was confined for a week. Once home, Donna gave her the last three shots. That quick action possibly saved her life. Another Salvation Army lady was also in the hospital after bleeding for five weeks. They all prayed for her and the bleeding stopped. PTL. Donna was just floating on air after that.

At the same time, a guest evangelist, Jim Davis, preached for several days at our church. He spoke on "Big Dreams for God" and the whole church came forward as he prayed that we would each find direction in our lives. Donna was weeping as she felt that God had been so gracious to her. She had a lot of answered prayers and was sure her other requests would be answered as well. Both of us had some deeper conversations together after that.

One night we went to Jay and Marsha Jackson's house for a delicious curry dinner, along with some USAID people, who had come to evaluate CARE's programs. When Donna mentioned to one guest that my dad had visited here, he said, "I was just talking to your husband about his father, and I hope that my own children admire and love me as much as your husband does his dad."

202. A WEEK IN KENYA

ON MAY 4, 1978, I flew to Nairobi, Kenya to attend a CARE conference for all the Assistant Directors on the Africa-Asia side of the world. Four of us arrived a few days early and hired a driver who took us 190 miles west to the Masai Mara Reserve. The landscape reminded me of Wyoming, where you could see for 100 miles. Now I knew why the Kenyan marathoners were so good. They had to walk or run for miles to get anywhere.

We stayed in a modernized lodge and took several guided tours to see the lions, elephants, giraffes, zebras, wildebeests, hyenas (the ugliest animals alive), leopards, wild boars, all kinds of antelope and more. It was a wonderful two nights before we started back to Nairobi, but our driver pushed the old van too hard and it broke down in the middle of nowhere. We wondered, "How are we going to get back by 6:00 p.m. for the start of the conference?" We all piled out with our suitcases and waited for somebody, anybody, to drive by. Within 30 minutes, all three cars that passed by had picked up the four of us — and we all arrived at the hotel within three minutes of each other. Best of all, we didn't become lion food along the side of the road.

Back in Colombo, Miss Perera, Sean's teacher, was pushing him to read. She said, "He really needs a push." Every morning for a week, Sean complained he was sick attempting to get out of going to school. Sarah liked school but was extremely tired by the time she got home, and it took her over an hour to put on her happy face. After school, Sean enjoyed swimming laps in the pool while Sarah would stand in the baby pool practicing the crawl. It wasn't long, however, before she was swimming from side to side in the big pool.

203. SERVING SOUP

AS SOON AS DONNA SAW the complete set: a large white pitcher, wash bowl, toothbrush holder, soap dish and a one-handled bowl, she just had to buy it. To get my approval for this somewhat unnecessary purchase, she quickly volunteered to spend her macramé teaching money. I appreciated antiques too, thanks to my travels with Uncle Frank, but she had another reason.

She wanted a soup tureen. I didn't think much about it but when we were later informed that soup tureens had two handles — we realized that our new tureen was a chamber pot. Since Donna lived on a farm and didn't have indoor plumbing until she was 13, I would have guessed she knew that. I sure didn't.

While Donna was busy preparing my 38th birthday dinner, my favorite Pakistani meal of ginger chicken and naan, Sarah was trying to help in the kitchen and said, "Aren't you glad you have a daughter who cooks?" Donna said, "Yes I am" and continued telling her stories about Great Grandma De Young and how Sean had seen her just before she died. Sarah responded, "Didn't she drink enough water?" At five years old, I already had her indoctrinated. This all started with Mom's constant reminders to drink eight glasses a day. Wrestling exacerbated the situation. The only way to weigh 5-6 pounds less from one day to the next, was by not drinking water, which made me want it even more for the rest of my life.

204. OUT IN THE MIDDLE

WHEN THE CARE DIRECTOR, Bill Schellstede, and his Korean wife, Sang Mie, were transferred to the CARE-New York office, we took a few days of local leave before the new Director, George Taylor, arrived on July 2, 1978. Once again, we travelled across the island to the Sea Angler's Club in Trincomalee. It was on one side of a U-shaped bay about a half mile wide. Sean and I took our masks and flippers, walked around the shore to the far side and then swam back. Out in the middle, about 10' below us, we swam over a huge pulsating jellyfish that was pure white and about 3' wide. I

The Long Ride Home

thought to myself, "What am I doing out here with a seven-year-old? We don't even have scales." I was somewhat relieved to get back safely. Right after that, I gashed my foot on a sharp shell and spent the rest of our vacation with my foot in the air.

Back in Colombo, we continued to have a busy social schedule. First a cheese fondue dinner at our house, next a Disney movie, "Gus," followed the next day seeing Earlene Bently, a black soul and gospel singer from the U.S., and some local dance groups. Before we saw a local production of "Camelot," some friends picked us up in their brand-new white Peugeot 404. Since we arrived a little behind schedule, they parked under a big tree that turned out to be the roost for hundreds of pigeon-sized birds. When the play was over, there wasn't a square inch of their car that wasn't covered by bird droppings. Droppings isn't the right word. They were much bigger.

Our friends, Arnie and Dawn Remtema, were missionaries who worked for Trans World Radio. Arnie had been working on a new 400,000-watt transmitter to beam radio signals to India. After their first test run, they received over 9000 letters from Indians who said the signal was loud and clear. On July 15th, we attended the inauguration of the new Christian radio station. Arnie and Dawn have remained intimate friends ever since but now reside in Colorado.

205. THE BUDDHA'S TOOTH IN KANDY

ON OUR NEXT TRIP TO KANDY in August, we saw the Perahera, a Buddhist celebration that went on for ten consecutive nights. Each night the parade got longer with more elephants and groups of dancers. The elephants were covered with huge decorated blankets and other adornments and there were more than 100 elephants the tenth night when one would carry the venerated tooth that had

The Perahera Parade in Kandy

supposedly belonged to the Buddha. The next night in Nuwara Eliya, we visited Hunas Falls and the botanical gardens, met Peter, the head gardener, who also showed us the gardens at the President's and the Prime Minister's homes. Back home in Colombo, he worked several days in our yard, brought us flowers, and even cut off a large branch from one of our flowering temple trees, dug a hole and stuck it in the ground. It kept growing and the leaves never even wilted.

206. ONE SICK DOG

A COUPLE WEEKS BEFORE the new CARE Director, George Taylor, arrived from Israel, he sent his old Cocker Spaniel on ahead. Somehow, I got elected to take care of it until he and his wife, Ellen, arrived. A day later, the old limping dog got sick. Donna took it to a veterinarian and the hospital for X-Rays, but the dog became unconscious and had to be put to sleep after it was diagnosed with hemorrhagic fever. I thought, "What a way to start off with my new boss!" We dug a hole in our small backyard and marked it with a stone. Sean was upset when he got home from school and started digging in the backyard to see for himself. When the Taylors arrived, they visited the dog's grave and seemed pleased with what we had done. They were great people and were surrogate grandparents to Sean and Sarah.

In August 1978, we hosted a farewell party for Jay Jackson, who was heading to Costa Rica, while poor Marsha got stuck packing up alone. In the evenings, we also went to a lot of other farewell parties for departing Americans who seemed to come and go in groups. We were losing our temporary friends who replaced our families while we were overseas.

207. JUST CURIOUS

SEAN WAS WORKING HARD AT SCHOOL, had excellent penmanship, and was reading quite well. In some ways he reminded me of a little Buddhist, very tender-hearted and unable to kill a bug. He'd pick up six-inch millipedes in his hand with no thought that they could bite. Both Sean and Sarah would help set the table and do other chores around the house. Sarah was sometimes silly and naughty at the same time, but she was very loving, vivacious, and curious.

One evening, when we were at the boss's house for dinner, Sarah was snuggled up and talking with Mrs. Taylor. Now Mrs. Taylor was a large woman and curiosity finally got the best of Sarah. She crawled up higher, pulled Mrs. Taylor's blouse forward and peered in to see what those big mamas were. Now she knew.

Sarah had a big fifth birthday party at the Dolphin House School. Donna made a Noah's Ark

A New Prima Donna

cake decorated with little animals that she had bought earlier in the U.S. The Swimming Club made a lot of the snacks and Sarah and all the kids had a great time playing games, winning prizes, and eating ice cream and cake. Sarah also started ballet lessons and was soon joined by Sean and a little Dutch kid, Matias, who also went to the Dolphin House School. It wasn't long before they were in a ballet program and did quite well. Sarah even got her picture in the paper.

One afternoon when Donna picked up Sean, Sarah and Matias after school, Sarah grimaced when Donna held her arm. Suddenly the kids were all frozen with fear when Donna wanted to know how she got welts on her arm. After the kids made Donna promise not to tell Miss Perera, they admitted that Miss Perera beat them with a stick when they messed up or did something wrong. That explained how sweet Miss Perera was able to get the kids to perform at a high level. Since Sean was at the age when we thought he should be starting to go to the International School, we took them out of the Dolphin House.

208. PUBLISHING SOYANEWS

IN OUR EFFORTS TO IMPROVE THE NUTRITIONAL QUALITY of foods in Sri Lanka, I had been working on a monthly newsletter that would provide information on how to incorporate soybeans into the diets of the local people. Soybeans contain about 20% protein and 40% oil, both of which were in high demand, but they also contained some antinutritional factors that had to be removed. That could be done by boiling the beans for several hours and throwing away the first batch of water. In our research lab, we were constantly developing new recipes which we distributed in our "Soyanews" newsletter, as well as information on other aspects of the program that included soybean cultivation and the development of new soy-fortified foods.

Our first monthly issue went to 2500 people in English and 3000 in Sinhalese. A bit later we also started printing the newsletter in the third official language, Tamil. I developed the soybean logo and wrote many of the articles but was fortunate to hire an articulate editor who also wrote a lot of articles in all three languages. The circulation increased every month as people requested their own copies. I provided the editor with a lot of information and proofread the English version. For some time, I had also been proofreading just about every report and project proposal that left the office. My ninth grade English teacher would have been proud.

209. MEETING THE PRESIDENT

THE ASSISTANT EXECUTIVE DIRECTOR OF CARE-NY, Fred Devine, had been a strong, healthy man but woke up one day paralyzed. Nobody ever figured out why, but he was coming to Sri Lanka, along with his new young wife, Bev, his former physical therapist. We borrowed a big Embassy car to carry Fred around, but we couldn't fit him and his wheelchair into a U.S. military helicopter to show him the country. Among others, we met the President of Sri Lanka, J. R. Jayewardene. Fred's visit went well, and we also had them for dinner along with all the American staff and two other couples, 14 in all. That was nothing for Donna who was used to giving big dinners. She even served flaming baked Alaska for dessert. Later, she hosted the American Women's Club Christmas Program for over 50 women. That's what you do when you have a big house.

Just after Fred Devine's visit, our new order of Datsun (Nissan) station wagons with air-conditioning arrived. Now we could travel in relative comfort. CARE-NY finally relented because it was getting difficult to find and purchase cars that weren't air conditioned.

210. LOSING OUT TO JONESTOWN

THE EASTERN HALF OF SRI LANKA was hit by a terrible cyclone on November 23, 1978, that killed almost 1000 people and damaged or destroyed 250,000 homes, 250 schools, 90% of the coconut plantations and more. As we flew over the east half of the island in a U.S. military helicopter, I was amazed at the devastation. CARE was first on the scene and we diverted cookies from the lunch program and provided tarps to cover their roofs. CARE, however, couldn't raise much money for the disaster because the newspapers were consumed by the Jonestown massacre that had happened just five days earlier. In Guyana, on the Northeast coast of South America close to Venezuela, 909 people had died from cyanide-laced Kool-Aid and gunshots, including the People's Temple founder, Jim Jones, and a California Congressman, Leo Ryan, who had gone down to investigate the "socialist utopia" with several journalists.

On January 2, 1979, Donna and I went to Kandy, where we attended a farewell party for Jim and Rita Spata at Carl and Grace Hittle's house. Jim had been responsible for setting up the soy foods research lab, deciding what machinery to purchase and developing all the soy-fortified foods that we were trying to incorporate into the local diet. Years later, Jim developed all the Kroger-brand generic foods and would say, "It's not good for you if you don't eat it." We were sad to see them leave but they have remained our good, long-distance friends in Cincinnati even though we seldom see them.

Sarah Loving the Beach

211. MOM AND DAD DE YOUNG VISIT SRI LANKA

A FEW DAYS LATER, Donna's mom and dad arrived on Swissair. After they recovered from 11.5 hours of jet lag, we traveled down the coast to Galle where we enjoyed the beautiful beaches and the new hotels with their wonderful Sunday buffets. We also visited Kandy, Hunas Falls and the tea country. As I drove around the very curvy, blind corners, they were quite nervous, as they had been in car accidents the previous two Januarys. After repeated requests to blow my horn, I finally relented and gave it a long blast. Instantly the scared monkeys in the treetops above bombarded my car with fruit. I said, "Now you know why I don't blow the horn." The timing was perfect.

Although Wally and Dorothy both preferred to stay nearby in Colombo, they did take a seven-hour, air-conditioned train ride (it did have a fan) with Donna, Sean and Sarah to Nuwara Eliya, where I met them after working at our Research Laboratory near Kandy. We stayed in an elegant hotel built by the English. Years earlier, the Queen had stayed there and when we walked through the library, the very proper English ladies looked up with some disdain wondering why two little kids were walking through their reading room. Then Donna noticed that both Sean and Sarah had lice in their hair, so the drugstore was our next stop. The four of us, excluding Donna's parents, rubbed the smelly medicine into our hair. That evening, as we watched a group of Kandyan dancers perform, they sat on our sides so others might not notice our plight.

Back in Colombo, we had a sit-down dinner for 27 people, which just about filled up our dining room. Our guests were mainly selected from Donna's Bible study group and six of the spouses were ministers. I didn't serve any wine that night.

On March 6, 1979, Wally and Dorothy flew home after their trip was delayed two weeks because of a health scare. Wally had a bad cold, cough, upset stomach and a fever, so we took him to Dr. Buehl, a heart specialist. His pulse was irregular, about 120, and an EKG showed some problems. Dr. Buehl wanted to admit him immediately but there wasn't a bed and the only nurse who could read the heart monitor was on vacation, so we took him home, gave him Ampicillin and Norpace to get his heart regular. The next day, after a second EKG and chest X-Ray, he was admitted. The motel-style clinic had open doors on both sides of the room. One day a cat wandered in his room and Wally wondered if he would have had the strength to knock it off his tray if it had decided to jump up for a bite of lunch. On Sunday, our Pastor, Lloyd Perera, prayed that Wally would wake up on Monday feeling better. That's what happened. Monday morning at breakfast, Wally announced "I'm getting better." A few days later at the airport, I got their seat assignments and checked them both in, so that when they arrived, they only had to walk straight to the departure lounge and wait ten minutes before they boarded the plane. KLM treated them royally and in Chicago wheelchairs were waiting for them.

Sean Flying High

The Soyanews newsletter kept me busy, as did writing a full-page newspaper supplement that was printed in English and Sinhalese on March 24, 1979, the day that our Soybean Research Laboratory was inaugurated. Work was interesting and we were receiving letters from all over the world, which often provided us with additional information. My editor quit for a higher paying job somewhere in the Middle East, but fortunately I quickly hired a new one.

The Research Center in Gannoruwa was 95% complete and was a high-quality research lab and production facility with all the different processing equipment inside. We hired a local manager and a number of employees to run the equipment and could make just about any kind of food, even soymilk. We also extruded different kinds of soy-fortified cereals and full-fat, soy-fortified flour for cookies, breads, and noodles. It surprised me that the packaging always cost more than the contents unless we used only a simple plastic bag. Businesses were getting interested in many of our products and we had trained over 100 volunteers to teach others how to cook with soybeans.

Glued to the TV

TV had recently arrived in Sri Lanka. Small 15" black and white sets were flying off the shelves and one ended up in our house. Sesame Street started at 5:00 p.m., but because government officials were concerned with how TV might affect family life, shows were suspended from 8:00 to 8:30 so parents could put their kids to bed. Then the old taped movies resumed until 10:00 p.m. when the transmission was abruptly cut off, whether the films were over or not. Quite often we missed the last five minutes.

212. THE HINDU KINGDOM OF NEPAL, 1979

GEORGE TAYLOR DEPARTED for home leave, which meant that I was the Acting Director for three months until he returned. That kept me extremely busy overseeing all the other programs as well as my own. As soon as he returned, I departed for Kathmandu, capital of The Hindu Kingdom of Nepal, for three months of temporary duty where I replaced the Director, Frank Brechin, while he went on home leave. Donna and the kids took this opportunity to fly home on June 27, 1979, for her dad's 66th birthday, the July 4th celebrations in Friesland, her 20th Randolph High School reunion where she won the prize for having come the farthest, and her niece Julie's wedding.

When Sarah was handing out packets of rice at Julie and Denny Wendt's wedding, she became upset that there was none for the bride. When she learned that it was for the guests to throw at the bride, she then worried, "But it might get in her eyes." In the following days, Sean wore the tires off his big wheel and under Uncle Chuck's tutelage became an even more enthusiastic fisherman.

I wanted to go too, so I could attend our Guatemala III Peace Corps reunion in Washington, D.C. and have a tour of the White House. It was hosted by Tim Kraft, my PC travelling companion and groomsman, who became President Jimmy Carter's Appointment Secretary. It seemed quite coincidental that in the PC, Tim was stationed in Flores with Carol Bellamy, who later served as President of the New York City Council, became a N.Y. State Senator, Director of the PC and the head of UNICEF.

213. HOLY COW

IN KATHMANDU, Frank Brechin met me at the airport, introduced me to the office staff, and took me to his house before flying to New York. It was sparsely furnished but full of mosquitoes as the rainy season had just begun. I did my best to hide under the sheet, leaving just my nose exposed, but the next morning it was covered with about 50 tiny bites. When I didn't have a drink at a cocktail party that night, Norma Smith, one of the CARE-Medico Nurses was surprised. She said, "I thought you must be a heavy drinker with that red puffy nose."

The one thing you learn quickly about Nepal is that cows are sacred and that you don't want to kill one. If you do, it's off to prison for 12 years. If you kill a person, it's eight years. The cows, which wander all over the place and eat whatever produce they want in the markets, are fortunately quite well-disciplined and confine themselves to the center line when walking up and down the busy streets. One United Nation's employee who did kill one, went to court and won with a defense argument that "the cow committed suicide."

I was pleased that our Pastor from Lahore, Al and Peggy Scholorholtz, were now in Nepal where they spent the last ten years of their missionary work. Al oversaw the United Mission to Nepal which consisted of some 350 missionaries who all got work visas to do developmental work only. I was glad they invited me over quite often, as Al remembered how he felt when he arrived alone for five months. They also had me over for weekly Bible studies and since I had plenty of time without my wife and kids, I also started reading the Bible, sometimes for hours at a time. There was also a Sunday church service which was held in a school and attended by about 150 English-speaking foreigners.

214. GETTING TO WORK

IN THE OFFICE I SPENT THE FIRST FEW DAYS READING all the project and evaluation files, trying to understand what had happened during CARE's first year in Nepal. There were a lot of mistakes in the paperwork and it became clear that no one in the office understood the new process of writing and evaluating project proposals that CARE-NY had recently established. Part of the problem was caused by terrible mail service. In New York, there had been a postal strike which was further complicated by the small amount of mail destined to Nepal. Letters sometimes got pushed to the side and sat in mailbags for months, like it had in Afghanistan a couple years earlier. After I figured out what had gone on and what the goals were, I spent a huge amount of time, at the request of CARE-NY, rewriting all their proposals and budgets and establishing how they could be evaluated. Since I had just done that for our projects in Sri Lanka, I was very familiar with the somewhat complicated process and had it completed after two months. After that I started to investigate possible new projects, such as small water systems for isolated rural villages. The big problem, of course, would be delivering water pipes to locations more than just a few days trek from any road.

After my assignment was over and Frank and his wife Sue had returned, he wrote me a letter of thanks for sorting out all his projects, files and paperwork.

In 1951, Nepal first opened its borders to the outside world when Sir Edmund Hillary became the first person to climb Mount Everest. At that time, 30,000 people lived in Kathmandu valley and virtually no one could read or write. By 1979, the population grew to 500,000 and 4% of women and 24% of men could read. In a country about as big as Tennessee, there were only 1,080 miles of paved roads, most of which were in the flat lowlands bordering India. The mountains were so steep that it was incredibly difficult to build and maintain roads which were frequently blocked by landslides after a rain. Sometimes I asked, "How do you get there?" They replied, "Fly to 'x' and trek, or hike, for 'y' days." It was exhausting to hike several days in a row, going up and down thousands of feet, to go just a quarter mile as the crow flies. People often joked that they suffered from trekking disease, which was simply the inability to put one foot in front of the other.

The first night I was in Kathmandu, I met Jack Baker, a friend from Colombo, who was in Nepal for a month. We took several Saturday morning trips to nearby towns and were constantly amazed. We had stepped back into the Middle Ages. The pagoda-style architecture, so common in Japan and China, originated in Nepal. Some of the tall pagodas were five stories high and the edges of the roofs were covered with erotic figures. The doors were intricately carved and barely 5' high, tall enough for most Nepalis. In front of the temples and other buildings, were huge carved lions and elephants and we even saw a huge, gold-covered bull, as described in the Old Testament. Dozens of little naked kids were everywhere and many of their mothers were sitting in the sun breastfeeding them. All this was in plain view of the tourist buses, full of stylish Argentine tourists on this particular day. For lunch we ended up at the International Club and ordered an American hamburger, onion rings and a coke followed by apple pie and ice cream. Then I dropped Jack off at the fancy Yak and Yeti Hotel and drove home during the afternoon rains. After a couple weeks, the clouds briefly parted, exposing Mt. Everest and the Himalayas. Even though we were 120 miles from Mt. Everest, it loomed large above us. It was an impressive sight.

For the first few mornings, I went jogging around the neighborhood but soon gave it up because it was evident that there was no central sewage system in the entire city of Kathmandu. People simply used the sidewalks, but by late morning the vagrant dogs, fortunately, had it all cleaned up. When walking down the very narrow cobblestone streets in the older parts of town that were bordered by four-story houses, I always looked upward to avoid getting splashed by a chamber pot being emptied. Being a better birder than a fisherman was an unexpected benefit.

In addition to a few cars, the office had a couple of Honda Hobbits, mopeds that could go about 20 mph. They were fun to drive around town but were rated unacceptable in one of Frank's Consumer Reports because the front brake would lock up and throw off the rider. When I warned our driver, he said, "Yes, I know. That's how I smashed the headlight." I drove them several times, sometimes to the Tibetan Handicraft Center, where I bought several brightly colored 3'x 6' carpets.

One result of working for a large, respected non-governmental organization like CARE was that we got to meet high government officials, UN representatives, ambassadors, and other American and foreign-aid leaders. In Nepal, I was invited to lunch by the U.S. Ambassador, Douglas Heck, and his wife at their residence. He had sprained his ankle ten days earlier, so he kept his foot elevated on the coffee table, bare toes and all. Ambassadors weren't so different from the rest of us.

215. THE POLICE IN ACTION

SEVERAL BIG HINDU CELEBRATIONS took place while I was in Kathmandu. Dozens of men struggled to carry the heavy religious objects while the bystanders threw cooked rice to placate some of their 33 million gods. It was quite a scene to behold. As I took movies, I found myself in a huge, tightly packed crowd of thousands and soon realized that I had been pickpocketed. I quickly reported the loss at a nearby police station with the slim hope that my wallet might be returned without the $100 bill inside. After a few minutes, the police rounded up about ten known suspects, and I was escorted into a room where they were all lined up. I had no idea, of course, who had taken it, as the policeman briefly questioned the suspects, kicking each one in the shins with his heavy boots and poking them with his club as he went down the line. When I left the room and walked down the hall, the interrogations intensified as the suspects hollered in pain from each kick and whack.

216. ANOTHER BEAUTIFUL BLONDE

SHORTLY BEFORE I RETURNED TO SRI LANKA, Donna returned from Wisconsin and planned to visit Nepal. Planning, however, was not easy. She had tried several times to call me from the U.S. but in frustration finally asked the operator, "Have you ever completed a call to Nepal?" The operator admitted "No." Fortunately, our letters arrived, and she managed to book a flight to Kathmandu. As I watched the passengers disembark, I didn't see Donna, but when I checked with the airline, her name was on the manifest. Minutes later, a beautiful blonde walked through the door. With her new hairdo and new clothes, I could hardly recognize my own wife. We had a great ten-day reunion seeing the sights as far away as Pokhara, 160 miles west of Kathmandu. We also took a DC-3 flight along the edge of the Himalayas to view Mt. Everest, which loomed above us at 29,029 feet. It was a beautiful day and the scenery was unforgettable.

Ever since I was married, Donna was our family's social director. I would ask, "Who is coming to dinner? Then a few days later would ask, "Who came to dinner?" It came as somewhat of a surprise to realize, after I had been in Nepal for a month and looked around at the church congregation, that I knew the names of about 150 people.

While exploring Kathmandu, we came across a little, black Lhasa Apso puppy. He was so cuddly and furry, we decided to buy him, thinking that the kids would love him and that he would be a companion for our other dog, Tashi. In retrospect, I can't believe we bought the little mutt. The kids, of course, were happy but "Baloo" did have some issues. Whenever it rained and thundered, he cowered and howled in fear.

217. NO PHOTOS, JUST MEMORIES

BACK IN SRI LANKA, we spent a five-day weekend once again in Trincomalee at the Sea Angler's Club. Sean woke up early every morning and fished with a short line on the end of a stick. Every few minutes he'd catch another little fish, using a piece of bacon rind for bait, which the little fish couldn't pull off. All of us went on a couple of deep-sea fishing trips but the third time I went with another Assistant CARE Director, Bob Luneberg, who was vacationing from Bangladesh. About ten miles out in 4000' of water, I hooked a 90" sailfish and had an intense 20-minute battle. It was exciting to see it jump out of the water and the boatman gaffing and hauling it into the boat. They said it was the first time since 1946 that someone had caught a sailfish off Trincomalee. My fanatical fishing partner from Bangladesh took my picture and then I took some of him with the big fish. He never sent me the promised photo, but we had the pleasure of eating it, one cross section after another. I wonder what stories he told.

As Vice-President of the American Women's Club, Donna planned a big Halloween Party held at the Deputy Chief of Mission's house. Sarah was dressed in her pink ballet outfit and Sean was dressed in a king's guard uniform from Greece that the Director, George Taylor, bought 18 years earlier for his son. Later we took a carload of kids trick or treating and after visiting 15 Embassy and USAID houses, the kids had quite a load of candy. In the middle of November, we attended the Marine Corps Birthday Ball where I wore the same black suit I had bought for Denny Hamill's wedding in 1962 as well as my own in 1966.

You might be thinking that all I did in Sri Lanka was take one vacation after another. CARE celebrated 15 American holidays each year but in Sri Lanka, every full moon was also a holiday, for a total of 27. In addition, we also had ten days of local leave and had about two months of home leave every 30 months. It is also more fun to talk about vacations than work.

218. ON THE MOVE

IN JANUARY 1980, I received a cable from CARE-NY that I would soon be transferred to Guatemala which was not particularly exciting news. For the next two months, we kept busy tying up loose ends and packing our belongings. In Sri Lanka we had accumulated a lot of antique furniture, including an 8' Ebony settee, an 8' Sandalwood settee, an Ebony-inlaid armoire, chairs, tables, and a Hemingway octagonal table. We also had some large furniture from Chile, artwork and other items that wouldn't benefit from more long-distance moves. Dad always said that "Three moves are like a fire." As a result, I took this opportunity to ship one large lift van directly to Mom and Dad's house in Madison, which would save both money and possible losses. We were fortunate that in all our moves we never lost more than a few inexpensive small items. One former CARE Director in India lost half his shipment because some new and inexperienced Field Representative refused to tip (or bribe) the ship's crane operator. The irritated crane operator picked up the lift van off the dock, swung it over the ship, and dumped it in the ocean.

Sarah and Sean with Two of the New Puppies

The four of us left Sri Lanka March 14, 1980 and headed to Wisconsin where we spent one week with Mom and Dad in Madison. Our night and day schedules were, of course, once again reversed. When the kids woke up at 2:00 a.m., they were in a panic and screamed, "The dogs are stuck together." That, I believe, was their first lesson about the birds and the bees.

That morning, Dad made pancakes like he always did. As I was standing next to him, I picked up the spatula and started to flip one over when he grabbed it out of my hand and said, "No, that's my job." Mom quickly replied, "Oh for heaven's sake, let him flip the pancakes. He's a middle-aged man." Dad was so capable and could do most things so quickly, he usually did. Years later he said, "I wish I would have let you kids do more." I never noticed we didn't.

219. BACK IN GUATEMALA: 1980

A FEW DAYS LATER, I WAS OFF TO GUATEMALA where I turned 40. Donna stayed behind with the kids and enrolled them in school in Friesland. It didn't make sense to haul them all to Guatemala because in just three months I would return for a couple months of home leave.

It had been almost six years since I had spoken Spanish, so getting up to speed was my first goal. Each morning I woke up early, read the newspaper, and tried to relearn what I had forgotten. At the office I worked mostly on the school lunch program like I had in Chile, Ecuador and, on a small scale, when I was in the Peace Corps.

Guatemala City had grown much bigger and even had some fast-food restaurants like Hardees and Burger King. In my little apartment, however, I did some of my own cooking. I'd buy a whole chicken, potatoes, celery, carrots, and other vegetables and make a big pot of delicious soup. It tasted great, but by the time I could consume it all, with several dinner invitations in the meantime, it would get moldy. It seemed cheaper to eat out.

One weekend I visited San Pedro Ayampuc, where I had lived 15 years earlier. My water project was still functioning, women were washing clothes at the pila, the road up the main street had been improved and it was fun to meet some of my old neighbors. During my days off, I visited various sites around the area, and with a 20-year-old kid whom I met at the Union Church, hiked up "Agua," the same 13,336-foot volcano that I had climbed in my PC days. It was a steep hike to the top, but before I knew it, I was back in Wisconsin with Donna, Sean, and Sarah.

Back in Friesland, Sean finished out the year in third grade and Sarah in first. This was a big change for Sean. He wasn't used to the totally different teaching methods and had a hard time with word problems. His teacher even remarked, "This kid is never going to college." He had beautiful cursive penmanship and was remarkable at memorizing, like he did in Sri Lanka where there was little money to buy books and teaching materials. But he didn't get any credit for understanding Spanish, Punjabi or being able to eat chapatis and curry with his fingers. I do wish his teacher could have lived long enough to see his college transcript.

220. JUST ONE PRAYER

MEANWHILE, DONNA'S SISTER SHARON and her mom took her to a Bible study held at a friend's house in nearby Randolph. The group's leader, a man from Milwaukee, later prayed for some of the ladies and for Donna's sore back, which had been aggravating her ever since Chile where she had been in traction for three weeks. Since her long flight home from Sri Lanka, it was hurting and lugging heavy suitcases without wheels didn't help. One side of her hip was higher than the other and she thought bed rest was the answer. Before the man prayed, Donna wasn't expecting much to happen but then she suddenly felt relaxed and straight. Months later, she realized that's when she was healed — and has been ever since. Many people claimed there was power in prayer. This was one of those times.

221. HOME LEAVE

MY EXTRA LIFT VAN FROM SRI LANKA arrived at Mom and Dad's house and we were able to store a lot of treasures on a shelf, made from the heavy lift van planks, that we hung from the ceiling above the garage door. Our bigger furniture ended up in their downstairs recreation room.

Donna and I, along with Mom and Dad, drove to Detroit to help celebrate Uncle John and Aunt Elizabeth Middleton's 50th wedding anniversary. It was entertaining to see them and visit with my cousins, Nancy, Mary, and June. It was a hot ride home in Dad's new Chevy Citation and the air-conditioning barely kept up. Mom, however, talked the whole eight hours, recounting moments from her childhood and dating years. Somehow, she even remembered what she ate and what dress she wore and what she was thinking. We could hardly believe what we heard. I needed a tape recorder.

During our drive home, I realized that I couldn't read the license plates in my rear-view mirror unless I squinted. After all, I was 40, so I had Paul make me an eye appointment who gave me the news that I had astigmatism and would benefit from glasses. That wasn't such unexpected news. With my present lifestyle, they wouldn't be too much of a bother. In fact, they might even make me look more intelligent. I was simply happy that I didn't need them in grade school or during my wrestling years.

Back at Mom and Dad's, Sarah and Sean loved swinging in the hammocks. Sarah said, "What a beautiful day, bumping butts and having fun," as they swung back and forth on a sunny afternoon. "Swinging, swinging, it's music to my ears," she said dreamily.

On this home leave we had to contend with our six Lhasa Apso puppies. Our parents must have loved us to put up with that. Fortunately, the puppies were born soon enough that we could sell them before we once again departed.

During this home leave, we decided to buy a house in Cambria even though we still had three years left on our land contract to pay off the 84 acres. With Jean Downen, the local real estate agent who worked at the bank, we looked at most of the houses for sale in Cambria and finally made an offer on

Our home in Cambria, Wisconsin

a brick house at 123 E. Edgewater Street. It backed up against the 34-acre millpond called Tarrant Lake and was listed for $29,900. We settled on $25,000 after Dad said, "This could be a nice house with a few changes."

We picked Cambria because Donna grew up five miles away in Friesland and her sister, Sharon, lived just two blocks away and we hoped she could keep it

rented. Paul was so surprised that we could buy a house for only $25,000, less than the $33,000 his friend had spent remodeling his kitchen, that he drove to Cambria to check it out. I put $6,000 down, and since interest rates were on the increase, was happy to pay only 12%. When the house finally closed a few months later in October the rate was 16%.

222. COSTA RICA: 1980-1983

BERT SMUCKER, HEAD OF OVERSEAS OPERATIONS in CARE-NY got it right. Instead of sending me back to Guatemala, where I had already lived for almost two years, he changed his mind and sent me to Costa Rica where CARE was managing a soybean program. I replaced Jay Jackson, who had been there since he left Sri Lanka two years earlier. We were the two CARE employees who knew the most about soybean production, processing, and consumption of soy-fortified foods. I was happy with the change since I'd already seen all of Guatemala.

On August 15, 1980, we left Madison on Northwest Airlines for San José, Costa Rica. After several delays, we missed our final connection with Pan American and ended up on Costa Rican Airlines, LACSA, that tried to land in the fog and rain. As we made our approach, I could see the right wingtip almost touch the runway. To my relief, the pilot revved up the engines and headed for San Andres, a Colombian island in the sunny Caribbean, where we waited a few hours until the weather improved in San José. After a successful landing, the passengers cheered and clapped. After that I thought perhaps, I should have waited for the next Pan Am flight. Over the next two days, all our nine suitcases arrived.

We played house in a small hotel, Apartotel El Conquistador, room 215, in Los Yoses. It had a stove, a mini-refrigerator and a 12" black and white TV. The walls were thin and the man next to us was a "throat clearer," but the noise made by Sean and Sarah probably kept things even. At least he wasn't around at breakfast.

Costa Rica was a peaceful country bordered by the Atlantic, the Pacific, Nicaragua, and Panama. San José, the capital, at 3900 feet, had a great climate and was surrounded by mountains and lush vegetation. The supermarkets were well-stocked, and the country was quite modern and Americanized. Like in Chile, the women dressed in the latest fashions, even to go to the supermarket in the early morning. American music was played on the radio and it was possible to make telephone calls home. We could even drink the water right out of the tap.

During our turnover, I met the President of Costa Rica, the Ministers of Health and Agriculture and the head of the National Production Council who had even been to Iowa.

223. REVERSE PSYCHOLOGY

WE IMMEDIATELY ENROLLED SEAN AND SARAH in the Country Day School, but Sarah soon complained about the unfriendly kids who were always fighting. At our first parent-teacher conference, at the suggestion of Mrs. Dee Sepulveda, whom we had met in the hotel, we used reverse child psychology and told the teacher how much Sarah liked school, hoping that the teacher would respond positively. She did and soon Sarah enjoyed going to school. We became friends with Dee and her husband, Luis, who was on a three-month assignment with USAID. Along with their ten-year-old daughter, we went to church, movies, bowling, and day trips. A few years later we even visited them in Denver, Colorado.

To commemorate Sarah's seventh birthday on October 10, 1980, Dad wrote her another illustrated poem, *"To Sarah on Her Birthday."*

Sarah, October 1980

*She has an independent bent
And goes her secret way
To view her explorations wide
Would take your live-long day.*

*An artist she, you'll quickly see
With carefully drawn lines
Details the world in miniature
Or colorful designs.*

*She quickly adds up two and two
In any situation
And in an instant oft presents
Surprise interpretations.*

*An active child as ever was
You're just as apt to see her
Hanging from a high trapeze
Or from a chandelier.*

*There is a pretty girl I know
Who just today turned seven
But if you judge her by her wits
You could believe she's eleven.*

*She has imagination keen
That works both day and night
It fills her private little world
And makes her days more bright.*

*For one so young her world is wide
She's travelled far and near
And lived in distant lands of which
Most people seldom hear.*

*To Sarah on her special day
Both Gramps and Grandma send
Congratulations and a wish
Her joys may never end.*

Sean was getting tutored at school and had a lot of homework. By the time he finished and after we helped him with reading for an hour, it was time for bed. He was also tested for learning disabilities. Spanish, Punjabi and now Spanish again had slowed him down in English, and compared to school in Friesland, Country Day was at least a semester ahead. After the first month, we moved Sean from fourth to third grade and he was a lot happier. During the six weeks of Christmas vacation, Sean who was nine, also had a tutor for two hours, three times per week.

224. CONFUSING ADDRESSES

AFTER A MONTH-LONG SEARCH, Donna found a good-sized house with help from rental agents. We had seen it earlier on a rainy night but thought it was too expensive and far from the office. When we saw it again, we realized it wasn't so far and the price had been lowered to $750. It had a 2-car garage below, four bedrooms, a dining room, and a large open entryway on the main floor, plus a kitchen, dinette and a spacious living room overlooking the street on the upper level. It even had a shallow pool below the open staircase up to the living room, around which we planted some tropical plants. The walled, private backyard had banana plants, sour-orange and grapefruit trees, and a solid wall of colorful bougainvillea.

Our address was 100 meters west and 150 meters north of the main entrance to La Guardia, Moravia. The houses weren't identified by streets or numbers, which made house hunting more difficult. When giving directions to our house, I would start by saying, "Turn left at the little store named 'x,' even though the little store no longer existed." Our office address was Street 19, Avenue 2 & 6. 50 meters north, Supreme Court of Justice, San José. This was no problem for long-time residents, but I wonder how Garmin has since resolved this issue.

Our four big lift vans from Sri Lanka arrived by truck from Guatemala on October 3rd, a huge relief to us after living out of suitcases for seven months. The freshly cut heavy planks used to make our lift vans were so wet that much of our furniture arrived moldy. The engraved, leather top of an end table was ruined and had to be replaced by a plain piece of leather but fortunately the rest of the furniture could be cleaned or refinished. Since we always packed our clothes in plastic bags to save space, they were all fine.

On October 15, 1980, Donna's mom and dad sent our dogs. After all our time at home, they had been stuck with them for two more months. They even had to get documents for them from the Costa Rican Consulate in Chicago. When Costa Ricans came to the door, they all seemed afraid of the barking dogs. Since security was always a problem, they made Donna feel a lot better. A month after we arrived in San José, Donna was a bit upset that she hadn't received any letters. I told her, "Relax, your parents are still recovering from the last six months."

225. SOYBEANS ON MY MIND

CARE HAD A 5000-SQUARE-FOOT SOY PROCESSING PLANT in nearby Tirrases de Curridabat where we made Nutrisoy, somewhat like the Thriposha made in Sri Lanka. A drink called Frescorchata, introduced in July 1980, soon became more popular and consisted of a 50-50 mix of soy, rice, powdered milk and a vitamin-mineral supplement, flavored with sugar, cocoa, cinnamon and cloves. We were also developing several new soy-fortified cereals, such as corn-soy-rice flakes, that were much more nutritious than cornflakes. We received a lot of technical assistance from Ron Tribelhorn, who came from Colorado State University. He helped set up the plant and trained our manager how to operate the extruder, just as he had done in Sri Lanka. The plant was working at about 30% capacity with room to grow along with the local production of soybeans. We also had two agronomists, who received assistance from INTSOY, the same group from the University of Illinois that helped us in Sri Lanka. They worked with the Ministry of Agriculture identifying the best varieties and planting practices.

In November, we planned a field day about 100 miles Northwest in the province of Guanacaste, where most of the soybeans were grown. It was attended by the Minister of Agriculture, representatives from the Central Bank and the National Bank (which gave loans to

Welcome to Our Field Day

the farmers), the National Insurance Institute (which provided crop insurance), USAID, agronomists, and about 100 other interested parties. I took my Pakistani *Shamiana* to add a little color to the festivities and gave a speech in Spanish. I even had baseball caps made, with our soybean logo, for all the guests. It was a successful day and did a lot to promote the program. The weather was perfect until a sudden downpour completely soaked the *shamiana* just as the program ended.

Even though the sun reappeared in no time, we couldn't wait for it to dry. For the next week, the 18'x18' canopy took over our living room until it was dry enough to roll up. Mold was always a problem.

A month later, Donna and I hosted a big official office Christmas party at our house. About 60 guests showed up for dinner, including the U.S. Ambassador and the Minister of Agriculture. Donna slaved all week making cookies, snacks and goodies. We bought boxes of grapes, pears, and Washington State apples, grilled tenderloins and discovered it took a whole lot longer to bake 70 potatoes than just a few. We had two maids in the kitchen and two waiters in white coats to serve the drinks and trays of goodies. It was a great party and almost everyone stayed past midnight.

In February 1981, I flew about 100 miles to Quepos, our other major soybean-growing area, where we had another soybean field day. It was a repeat of our first field day in Guanacaste, except this time I was interviewed on TV for about five minutes with one of our two agronomists.

The CARE Director in Panama, Jim Puccetti, who replaced me in Ecuador just before we left for Pakistan, came to evaluate my work in Costa Rica. Fortunately, he gave me an excellent evaluation and said I was just the right person for the job. That was gratifying to hear. I was working hard and according to Donna stayed at the office late on a number of occasions.

226. CRYSTAL CLEAR BLUE WATER

OUR LANDLORD, WIFE AND THREE KIDS who lived next door, invited us several times to go to their Pacific beach house. From there, we zipped over the water for 90 minutes in his speedboat

Sean, "The Costa Rica Kid"

before we arrived at a beautiful white sand beach with crystal clear water of various shades of blue. The swimming was great, and they even treated us to a fish dinner on another nearby island. Once we returned to our car, however, we were rear ended by a tipsy Costa Rican. His Jeep didn't have a scratch, but he did give me some cash to avoid any problems or delays with the police. Donna suffered from a little whiplash and a sore neck for a few days, until the three of us prayed for her.

When Sarah was seven, and in the joke-telling stage, she made up crazy, silly jokes and soaked up a lot of Spanish playing with girls in the neighborhood. She kept her room extremely neat and always made her bed. Sean made his bed too, but his room became messier each day until it needed a complete overhaul by the end of the week. He finally grew into his bicycle which we had purchased five years earlier. He loved to ride but crashed in a ditch and got all skinned up.

For his tenth birthday, Grandpa wrote him a poem called "The Costa Rica Kid" in the unusual form of a quintain. Notice that lines 1, 2 & 5 rhyme as do lines 3 & 4. I was amazed that Dad wasn't just an architectural engineer but also a part-time poet.

Our young star, in Chile born
Has watched the sun rise in the morn
In Ecuador, then Pakistan
Then o'er Sri Lanka's golden sands;
Now Costa Rica he adorns.

A fearless, energetic gent
He puts his heart in each event
Run, swim or snorkel...at age five
Jumping from a high, high dive
Or riding on an elephant.

He loves all creatures great and small
That walk or fly or creep or crawl
Birds, bees, bugs, and buffalo
(Oh, I forgot...hornets must go!)
All living things his life enthrall.

In Grandpa's woods our hunter bold
With bow and arrow forth he strode
Squirrels and bunnies everywhere
(But sometimes creatures much more rare)
Wild, close-encounter tales unfold.

Like other boys, he pesters his Sis
But left to their own devices, hear this
They sometimes spend the live-long day
In wonderful creative play;
A sibling relation full of bliss.

In Miss Perera's Christmas endeavor
(A Christmas play with a year-round flavor)
'Tis here our hero stole the show
As "Little Boy Blue" ...
now wouldn't you know
This Thespian's fame will live forever.

A fisherman he, with pole and net
Out-fished his Uncle Chuck, and yet
No matter how we all appealed
He still refused to us reveal
His "Ancient Chinese Secret."

So at ten years we'll put the lid
On the story of "Costa Rica Kid"
But as the lively tale unfolds
We'll publish future episodes
Just for now, "Adieu" I bid.

227. AN AWAKENING

EVERY THURSDAY DONNA ATTENDED A BIBLE STUDY with about twenty women, and we all attended the Union Church, an English-speaking congregation of mostly Americans, missionaries who attended the Spanish Language School, and a few bilingual Costa Ricans. It was an interesting and constantly changing mix of people who came from many denominations. The one thing I came to appreciate most was the wide variety of Christian experiences that we encountered. We heard firsthand accounts and testimonies of what God had done in their lives, how prayers were dramatically answered, and even stories of raising people from the dead. I had never heard such stories back home in Wisconsin, where most of the parishioners I knew led more mundane Christian lives and seemed to stay the same for decades. Exposure to all these new people made Christianity more real and exciting.

A lay-witness mission of eight people came to our church from Tennessee and Texas for an extended weekend of meetings, potlucks and testimonies. It was a remarkably interesting time as they prayed for people and told what Jesus meant to them. During that week, Sarah went forward and asked Jesus into her heart. Sean said, "I've already asked him into my heart." A few months later he joined the church. He was ten.

Right after the lay mission ended, our friends, Jim and Gloria Chapman, whom we first met in the Apartotel El Conquistador, asked Donna if we wanted to start a Bible study with a few other couples. To Donna's surprise, I said, "Yes." I realized that at age 40, I didn't know as much about the Bible as I thought I should after attending church my whole life. You don't learn stuff just by getting older. It takes effort, and the older you are, the more effort it takes.

Our core group turned out to be rather diverse. Jim Chapman met his Peruvian wife Gloria, who was from a Catholic family, when he was a PCV in Chiclayo, Peru. They had twins, a boy and a girl. Bob Katz had a Jewish father and a Methodist mother and his wife, Jeannie, was a Christian novice. That was helpful for me because she asked all the questions that I wanted to ask. They had five little kids who had free range in their house. When Sean went there for dinner one night, he was horrified when they threw spaghetti on the wall clock. The Lathrops, who were music teachers at the Country Day School, also joined us. Our leaders, Jim and Pat McInnis, were missionaries from Canada, who had been living in Costa Rica with their small kids for a few years. He was also an electronics engineer. We met each Wednesday evening, usually in our living room. Jim, assisted by Pat, first started teaching the basics and asked the question, "Who was Jesus and who did he say he was?" We soon discussed many other topics and our group stuck together until we left the country. It was an interesting Bible study that none of us ever wanted to miss.

As the weeks went by, Jim and Pat related different stories about their prayer life. Once when they were a long way from home, they had car problems. Even though Jim was a seasoned mechanic, he couldn't figure out what was wrong. Pat suggested, "Let's pray." When they did, she got a vision of the problem part, told Jim what it looked like, and Jim fixed it. This story shocked me. First, I couldn't imagine praying for a broken-down car, and getting a vision of what the broken part looked like was an even greater surprise. There seemed to be more to Christianity than I thought.

Sometimes people come into your life who were meant to be there, who served a purpose, who were there to help teach you a lesson about what's important. Jim and Pat were some of those people. Everything happens for a reason. There are no coincidences. We just call them that to avoid deeper discussions about life.

228. TO STAY OR NOT TO STAY

DURING THE LAST TWO WEEKS in March my life got extra busy. I learned that CARE's new Executive Director, Dr. Phillip Johnston, along with the CARE-Panama Director, Jim Puccetti, were coming for over three full days, from March 29 to April 3, 1981, to determine what would be done with CARE in Costa Rica. Costa Rica was classified as a middle-income country and CARE had considered pulling out and using its resources in more needy countries. There had been a lot of talk about making CARE-CR self-sufficient, which it already was, and forming an organization that could take over whenever we left. Being self-sufficient simply meant that CARE-CR didn't receive any dollars from CARE-NY. The Board of Directors suggested that a final decision be made and that is why Dr. Johnston and Jim Puccetti came for a visit.

Suddenly, the timing of their visit was less than ideal. A bomb blew up a U.S. Embassy van transporting three Marines and one was critically injured. There was also a bomb threat to the Embassy in Honduras. At the same time, the Italian President was scheduled to arrive for a state visit. Based on this, I decided not to schedule any big receptions but just made the needed appointments and drafted some position papers on what I thought should be done.

On Sunday, after I picked up Dr. Johnston and Jim Puccetti from the airport, we spent the rest of the day talking at our house while enjoying a delicious dinner that Donna prepared. The next day, we had a meeting with the Minister of Health and visited the soy processing plant. Then more discussions. In the afternoon, we met with the German Ambassador whom Dr. Johnston wanted to see since he had worked closely with him four years earlier when he had been in charge of setting up CARE-Germany and CARE-Europe, which became fundraising offices for CARE-International. In the evening we ate at the hotel and learned that President Reagan had been shot in Washington, D.C. On the way to the hospital, Reagan quipped, "I sure hope the doctor is a Republican."

On Tuesday, we had more meetings with our counterparts who funded our programs. All went well. That was followed by a meeting with U.S. Ambassador McNeil and lunch with the CARE staff at an expensive steak restaurant. We also met with the Canadian Ambassador who spent the first hour complaining about how busy he was trying to cover five countries without enough staff. That evening, Donna prepared another big dinner of Beef Wellington so our Executive Director could meet about twenty more people who worked with us. Donna slaved in the kitchen for two days and the food was fantastic. After all, the Executive Director of CARE-NY didn't come every day.

On Wednesday, we talked with the Minister of Agriculture and then went to President Carrazo's office. This year the President of Costa Rica and the U.S. Ambassador both got involved. After a two-year lapse without getting any PL480 commodities through the USAID program, they decided that CARE, once again, should be getting some for the school feeding program. The U.S. Ambassador was looking for some favorable publicity after the recent bombing of the Marine van. After a meeting with the President, at which I translated for Dr. Johnston, we were all ushered into another room where TV cameras were set up — to watch as our new annual agreement was signed. The President, the Ambassador, the Ministers of Health and Agriculture, Dr. Johnston and I were all lined up. I also had to make a few remarks, which fortunately came out okay.

The visit went smoothly, and our Executive Director seemed impressed with all the work I had done. In summary, CARE wouldn't be pulling out of Costa Rica soon because we first had an obligation to increase the production of soybeans and soy-fortified foods at our processing plant. Virtually everything I recommended was accepted by Dr. Johnston who later presented it to the board. The week went extremely well but it was tiring and I was relieved it was over.

229. A NEW HOPE AND GOOSEBUMPS

OUR WEEKLY BIBLE STUDY CONTINUED, and I was looking forward to May 30, 1981, when we planned to attend a class on the Holy Spirit taught by John Huffman. Although he was the Director of the Spanish Language School, we had never met him. After listening to him all morning explaining the characteristics of the Holy Spirit and describing many of the 28 spiritual gifts, he asked if anyone had a desire to know what spiritual gifts they had. After several people had raised their hands and had been prayed and prophesied over, I finally got up enough courage to raise mine. I sat down on a chair in the center of the room surrounded by everyone. Then John asked, "What do you want to be prayed for?" I said, "In other countries, I met several people who I thought were authentic Christians and I hope to be like them." That sounded fuzzy to me and I felt a little embarrassed, but John Huffman and his prayer partner, James Barry, seemed to think that was enough.

James Barry started out by prophesying the following that was recorded and transcribed for me by our Bible study leader, Jim McInnis: "This morning, I say to you this one small truth, that I have won the victory and that everything you will be doing on this day is nothing more than appropriating what I have already done. This picture of being seated signifies rest, signifies victory, because all enemies are put under my feet and you are with me in this place. We are together at the right hand of our Father God and I say to you my children that you are in me. I am with you at this time, and I have won the victory in my death when I died on the cross. I gained the whole victory for you and whatever happens today is nothing more than appropriating what I have already gained and done. Remember that you are seated with me. I would have you rest in me and center your thoughts and your attention and affection on me because I am the fountain of strength, I am the fountain of gifts, I am the fountain of liberty, I am the fountain of healing, I am the fountain of whatever you need in your spiritual life. It is in me that you will find these gifts as you rest in me."

John Huffman continued, "I have put you in a position where you will talk to both great and small in the government. I want you to talk to them for me, and one thing I don't want you to be afraid of is thinking that I won't bless my word. The way I have called you is such that as you learn more about it, you will know exactly what it is I want you to do and say but this much you need to know: When a sign or a wonder is necessary, when someone needs a touch from me that is miraculous and marvelous and beyond what you can believe, when you feel the sensation you are having at this moment, pray for that and don't be afraid, and I will bless. As my word goes out from you, I will bless it. I will prove it. I will establish it and those whom you will minister to who will need this kind of evidence and proof of my presence will see it and feel it and it will happen. And those where it is not necessary, sometimes it will happen too, for among other things you have the gift of miracles."

Just what was the sensation I was feeling when John was prophesying? I was embarrassed at being seated in the middle of the room and being the center of attention. Most of all, I felt like Sylvester the Cat who had just stuck his paw into a live electrical socket. I had goosebumps and the hair on my arms stood straight up as if I were freezing.

James Barry continued, "I would say unto you my son that this will require that you take up your cross daily and follow me. I would say unto you my son that this is a daily requirement that I put before you of taking up the shame of the cross, of taking up the death of the cross because when these opportunities arise, you will have a choice. You still have a choice of the possibility of having to suffer shame for my name and seeing my glory or standing back and not seeing anything come to pass but I say unto you my son be bold. Be bold and you will see the glory of God."

John Huffman finished, "You will be tempted to go into the ministry on a full-time basis. Because of the wonders that will take place, many people will ask you to and that isn't what I want for you now. Sometime in the future it may be that it will both be what you want and may actually be the best for your family. That will depend on many things that will come to pass. However, at the present I want you to be an anointed layman for me. I don't want you to think or to accept the offers that will be given to you for involvement. I don't even want you to take positions of authority in Christian organizations because these positions of authority will take away the time that I want you to give to people who need it in the anointing that I've given you.

You can feel free to speak at these occasions or go to pray with those men but it is my desire that you not be a part of the organization as a member of the board or anything that will take time."

What happened next? My appetite to read the Bible suddenly grew. On Sunday afternoons especially, I spent a lot of time, often four or five hours at a time, reading the Bible. We also kept going to our weekly Bible study. Donna had been attending Bible studies, in addition to our Wednesday group, for the last seven or eight years. I was finally getting up to speed.

230. FRESH OYSTERS

DONNA'S MOM AND DAD MAILED US our round-trip Amtrak tickets from New Orleans to Columbus, Wisconsin, to start our two months of home leave on June 16, 1981. While we were waiting at the train station, across the street from the Super Dome, Sean discovered an oyster bar where he spent $5 of his hard-earned money to buy a big plate of fresh, raw oysters. A year earlier, before Donna and I opened a can of oysters, I carried on and on about how fantastic they were, believing that no little kid would voluntarily eat the oily looking little creatures. Sean was convinced and ate a lot of them. After eating just two, Sarah concluded that we could have the rest.

As the train headed north, past the backsides of houses and businesses, the south looked like a third-world country, but the farther north we rode, the better it became. The first few times I asked the waiters for food or drink, I spoke in Spanish, forgetting where I was, but by the time we arrived in Columbus, Wisconsin eighteen hours later, I was back to normal. Never had we seen so many millions of acres of corn and soy. In Costa Rica, we were proud that our 1100 acres of soy had just doubled to 2200.

This vacation wasn't like our previous home leaves, as it seemed we worked full-time on our 100-year-old brick house. With many assorted workmen, we converted a hallway into a downstairs bathroom and closet, put in a new kitchen countertop, added attic insulation, and completed assorted repairs and painting. I was grateful for Dad who drew up the plans, supervised the job and even worked a few days himself.

Once again, we enjoyed seeing family and other relatives. After fourteen years overseas, we no longer had to go on a buying spree. We just had to worry about making our once-a-year, 84-acre, land-contract payment, and our new monthly house payment. Fortunately, Donna's sister Sharon found a renter for the house the day after we left Wisconsin on Amtrak.

231. CHEATING DEATH

FROM NEW ORLEANS, we first landed in Managua where we were again delayed by the afternoon rains. When we landed in San José, the passengers cheered and clapped as once again we had cheated death. Back at the office, the staff had a welcome-back party and a bouquet of roses for Donna. My Chinese agronomist, Francis Hsu, even prepared a Chinese dinner for us. Whenever Francis had a cold, he wore a coat and tie so he'd look enough better that people wouldn't ask him how he felt.

We soon celebrated our fifteenth anniversary and Donna's fortieth birthday. Sean and Sarah were doing well in school and this year they had more playmates living close by. Sean loved Monopoly and played with the babysitter for hours. He looked forward to *Ranger Rick* magazine's nature stories. He even went on his first date to see the play, South Pacific, with the neighbors and their ten-year-old daughter. Sarah went to her first slumber party, stayed up until 1:00 a.m., six hours past her bedtime, and came home grumpy the next day. We had Donna's cousin, Ron Smits (the son of Martha, who was Donna's mom's older sister), his Costa Rican wife, Betty, and kids over for dinner. One of their four kids, Gavin, was in Sarah's third grade class which was quite a surprise. Ron was a dermatologist who also had a clinic in Los Angeles.

To keep me on my toes, the soy plant was evaluated by USAID, a Chilean, and Ron Tribelhorn, our friend and technical advisor from Colorado. All went well and Donna and I had all 22 people involved over for dinner. They took us out the next night for lobster and the USAID lady invited us all over the third night.

232. SHARK MEAT

WE THEN TOOK OFF FOR THE BEACH at Tamarindo on the Pacific coast. We stayed at a small hotel and spent hours walking on the almost uninhabited, white sand beach, which went on for miles. Ron Tribelhorn and I went deep-sea fishing and in addition to filling up our cooler with big red snappers, I caught a six-foot, 110-pound shark. The boatman didn't want us to keep it because the guts attracted undesirable scavengers but we insisted and took it home. After we hoisted it up on the kitchen counter, Ron and I discovered that cutting it into steaks was a man-sized job. I picked out our stoutest, sharpest kitchen knife and stabbed the shark as hard as I dared without breaking the knife. After two or three stabs, I broke through its sandpapery skin and sliced one side. Ron then took my hacksaw and cut through the notochord, it's cartilaginous backbone, while I sharpened my knife for the other side. This was a slow process, but we ended up with a lot of delicious shark steaks. We then drove Ron to a nearby town, Sarchi, where they made hand-painted decorative ox carts which most people used as a liquor cabinet. Ron bought one and later, we did too.

233. EXPANDING SPACE

OUR PROJECTS WERE GOING WELL. Next to our plant, we finished building a new 5000 sq. ft. warehouse. Using local currency, I purchased $21,000 dollars so CARE-NY could purchase a bulk tank and grain elevator that enabled us to receive beans and other grains in bulk. I signed contracts to clean and dry about 1500 tons of soy, as well as for processing beans for seed. In the province of Guanacaste, I met the USAID Director from Washington, D.C., a former PCV who had made good, so he could see our soybean plots. Next, back in San José, I showed him and the USAID-CR Director our production plant and new warehouse. It seemed that our CARE project was one of the best ones that the local Director could show off to demonstrate that their money was well spent. USAID had given CARE about $500,000 over the previous five years to construct the plant. CARE had provided another $350,000, while the government provided the land, all the administrative expenses and other materials. Our plant had 25 employees who kept busy making soy-flour to fortify cookies and noodles, instant soy-black beans, a soy-rice drink with chocolate and spices, and soy-corn flakes. The Food Technology Institute at the University of Costa Rica helped develop and test the products as well as design the packaging.

On December 6, 1981, we hosted another office Christmas party for over 70 people. Donna worked for over two weeks, always without pay, making ten different hors d'oeuvres of 100 each, including mini-pizzas and Chilean-style empanadas. The main meal included five filet mignons, two big hams, 11 pounds of sausage, 100 baked potatoes, tomato salad, three big pots of baked beans, rolls and four desserts. We also made a delicious punch from oranges off our tree that we mixed with the juice of five pineapples, orange sherbet and ginger ale. We washed a lot of dishes that night. Our Pakistani Shamiana was a big hit as about 35 people could eat outside.

Inflation was getting serious. The exchange rate had increased from eight Colones to over 40 for one dollar. Since my salary was based on the official rate, I benefited greatly but the locals took a beating. Inflation made it much easier for us to make our land and house payments.

234. CONGRATULATIONS

CHUCK AND SHARON'S DAUGHTER, Linda, arrived on January 5, 1982, to spend the next 25 days relaxing with us in Costa Rica before taking her state boards. She had just graduated from UW-Madison in nursing and we wanted to congratulate her for her accomplishment. We spent a week at the beach but the one day I remember best is when Linda and I drove to the coast to take an excursion to a nearby island. Poor Donna had to stay home with the kids because Sean was sick with a fever after being stung by a jellyfish. Sarah was a little upset that I drove off to spend the day with Linda and asked Donna, "Is Linda going on a date with Dad?" We headed to our island destination in a boat filled with Costa Ricans, who were gaga over tall, blonde Linda. One of them handed his fishing pole to Linda who knew just what to do. She quickly reeled in a foot and a half long fish and now they were even more gaga.

235. A LETTER HOME

SOON AFTER, MOM AND DAD VISITED US in March. Dad wrote to Paul and Elaine, "Having a wonderful time, wish you were here. Beautiful weather. Flowers are everywhere — mostly vines and bushes but also exceptionally large flowering trees. We are eating fruit like it's going out of style, fresh orange juice, pineapples, bananas, strawberries, grapefruit, and a lot of salads. Donna makes whole-wheat bread with soy-flour added. All this with meat and desserts makes it hard to hold the line. This afternoon, John, Sean, Esther Jane and I will go to the ocean for deep sea fishing tomorrow. The countryside is all a picture postcard with rolling hills and a ridge of mountains in all directions. There are a few small fields of sugar cane and some terraces. Coffee is in abundance and they use it accordingly. Restaurants often serve hot water and hot milk with it for the gringos. We ate in the evening at a mountainside restaurant overlooking the city — spectacular! Went up a big volcano, Irazú, to see the crater but the rainy season was upon us and it was all in the clouds. We have been to a beautiful Jade museum, a pottery shop hidden out in the hills, some interesting villages and shopping in the city markets. We have been invited to evening get-togethers to meet other parents and also John and Donna have invited others here. The social whirl continues. Went to church and have had two Bible study classes here. The kids are in school, so it is difficult to get away as a family. John keeps busy and Donna has gone all out to keep us busy and to get us to all the points of interest. Also, she has no maid since they returned from their last home-leave and does all the cooking."

In late March 1982, I attended a CARE conference in Santo Domingo, Dominican Republic, for all the Assistant Country Directors in Latin America similar to the conference held in Nairobi, Kenya. At the end of it, I discovered I could fly home to Wisconsin for just $50 before returning to Costa Rica. Dad picked me up at the airport on what seemed to me was the coldest day of the year, as I didn't even have a T-shirt to go under my short-sleeved Guayabera shirt. It was a quick and very unexpected trip, but it was fun to be home for a few days. When I arrived, I noticed I had a spot on my arm that I thought might be ringworm. Paul made an appointment with Dr. Moss, his dermatologist friend, who quickly rubbed some salve on it and said, "It's just a bit of dry skin." I responded, "But I live in Costa Rica and have just been in the Dominican Republic for a week." He looked stunned but that was the end of my appointment. Back in San José, Donna's dermatologist cousin, Ron Smits, prescribed the right medicine and my spot of ringworm was soon gone.

236. GOOSEBUMPS

OUR WEEKLY BIBLE STUDY CONTINUED every Wednesday and we were now getting bold enough to pray for each other. Gloria Chapman, the girl from Peru, was pregnant and her due date was just two weeks away. During our study, she started having contractions and was getting upset because she hadn't gotten ready or packed her suitcase. While others were praying, I silently prayed for Gloria that her contractions would stop and that she wouldn't give birth for two more weeks. As I prayed, the hairs on my arms stood up and I was covered in goosebumps. I thought back eleven months when we had learned about the Holy Spirit and wondered, "Is this for real?" It sure seemed like it. To put myself on record, I quietly said to Gloria as we left, "Don't worry, Gloria, everything is going to be all right." The next day I could hardly wait to see what happened. Gloria told Donna, "Right after we left, my contractions stopped." Two weeks later, she had her baby. That was my first answered prayer. Or was it just a coincidence?

From then on, every time I prayed for people suffering from a variety of ailments and felt the same way with goosebumps on my arms and tingly all over, my prayers were answered. During those moments, I'd request as much as I could in prayer until the feeling went away. This happened eight times in the next nine months. I kept track on a 3x5 card. From then on, I became convinced they weren't coincidences. God was actually blessing my word, just as John Huffman prophesized.

Why didn't this happen years earlier, or all the time? Could it be because I wasn't ready? Or because I didn't expect anything to happen? I, for one, had never seen much happen before. But when it did, they were the happiest moments of my life.

The Sunday School Superintendent came to me one Sunday and said, "God told me to tell you that you are supposed to teach the adult Sunday School class next month on Exodus." What was I supposed to do with that statement? Argue with God? So, I reluctantly said, "Okay." At that point in my life, I don't think I had ever even read Exodus. But I soon started. Each night after dinner, I read and studied Exodus all evening long, all week until Sunday. I read the Bible commentaries and all the references, took notes, and finally had my first lesson prepared. It was exhausting but what choice did I have? Half the class consisted of missionaries and I didn't want to look like a moron. After all, I was now the teacher. Unfortunately, there was little class discussion, so it was up to me. The first class went rather well, I thought. For the next three weeks, I followed the same nightly routine. After four weeks, I didn't think I could do another as I looked at the calendar and discovered that May 30, 1982, was the fifth Sunday in the month. Then the Superintendent said, "Since next week is Pentecost Sunday, you are done for the month, and we'll be doing something different. I was done all right. What a relief. Bob Katz from our Wednesday night Bible study group said, "You did a good job. I was impressed." Bob, you may remember, was the one with the Jewish father. I'm sure he knew about Exodus. I could have wondered, "Why didn't God ask him to teach?" During my studies, however, I became amazed at how consistent the Bible message was from one book to the next, and from one author to the next over thousands of years. God's decision had been right for me after all.

237. THE LATEST AND GREATEST TRS-80

AFTER TWO YEARS OF BEING THE ACTING DIRECTOR in Costa Rica, I went back to being Assistant Director when George Menegay was sent by CARE-NY to be the Director. Shortly after he arrived with his wife, Anita, and a boy Sean's age, we flew home for over a month's vacation. While home, we purchased the latest and greatest computer, a Radio Shack TRS-80, which had just been upgraded from 4K to 16K, for just $400. Sean even took a coding class at Radio Shack where he learned some basics. We also spent a week at Whispering Pines Methodist Church Camp at Frederick, Wisconsin, rode the Ducks at Wisconsin Dells, were visited by Bjorn and Hannelore Edstav, our Swedish neighbors in Guayaquil, and reinforced the foundation of our house in Cambria.

We returned August 6th on the Honduran airline, SAHSA, which since our PC days we called the "Stay at Home, Stay Alive" airline. We stopped in Belize, San Pedro Sula, Tegucigalpa and then during our fourth stop in San Salvador, the lights went out, so we had to change planes. We were then delayed in Nicaragua for another hour, our fifth stop, before continuing to San

José where we circled for an hour because of rain and fog. Once again, everyone clapped, whistled, and cheered for the crew. When we finally got home, we found our new maid, both dogs, and our house were all fine.

Back at the office, work was accumulating because I had to spend so much time getting George up to speed. We had been trying to get our annual contract signed and had it just about settled when USAID offered to pick up the entire bill. Although we benefited, I didn't want to be so dependent on USAID. We did, however, get along very well with our American benefactors who were offering us non-fat powdered milk, cheese, clarified butter and oil. Because of the government's huge surplus of powdered milk, it cost just $0.05 a pound. On the same list, rice cost four times more.

According to their teachers at the Country Day School, Sean had a hard time keeping quiet with a straight face and Sarah had a hard time sitting still. She was a lot smaller than her classmates, and it was hard for her to physically keep up. If she didn't get her homework done by 7:00 p.m., there was often a meltdown and it didn't get done. Sean liked his TRS-80 computer and coded some simple games which he copied on cassettes and then played on the computer. This was in the days before floppy discs. We also bought a few games and his scores were far higher than his friends.

238. UNDER NORMAL CIRCUMSTANCES

SEAN, 11, WAS A DEPENDABLE KID under normal circumstances, but when he was with certain friends, he was capable of a bit of mischief. One day when he was with Dan Moriarty, the son of the Catholic Relief Services Director, they decided on their own to take a taxi to an amusement park on the other side of San José. After they spent the day and all their money on rides and food, they found themselves stranded and had to call home. As they waited in the rain and dark, we finally found them at another amusement park.

Together with the new boss's son, they decided to throw the hard, bitter oranges that grew in our backyard over the back wall onto the house behind. For four days in a row, they thought it was funny hearing them crash onto the metal roof. It was even funnier when they threw some much larger grapefruit. That was until the homeowner got a ladder and peered over the wall with a pistol in his hand. Speaking in broken English, he shouted, "If you no stop, I shoot you." That ended the fun as Sean pushed his buddy out from behind the banana plant. The man then yelled, "You come out too." Sean swore to me he had only thrown one orange over the wall. Upon further interrogation, he finally admitted to a second. Nobody got shot and that was the end of it until Donna and I took a walk around the block. When we saw several more oranges in the street, a bit more of the truth eked out. Almost 40 years later, when the statute of limitations had expired, Sean admitted he had thrown maybe 100 but that was probably an exaggeration.

For Sarah's ninth birthday, we took her class and Sean's too, roller skating. The 45 kids ate ten pounds of sloppy joes, popcorn, corn curls, 60 cupcakes and nobody got injured or sick.

239. PARADISE IN TAMARINDO

FROM DECEMBER 28TH until January 12, 1983, Donna's sister June, her son Fritz, along with Sharon and Chuck, came for a visit. Sean said, "Having Uncle Chuck come is better than giving me $100." We spent one week at our favorite Pacific beach at Tamarindo. To get ready for the trip, Donna prepared a lot of food so all eight of us could save a pile of money eating in our rooms. At the end of the week, Donna was amazed that just one meal for two was left over, because Chuck and Sharon wanted to eat one meal in the restaurant.

At night we witnessed a giant 500-pound Leatherback Turtle walk up on the beach past the high tide mark, dig a hole in the sand, and lay over 100 eggs, each about the size of a ping pong ball. Then, with great effort, the giant leatherback buried them in the sand and struggled back to the ocean. Unfortunately, wild pigs and even the local people often dug them up for food, and those turtles that did hatch and make a mad dash en masse to the ocean often got picked off by the gulls. Very few survive to adulthood.

While we were swimming in the Pacific, Dad was back home in cold Wisconsin composing a poem for Sarah. He titled it, "Little Winter Scenes Outside the Window of a Wooded Hilltop."

Baby Sea Turtle, photo by Max Gotts, Unsplash.com

The winter woods are bare and brown
With just a little snow
And where the birds and beasts find food
It's interesting to know.

The bugs and worms have crept away
   The seed supply's receding
I supplement the meager fare
   With table scraps and peelings.

I saw a big fat squirrel
   Who was trying to remember
A walnut he had buried
   Way back in warm September.

Three cock pheasants in a row
   Parade across the lawn
They pick at bits of nothing
   And soon all three are gone.

A pair of bright red cardinals
   In a dark fir tree appear
And pipe their usual question
   What year? What year? What year?

I saw a nuthatch hunting bugs
   And it was very plain
That right side up or upside down
   To him was all the same.

A dozen crows land in the yard
   And quickly 'round they look
Then they eat the seeds and peelings

The crows rise up with raucous cries
   In wild and wide gyrations
Then chase a Great Horned Owl
   It's their favorite occupation.

They circle toward the setting sun
   The sky is rosy bright
And quietly they settle down
   To seek shelter for the night.

A bunny rabbit hops about
   In the fading light
His tummy filled with Sumac bark
   A special bunny delight.

Darkness falls . . . the Great Horned Owls
   Call out their who ...who ...who's
Another plaintively inquires
   And who, who, who, are you?

Out the window Grandma dumps
   Some chicken bones and scraps
A 'possum and a big raccoon
   Share a flavorful repast.

A crescent moon surveys the scene
   A world of dark and light
And keeps her secret diary
   On the doings of the night.

240. MORE GOOSEBUMPS

A MISSIONARY whom I didn't know, Mark Rudeen, was in a terrible motorcycle accident in March 1983. He broke a lot of bones and his treatment was further complicated by some heart problems. When our Bible study leader, Jim McInnis, told us about the accident and we started to pray for him, I got goosebumps and the hairs on my arms stood straight up as if I were electrified. After a week, they finally were able to fly Mark to Houston, Texas, where he could get better care. Every few days for the next month while he was in the hospital, I felt the same way every time I prayed for him. I was absolutely confident he would fully recover. Finally, one week before he was scheduled to leave the hospital and fly back to Costa Rica, we heard that he would be coming back in a wheelchair. I thought, "No, that is not what is going to happen. That is not the answer that I was sure would come true." On the day Mark returned, there was a mix-up and his plane arrived over an hour before dozens of his friends gathered to meet him at the airport. Since Mark knew they would be coming, he stood around — without a wheelchair — and waited as his last-minute X-Rays showed no signs of broken bones. The next Sunday in church was a huge celebration as he told his story. It was a miracle.

Sometimes, however, I was too timid and didn't experience the blessings of great joy that I felt after Mark was fully restored. How awful it is to realize that God didn't reveal more just because I was sometimes too bashful, unsure of myself or even unwilling to pray, for fear that my prayer wouldn't be answered. Being satisfied with a powerless life should not be normal. Just like a TV set turns invisible signals into something visible, it is the Holy Spirit's job to deliver God's messages to us. We have to turn on our receptors and listen.

241. PROMOTING THE U.S.A.

TO ENCOURAGE TOURISM, U.S. airlines were offering inexpensive 30-day fares to anyone who bought a ticket outside the United States. For peanuts, the four of us took advantage of the deal by flying to Mexico, San Francisco, and Boulder before going home. In huge Mexico City, we met two of Sean's friends from school and took taxis to Chapultepec Park and some other tourist spots, including the pyramids. In Guadalajara, where Mariachi bands played all over town in the evenings, we purchased a big brass toucan for Mom and Dad's upcoming golden anniversary on Memorial Day, 1983. From there we flew to San Francisco, where we stayed with Vance and Dorothy Austin at their condo in nearby Walnut Creek. We took the Bay Area Rapid Transit (BART) into the city, rode the cable cars, went to Fisherman's Wharf and saw the Golden Gate Bridge. On the way east, we stopped in Las Vegas for a night to see the show "Circus-Circus." In Boulder, we stayed with Donna's cousins, Marilyn and Dick Steig, who let us use their spare car so we could drive up some of the nearby mountains. We also drove to Wellington to visit my wrestling buddy, Steve Martin, who lived in a huge rambling ranch. He owned a big building full of word processors and had 21 Ph.Ds. working for him doing ecological-impact studies.

Sean and Sarah loved going home to Wisconsin where they were doted on by grandparents, cousins, uncles and aunts. Paul would treat them to a movie and ice cream and then make a stop at "Paul's Toy Store" at the nearby Westgate Shopping Center. Since they knew about kids being adopted if something happened to their parents, Sean wanted to make sure we knew that Uncle Paul and Elaine should be considered as future adoptive parents. They could see that their spacious house would be a ritzy place to live. Years later I was surprised to learn that they thought Uncle Paul owned Paul's Toy Store at Westgate Shopping Center.

On this home leave, I made another eye appointment. While his nurse was checking my eyes, she nonchalantly said, "Humm, you may be into bifocals." Bifocals? That hit me like a ton of bricks. I felt I had just been diagnosed with the big "C." I thought bifocals were for old people. Ten seconds later I pulled myself together and thought, "Who cares?"

242. A ROMANTIC EVENING IN SAN JOSÉ

OUR AIR FLORIDA FLIGHT to San José on August 15, 1983 went smoothly, but while we were gone there was a scary earthquake, several items rattled off the shelves and our new maid, Alicia, had been terrified. Everything was fine except the grass was a foot long, giving my push electric lawn mower a tough workout.

For our anniversary, I asked my office staff where I should take Donna for a romantic evening. It was a fancy club on the top floor with a great night-time view of downtown San José. The waiters were super, the food was delicious, and Donna was impressed with my selection. She wrote to Mom and Dad saying, "It was a romantic evening. Maybe 17 years is a magic number. Really glad I married your son!" I was the lucky one.

Sarah, Costa Rica

When school began, Sean started sixth grade and we moved Sarah back to fourth. She was now much less stressed and was finally surrounded by kids her own age and size. Like all the other Costa Rican girls her age, she got her ears pierced.

On October 19th, I was pleased to get a letter from CARE-NY's Executive Director, Phil Johnston, who enclosed an article which appeared in Horizons, a USAID publication. The article described CARE's involvement in Costa Rica's first soybean processing plant and Phil wanted me to know that he appreciated my efforts which helped generate such kind words about CARE.

At a meeting with the U.S. Ambassador, I suggested that some of the new people visit our soy processing plant. He replied, "Yes, I'd like to go too sometime." I quickly replied, "I thought that is what we were going to do today." He seemed a bit embarrassed but after he had his secretary check his schedule, he said, "Let's go." We left in two big black Embassy vehicles with bullet proof glass and several bodyguards carrying machine guns. Sean would have loved it, but I didn't feel any safer.

On Sunday, October 30, 1983, Pastor Phil Truesdale asked me to make a presentation in church, "A Challenge to Stewardship," encouraging people to give more generously so we could meet the budget. It went amazingly well, and I wish I had a copy of what I had said because a week later, when I helped collect the pledges, our funding drive was successful. Donna continued teaching Sunday School, ages 7-11, and gave her testimony at an Aglow meeting.

The next day, the Language School held a spiritual emphasis week. The preacher from some church in southern California brought along six college kids, three boys and three girls, who had the spiritual gifts of healing and knowledge. It was the first time in my life that I had publicly seen such gifts in action. An English teacher I knew at Sean and Sarah's school had broken some cartilage in his knee, couldn't pivot on his foot and had been debating if he should go home for an operation. After they prayed for him, he ran outside up and down the hill. Talk about someone being happy! Several others were also healed. When you see such things on TV, you always wonder about it. When you are there and know the people, it is different.

243. MOVING ON

ON NOVEMBER 15, 1983, I received a call from CARE-NY that I was being transferred to Tegucigalpa, Honduras to manage a large Emergency Food for Work Project in the southern part of the country that had been decimated by floods followed by a severe two-year drought. If the drought ended and a crop could be harvested, the project would end in August 1984.

This news was greeted with some hesitation because during the week, I'd be separated from Donna and the kids. I also wondered how well I could work with the Director, Jay Jackson, who I had also followed to Sri Lanka and Costa Rica. We had been friends since the PC, but our management styles were totally different. Jay got involved with every detail while I tried to give the employees more freedom to do their jobs. Instead of ordering employees, I asked if they could do whatever needed to be done. Making suggestions, which they gladly followed, worked for me.

After I heard about my transfer, Donna and I were trying to decide if I should resign and return to the states or soldier on. Jim and Pat McInnis, our Bible study group leaders, encouraged us to go for prayer with some of the missionaries at the Language School. We did and they prayed that the kids would get into the best school, we would make many new friends, and our living situation would work out. They also prayed for Sean, Sarah and our family and that we would all grow closer, that on weekends we could make up for the time when we weren't together, that Sarah's stomach problems would be healed, and that Sean would become a bold, spiritual leader.

John Huffman then prophesied, "My son, I have called you to feed the poor and the hungry — but more than that to minister to them, for there are thousands and thousands of them praying to me and asking for food. I have sent you to them to fill this need. I want you to feed them and to share with them about me. I want you to minister to their needs both with food and heal the sick. Don't be afraid to share about me. I have sent you after hearing the prayers of these people." Several others confirmed this message. Our minds were made up, and Donna no longer felt like kicking and screaming over another move.

We first inquired about schools in Tegucigalpa. The best one, we learned, was a Christian school called "Los Pinares," but it was full and not so easy to get into. When we called and talked to the Director, Sam Herringa, we found out he was from East Friesland, a tiny "suburb" with perhaps a dozen houses about a mile east of Friesland where Donna grew up. Our first prayer request was answered. Was it a miracle or an unbelievable coincidence?

On Thanksgiving Day, we finally cooked the frozen turkey that Chuck and Sharon had brought us almost a year earlier. We invited some of our friends, the Tweedies, McInnises, and Galen McLeod Fung and her family. Galen was from Michigan, not far from where Dad's grandmother had lived, and she looked like one of Dad's sisters. Since her dad had been an orphan, we couldn't come to any conclusions, but I thought we had to be related.

244. HONDURAS: 1983-1985

I FLEW ALONE to Tegucigalpa, four days later on November 28, 1983, leaving Donna and the kids behind to continue packing. I was surprised that Jay was in the states (his mother-in-law had just died) so I spent the first week preparing to conduct a survey in the project area which was around the city of Choluteca. We assembled five survey teams, each consisting of two Supervisors from CARE and our counterparts.

As we departed the next Monday in five CARE Jeeps, I briefly said "Hello" and "Goodbye" to Jay. During the week, each team visited at least five municipalities where they filled out a three-page questionnaire in each one and talked to at least ten families. The corn crop had failed three years in a row and the typical family of eight was eating just 3-4 pounds of corn and 1-2 pounds of beans each day. One family had 26 kids, all naked and filthy. The poverty was the same everywhere we went.

The first day I spent in La Venta, south of Tegucigalpa. Then I continued to Choluteca, a city of about 40,000, squeezed between El Salvador and Nicaragua. Choluteca wasn't a tourist destination but on the edge of town there was a basic, but pleasant hotel, The Camino Real, that had a pool, decent food, small refrigerators in each cabin and cold water. The following day I went with a second team to Duyure, Northeast of Choluteca and less than a mile from Nicaragua. The people talked about refugees, fighting and explosions that they could hear in the distance. They complained about getting sick from all the dust and mentioned that the Honduran army had dug an anti-tank trench along part of the border. On Wednesday we drove south to El Triunfo to visit three CARE Food-for-Work projects. Crews of men were building new roads, retaining walls and houses. They were paid with beans, corn and oil. On Thursday, we went to the island of Amapala, which was in a sorry state ever since the port had been moved to San Lorenzo. The volcano at Amapala was well-fortified and San Lorenzo was overrun with Honduran and American soldiers. U.S. Army trucks and helicopters were all over the place. A few days earlier, a 70' Nicaraguan gun boat got into a skirmish with several Honduran PT boats of WWII vintage. To settle the matter, the Honduran Navy called in a couple jets which sank the Nicaraguan boat. That wasn't in the papers. On Friday I went north with the fifth team to Liure and saw more hungry people. Their stick houses were right out of "The Three Little Pigs." The roads were unbelievably rough and I was amazed at how many places we could go with our Jeeps, up and down rocky gullies that they called "all-weather" roads.

At the Tegucigalpa Union Church, I met Sam Herringa, Director of the Los Pinares school. It was a small world. That afternoon, I explored Tegucigalpa with a Canadian Field Representative and his Peruvian wife who had arrived four days after me. Monday was my first day with Jay.

The office was a bustling place. About a month earlier, a Wang computer, costing $102,000 and financed by USAID, was installed in the office. The brains of the computer occupied a small air-conditioned room which supported four-word processors and two printers. A computer technician had been hired to keep it all working smoothly. The processors were a huge help to the secretaries when they made corrections or additions compared to the IBM Selectric typewriters that they had been using.

Even though the project agreement hadn't been signed, we proceeded in good faith as if it had been. I started planning to set up the new temporary office and warehouse in Choluteca and hire a staff of about twenty people which would include eight agronomists to organize the work groups. I wondered if I could find that many productive workers. Since the unemployment rate was 30%, maybe it wouldn't be as hard as I feared. Furthermore, it was prestigious to work for an international organization. We would also need a fleet of new Toyota Jeeps. I spent the rest of my short stay reading, writing, modifying, and proofreading the proposal.

I returned to Costa Rica on December 16th, just three days before the movers arrived. Then we attended a swirl of farewell and Christmas parties, including one at the hilltop farm of Ladoit and Ruth Stevens, a missionary couple, where we said goodbye to about 70 people. We moved into the hotel for our last week. Sean loved the big pool and when I offered to pay him a nickel for every lap, he just kept swimming and swimming. Donna was upset that he might get too tired, but I replied, "If he gets too tired, he'll stop." He never did and later became a lifeguard.

We all left for Honduras on December 29, 1983, except for the dogs, Tashi and Baloo, who arrived a bit later. As soon as school started, Sean and Sarah had to be at the bus stop at 6:45 a.m. for the 40-minute ride up the hill to Los Pinares. Both were soon doing fine, and Sean joined the soccer team and played games on Saturday. They wore their green uniforms every day, and Sean had to wear a vest on Fridays during chapel. They also had a daily Bible class. We soon joined the Union Church, pastored by Bill (Marlys) Johnson, and went to their Bible study as well. I spent a few days now and then traveling to Choluteca looking for office and warehouse space but most of my time was spent looking at employment applications, interviewing people and working on the proposal.

Our shipment of personal effects arrived quickly on January 6, 1984, but my old boss, George, didn't send us the papers to clear them through customs until the 17th. Then it took a couple more weeks before I got them.

In the meantime, Donna spent the first six weeks looking at houses with rental agents and found a four-bedroom, six-bath house with a spacious kitchen, a spiral staircase, private yard with flowers and roses, and maid's quarters. It even had a big, tiled indoor water tank and pump so we had running water all day. To keep Donna from being stranded, we bought a new Toyota Corolla for $6800. Luckily CARE didn't pay import taxes, or the price would have doubled. I was now 42 and it was the first car I had ever bought. It wasn't long, however, before someone climbed over the fence and stole the radio cassette.

245. A LANGUISHING EMERGENCY

IN THE MEANTIME, the Food for Work project proposal was languishing. It seemed unbelievable how long it was taking to get an emergency program approved. The USAID bureaucracy was slow, key people were on vacation and two government entities, the Ministry of Natural Resources (MNR) and the National Agrarian Institute (INA) were haggling over very minor points that represented maybe two percent of the total. There was a lot to do, but without an agreement, I couldn't hire anyone, rent an office, a warehouse or order vegetable oil from the U.S. I did, however, have time to design a lot of the fifteen forms we eventually needed to control the input and output of tools and food, as well as keep track of all the participants and their hours worked. After weeks of unnecessary and frustrating delays, Jay and others in the office began to doubt the project would ever get off the ground. Because of the prophecies we had in Costa Rica, however, Donna and I were convinced it would be approved. We stayed calm and I kept planning.

During the delay, Mom and Dad came for their eighth overseas visit. Donna showed them around as much as she could and they helped can some pickles and jam, plus Dad even did some repairs around the house. Right after they returned home, we were visited by the wife of our former Bible study leader, Pat McInnis, and the pastor's wife, Marjorie Truesdale, who next flew up to the north coast to visit a missionary, Doctor Caparelli, and his family. Every week, Donna bought about thirty pounds of fresh vegetables for the Caparelli's, which were delivered by our friend Jack Hamilton, a Missionary Aviation Fellowship (MAF) pilot.

246. GET READY, GO

WHEN PROJECT APPROVAL LOOKED IMMINENT at the beginning of May, I held an organizational meeting in Choluteca to explain how the project would proceed. It was attended by some 35 participants from the MNR, INA, and my newly hired CARE employees — including eight agronomists, warehousemen, an accountant, and a secretary who spoke English. We bought five new Jeeps for a total of $55,300 and borrowed four more from CARE. Even though we still didn't have any money from the government, I went ahead and rented an office and a big vacant warehouse that was perfect for our needs.

Finally, five months after I had arrived in Honduras, we signed the six-month Emergency Food for Work Project agreement and the marathon started. Each Monday morning about 6:00 a.m., I said goodbye to Donna, Sean and Sarah, and drove my brown Toyota Camry to Choluteca, over two hours south. The scenery was beautiful as I descended into the lowlands, with the blue Pacific in the distance. The foliage had turned green earlier after just a couple of rains and was quite different from January when the land was dry and parched. At first there were many beautiful flowering trees but soon all was just green.

Each morning we were greeted by several huge toads that sat contentedly on the front stoop of the office where they had spent the night gulping down some of the thousands of insects attracted by the overhead doorway light. We swept away the rest.

A total of 30 work-group organizers from MNR, INA, and CARE began to organize what turned out to be a total of 446 work groups. Our agronomists worked from dawn to dusk to rapidly form work groups, usually consisting of about 30 men each, who worked on many different kinds of agricultural, forestry, and infrastructure projects — whatever the participants felt was the most pressing need in their community. To help meet the goals of each group, we purchased thousands of hand tools, such as shovels, hoes, picks, crowbars, wheelbarrows, machetes, files, levels, axes, hammers, and a whole lot more from local hardware stores, so the men could work more effectively. In fact, we bought just about every available hand tool in the country. The participants were required to work 90 hours each month, and in return received 150 pounds of corn and 33 pounds of red beans grown in Honduras, as well as a gallon of soy oil which came through the USAID PL 480 program.

The Embassy decided that living in Honduras was now a 20% hardship post, up from 15%. This meant CARE would also benefit from the new regulation. As a result, we now got a week of R&R and a free trip to Miami. This came at just the right time for Donna and the kids, who flew home to Friesland for the July 4th celebrations, her 25th high school reunion and her parents' golden wedding anniversary. I stayed behind and kept so busy that time flew by.

At the end of July, the USAID-CR Director, the Minister of Natural Resources, and the Minister of the National Agrarian Institute (land reform) came to visit another USAID-financed project, a new Natural Resources Regional Office, that helped support our Food-for-Work project. It was interesting and amusing to watch the ministers talk with the people being helped. All the beneficiaries could say was "Thank you CARE for the tools and food." After the ministers inaugurated the new regional office, they visited the CARE office, where I got a chance to talk with them about the project. I also took the opportunity to bring up their late reimbursements and let them know that if they wanted to extend the project, they would soon need to take some action.

Later, when we drove them, along with their photographers and writers to see several CARE projects, we had additional time to show them our accomplishments. As a result, the TV crews returned to film our warehouse and a road building project close to the Nicaraguan border.

After they departed, one of my agronomists and I drove a couple miles to the border where the bridge at the entry point had washed out in the floods three years earlier. There were just two Honduran soldiers stationed at the border guarding a new building, but with little else to do. We talked to the guards for a few minutes and departed. Shortly after, relations between Honduras and the Communist-supported regime in Nicaragua totally fell apart. Fortunately, that didn't affect our project. Sometimes on the way back to Tegucigalpa, I'd stop at a USDA-inspected meat packing plant and buy a 32-pound box of frozen beef tenderloins destined for restaurants in New York. They were only $2 per pound and just delicious.

Now that the project was running smoothly, I had more chances to visit the work sites. That was the fun part. It was amazing to see how much work was getting accomplished but there was so much more to do. Most people just had a piece of rocky land, six kids, a stick house, and no education. As a result, they were willing to work hard for the corn, beans and oil. When I had the chance to talk directly with the men, they would tell me how the project was saving their lives. Several men finished by saying, "You were sent by God." Even some of our government counterparts who were responsible for monitoring the project made the same comments as we discussed various ideas. It was an amazing experience to be in the center of God's will. Those language school missionaries back in Costa Rica sure got it right.

247. THOUGHTS IN MY HEAD AT THE CAMINO REAL

EACH EVENING, AFTER WE STOPPED work for the day, I would return to the nearby "Hotel Camino Real," order dinner, maybe take a quick dip in the pool or jog up and down the highway towards Nicaragua for a mile or two. For the rest of the evening, I read "The Spiritual Man" by Watchman Nee, which held my attention as I digested a few more pages each night. This book taught me the difference between spirit and soul, words that are not interchangeable. The spirit consists of our conscience, intuition, and communion. Our soul consists of our volition or our power to choose, our intellect and our emotions.

As I read each evening, thoughts would suddenly pop into my head which were crucial and important for the project's success. I would think to myself, "How could I not have thought of that until now?" Somehow these thoughts always came to me just in time to implement them. It's like I had a secret genius next to me keeping track of my decisions and making sure I knew what to do at just the right time. It almost seemed embarrassing to me that I hadn't thought to inform the supervisors, the accountant, or the secretary a day or so earlier to warn them that we now needed to do such and such. When I gave them these new last-minute instructions the following day, however, it was always at just the right time. *"If you listen to me, you will know what is right, just and fair. You will know what to do."* (Proverbs 2.9)

With Donna and the kids in the U.S. until the middle of August, I had to fend for myself on weekends back in Tegucigalpa. Even though the maid prepared food for me, I never ate much of it, as coworkers and friends from church frequently invited me for meals. Tom and Cheryl Sorens, Dutch Reformed missionaries from Wisconsin, who lived next door, were some of them. They had a comfortable home too, but it seemed as if much of their life was consumed dealing with the government and just living. I was fortunate that CARE had a driver to pay my bills, fill up the gas tank, wash the car and get repairs done, saving me from a lot of daily tasks. The driver felt fortunate too, I suppose, as he drove around town in a car with International Organization license plates.

248. STOMACH ACHES AND SCORPIONS

WHILE I WAS IN CHOLUTECA, Sarah continued to have painful stomach aches and said that once when she looked in the mirror, the face of a devil looked back at her. Donna immediately called a missionary couple from her Bible study and they came over and prayed throughout the house. When I arrived on Friday, I was a bit surprised at what had transpired. Later in the evening, when Donna and I were sitting in bed, Donna started praying for Sarah who was lying between us. Then I thought maybe all this was because of a demon. As I silently prayed for the demon to depart from Sarah in the name of Jesus, Sarah suddenly let out a blood curdling scream. We were shocked but after that her stomach aches were gone. During the same week, as I walked into Sean's bedroom to check on him before we turned off the hall light, I noticed a big scorpion in the doorway. I had never seen one before but this one got whacked with my shoe. I always wondered how it entered the house and I kept looking for any siblings.

The Tegucigalpa office hosted a regional accounting update conference for all the CARE people in Central and South America and it was interesting to catch up with my co-workers. Soon after, CARE-NY's Assistant Executive Director, Fred Devine, drove from Nicaragua to Choluteca where I met him and showed him the project before we headed to Tegucigalpa for more meetings and big dinners.

249. WRAPPING IT UP

AFTER SIX HECTIC MONTHS, the Emergency Food-for-Work Project came to an end in November 1984. As the auditors went over the books, I kept busy in Choluteca assembling all the work results, the numbers of participants, the amount of food and tools delivered, the vehicles repaired and the money that we spent for each activity. I then wrote the final report in English and had it translated into Spanish by my secretary. It consisted of 15 pages and 40 attachments and was sent to all our counterparts and CARE-NY. It turned out exceptionally well and I was pleased. Even Jay said it was complete and very well written.

The program quickly grew from 3828 families in late May to 10,566 by September. During the program, over 140 miles of various kinds of retaining walls were built, 20,000 acres of land were prepared and seeded, 40,000 pineapple seedlings were planted, 260 acres of trees were reforested, 300 compost piles were built, 62 miles of new roads were constructed, 158 miles of roads were repaired, 14 miles of fences were built, 23 miles more were repaired and many more projects were completed, including hundreds of latrines, water tanks, community laundries, school repairs and 4 miles of trenches for water projects.

In payment we distributed 6,295,523 pounds of corn, 1,405,698 pounds of red beans, and 41,745 gallons of oil. Compared to the amounts budgeted, 99.4 % of the food was distributed to the workers. Considering that we started with a rough proposal and had no solid information about how many workers we could actually enroll and then get to participate in the program, the 99.4% figure was unbelievable. It was not a "coincidence" — as some might think. We also distributed 16,529 hand tools, as well as agricultural inputs including seeds, fertilizers, pesticides, and construction materials such as cement, pipes, bricks, and roofing sheets, which were all retained by the work groups. All the employees I hired willingly worked an average of 12 ½ hours per day including every holiday.

Our small crew of 8 agronomists organized 220 work groups of 30 workers in each. By comparison, the 30 group leaders from INA and the MNR organized 226 groups with an average of 17 workers in each. The amount of work accomplished, as noted above, was amazing. Our entire Choluteca office had worked extremely well together. A USAID employee told me later, "I don't think anyone but you could have managed this project." It did seem as if it were in God's hands and that I was doing exactly what I was supposed to be doing. When it was over, it all seemed like a dream.

As soon as the project ended, there were more discussions to start a new program for three more years at a cost of $12 million. As a result, I was asked to write up another project proposal. John Warren, a USAID official wrote, "CARE expects Mr. John McLeod, who very effectively managed the Southern Emergency Food-for-Work program, to coordinate the development of the proposal for the new integrated development project for the south. McLeod will be in Tegucigalpa to begin this assignment on Friday, November 17, 1984." He also noted that he was generally opposed to such Food-for-Work projects because they generally left little behind of value. He continued, "However, I am very favorably impressed with CARE's results and am convinced that what they delivered is indeed something of lasting value …."

250. AN AIRPORT INCIDENT

PART OF A NEW PROJECT involved reforestation and Jay had been talking with a forestry consultant who was sent by CARE-NY to help with that part of the proposal. On his last day, we kept him busy until the very last minute, when he insisted, he had to go to the airport to catch his flight back to New York. Jay then joked that we would have to cancel his flight so we could continue our discussions. This was overheard by a secretary who dutifully called the airport, unbeknownst to us, and did exactly that. When we arrived a few minutes later, the airport was packed, and we discovered he had been bumped as a result. Jay argued and explained and begged some more. Then we waited for a reply. Every few minutes we inquired again. After a half hour, I could see that our forester friend was getting anxious, so I turned around and prayed that he would get on the overbooked flight. Almost as soon as I finished my short prayer, I watched an airline representative turn around, walk over to us and say, "You are all set to go." That was a miracle. I was the only one who knew it.

251. NO ESCAPE

AFTER CHRISTMAS AND NEW YEAR'S, the four of us went on a vacation to Guatemala. I borrowed a little blue Jeep from CARE to show Donna, Sean and Sarah the village of San Pedro Ayampuc, where I had lived in the Peace Corps. As we drove up the street, four years after my last visit, I could see that things looked a bit better in town, as some of the ruts in the road had been repaired. When we reached the plaza, the water project looked fine, but I heard that occasionally they still ran out of gasoline. I soon knocked on the door of my best-known acquaintances, the Sasos, but was saddened to hear that Mr. Saso had died just a week earlier. Mrs. Saso instantly recognized me and said, "Juan!" She then looked at Donna and said, "Nancy!" "Who's Nancy?" the kids asked. There was no escape. I was caught. Red-faced, I had to explain to Sean and Sarah that my old girlfriend Nancy had visited me here twenty years earlier. I could see the humor in this situation but also thought, "How could Mrs. Saso possibly remember her name after 20 years?

As we walked down a busy street back in Guatemala City, I noticed a couple men arguing with a woman as we blithely approached. As we got closer, too close, I suddenly saw one of them brandish a Clint Eastwood-sized pistol. Unknowingly, I had walked right in front of the gun. The short man's face met my chest as I watched him slowly turn his face to meet mine, a foot above his own. He decided not to shoot. They abruptly turned, ran to their car, and sped off down the street. The woman thanked us profusely for interrupting their attempt to steal her BMW.

252. BARGAINING TECHNIQUES

NEXT, WE DROVE TO THE PICTURESQUE COLONIAL CITY of Antigua and then on to Chichicastenango. When I was a PCV, the market in Chichi was open just one Thursday morning each week but had since become a permanent fixture with booths completely filling the plaza. The Indians couldn't resist selling their wares every single day to the huge numbers of tourists who arrived daily. The tall booths even hindered the view of the Santo Tomás church where the Indians swished incense on the front steps.

Once again, I had the chance to refine my bargaining techniques and the kids were fascinated. They were more cautious spending their own money and wanted to learn how to spend as little as possible. I explained, "Just don't act too excited or anxious to buy something and turn away if the price seems too high. And take your time. Be friendly. Once you agree on a price, make sure you have enough money to buy it or it will be more expensive when you return. One more thing, if you want it and won't be back again, just buy it or you'll wonder later why you were so cheap." Back home it would cost five times more.

Next, we drove back to Sololá and down the steep switchbacks to Panajachel, where we stayed in a lovely new hotel by the lake. The view of Lake Atitlán surrounded by volcanoes was stunning. It was the most scenic place in Guatemala.

253. WHAT'S NEXT?

BY THE TIME WE RETURNED TO TEGUCIGALPA, we started thinking more and more about returning to the States so that we could turn Sean and Sarah into Americans instead of overseas vagabonds. Many people told us, "If you don't return before your kids leave high school, they will never feel they belong in the U.S." We also thought CARE might transfer me to Liberia, which meant we would have to send Sean and Sarah to a boarding school in another country.

When Jim and Gloria Chapman, our friends from Costa Rica, visited us for a few days, he showed me how to make a more current resume. I thought maybe I could get a job with some missionary organization, be a coordinator of some university's international program or even be a travel agent. I was wide open for suggestions. When we talked to the kids, Sean was concerned he wouldn't get to eat so much shrimp and filet mignon. When Sarah learned she could walk to school instead of riding the bus for 45 minutes each way, she got more enthusiastic.

Then we got the news that Mom fell and broke her ankle on a late evening walk down the hill. Fortunately, just after dark, Al Toon, the Wisconsin and New York Jets football player, heard her cries for help, picked her up and took her to the hospital, where she received a lot of extra attention due to her rescuer's fame. Sarah, 10, wrote her a letter, "I heard you had an accident. How are you feeling? It must be boring. Do you do any knitting? If you're sick of that,

Day Care at the Market

did you try reading a book? If you're bored of that too, I guess you're stuck. Every day this week, we have unit tests. The bus driver goes 5 mph all the way down the hill from school and it keeps jerking your stomach so you feel so terrible you could die. Is that how you're feeling? Too bad you can't send us any snow. I have to go now."

In the middle of January 1985, I flew to Belize, an English-speaking, former British colony on the Northeast edge of Guatemala, where I met with George Radcliff from CARE-NY about my future with CARE. After some honest conversations, I decided to request a temporary leave without pay from CARE, which would give me a chance to look for a job before returning, or to resign and return to the States. As I expected, CARE-NY didn't approve my request to take LWOP, so we decided to resign in June. It was time. I had been overseas for twenty years and thought, "If I don't leave now, I never will." I would be 45 when I returned.

To prepare for this big change, we had five garage sales with some of our nearby friends who would also be leaving at the end of the school year. Until then, our transfers from one country to another had all been at the last minute and we never had a chance to get rid of our baby clothes, toys, electronics and some furniture. Two hours before our multi-family sales opened, buyers were lined up at the front gate. They threw everything they wanted into a bag without even looking at the price. For us, selling our used stuff for practically the price we had paid was a blessing. The buyers were happy too. We arrived in Honduras with 15,000 pounds of personal effects, sold 6000 pounds, and miraculously ended up with 9000 pounds, the weight limit imposed by CARE.

I was pleased that we sold all our big appliances, our Toyota Corolla, some easy chairs, a sofa, and our piano, which the kids no longer played. The best part was that we lived off our earnings for most of our last five months. It had been a smart decision to send one big lift van home from Sri Lanka five years earlier.

In preparation for the move, I went to a local sawmill and picked out enough large planks of Honduran Mahogany to make a big lift van. I thought I could later use the wood to make a desk and shelves in our Cambria house. I then air-dried the planks for several weeks before the movers came, and my plan worked out perfectly.

Sarah and Sean were doing well in school. In the third quarter, Sean got a 95 in Science, 98 in Social Studies, 95 in Spanish, 91 in Math and 90 in English. He had become conscientious, more grown up, and at 14 he even parted his hair. In April, he was the student of the month. In May we had more gratifying news when Sarah was selected as student of the month, and then a lady who worked for USAID decided to take our two dogs, Tashi and Baloo. She promised the kids she'd take wonderful care of them and would write them a letter. She never wrote but the kids were satisfied. We never told Mrs. Neff, our dog-lover friend in Wisconsin, that we had left part of our family behind.

Our last weeks were hectic and work was frustrating, but we finally finished up, moved into a hotel for a week, and flew to Miami and then Orlando for a five-day vacation at Disney World. On Sunday, June 16, 1985, Donna, Sean, and Sarah took Ozark Airlines to St. Louis and Madison, ending their overseas odyssey. I flew to New York for the week and didn't arrive home until Friday night, the 21st, which brought my twenty-year adventure to an end. It was stressful going home unemployed, and I wished that CARE would have paid me for the 360 days of unused sick leave that I had accumulated. As a newly unemployed person, I sure could have used it. We would miss the many hundreds of friends we had over the years. It had been an extremely rewarding experience for all of us.

PART IX. 1985-2020
HEADING HOME

254. CAMBRIA, WISCONSIN

AFTER WORKING OVERSEAS FOR CARE in nine different countries for 18 ½ years, home was now Cambria, Wisconsin, a small town of 792 people located about 45 minutes northeast of Madison. Our old brick home at 123 E. Edgewater Street, that we had purchased five years earlier, was just a block east of the main intersection in the center of town and backed up against the old mill pond called Tarrant Lake. There was a small grocery store, a bank, a post office, the village office, two bars, two restaurants, Chuck's Barbershop, a thrift and hardware store, three gas stations, a convenient park on the pond and a fairly new middle and high school. It was about 20 miles to Portage, Beaver Dam or Columbus — where there were stoplights.

Since our house needed a lot of work before we moved in, we were pleased that Chuck and Sharon were happy to let us stay with them for over two months during renovations. As my dad previously said, "This could be a nice house with a few changes." He had plenty of ideas and experience remodeling old houses and had drawn up the plans, which we followed. Again, I hired the same two local carpenters, John Tamminga and Joel Koopmans, who ripped out a lot of the old lath and plaster and a whole lot more before they could start making the needed changes. It was my full-time job to clean up after them. I filled up dozens of paper shopping bags and stashed them on the front porch until I hauled them to the dump. I loaded my father-in-law's three-quarter-ton Chevy pick-up with so much junk that the front tires barely touched the road and I could hardly steer.

Two old ladies, the Jones sisters, had lived in our house for years and never touched a thing. That was fortunate because we wanted to restore it the best we could. The main task was to make a short hallway so Sean could enter his bedroom without first going through the bathroom. We also added a lot of insulation and electrical outlets, new drywall, closets, a built-in desk and closet for Sean, carpets in all three bedrooms and new vinyl in the bathroom. We then replaced the old oil furnace with a 96%-efficient gas furnace and dumped the ancient electric water heater. We even got air-conditioning thanks to a gift from Donna's parents. I paid off my mortgage, purchased a dark blue 1974 Cadillac with white leather seats, and then started thinking about what I would do for a living. We had spent a lot of money on the house and I began to think, "Maybe it wasn't so smart to pay off the home loan," but at least we were debt-free. We had a house, 84 acres of trees, and the kids soon learned that money didn't grow on them.

255. ON THE FRONT PAGE

JUST THREE DAYS BEFORE SCHOOL STARTED, our home renovations were finished and right on schedule we received our shipment of personal belongings from Honduras. With our five big lift vans sitting on a truck in front of our house, we were interviewed by the "Randolph Times," followed by a big splash on the front page. Everyone now knew who we were. Of course, a lot of people already knew Donna and her mom and dad because they lived in nearby Friesland. They also knew her sister Sharon, the school nurse, and her husband, Chuck Dykstra, the barber. Now we had to learn who they were. It wasn't always so easy. Sometimes when I made the effort to introduce myself, they replied, "Yes, that's who I thought you were," without ever mentioning their own names. With so many new names to remember and relationships to figure out, I felt like I was back in Pakistan suffering from jet lag.

In the fall of 1985, Sean started eighth grade and Sarah began sixth. Before the first day, Sarah had the jitters about going to school in the U.S. It was a real answer to prayer when her new friend, Jenny Dysktra walked her to school and helped her navigate those first few days of opening lockers, finding classrooms, and getting used to six new teachers. She enjoyed talking with the migrant kids who were surprised to hear a blonde gringa speak Spanish. Sean had an easy time making friends and enjoyed the freedom of taking Paul's old canvas-covered kayak to go fishing whenever he wanted. He discovered basketball and probably because of me, even went out for wrestling. I helped the coach out for a few months. I worked with senior Andy Agnew, taught him some basic moves which he mastered, and was pleased when he won the conference title.

256. WHAT AM I GOING TO DO?

AS SOON AS SCHOOL STARTED, reality set in. Here I was, 45 years old, and living in a rural village which made me feel like I was in another country. I needed to find a new career, soon, before what little money we had left was consumed by everyday expenses. I had turned down a couple of well-paying job offers in Guatemala and Honduras, a possibility at Texas A&M University in Prairie View and maybe one in Washington, D.C., but we soon rejected all of them. The reason we had returned to the U.S., after all, was to be close to our families and to turn our kids into Americans. I devoted most of each day to finding a new job and my search had to be local. I interviewed to be the Director of Pilgrim Point, a small UCC church camp on Green Lake but the pay was so low I knew we would soon be impoverished. Wally, Donna's dad, suggested I get a job as a prison guard and we even drove to Racine to investigate the possibility of starting a carpet cleaning business. That was my most desperate idea. My search had to expand.

You might think it strange that I never thought about teaching Biology. The answer was simple. After 22 years, I had forgotten almost all of it. I still had all my books and lecture notes which I paged through before dumping them in the trash. I couldn't believe how much I had learned and forgotten.

And much of what I knew about living and working overseas wouldn't be much use to me either. I was starting over in a strange land.

257. ON MY OWN

I KNEW I WANTED TO WORK FOR MYSELF. After getting a salary my whole life, not to mention a free car, house, and utilities, I wanted to see if I could make a living on my own. What would I enjoy doing? Five years earlier when we bought our house, I thought the process was interesting and was something I could get into quickly. To start, all I had to do was take a class, pass an exam, and find a broker where I could work. I finally decided on Real Estate.

At the Wisconsin Realtors Association, I bought the two manuals I would need to learn, took the two-week class, and studied for two weeks. Three days before the exam, I took a practice test and got a 69. I was shocked. As I reviewed my answers, I discovered, to my relief, that I simply hadn't read the questions carefully. I had forgotten my own advice: don't assume anything. Read the question. When I got my test results in the mail on Pearl Harbor day, I was relieved. Passing had not been a problem. I was now a licensed Real Estate Broker.

By joining a company in a bigger market, I thought I'd have more opportunities to learn. I updated my resume and then interviewed with Herman Kraus, the broker-owner of ERA Kraus Real Estate and Builders in Sun Prairie. Herman was glad to have me and invited me to their New Year's Eve Party. I started two days later, joined the Wisconsin Realtors Association, paid my MLS dues and was now an independent contractor and a Realtor — not a Ree-later but a Real-tor. I drove my big blue Cadillac 33 miles each way to the office and got 12 mpg uphill or down, not 18 as the seller had promised. I soon discovered I was buying a lot of gasoline. At least I encountered only a few cars on the way to work.

My new career in sales started by knocking on dozens of "For Sale By Owner" doors all over Sun Prairie and Madison as I tried to drum up business — without success. I guess they could see I was a beginner and perhaps not very convincing, but I did begin to learn what not to say and how to rephrase questions. When knocking on doors one day, a young-looking girl answered and I asked, "Is the owner of the house home?" She replied, "I am." From then on, I asked, "Are you the owner of the house?" I worked hard and soon had several signed contracts, but they regularly fell apart because of sheer inexperience. Just because I had passed the state real estate exam, didn't mean I knew how to sell a house. My problems were far worse than a week of jet lag. I had never been to Sun Prairie before joining ERA-Kraus, didn't know where anything was, who the bankers were or much of anything. My hard work was getting me nowhere. I wrote an offer with a VA loan and included the income of the veteran's girlfriend (for VA loans only a spouse's income could be counted) which doomed the transaction from the beginning. The Sales Manager, Frank Netzer, thought my many problems were quite amusing. Nobody cared if I made any money, in fact the other Realtors didn't want any competition at all. After two months, I finally wrote an accepted offer and had my first closing at the end of March. That was good, but since arriving in Cambria, I had gone over nine months without any income. My second closing didn't happen for five more months until late August. By then I had chewed up more than $27,000 paying off my mortgage, the house renovations and just living. Our savings were gone which forced us, from time to time, to borrow money from Sean and then Sarah. After September, however, I became somewhat more successful and managed to close eight more transactions by the end of the year. Sean and Sarah got paid back and I was catching on, but we were grateful when Donna's parents occasionally brought us a gallon of milk. Years later, I would tell people, "It's not a good idea to hire a new Realtor." There was more to selling a house than devoting a lot of time to the effort.

258. TOO MANY RULES

AFTER WE ARRIVED IN CAMBRIA, we were trying to decide where to go to church. Donna didn't want to attend her old church where we were married because she didn't want to have to follow all the unwritten rules of dress and behavior. We also wanted to be free from parental influence. Since we wanted something new, we started going to an Assembly of God Church in Rio, about 20 minutes away. The pastor and people were great, but we soon realized that they had a lot of rules, too, which greatly surprised us. We weren't supposed to go to the movies and Donna was expected to wear a dress. In addition, the 20-minute drive in our big Cadillac cost more than I could afford and hindered us from getting involved with other activities. After about a year, we decided to try the Evangelical Free Church in Randolph, five miles straight east of Cambria. That suited us fine for the next couple years and we joined a Bible Study with two farm couples.

Sean turned 15 in the summer of 1986 and got a job at Jungs, the big seed and flower company in Randolph founded in 1908. He detasseled corn, hoed and did other farm work. On the hottest days, he arrived home dragging his feet, sometimes because he had several pounds of mud caked on his boots or because he was dehydrated when there was no time to drink water. After suffering from a bit of heat exhaustion one day, he traded his sandwich for a bottle of "Jolt," a soft drink containing "double the caffeine and all the sugar." After that he begged for more.

259. A SIX-WEEK'S DIVERSION

IN SEPTEMBER 1986, I was asked to teach Spanish at the Cambria-Friesland High School for the first six weeks because the teacher, Mrs. Wagner, just had a baby. That sounded doable and would give me some regular income. So, I agreed. Finally, my teaching credentials earned in my fifth year at the UW came in handy. Sean started ninth grade and was put in a second-year Spanish class. Sarah was doing well and joined the 4-H Livewires.

I thought that by teaching an elective, I would be encountering only the better students who wanted to do well. Most were but I was shocked that several of them never did a lick of homework. After a few weeks, I gave them a 40-word vocabulary test and one kid got 36 wrong. It wasn't easy correcting his test because I kept thinking I was marking everything in reverse. Several times I had to stop and check what I was doing. He was obviously more interested in basketball, and yes, he was from Randolph, where that is all they thought about. I just couldn't believe that not everyone would try to do well. That confirmed it. I had made the right decision when I decided teaching might not be the best profession for me. Shortly thereafter, my real estate sales in Cambria started to improve, thanks in part to the connections I made at the school. We were, however, still living from hand to mouth.

In ninth grade, Sean went out for basketball and was on the JV team. When he scored a basket, I could hear the girls exclaim, "Sean scored a basket!" Good for him. That's more than I ever did. Both Sean and Sarah were doing well in school.

260. OVERCOMING FEARS

LIVING FROM HAND TO MOUTH is why Donna decided to get a job, but since she hadn't worked as a nurse for twenty years, except to fill in for a few days here and there at the U.S Embassy, she was worried. She had obviously forgotten a lot and of course a lot more had changed. She decided to take a refresher course which only reinforced her fears. Despite all this, she decided to interview at the Columbia County Nursing Home in Wyocena, thirteen miles west of Cambria. They needed assistance and promised they would help her get oriented. She was scheduled to work part time, two or three PM shifts a week, plus just one weekend out of four. The pay was good, and we would all get health insurance. Since none of us had any health issues and I never even went to the doctor for the next 10 years, the insurance part didn't seem like a big deal to me, but everyone around us seemed to think it was extremely important. We then bought a used Buick Century so Donna could get to work. It turned out to be a piece of junk contrary to the recommendations of Consumers Reports.

261. ECSTASY AT THE PUMP

I NEVER WASTED TIME at work because just getting there and back cost me six gallons of gas a day. To reduce this expenditure by more than half, we decided to buy a new Honda Accord. I had a chain of four pending closings all lined up and would pick up the car in three days. When Uncle John, Mom's brother who lived near Detroit, heard about my gasoline woes, he gave me a call and said, "I have just the car for you, my wife's 1981 diesel VW Jetta that gets over 50 mpg. Would you want it for $5000?" I jumped at the chance and said, "Yes." Not only did I save $9000 but my uncle and the three-day right-of-rescission law saved me from myself. My chain of pending closings to finance the deal all fell apart and I'll never forget the first time I filled it up. After driving over 300 miles, the diesel fuel, which was then cheaper than gas, cost me $5.00. Filling up the Cadillac after just 225 miles cost $25. I almost started laughing for joy, and after that I never counted my chickens before they hatched. From then on until I retired, I only drove Jettas.

In the summer of 1987, all four of us hopped in our little Jetta and headed east to visit some of our overseas friends. As we buzzed along I-80 with a tailwind, we got 58 mpg. The diesel seemed almost free. Near Akron, Ohio, we visited Gary and Carol Eiber, whom we knew in Chile where Gary worked for Firestone. He was at least 6'6" and used to say, "I'm not a connoisseur, but I do like to eat a lot." Then we drove to Williamsport, Pennsylvania, where we met Jim and Wendy Etzel, our card-playing and gambling friends from Chile. Of course, they had to teach me once again how to play pinochle, and while Donna and Wendy were in the kitchen, Jim stacked the deck so everyone had a perfect hand. The girls were so excited they just couldn't believe we all had perfect hands. In Philadelphia, Harry, and Mary Tweedie, from our Costa Rica days, showed us Independence Hall, the Liberty Bell and Gettysburg. Finally, we ended up in the Pocono Mountains and stayed with Sterling and Jackie Edwards, who had been Sean's science teacher in Tegucigalpa, Honduras, and were our Christian friends who participated in our garage sales. In the evening, we watched the raccoons climb high up into a tree to eat snacks and by day we played in their rocky creek before making the 954-mile trip back home. Later in the summer, they returned the visit. That's when I gave Sterling my stuffed Great Blue Heron for his Mennonite Camp museum. Unfortunately, it was soon confiscated by the Pennsylvania DNR.

Sarah, now in eighth grade, always kept busy with her many projects. She was also happy to play one of the little children in the high school play, "The Sound of Music." During the same year, Sean joined the "New Action Singers" youth group. It was great to see 20-30 kids singing and telling about their faith. At the urging of our kids, we decided to leave the Evangelical Free Church in Randolph and joined the nearby Rosedale Presbyterian Church so they could be closer to their new friends. That's when I started learning about reformed theology which made perfect sense to me — that is if you pay attention to what the Bible says.

After Sean's sophomore year, he spent the next four summers working as a lifeguard in Cambria's new pool in the park, just one long block from our house. All those hundreds of laps he did for a nickel finally turned into a full-time job. He also gave swimming lessons, and for several years after he left home, I sometimes overheard young girls walk past our house, with longing in their hearts, saying, "This is where Sean lives."

262. THE ROLLOVER

IN EARLY 1988, AS SEAN WAS DRIVING the big 1974 Cadillac back from youth group with Sarah and three other kids, Marty, Jean, and Katy, he missed the curve on the edge of Cambria, rolled the car over and ended up 10' below in the ditch. They crawled out of the wreck and ran back to the nearest neighbors for help. Sean's face, which hit the windshield because his seat belt broke, was bleeding everywhere and Sarah had to hold her broken arm to keep it from flopping up and down with every step. The ambulance took them to Beaver Dam Hospital, but since the doctors thought that they both needed surgery, they were sent to Madison General Hospital in Madison. When I got the call, I was at Mom and Dad's house after working late in Madison. The nurse was still picking glass from Sean's face when I arrived, and he ended up with 58 stitches. A policeman then entered the room and gave Sean a ticket for inattentive driving. I thought, wasn't he just punished enough? The next day Sean had surgery on the end of his little finger which was barely attached. In the rollover, Sarah ended up in the front seat with Sean and his friend Marty, who was fine, but Katy hurt her knee. Sarah's broken upper arm healed without surgery, but she had to sleep sitting up for the next two weeks. The weight of the cast below the break held her humerus in place which seemed a strange way to treat the break which was almost straight across. Sean felt responsible for wrecking the car, which had just been painted, but I was glad to get the pretentious gas-guzzler out of my life.

As I left Sean and Sarah's double room, I had a long walk back to my Jetta — which wouldn't start. I hurriedly walked back to their room where Donna kept watch for two days and called Dad. I didn't think about it at the time, but Dad was now almost 80 years old, and for the first time in my life, he wasn't able to help. Paul came to my rescue and called AAA. The mechanic finally came again after I missed him the first time and started the car. Late that night, I dropped it off at the VW garage and somehow came up with the $350 to pay the repair bill. After two frantic years of struggling to drum up business with limited success, my kids were in the hospital and we were still living on the financial edge. We couldn't even afford the newspaper. Overseas I was a VIP with maids, drivers, employees to supervise, paid vacations and cocktail parties to attend. What a dramatic change. That night I was miserable, frustrated and had hit rock bottom.

A couple days later, I was suddenly rescued out of the doldrums. A big house, which I had listed and sold, closed and I was paid $4000. That was a huge blessing. A couple years later, the county rerouted the road into Cambria that ended the long list of accidents on that deceptive curve — which I had almost missed myself more than once.

263. REAL ESTATE GURUS

I LISTENED TO EVERY REAL ESTATE GURU that came to Madison, bought their overpriced cassettes, and tried to implement as many of their ideas as I could. My listing presentation improved and by the end of the fourth year, I became the top salesman in the office. That sounds a bit better than it was, since most Realtors don't make all that much. In fact, 76% of all newly licensed Realtors quit before 18 months and just 20% sell 80% of the houses. I never got rich but with Donna's salary and health insurance, we soon had enough to do what we wanted to do. Things were looking up. Whenever I thought we would have a little extra, however, state and federal taxes, plus the 15.3% self-employment social-security tax took the rest. I was convinced that if everyone had to pay their taxes quarterly, instead of seeing them dribble out of their paychecks every week or two, there would be a huge tax revolt. While overseas, I didn't have to pay any federal or state taxes, which made all these taxes even more of a jolt.

One guru demonstrated a new real estate program called "Top Producer." It sounded great, so I bought a new laptop computer, purchased an expensive-looking leather briefcase to impress new clients, and a laser printer — all for $6200. When I came home, Donna said, "What? That costs more than a car." No, she was not a happy camper. The other Realtors were surprised too and made bets at our weekly sales meeting. They each put $0.50 into the pot and guessed how many weeks would pass by before I got frustrated and quit using the program. I never did and months later won the $3.50 pot. Until I became adept at using the program, my income didn't increase — but it finally did a year later. Luckily, it was tax-deductible. What I needed, however, was income, not deductions.

By the end of 1988, we had saved enough money to build a two-car attached garage in between our house and the existing single garage. It was designed perfectly by Dad, and once the garage door opener was installed, I felt like King Tut. Now I could enter the house without getting wet in the rain and had plenty of room for our cars. To landscape around the new three-car garage, I lugged boulders from a nearby farm and built a rock garden surrounding it all. I'm glad I did that before I was fifty.

Sarah went to two youth church camps, visited a friend in Illinois and went to a Christian Athletic Volleyball Camp. She returned home for a few days, washed and repacked her clothes, and left again to help some missionaries build a log home up north where they camped out in an Indian reservation. She loved it.

For the first time ever, Sean was asked to go out for football in his senior year. The team needed two more kids, 28 in all, so they could hire a third coach. Sean at 6'1" and 153 pounds, had never played football or lifted weights, but they discovered he had played soccer and tested out his kicking skills. He could do that. The team had a successful season, scored a lot of touchdowns, and got into the playoffs, which gave Sean the opportunity to kick a lot of extra points. When Sean became the All Conference Kicker, I was impressed, especially since he did it with his left foot. Sean also went out for wrestling in his senior year at 156 lbs. I can't remember encouraging him to do it. He never had to lose weight and it toughened him up.

I CONTINUED GOING TO REAL ESTATE CLASSES and earned my Graduate Realtors Institute (GRI) designation. Later in the year, after I had completed 100 closings, I also earned my Certified Residential Specialist (CRS) designation. I was gaining confidence and finally earning enough to survive. Donna was helping a lot, too, as she continued working part-time at the 150-bed nursing home in Wyocena. She was now the P.M. Supervisor.

In the summer of 1990, some of the men and boys and our two pastors from Rosedale Presbyterian Church went on a week-long canoe trip to the Canadian boundary waters. We had beautiful weather, caught plenty of fish, but spent our last day paddling against the cool wind and rain. When I stood up to get out of the canoe, my toe hooked on the gunnel, thanks to my tight wet Levis, and I fell flat on my face in the shallow water — my face just missing a rock. Nobody dared laugh until I popped up and they could see I hadn't killed myself. All in all, however, we had a great trip.

Within the year, our lead Pastor Tim Bayly moved on and his newly hired assistant, Nathan Kline, became our full-time pastor. This all happened after our church voted to break away from the increasingly liberal Presbyterian Church USA. We left everything behind including the building, hymnals, tables, chairs, and a few people who chose not to leave for sentimental reasons. During the next couple years, which was a time of spiritual revival, we held services at the Marcellon Elementary School, purchased twenty acres, built our new Grace Presbyterian Church just north of Pardeeville, and joined the Presbyterian Church in America, a southern denomination. I continued teaching an adult Sunday school class and a year later, after studying The Book of Church Order, became an Elder until 2020.

Liberalism in churches doesn't result from interpreting the Bible differently. It is simply a rejection of the Bible. It is not just a different view but a competing religion. When such splits occur, Evangelical Christians should rejoice that they are no longer taking part in a non-Christian religion. Liberalism is founded on the changing emotions of men who try to decide for themselves what seems right and wrong at the moment. Not following the Bible's teaching is what has led to declining church membership for the last half century. There is a strange thing about heresy; nobody who falls into it thinks he is a heretic.

265. KNOWING WHAT HE WANTS

IN SEPTEMBER 1990, SEAN WAS 19 and headed off to the UW in Madison to study finance. He was fourth in his small Cambria-Friesland High School graduating class, yet I had no idea how he would do at university. His grades had been good, but he didn't seem to know the same things that I had learned years earlier. Maybe that was all right because most of what I learned was either forgotten or useless to me now.

After Sean was settled in, Donna and I visited him in Sellery Hall on a beautiful Sunday October afternoon. He was in his dorm room studying while most kids were outside playing basketball or lounging in the sun. As I looked out the window, he said, "Those are the kids I'm competing against." I was silently shocked and stopped wondering how he would do. The one thing I didn't know at the time was that he had a goal — to get better grades than his girlfriend, Sara Jerred, who was the Valedictorian in Pardeeville. She could have attended any Wisconsin State School with free tuition, books and fees but instead became a nursing student at Olivet, a Christian School in Kankakee, Illinois. That was a wise decision for them both.

266. UNNECESSARY PRESSURE

AS A HIGH SCHOOL JUNIOR, Sarah was busy with pom poms, volleyball and other activities. She was getting all A's and we were proud of her. Once when she got an A-, I said, "What happened here?" I was joking but Sarah didn't think so. I didn't realize how much pressure I was putting on her and sure wished I'd never said it.

It was great to see Sarah hugging her Grandpa McLeod after she was inducted into the National Honor Society — just like he was 65 years earlier. She continued going to "Quest," the new name of the "New Action Singers" youth group, now held at our Presbyterian Church. The next year, Sarah was the Valedictorian, gave an excellent speech, and headed off to UW-Eau Claire. We loaded up not only our car but also Chuck's pick-up with all the essentials she needed to survive the year.

We enjoyed Thanksgiving and had Mom, Dad, Paul's, and Margie's families over for a big turkey dinner. We showed my movies taken in Chile, Ecuador, Pakistan, Sri Lanka, Costa Rica and in the U.S. It was a movie marathon but fun for everyone to see how we all used to look.

In 1992, Donna wrote a poem for our Christmas newsletter:

It's Christmas time which brings to mind
Our friends both far and near.
We've had a good year and are looking ahead
To the year of nineteen ninety-three.

Our nest is now empty and we have time to enjoy
Less washing and cooking
and phone calls that annoy.
Our thoughts turn to our kin, dear Sarah and Sean,
Who are off on their own and doing their thing.

Sean is in Madison studying business in class
While his mind is dreaming about one special lass
Who's miles away trying to study and pass
To be a nurse is her special task.

Sarah worked hard and brought home a surprise
First in her class and four years tuition as prize.
We all sighed with relief and were happy as clams
For this helped avoid a financial jam.

Sarah's at Eau Claire taking Spanish and Art
She's thought about home but is sticking it out.
She calls about studies, boys and that's all
And we try give her advice as to what is her call.

We are hoping this "poem" finds you healthy and hale
With visions of Christmas while reading your mail.
This greeting from us and from all those you love
Is just to say with a smile
Merry Christmas and a Happy New Year!

National Honor Society Inductees,
65 Years Apart

267. TWO GREAT DADS

1993 WAS A TRYING YEAR. In the winter while walking to the mailbox, Dad slipped on the ice, fell, and hit his head. For six weeks he seemed fine but then suddenly got an excruciating headache. He had a brain-bleed, got better, then worse and died in Meriter hospital on April 29th, four days before his 85th birthday. Dad was a huge influence on me. He was big, strong, and smart. He could do or figure out most anything. He was also a peacemaker, gentle and under control. He had my respect. I loved him.

During several years before Dad died, Mom sometimes got a bit frustrated because she didn't seem to realize that he was aging faster than she was. When he was engaged in stimulating conversation, he perked up noticeably, but he was slowing down, required more rest and was not

Walter and Donna

able to do everything quickly as he had always done. As soon as he died, however, she did understand and her whole countenance changed.

When Donna's dad retired from DeKalb, he was asked, "To determine your monthly retirement income, how long do you think you'll live?" Wally said, "80." I would have said, "120 years," but he probably thought 80 sounded like a ripe old age. On September 25, 1993, when Donna and I visited them in Friesland, they were both fine but her dad kept giving us instructions, like what should be done with his loudspeaker that he used for auctions, and what his wife should do with their 60-acre farm. Donna joked, "What do you know that we don't?" He just smiled. That night, he had a stroke, went to Meriter Hospital, followed by his wife, Dorothy, Donna and Sharon, and died the next morning just after June arrived. Everybody knew and loved Wally. He was kind, patient, considerate and a true salesman. When he died, his wife said, "Absent in the body, present with the Lord."

268. CAMBRIA: 1844 TO 1994

JUNE 18, 1994 was Cambria's sesquicentennial. A lot of activities were planned, including a tour of some of the oldest and newest homes. Ours, from about 1870, was one of them. For two months in advance, we started fixing, painting, decorating, putting up new curtains, and cleaning. I even replaced the old concrete walkways with bricks. The day of the tour was hot and muggy, and we just got hotter as the people poured in and out. My air conditioning just couldn't keep up — until the next day when I replaced the totally clogged air filter.

269. OFF AND RUNNING

1994 WAS THE YEAR that Sean and Sara Jerred got married. Before their big day, Sean and I took a flying ten-day camping trip to Yellowstone and the Tetons, where I had spent the summer 28 years earlier. I had an AAA travel book and with a new cell phone in my car, we could call ahead and make reservations before the campgrounds filled up. When I told Sean that we were going to the nightly rodeo in Cody, Wyoming, he didn't want to go but I replied, "We're going anyway, and you'll like it." When a bucking bronco violently threw a cowboy against the chain link fence in front of our noses and stuck there like a squirrel, Sean changed his mind. A day later he got a bit too close to a moose and took shelter behind a tree as we hiked to Swan Lake, one of my favorite spots in the Tetons. We even fished in the Snake River in the rain, fried a pan full of our freshly caught trout, and visited all the tourist attractions along Yellowstone's figure 8 loop, such as Old Faithful and Yellowstone Falls.

On our way back, buzzing along in my diesel Jetta, a State Trooper coming the other way detected I was over the 65-mph speed limit. In my rear-view window, I watched him do a U-turn, cross the median and follow me. As he got closer, I decided to exit and passed a car stopped on the side. With the trooper right on my bumper, my luck ran out — until the two stranded boys waved their arms and yelled for help. The trooper stopped while Sean and I nervously headed into town for a milkshake. When the coast seemed clear, we continued east, drove all night, and arrived home the next day for lunch. That was the last time I ever drove all night.

On August 13,1994, Sean married Sara Jerred at Grace Presbyterian Church. Sara and her mom, Claire, made a lovely silk wedding dress, plus four bridesmaids and three flower girl dresses. During the hour after the service, presided over by Pastor Nathan Kline, the sanctuary was transformed into a beautifully decorated and elegant dining room. The newlyweds flew to Cozumel, Mexico, for a week, as Donna insisted that they have a proper honeymoon — better than the 2000-mile, four-day camping trip that she endured on our way to Arizona. Sean and Sara got off to a more luxurious

Sean & Sara McLeod

start and never looked back. After all, they were each voted by their high school classmates to be the "Most likely to succeed."

Sara, now an RN, got a job with the Red Cross. They were now financially independent and living in their own apartment in Madison. In the fall, Sean started his ninth and last semester before he graduated with a Bachelor of Science degree in Finance, Investments and Banking. He then became one of the 14 students and the only underclassman selected into the Applied Program in the newly constructed Grainger Hall Business School. They were divided into two groups, picked stocks under the tutelage of former UW graduates and finance professionals, and had several million dollars of real money to invest. This was a tremendous opportunity, which led to a series of bigger and better things.

During the same year, The Milwaukee Journal started an investment contest. They selected about 30 well-known individuals, finance companies and some pro-athletes. Each participant picked five Wisconsin stocks and then waited to see which increased the most. Sean, with two of his classmates, also entered the contest, and for fun, the journalist entered his dog which fetched five tennis balls representing five companies. Each month, the paper published the results and month after month Sean's team remained on top. Until the last couple months of the contest, the dog remained in second but faded near the end.

In January 1995, with diploma in hand, Sean was headed for a new job as a research analyst for the Red Chip Review in Portland, Oregon, but the Director of the Applied Program intervened. He told Sean, "You can't quit the Applied Program in the middle." What could the Director do to stop him? He offered Sean guaranteed admission to Graduate School and said he didn't have to worry about passing the big GMAT entrance exam. Sean agreed, took the test, answered all the questions without reading them, and finished the GMAT in record time minutes later. After three more semesters in graduate school, Sean had his master's degree and was ready to take on the world. He soon got a job as a Research Analyst with Strong Capital Management in Menomonee Falls, just north of Milwaukee and I wrote an offer on the house he bought in nearby Germantown. Sara worked at the Menomonee Falls Hospital coordinating new admissions and their insurance benefits. Now they were really on their own.

270. SETTING THE DATE

DAUGHTER SARAH CONTINUED AT THE UW-EAU CLAIRE, majoring in Graphic Design and Spanish. She took two trips, one to Mexico, where she helped build houses with Habitat for Humanity, followed by a month-long trip to Chile in 1994 with the Navigators, where she lived with a missionary couple. Earlier the same summer, her college boyfriend from Eau Claire, Robert Leafblad, was in the Dominican Republic and by chance called her on Sean and Sara's wedding day — just because he missed her. A year later they got engaged and set the date for June 1, 1996.

Back in high school, Sarah had entered an American Legion essay contest. She soon learned that she was the winner in Columbia County but then didn't hear anything more. Finally, she asked her teacher, "Who won the state essay contest?" Her teacher replied, "Oh, some kid from up north." Yes, the statewide winner was Robert, as the two of them discovered later. It was meant to be.

On June 1, 1996 Sarah and Robert had a beautiful wedding and reception at Grace Presbyterian Church, like Sean and Sara's. At the reception, her Maid of Honor, Annie Boldt, a music therapy major, belted out a song that amazed me. They spent their week-long honeymoon in Fish Creek, Door County, Wisconsin – and Donna could relax.

Robert & Sarah Leafblad

A semester later, they both graduated from UW-Eau Claire. Robert got a job at the Pleasant Company in Eau Claire and Sarah worked for the newspaper and then for Michael's where she also taught art classes.

We were empty nesters after 30 years of marriage. Donna was sad, but I thought it meant we had been successful. Wouldn't it be far worse to have a couple of flunky kids hanging around the house with nothing to do?

Over the next twenty years, they bought four houses that needed a lot of improvements and we enjoyed the back-breaking labor that ensued.

Donna and I started a different kind of Bible study, called "Sonship" from World Harvest Ministries. Each month we called our counsellor in Pennsylvania for advice and accountability. It involved a lot of soul-searching but we both felt the benefits. The central theme was to make us realize that unlike orphans, we should live like a son or daughter of God who will receive a huge inheritance. From Dad especially, I had learned to do a lot of things which made my life go smoother. While useful, it tended to make me live by rules instead of by the freedom that I had by being a believer.

271. A WORKING VACATION

IN MAY 1997, DONNA SPENT her two-week vacation taking a real estate class and passed the exam on a computer. That was quite an accomplishment. Then she resigned from her more lucrative job at the Wyocena Nursing Home and started working with me in December. We were now on the same schedule and it was understandable that she wanted to leave before she became a patient herself. This wasn't the best financial decision we ever made. We lost her steady income and had to buy health insurance. The first year I paid $360 a month and each year the premium increased, first to $460, then

The McLeod Team

$660, then $850, and finally $1024, which I deemed unaffordable, since we never used it because of the high deductible. Then we heard about Samaritans. Starting in the year 2001, we each paid our monthly premium of $85 directly to someone who had a health expense and included a note of encouragement. When we had a medical bill, we received enough money from several other members to pay it. No middlemen or big glass buildings wasted our premiums. It worked great until we started Medicare. I thought this should be the model to solve our health care problems.

In late 1997, Sean got a new job as a securities analyst at M&I Bank and managed their Marshall Growth Fund. The pay was much better but with a slightly longer commute. In March, Donna and I flew to Las Vegas for the ERA Real Estate Convention. We had a great time seeing some shows and virtual-reality movies, such as Jules Verne's "20,000 Leagues Under the Sea." I loved it but Donna was dizzy for several hours. When we returned, she attended two four-day classes towards her Graduate Realtors Institute (GRI) designation but was happy that I took care of all the problems at work. Meanwhile, Sarah began a new job as a graphic designer for the Leader Telegraph Newspaper in Eau Claire.

On December 11, 1999, Sean and Sara delivered our first grandchild, Molly Mae McLeod. She was cute and healthy, and we were excitedly waiting see her. What could be better?

Molly Mae McLeod

272. A NEW MILLENNIUM

WE FLEW TO ANOTHER ERA CONVENTION, this time in San Diego, where we attended some top-notch training seminars and saw some great entertainment. We also had fun wandering around and shopping in Tijuana, Mexico, for a day and speaking a little Spanish once again. Back home and for the first time since Sri Lanka, Donna started taking piano lessons on our new Yamaha piano. We continued to keep busy gardening and I greatly enlarged our brick patio.

In the year 2000, Donna planned a big surprise 60th birthday party for me at the village hall. She bought and made a ton of food, including two huge lasagnas, cakes, ice cream and soda for 100 people. She fended off my questions saying they were for her mother's party. When I got a call from Harry, who inquired about the time, I asked Donna, "Who's Harry?" but she deflected. On the big day, I still had a terrible cold and drugged myself with antihistamines and cold tablets before I walked down the street to the party at the last moment. When I arrived, everyone yelled "Happy Birthday" but for a few seconds I still didn't comprehend that the party was for me until I saw Mary, who had come all the way from Texas, and my Realtor friend, Len Knitter, who for sure wouldn't be invited to a party for Donna's mom. Everybody was there, including Paul, Margie, Mom, and "The Blue Denim" two-person band, Harry and his wife, Arlene. He played the bass and Arlene the accordion and several guests danced to their music. Donna discovered them at the nursing home where they sometimes played for the old folks. How appropriate. I received a lot of "over the hill" presents, like a cane with a horn and a rear-view mirror, so I could see where I had been, and a motion-activated, singing "Billy Bass." I had finally reached middle age — if I lived to be 120.

Meanwhile, Sarah and her husband Robert moved to Burlington in southeast Wisconsin. Robert got a totally new kind of job welding in Kenosha. Sarah worked as a graphic designer in Lake Geneva.

Our real estate business was going great and we could be reached at John@McLeodTeam.com. I was taking advantage of my Top Producer real estate program and could type personalized letters to dozens of people with a few clicks of my mouse by using inserts that changed for every recipient. Donna spent a lot of her time searching for new property listings that she mailed to future customers. Donna was happy she had a lenient boss who let her off to babysit for Molly. Sean and Sara even became short term foster parents by taking care of little Eddie until he was adopted a few weeks later. Donna's mom, now 87, moved temporarily into an assisted living apartment in the Randolph Nursing Home. She did get a lot of visitors and knew just about everyone in the home. Shortly thereafter she moved to the new Cambria apartments next to Chuck and Sharon's house.

In March 2001, we flew to Tampa to attend another ERA convention. Being so close, we visited Chuck and Sharon in Tiki Village in the town of Holiday, where they would spend many more winters. At a nearby deli, we also met Al and Peggy Scholorholtz, whom we hadn't seen since Nepal 22 years earlier. When a gray haired man walked in, Donna instantly ran up to him, gave him a hug and said "Hi Al." I couldn't stop her. The man loved getting an unexpected hug from a strange blonde.

273. SEPTEMBER 2001

SEPTEMBER WAS A TRAGIC MONTH. After a long battle, Paul's wife, Elaine, died from breast cancer on the 6th. She was only 61. She also left behind three kids, David, Jennifer and Eric, and their families. Five days later on September 11, 2001, as I walked out the kitchen door to go to work, I glanced back at the TV and saw a plane crash into the World Trade Center. Minutes later I realized it was no accident when another plane hit the second tower. I watched in horror as people jumped to their deaths to avoid the gasoline-fueled flames just before the buildings collapsed. Planes throughout the country were immediately grounded, which prevented Elaine's oldest brother, Carl, who lived in Florida, from attending the funeral officiated by their former minister, Tim Kehl. The death toll was worse than Pearl Harbor and all our lives changed forever. Now we suspect and frisk everyone, wasting millions of dollars and hours of productivity.

A few days later, the kids surprised Donna with a 60th birthday party at our church in Pardeeville. Donna thought she didn't want one, but had a great time seeing so many friends and family. Everyone was much kinder to Donna than they had been to me — she didn't receive any gifts that even hinted she was over the hill. At the same time, she wasn't immediately aware that all her presents were white elephants. She did her best to sound sincere when opening the tacky gifts until it finally became way too obvious — to everyone's delight.

274. FISH CRACKERS

ONE AFTERNOON when I was extremely busy at the ERA office in Sun Prairie trying to finish some last-minute paperwork, Donna called and asked me to pick up a box of goldfish crackers, and pampers for Molly. The last thing I wanted to do right then was to take time driving down the street to Walmart. At least I knew right where the crackers should be, but on my first trek down the aisle, I didn't see them. As I turned around and looked back down the vacant aisle, a box fell off the shelf onto the floor. Who did that? I walked back, picked up the box of crackers, grabbed some pampers and was quickly on my way. I think God could see I was frustrated and in a hurry.

275. A TWO-YEAR PROJECT

IN 2002, SEAN AND SARA BOUGHT a vacation house on Park Lake in Pardeeville. It was a big A-frame, and over the next two years various carpenters and I filled up twenty 30-yard dumpsters as we gutted the house, reinforced floors, and made extensive changes. It was a huge project, much bigger and more expensive than anyone thought at the beginning, but it turned out great. I worked on the house almost full-time for a year as I was starting to get tired of selling houses. This was more fun and at 62, I was in great shape after lugging so many tons of rubble up the steep hill.

One morning when I was demolishing the old two-story boathouse, it suddenly collapsed and knocked me flat on the concrete slab. I was stunned, but after a minute slithered out, stood up slowly, looked around and realized that a tree had kept it from squashing me. I walked up the hill and noticed that every time I turned around my left foot felt like I was standing in a pile of mush. Then I realized my ankle was twisting but not my foot. I drove home, took a hospital dose of Ibuprofen, and drove to the Meritor Hospital Emergency Room in Madison. While the nurse was asking me questions, she lifted my T-shirt and looked at my back. I said, "My back feels fine," and she replied, "But you have blood on your shirt." My ankle wasn't broken, just very badly sprained. When I got home and looked in the mirror, I saw the red indentation across my shoulders where the 2x6 had knocked me down. My back never hurt, but I did keep my foot elevated for four straight days. After hobbling around for a few months, I resumed work on the house.

On October 1, 2002, I became President of the Cambria Kiwanis Club, the first of four different times. We enjoyed babysitting for Molly who had just turned three, Mom turned 94, and we sold Donna's mom's house and 60-acre farm. Her mom generously gave her three kids an early inheritance and we used our share to remodel our kitchen and downstairs bath. We gutted the kitchen and by noon the first day had to order a second 20-yard dumpster as we ripped out everything down to the studs. When the ceiling came down, we were knee deep in insulation and soot, but Donna and I had it cleaned up by the time the carpenters, John and Joel, returned from lunch. After over three months of cooking on a two-burner hotplate, we had all new custom cherry cabinets, new appliances, granite countertops, a tile floor and a bigger picture window that more birds flew into. Donna loved it, and by spring in 2003, I loved all the food she prepared. That wasn't anything new for me, of course — just more convenient for her.

276. NEARING THE END OF A SECOND CAREER

IN MAY 2003, WE RECEIVED A CALL from Chuck's brother, Al Dykstra, letting us know that there was a double-wide coach for sale in Tiki Village, down the street from Chuck and Sharon's. We decided to make an offer, sight unseen, and soon became owners of our winter get-away. We had to be patient because we didn't return to Florida until after Christmas.

Late the same summer I flew to Mahwah, New Jersey, to celebrate our 40th anniversary of

Older, Wiser and Wearing Name Tags in Mahwah, New Jersey, 2003

joining the Peace Corps. It was a cheerful reunion, hosted by Charlie Carreras in his shaded backyard. We sat in a big circle and all had a chance to give an update. It was good to see everyone again, but some people had changed so much they didn't recognize me.

I was surprised when Jim and Celeste Corzine said that I had saved their marriage — on numerous occasions. Back in PC training, Celeste was progressing faster in Spanish than Jim, but he was adamant that he didn't want her to be moved up one group. I was shocked and thought he should be happy to be with someone who could help him. When I heard about it, according to Jim, I told him, "You're such a jerk." I remember thinking just that, but I couldn't believe I said it. From then on, whenever they had a fight, one of them would repeat my line, they would laugh, and it would be over.

Soon thereafter, Sean and Sara had their second baby girl, Meghan Claire McLeod, on November 11, 2003, exactly one month before Molly's fourth birthday. That made it easy to remember. She was, of course, a little cutie and now we had two little ones to admire.

Meghan McLeod

Just after Christmas, we drove to Holiday, and discovered that our 1972 Dodge Coach had a decent kitchen and floor plan but was grubby and needed a lot of elbow grease. For two weeks, Donna and I worked like slaves, washing, and painting the walls, replacing the toilets and all the flooring. A day after we finished, Donna's mom and sister June arrived for a visit.

When we returned to Cambria in early April 2004, I found "For Sale" signs around town from several other real estate companies. More than one seller told me, "I tried to call you, but...." I quickly realized that I couldn't be vacationing in Florida and expect to stay in business.

Without thinking much about it, I had already decided. I had been easing into retirement ever since I started spending a lot of time helping the carpenter remodel Sean and Sara's lake house. To make up for the loss of income, I started Social Security at 62.

My number-one ranking in the office quickly ended and I was losing interest in selling houses. I didn't officially retire from ERA-Kraus Real Estate & Builders, however, until I was 65. My twenty years overseas had been followed by twenty more selling real estate. An accountant reviewed our finances and said, "Yes, you should be okay. You can always sell the land." That's how we "planned" for our retirement.

People asked, "Why do you want to spend your winters in Florida?" It was the warm sunny weather, picnics on beautiful beaches, walks along the boardwalks through the cypress swamps, as well as resale shops, garage sales, and meals with friends. Everything was so close and convenient.

In April 2004, Sean got a new job with the U.S. Bank in Minneapolis, moved to Woodbury and lived on the same street as Chuck and Sharon's daughter Linda and her husband, Brooks Berg. After two years, he accepted another similar job at Windsor Financial Group for the next four years. It was a family friendly place to bring up kids.

277. MORE GRANDKIDS

Bjorn Leafblad

SARAH AND ROBERT had their first baby, Bjorn Thomas Leafblad, in Burlington, Wisconsin, on December 11, 2004 which coincidentally just happened to be Molly's fifth birthday. We were all warned that he might have a cleft lip and palate but when I saw the crystal-clear ultrasound taken at Milwaukee Children's Hospital, my heart just sank. Sarah suffered through a rough bout of contractions, followed by a C-section, and was physically beat up for the first two weeks.

She needed a lot of help which Robert and Donna provided. The first few months were a real struggle for Sarah. Milk had to be squirted into Bjorn's mouth to keep it from coming out of his nose. Fortunately the Cleft Palate Team at Milwaukee Children's Hospital showed Sarah what to do and how to tape his upper lip, a seventeen-step process, which helped close the gap until he was big enough for his first surgery four months later in April. When Bjorn turned one, he had his second surgery which also went amazingly well. There would be more, but he looked much better and was walking everywhere. Things were all coming together, and the hardest part was over.

278. AFTER FORTY YEARS

I HAD MISSED THE FIRST PC REUNION in Washington, D.C., attended the big one in Mahwah, New Jersey, at Charlie Carreras' house in 2003, and didn't want to miss this next one a year later in Guatemala. It would be interesting to see how the country had changed in 40 years.

My PC house still needs paint 40 years later

Almost half our PC group, 23 in all, went to Guatemala. As Donna and I flew into the country at night, I tried to figure out what cities we were seeing below. Only one thing was certain. Guatemala City had grown much bigger and extended far beyond its old boundary. We couldn't stay at our old meeting place, the Palace Hotel, because it had been converted into a bank. The next morning, we boarded a bus and started our tour to Antigua, Chichicastenango and back to Lake Atitlán. When the driver was asked if we could stop at certain project sites, he said, "No, it's too dangerous," and we could see the fear in his eyes. It was sad to see how the huge population increase since 1965 had resulted in so many social problems. As a PCV, I never felt unsafe or even thought about it, despite what was going on behind the scenes. Besides seeing the sights, we also enjoyed a delicious "Paella" dinner one night at Mike Schwartz's house prepared by his Chilean friend.

After our bus tour, several of us flew to Flores in El Petén to see the Mayan ruins at Tikal. Since our "tours of duty" in Guatemala, many more pyramids had been uncovered from the dense jungle and Tikal had become a major tourist destination.

After we flew back to the capital, Donna and I borrowed a CARE Jeep and headed towards San Pedro Ayampuc. In my PC days, the bus left Guatemala City behind after just a couple miles. This time we drove through the outskirts for about ten miles before we reached the countryside and headed down the steep switchbacks to my former village. The rutted street had now been paved with concrete and, as I soon found out, most everyone in town had running water. I could see progress.

As we entered the plaza, we stopped in front of my former abode and could see that it was the same as when I had first seen it. Major repairs were once again being done after a mudslide filled up the backyard. I stopped a passerby and asked if he knew the whereabouts of a a girl named Sonia, who would be about 45, and who used to live in the house in front of mine. He did. She was now a teacher at the new high school between the church and the dispensary. Since recess had just started, I soon found Sonia, who was incredibly surprised and happy to see me. She left her class for a half hour and showed me where several people, whom I had known the best, were living. As they came to the door, they instantly yelled, "Juan!" It was a short but fun return trip.

279. BURMESE PYTHONS

"Popnoculars"

WE BEGAN 2006 IN ORLANDO where Donna and I met Paul and Barb, his new wife, at the Capital One Bowl. There we saw Wisconsin beat Auburn 24-10. We then continued down the Florida Turnpike to Jupiter on the Atlantic coast, where we stayed for the next few days at their condo, just a block from the beach. On our way back we toured the Everglades and did some bird watching. I loved the Everglades but worried about the Burmese Pythons that have already decimated 98% of raccoons, skunks, foxes, opossums, and rabbits. They are even eating the alligators, some up to 6 feet. How did the pythons get there? When pet pythons get too big, they get dropped off in a nearby swamp. It will be all but impossible to eliminate them.

280. A NEW HOBBY

CHUCK'S BROTHER, BILL, was giving bird-carving lessons back in Holiday to a few old fellows in his garage. Chuck and I thought that might be interesting, so we both decided to go. I bought a set of knives and was all set. Our first lesson was about how to hold the knife so we wouldn't slip and slice our fingers or worse. Carving was a slow process but after a few days my first project, a dolphin, turned out quite well. From there, I carved a small pelican, a decorative

At the Madison Carving and Woodturners Show

spoon, then my first full-sized bird, a killdeer. I had to learn to keep drawing the center lines so my carving would be symmetrical. The bird's beak, eyes and face were the most important. If they were poorly carved, everything else wouldn't matter. Fortunately, I knew what birds looked like, which made it much easier for me than for some of the others. Since Chuck was a fisherman, he preferred carving fish.

Back in Cambria, I purchased a Dremel, an assortment of bits to speed up the carving process, and one of Bill's old wood burners for detailing feathers. Until I bought my own equipment, Bill continued to help by cutting out some more birds on his band saw which included a Red-Tailed Hawk. That kept me busy for the next few weeks. The painting lessons came next which was an entirely different challenge.

Molly McLeod

That same summer, I bought a 12-foot kayak, the shortest one that would easily go in a straight line, a paddle, and a roof rack. Now I could explore the Grand River Marsh, north of Cambria, and Horicon Marsh, the largest freshwater marsh in the world. From the town of Horicon, I'd paddle north from a small boat landing, never knowing what I'd see next. There were beavers, muskrats, otters, carp by the thousands, and many kinds of birds, which I could sometimes glide quietly up to unobserved. The best thing about a kayak, compared to a canoe, is that the wind doesn't affect it.

We always looked forward to seeing our grandkids. Molly was now in first grade at a Spanish-immersion school, where all her classes, all day long, were in Spanish. Meghan was a highly photogenic and affectionate three-year-old with sparkling brown eyes. Bjorn was two and loved to sing loudly. He had his third major surgery in December and was now doing much better.

In June, Donna and I, along with our friends and Kiwanis members, Glenn and Sue Williams, drove north to Ear Falls in Ontario for a week of fishing. We shared a cabin and ate all the walleyes we could hold. We enjoyed the peace and quiet of the wilderness and even brought home some Walleyes and Northern Pike for summer fish fries. We took the same trip for the next three years as well.

281. GRANDKID NUMBER FOUR

ON JULY 31, 2008, Aiden Manning Leafblad, was born to Sarah and Robert, 100 years after my mom and dad were born. I hoped he would be born on the 11th, like the other three, but at least the date ended with a "1." Sarah had some blood pressure problems and the doctors almost lost her, but all turned out fine. For Grandpa and Grandma, it was an exciting time to meet our fourth and final grandchild.

Aiden Manning Leafblad

A few months later, Mom turned 100 on December 14, 2008, but we celebrated early in October, so all the cousins, nieces, nephews, and great grandkids wouldn't have to worry about school or a snowstorm. The party was held at the First United Methodist Church, where everyone enjoyed a big assortment of elegant foods and desserts. Mom was in her element busily talking with many old friends she hadn't seen in years. In preparation for the event, I edited all Mom and Dad's dozens of three-minute home-movie reels onto a couple of big reels, which were projected on a huge movie screen. Editing all those little reels in order was no small task since many of them were dated "the last roll."

Mom was doing great and still living in the home she and Dad had built in 1964. She enjoyed walking up and down the hill, playing the piano and observing the foxes, owls, turkeys and even deer in her backyard. Paul lived just a mile away, checked on her every day and usually

Meghan, Bjorn and Molly
Easter in the Pergola, 2009

made her lunch. I mowed her lawn and took care of the yard and Margie drove over from Milwaukee every week or so to clean and help out in many other ways.

I wanted to use up the leftover treated lumber at Sean and Sara's lake house so they could put a car in their garage, and I could build a pergola in our backyard. After paging through a dozen garden landscape books, Donna and I agreed on a design. In just two days, John Tamminga, who did all the carpentry work on our house over the years, and I built a solid 11'x6' pergola just in time for a big family reunion. We used all the old lumber, and it was a great addition to our backyard which we've enjoyed ever since.

For the sixth time, we headed to Holiday, Florida where we stayed over three months. Once back in Cambria, Donna got the idea of hosting a picnic for her 50th Randolph High School reunion. Getting ready involved weeding, planting more flowers, trimming, mowing, and

Meghan McLeod, great-niece Brailyn Kemink,
& Bjorn Leafblad, 2008

mulching to get the yard in tip-top shape. We put up our Pakistani Shamiana and the Randolph firemen put up another tent where we had tables and chairs for about 40 classmates and spouses who reminisced about their youth. We grilled filet mignon and served hot fudge sundaes, and everyone reconnected and had a great time. The weather was perfect and the flowers looked wonderful.

282. A NEW STUDIO

AFTER DONNA'S 2009 HIGH SCHOOL REUNION, we started building a fourth stall on the end of our garage where I could do my bird carving without covering the cars with dust. It ended up being a 14'x21' "studio" with two big 9' windows overlooking the lake and our side yard. The word "studio" seemed a bit pretentious and it was hard for me to say since I thought only artists had studios. We trimmed it out with lights, shelves, tables, a dust collection system, gas heater, air-conditioning, a sander, a bandsaw to cut out birds, plenty of outlets and even a TV connection— just in case. It soon filled up with books, patterns and photos, a few stuffed birds and dozens of carvings which have overflowed into the house.

I was lucky to find several big basswood trees in Watertown and Portage which we cut down and hauled to a nearby Amish sawmill. After it was all cut up into various sizes, I had a lifetime supply of wood. At 69, I finally had my very own private space and could stay there for hours. In the following ten years, I carved and painted with acrylics a wide variety of some 200 birds — from hummingbirds, songbirds, woodpeckers, shorebirds, ducks, loons, hawks, crows, and owls. By the time this story ended, I had sold, donated, or given away 80 birds that I mounted in various ways, most often on driftwood.

283. AN AMAZING EXAMPLE

IN MARCH 2010, we returned early from Florida because Donna's mom wasn't doing well. Donna spent much of March at the nursing home with her mom, who on March 20th, her 96th birthday, became very alert, dressed up in her finest and enjoyed the party. She was an amazing example to all who knew her. I never met anyone so sure of her faith in heaven. Her three daughters, Donna, Sharon, and June, were with her singing hymns when she died a bit later that year on April 2nd. *"Good people will be remembered as a blessing."* (Proverbs 10.7)

Sarah and Bjorn Leafblad, June Vorlop,
Donna McLeod and Dorothy De Young,
Randolph Nursing Home, August 2009

284. THE GARDEN PARTY

DONNA WAS SO PROUD OF HER FLOWER GARDEN which had grown larger after we gave up on our vegetable garden, that she volunteered to host the July meeting of the Pardeeville Garden Club. For many days, we worked in the garden, planted flowers until it was as magnificent as we could afford — but then Donna noticed some weeds in the lawn which she asked me to eliminate. That would be easy. I had a container of 2-4-D broadleaf weed killer and a 3-gallon backpack sprayer to take care of the problem. After a few days, Donna noticed that there were dozens of spots, some large and some small, that were turning brown. I wasn't worried because, I had applied the same chemical on previous occasions. After a couple more days, the spots were becoming more noticeable and Donna was getting more upset by the day. The lawn looked like a leopard. That's when I realized I had accidentally used Roundup — which kills everything. What could I do? As it turned out, nothing. But I did learn one thing. There was no shade of green spray paint that matched the color of grass. Those Pardeeville Garden Clubbers all laughed and there was no blame-shifting that day, just feeble excuses. Hearing stories of other husbands who had done the same thing helped a little.

Robert and Sarah had sold their house in Burlington and moved to nearby Lyons where they lived just about rent-free in a big, newer two-story home. Bjorn was in kindergarten and Aiden was a rambunctious two. Grandma McLeod was still doing fine at home where we celebrated her 102nd birthday and Christmas with her kids, grandkids, and great grandkids.

.......Donna wrote a little poem to celebrate the occasion:

As the days and years fly by
 We can't help but say "thank-you."
For birds and flowers and health
 We can't help but say "thank-you."
Each day's a gift and for each person we love
 We can't help but say "thank-you."
For children and precious grandchildren
 We can't help but say "thank-you."
For mothers and fathers on earth or in heaven
 We can't help but say "thank-you."
For friends and family
 We can't help but say "thank-you."
For Christmas and the New Year ahead
 We can't help but say "thank-you."
As 2011 draws near pause with us
 As we count our blessings.

As usual, we spent the winter in Holiday, Florida, where once again we were visited by both kids and grandkids. We visited Disney World, Busch Gardens and had a lot of picnics at nearby parks and beaches. After the kids left, Donna had arthroscopic surgery on her knee so she would be healed up in time to work in her garden. When we needed a break from our yard work in Cambria, we relaxed in our pergola.

In September 2011, Sean started a new job as a portfolio manager at Northwestern Mutual in Milwaukee. He commuted from Woodbury, Minnesota for several months before buying a house in Shorewood on the north edge of Milwaukee. Over the next seven months they had it extensively remodeled, sold their house in Woodbury and finally moved into their "new" 1925 house in October 2012.

Robert and Sarah also bought a new house in Burlington. Robert made plans to go to school to get his master's degree in adult education in order to teach welding at a nearby technical school. This meant he quit his job, got a part-time welding job, and Sarah ended up getting a job delivering mail on several rural routes.

I continued to spend a lot of time in my studio carving, painting and mounting birds. I joined the Duck Creek Arts Guild, a local group of about a dozen artists, which for several years put on art exhibitions in both Cambria and nearby Beaver Dam. Each fall, I'd cut out about 20 birds which I finished power-carving in Florida. Luckily, my neighbors were gone during the day when my grinding machines were humming for hours on end.

John and Mary in May 2018
Still the Same Age

On our way home from Florida, we drove to Mobile, Alabama, where we toured a battleship and a submarine before visiting Bellingrath Gardens, as I had done in 1953. In New Orleans, which was crowded with Final 4 basketball fans, we ate an awfully expensive lunch, and then drove on to Natchez, Mississippi where we toured several ante-bellum homes.

Back in Cambria, with my favorite carpenter, John Tamminga, we replaced the foundation, floor, pillars, and railings of our front porch making it better than new. Next, we had the house's fascia, soffits and porch painted professionally and even installed Leaf Guard gutters, so I no longer had to risk my life at the top of a tall ladder. With the new Window World windows installed two years earlier, our house was looking its best. We liked the look of the original single pane wavy glass windows that rattled whenever a truck drove past, but the new ones made our house almost silent and our heat bills dropped noticeably. Best of all, I no longer felt guilty about not scraping, caulking, and painting the old windows.

After Thanksgiving, we continued to celebrate the De Young Christmas where we exchanged and stole gifts from each other until there were no turns left. A few days later, Donna and I dressed up as Santa & Mrs. Claus for the Village of Cambria's Kid's Christmas Party in the village hall. We arrived on the fire truck, with sirens blaring, and listened to all the little kids explain what they wanted for Christmas. It was a lot of fun and we did it for several years until we started leaving earlier for Florida. I missed the camels.

285. THE END OF A GENERATION

WE CELEBRATED MOM'S 104TH BIRTHDAY on December 14, 2012. She was doing well and we had an enjoyable dinner. Next, Paul, Mary, Margie, and I, along with our kids and grandkids, celebrated Christmas Eve at Mom's. It was great being together as we sang carols and watched Mom and the grandkids dance to the "Happy Feet" song. In the morning, after a delicious breakfast, Donna and I hopped into our loaded Honda Odyssey and headed to Florida.

In June 2013, I went to Mom's house, mowed her lawn, walked down the hill and back with her and had a relaxing talk on her swing. The next day, Margie's daughter, Karin, and her girls came for a visit. While talking and swinging, Mom suffered a stroke and slumped down in her seat. After a day in the hospital, she appeared to be better and was about to go home when she had another. After a week's vigil at hospice, Mom died on June 23, 2013. We later had a memorial service at her home moderated by the Methodist Pastor. It was a wonderful time to hear all the stories and memories. She was a great mom, a real dedicated mother whose major interest was us. All of us kids experienced her a bit differently. I never analyzed her. I just thought she was a great mom.

Mom Baking Bread at 100

Mom had a contrarian streak, was somewhat outspoken, and sometimes made comments that her more politically correct kids (not me) thought she could have kept to herself. Such comments sometimes were suggestions on how we, or our kids, should be doing something a bit differently. Once when she was confronted about a remark, she said, "Give me credit for all the things I don't say." That was a memorable line that I have since appropriated. My siblings didn't need to. When we were younger, Mom often said, "Don't believe everything you hear," and when we were older, "You don't have to tell everything you know." Somehow, she also taught me (or was it Dad?) not to show affection in public, something they never did. When Donna attempts to hold hands when we are out for a walk, my hand automatically feels uncomfortable and pulls away.

286. PEANUT BUTTER AND A DIAMOND RING

ON THE LAST DAY OF NOVEMBER 2013, Donna and I flew to Florida with Sean, Sarah, Molly and Meghan, and embarked on a seven-night Royal Caribbean cruise to Haiti, Jamaica, and Cozumel. In

Cruisin' at Christmastime
Molly, Sean, Meghan, Sara, Donna & John

Haiti, Donna and I took a short excursion to a "typical" Haitian village where we watched a woman grind up a handful of peanuts, using a mortar and pestle, to make peanut butter. Sean and Sara were surprised at our choice of land excursions after we had seen thousands of similar rural villages during our years overseas. We were too.

Back on the ship, Donna listened to every presentation made by the cruise's offshore-shopping expert who told us what to buy and where to find the best tax-free bargains. You guessed it. After 46 years of married life, she began to believe she needed a diamond ring and I realized that I had been cheap long enough. At the next stop, Donna became the proud owner of a "Hearts of Fire" diamond ring. She was happy but I frequently had to cover her hand because the sparkles were too bright for my eyes. It was a real bargain thanks to Sean who subsidized our voyage. In Cozumel we visited the tourist shops and snorkeled for the first time in 34 years. It wasn't the Maldives but we got plenty of exercise so we could justify eating more on the ship.

Back home, we spent our last McLeod Christmas in Mom and Dad's house at 80 White Oaks Lane off Schroeder Road. Margie had worked hard for weeks cleaning, painting, repairing, and sorting their belongings. Everything was divided up between the four of us and the grandkids — without hassles, I'm happy to say.

We kept busy with church, Kiwanis, gardening, bird-carving and daily life until December when Sean, Sara, Molly and Meghan flew to Tampa. We then drove to Fort Lauderdale where we all boarded another huge Royal Caribbean Ship for our second week-long cruise in the tropics. This gave Donna a chance to complete her diamond collection by buying a set of sparkling earrings. I was now almost forgiven, I think, for my lapse in judgement so long ago.

Back home in Cambria, we modernized our upstairs bathroom and made it more useful. We ripped out the old cast iron tub and pedestal sink, built a tiled shower, a vanity with a granite countertop, a big new cabinet which held a ton of stuff and shelves for towels and more. There was nothing more we could do. Our 1870 house finally made it into the 21st century.

The Rio Grande at the Big Bend

IN OCTOBER 2015, Donna and I headed to another Guatemala III Peace Corps reunion at New Mexico State University, where we had trained 52 years earlier. On the way, we visited my former CARE boss and his wife from Ecuador, Charles and Ingrid Niemann, in Camdenton, Missouri. Charles was the one who pushed for my promotion to Assistant Country Director and we enjoyed reminiscing at their lovely house overlooking the Lake of the Ozarks. Next, we visited my sister, Mary, in Austin, where she showed us some attractive houses she had designed and built. We enjoyed the river walk, some nearby sites, and a delicious dinner on her deck. For the next three days we explored the Rio Grande, saw the fantastic scenery in Big Bend National Park, and a lot of wily Roadrunners.

In Las Cruces, we reconnected with 22 PCVs and several spouses and we talked and talked. We also became the talk of the campus when they learned about our return. The professors who had supervised our training had buildings named after them. The tiny campus had grown significantly and looked like a real university. We toured the area, visited the same haunts that we had frequented years earlier and enjoyed catching up with everyone.

I was amazed at how many in our group had continued assisting various projects in Guatemala.

The Three Latin American Explorers
50 Years Later:
John McLeod, Bryce Hamilton & Tim Kraft

Working for CARE in nine different countries, I had done the same thing but had gotten paid for my efforts. Since then, I guess I had become much more of a capitalist. The others, except for a few who kept their political thoughts to themselves, were so liberal that they just adored and cheered every word uttered by President Obama as they watched his speech in the bedroom of our guest suite. I sometimes agreed with his rhetoric, but his actions were often the opposite or nonexistent. When he was a senator from Illinois, he voted "present" 129 times, thus avoiding many controversial positions that might have been used against him later during his presidential run. To me that was a clue he was not a leader but was "all hat and no cattle," as they say in Texas. In

Arches National

Wisconsin that meant "all talk and no action." After traveling in Afghanistan just a few years before the Russians invaded in 1979, I couldn't believe he or anyone could think that is where we should take a stand in our battle against terrorism. There was nothing there worth anything except poppies.

We continued to White Sands National Monument, stopped in Ruidoso and Corrales, New Mexico, where we visited Donna's nursing school classmate, Barbara, and her husband Jerry Marx in their beautifully decorated, classic, desert-setting adobe home. I also had lunch with Jerry's buddies that included two former CARE employees.

Next, we visited Natural Bridges National Monument, Valley of the Gods, where the John Wayne movies were filmed, and Arches National Park in Utah. In Colorado, we visited Black Canyon of the Gunnison and Crested Butte, now a fancy ski resort, before heading north to Gothic and the Rocky Mountain Biological Laboratory where I had spent the summer of 1961. The old two-story shack where Ulysses S. Grant and I stayed years earlier was still standing. Eighteen days and 4800 miles later we were home.

288. BEST OF SHOW

Kestrel and Mouse — Best of Show

WE NOW HAD SIX DAYS TO CLEAN UP OUR YARD, decorate the flowerpots in downtown Cambria with winter greenery that we collected from our 84 acres, and get ready for the Madison Carving and Turners Show on October 25, 2015. The size of the show had increased and was now held in the two big gyms at the Madison City Church School on Buckeye Road. This time I entered my Kestrel and mouse and won "Best of Show."

A day later, Donna had arthroscopic surgery on her other knee. This time the doctor, recommended by Paul, did much better than the one in Florida. She recovered quickly and we continued our active lifestyle. Church, Kiwanis projects, gardening, working out at the YMCA, visiting people, and little trips here and there kept us busy.

Still Smiling 50 Years Later

DONNA AND I CELEBRATED OUR 50TH wedding anniversary two months early on July 2, 2016, before everyone headed off to school. Fifty years! How did that go so fast? We celebrated with about 150 people in our backyard on a perfect, sunny day with all the flowers blooming, and feasted on a ton of grilled chicken and brats, salads, and hot dishes. We served the cakes and ice cream in my air-conditioned studio where we displayed Donna's wedding dress and the same gold colored brass toucan that I had bought in Guadalajara for Mom and Dad's 50th.

How did we stay married all that time? We had committed examples. Our parents stayed married, as did the parents of our friends. By the time I was 26 years old, I knew what I wanted in a spouse and I'm sure Donna did as well. We shared the same values and worldview, and from Dr. Schultz, who voluntarily gave us some pre-marital counselling (I used to babysit his kids), we learned the importance of resolving any disagreements before we turned out the lights. Over the years, I heard bits of advice while listening to Mom and Dad's courtship stories which I filed away in the back of my mind. I even got a bit of advice from Mom and Dad's friend, Mike Neff, who said, "Don't get married until you are too old to do anything else and then marry a nurse to take care of you." I got that part half right. I also tried to follow my own advice: Beware of the little things before they accumulate and get to be big issues. Along the way I've learned that love covers a multitude of sins. For a relationship to flourish, it is important to share thoughts and feelings, which for me was always a bit difficult to do. Maybe it was because I was born at the tail end of the silent generation and didn't need to talk so much. Talking too much just got me in trouble. For me, it has always been a challenge to give up the security, independence and privacy that held my life together since I was a kid. Each year of marriage keeps getting better. That's the best part.

Did you ever notice how happy people were when they had next to nothing? Mom and Dad often talked about how happy they were during the Great Depression when they barely had two nickels to go to the movies. Every time you buy something, you have more worries and responsibilities. For a new car, you need money for oil, gas, repairs, tires, insurance, license plates, taxes, and you must wash it. Now that I have more stuff than I need or want, that's easy for me to say.

Back: Sean and John McLeod, Robert Leafblad Front: Sara, Meghan & Molly McLeod, Sarah & Aiden Leafblad, Donna McLeod, Bjorn Leafblad

290. BENNINGTON, VERMONT

IN OCTOBER 2017, I headed to Vermont for another Peace Corps reunion. Donna decided she didn't need to hear more war stories and stayed home — but everyone missed my better half. At the Albany, New York airport, Bernie Engel met Jay Jackson and me and drove us to Bennington where we congregated. We had several social events together, organized by Carolyn Plage, and then drove around the area to see some historic sites, such as Robert Frost's gravesite, and of course admire the

Caw Caw Caw

famous fall colors. The big hills were ablaze, and it was more colorful than Wisconsin because there were mainly maples without a mixture of pines.

Since the Peace Corps was signed into law, about 200,000 volunteers have served in 60 countries. For sure that positively affected the world. Even more, it changed all of us and redirected our lives as well.

Once again, I attended the Madison Carving and Turners Show and won first prize, this time for a crow, in the open division. It was a fun show that filled two big gyms and was attended by over 1400 people.

Back in Holiday, Living Word Church had a chili cookoff. There were two categories: traditional chili and non-traditional white chili. Donna, using her sister June's recipe for chicken-tortilla soup, made a big batch and renamed it "Mexican Chili." It came complete with tortilla chips and sour cream and was delicious. It's our favorite chili.

Our children and grandchildren were doing well. Molly was visiting colleges, Meghan was in eighth grade, while Sarah was still homeschooling Bjorn, 13, and Aiden, 9.

291. RENOVATIONS

*Donna Holds the Proof
Chili Cook-off Winner*

IN HOLIDAY, FLORIDA we upgraded our doublewide coach in January 2018. A neighbor, Vasco, and I did all the work. In two months, we eliminated the patio door between the living and Florida rooms, installed 17 new windows, 2 new doors and trimmed it all. After it was all caulked and painted, we had vinyl plank flooring installed, which made our abode easier to clean, more spacious looking and up to date. It was a lot of work, but Donna loved it. That's what I've learned is important.

When we returned to Wisconsin, we immediately helped gut and renovate Sean and Sara's recently acquired two-story lake house in Pardeeville. Eight years earlier, they got frustrated with their big A-frame after a pipe froze and flooded the house just before they arrived on Christmas Eve.

The insurance paid $34,000 to clean up the mess but that was the final straw and they sold it. Then they did it again, their third complete renovation, which surprised me. They again hired John Tamminga, who was scheduled to start work early in the year but broke his hip falling off a ladder. By April, he was somewhat recovered and I happily became his assistant who carried all the lumber and supplies into the house and all the junk to the dumpster. Just keeping the floor somewhat free from debris was a full-time job. We ripped out almost everything, rearranged doors, put in all new windows, doors, cabinets,

Aiden and Bjorn Leafblad

and trim just in time for Molly's high school graduation party on June 10, 2018. It was a big event, catered by Molly's favorite Indian restaurant in Milwaukee. The Indian waiters were surprised to see my Shamiana set up in the backyard, which helped keep the wind from blowing us away. By then, I had a painful case of sciatica and could hardly bend over. For almost the first time in my life, I had a physical ailment.

Erin & Pastor Chuck Walton, John & Donna, Sharon & Chuck Dykstra

292. NORTHWEST TO ALASKA

SCIATICA DIDN'T KEEP DONNA AND ME FROM flying to Fairbanks, Alaska, in July 2018 to start a two-week Royal Caribbean vacation, one week on land and one week at sea. It was another trip of a lifetime, even though Donna claims I was a bit loopy because I was overdosing on gabapentin which, unfortunately, didn't help. After a few days wandering for miles all over Fairbanks on our own, the tour started. We first took a 900-passenger paddle boat down the river where we saw a dog sled demonstration. I was amazed at their speed and power.

We next went to Denali, and then headed south taking several boat excursions to see

Denali National Park, Photo by Joris Beugels on Unsplash.com

glaciers, whales, grizzlies, moose, caribou, many new birds, mountains and rivers. It was here that my old wrestling buddy, Steve Martin, got stranded in a tent for 11 days during a snowstorm while leading an expedition.

We travelled on a luxurious train past Wasilla to Anchorage and Seward where we boarded the ship, our fourth cruise. We then sailed to Skagway, Juneau and Kechikan on the inland passage to Vancouver. It was interesting to see all the towns on our way south, many accessible only by boat, including the capital, that were long and narrow with no room to expand because of the steep mountains behind. After all this trekking around, I got a cortisone shot and felt instantly cured, just before my 60th West High School reunion.

PART X. 2020

THE OTHER SIDE
OF THE HILL

293. WHAT'S IMPORTANT?

DURING INDIVIDUAL CONVERSATIONS with classmates at my 60th West High School reunion in 2018, we all answered a few questions about ourselves. Later I wondered, what if someone had suggested that each one of us stand up and tell what we had been up to since graduation? Fortunately, our class was too big for that — but what would I have said? If put on the spot, would I have been able to rummage through so many years and say something meaningful? Or would I simply recite where I went to school, where I worked, and how many wonderful, accomplished children I had?

If the first lady who spoke had said, "At 39, I was in a terrible accident, my husband left me, and then I had a life-changing encounter with Jesus who transformed my trajectory from hopelessness and fear to a life full of joy and power," would you believe her? What would a proper response be?

From the time I was a kid, I had been learning about Jesus most every time I went to Church, but I didn't understand what believing in Him really meant. I just went with the flow and didn't pay serious attention to what Jesus said. Occasionally, I got to know things about Him, but it wasn't anything intimate. Most of the time, I just didn't care that much. But the more I got to know Jesus, the more I realized His blueprint was right and that I had a difficult time following it.

Like a typical unaware husband, I thought I was happy, worked hard, enjoyed our many social events and playing tennis, but I was mostly unaware of how frustrated and discontented Donna felt when we left Ecuador. She was the first in our family to reach out to Jesus when she prayed to be "born-again" shortly after we arrived in Pakistan. That's when her whole countenance changed, and even changed me and those around her. It took me seven more years before I came to the same realization. I was fortunate she changed when she did, or the consequences could have been severe for our family. But God patiently waited and reached out to both of us.

God's "Gospel" (the death, burial and resurrection of Jesus) or "Good News" literally means salvation or liberation from sin, brokenness and estrangement from God. Jesus wants to reign over our lives and doesn't want our sin, which we overlook and diminish, to separate us from Him any longer. He simply asks us to believe in Him. How? By trusting only in Him, who sacrificed his perfectly lived life to provide the payment big enough to clear our "sin-debt" against a sinless God.

I believe there are a lot of ways to be "lost," or miss God's desires for your life. Anyone can be lost and miss out by believing whatever they want. The list is endless, but there is only one way to be "found." Jesus said, *"I am the [only] Way [to God] and the [real] Truth and the [real] Life; no one comes to the Father but through Me."* (John 14:6)

He also said, *"Come to me, all who labor and are heavy laden, and I will give you rest. Take my yoke upon you, and learn from me, for I am gentle and lowly (humble, accessible, approachable, accommodating, understanding and tender) in heart, and you will find rest for your souls. For my yoke is easy (like a life preserver to a drowning man), and my burden is light."* (Matthew 11:28-30) His arms are open to those who cry out to Him for help. But to those who don't, the earlier verses 21 and 24 warn "...because they did not repent [and change their hearts and lives]..."Woe (judgment is coming) to you..."

Today could be the day you find that God has provided the way for your sins not to be counted against you... to be rescued from that separation from God that happens by going your own way. If you're still alive, you haven't yet missed out; your past can still be redeemed. Trust Jesus and obey Him. After all, as I did back in Costa Rica, you're only a humble, desperate prayer away from God doing a great work in your life. The thing about eternity is, it's a really *long* time — too long to get wrong. And if I'm wrong, it won't matter in the end; but if I'm right, then everything's at stake.

A lot of years passed by when I was apathetic about Christianity, and for a while I seemed to get along just fine without God. As a result, it amazed me that God grabbed my attention, finally, when I was 41 years old. On that day in May 1981, when I stepped forward with trepidation to discover my spiritual gift, I first encountered Jesus in a meaningful way. It was then I first realized that His words kept proving true — over and over. I became convinced that I could believe this Jesus and take him at His word. He showed me that there was more to life than I imagined. Being a Christian was no longer boring, but exciting and risky. For me it's been a whole new adventure — whenever I'm bold enough to do what I know I should do. Are you ready for the ride?

ACKNOWLEDGMENTS

Before Computers
& La-Z-Boys

AFTER SITTING IN MY LA-Z-BOY for the better part of a year, reading old letters, diaries, baby books and typing on my laptop in my spare moments, I want to express my appreciation to Donna, my patient and loving wife, who did most everything else around the house to keep me alive. And thank you to my three siblings, Paul, Mary, and Margie who made suggestions along the way. Also many thanks to my daughter Sarah, for formatting the book, for teaching me how to attach a photo to an email, and for letting me change the title several times a day.

Before I started to write, I was quite confident that at least ten people, my immediate family, their kids and my three siblings, would be willing readers. Then my son asked, "How many pages have you written?" "More than 300," I replied. That's when he announced, "Then I'm not reading it. It's too long." And then there were nine.

ABOUT THE AUTHOR

JOHN GREW UP in the 1940's and '50's in Madison, Wisconsin. It was a great location between two lakes, a short bus ride downtown and just a few blocks west of the University of Wisconsin where he received his BS-SED degree in 1963. After serving in the Peace Corps in Guatemala, he was graduated from the American Institute for Foreign Trade in Glendale, Arizona in 1967. He lived in nine countries, passed through over 40 more, and since 1985 has resided with his wife, Donna, in Cambria, a small town 45 minutes Northeast of Madison, Wisconsin.

In the early 1940's, Madison's homogeneous population was about 70,000 and kids played outside until dark without supervision. It was a simpler time as the four-digit telephone numbers increased to five and then seven. By the time John finished university, the city had nearly doubled in size but was still a great place to live. America was the new superpower, good and evil was black and white, and we were confident in our future. All the advantages the world had to offer were at our fingertips.

CPSIA information can be obtained
at www.ICGtesting.com
Printed in the USA
BVHW011804150222
629081BV00005B/136